The problem of internecine conflict in Europe dominated the thoughts of U.S. statesmen during the four decades after 1914. This study in the varieties of modern American experience of Europe traces the development of three distinct personal answers to the question of what to do with Europe: Roosevelt's partial internationalism, aiming at the retirement of Europe from world politics while avoiding American entanglement; Kennan's partial isolationism, aspiring to restore Europe's centrality and autonomy through temporary American engagement; and Acheson's accommodating interventionism, establishing the United States as a permanent power in Europe at the behest of European and U.S. interests.

Three learned and elegantly written portraits are set against the background of the dramatic events and foreign policy controversies of the twentieth century. Using a remarkably wide range of sources – including memoirs, original documents, and contemporary fiction – Harper describes how direct experience of Europe and Europeans helped to shape the feelings and attitudes of the three subjects, while providing a sophisticated and subtle analysis of the political and cultural influences that made up the mature vision of each. The seemingly eternal European Question shows few signs of diminishing in importance during the final, post–cold war years of the century. The book's conclusion shows the postwar resonance of the three visions and the way in which they retain their power to influence future U.S. policy toward the Old World.

AMERICAN VISIONS OF EUROPE

AMERICAN VISIONS OF EUROPE

Franklin D. Roosevelt, George F. Kennan, and Dean G. Acheson

JOHN LAMBERTON HARPER

The Johns Hopkins University
Bologna Center, Paul H. Nitze School
of Advanced International Studies

CAMBRIDGE
UNIVERSITY PRESS

Published by the Press Syndicate of the University of Cambridge
The Pitt Building, Trumpington Street, Cambridge CB2 IRP
40 West 20th Street, New York, NY 10011-4211, USA
10 Stamford Road, Oakleigh, Melbourne 3166, Australia

© Cambridge University Press 1996

First published 1994

Reprinted 1994

First paperback edition 1996

Printed in the United States of America

Library of Congress Cataloging-in-Publication Data is available.

A catalog record for this book is available from the British Library.

ISBN 0-521-45483-2 hardback

ISBN 0-521-56628-2 paperback

To the memory of
John Porter (Jack) Lamberton,
Cpl., 19th Tank Battalion,
9th Armored Division, United States Army
Born, Philadelphia, March 27, 1922
Died, Luxembourg, November 10, 1944

Contents

vii

Acknowledgments

Writing this book has been an intellectual odyssey back and forth across the history of the twentieth century. It has taken me, in the literal sense, to libraries and archives scattered across the eastern half of the United States. Many people were there to lend a hand. I began my research at the Franklin D. Roosevelt Library, Hyde Park, New York, in the summer of 1987. Its director, William Emerson, was a gracious host and took time to introduce me to the intricacies of FDR and World War II historiography. On the same occasion I was lucky to talk to Geoffrey Ward, whose book, *Before the Trumpet: Young Franklin Roosevelt, 1882–1905*, served as a model for me at the time.

During my trip to Independence, Missouri, the staff of the Harry S. Truman Library, in particular Neil Johnson and Elizabeth Safly, provided the special hospitality and service for which they are famous. I would like to thank Nancy Bressler and Nanci Young of the Seeley G. Mudd Library, Princeton University, Bill Massa and Judith Schiff of the Sterling Memorial Library, Yale University, Larry Bland of the George C. Marshall Research Foundation, Lexington, Virginia, as well as the staffs of the Library of Congress, the National Archives, and the Public Record Office, London. The book was written in Italy, which would not have been possible without the excellent library of the Johns Hopkins University Bologna Center. My special thanks go to the people who run it so efficiently, Alfredo Di Marino, Gail Martin, and John Williams.

My interest in "American visions of Europe" grew out of an earlier project in which I elaborated several political-ideological programs that emerged in the United States for the transformation of Italy after World War II. I traced the fate of those programs in encounter with local interlocutors weakened by the war but politically experienced and astute. For encouraging me to broaden my horizons after that rather narrow study, and for reading parts of the manuscript with a discerning

ix

eye, I thank my former dissertation adviser at the Johns Hopkins University Paul H. Nitze School of Advanced International Studies, David P. Calleo. Patrick McCarthy, my teacher at Haverford, now friend and colleague, inspired me to try my hand at the craft of which he is a master, the depiction of particular cultural milieus. My friend James E. Miller read the entire manuscript and made valuable suggestions. At Cambridge I was fortunate to work again with Frank Smith, who handled the manuscript in his characteristically expeditious and professional way. Tom Wallace of the Wallace Literary Agency provided valuable assistance, as did my copy editor, Mary Racine.

Alan Milward's invitation to prepare a presentation for his seminar at Fiesole in 1987 forced me to collect my thoughts at the beginning of the project. Chapter 4 was presented at a seminar organized by the Washington Center for European Studies in September 1991. For their helpful comments on that occasion I would like to thank, among others, the Hon. Charles McC. Mathias, Edward Luttwak, and Thomas Hughes.

David C. Acheson, Ronald Steel, John Lewis Gaddis, Elena Aga Rossi, Geoffrey Warner, and my Bologna colleagues David Ellwood, David Schoenbaum, and Craig Nation took the time to read parts of the manuscript and to make comments or corrections. Mrs. Gerald K. Lake and Anthony Lake also have my thanks.

Mr. George F. Kennan was kind enough to read and comment on a preliminary overview of the project as well as the two chapters I eventually wrote on his life. Mr. Kennan did not think it appropriate to pass judgment on the argument concerning himself, but I always felt encouraged by his prompt and courteous replies and am grateful to him for correcting various factual errors.

After calculating what it had cost him to write his *History of the United States of America During the Administrations of Jefferson and Madison*, Henry Adams concluded that history is the most aristocratic of the academic disciplines. To do it properly requires independent means and unlimited leisure time. Most of us depend instead on the charity of foundations and friends. The German Marshall Fund of the United States provided indispensable help in the form of a research fellowship for the academic year 1989–90. My friend Howard Levine provided me with a comfortable East Village base of operations from which to sally forth to Hyde Park, Princeton, New Haven, and points west.

A number of students and research assistants at the Bologna Center of SAIS helped me at various stages with this project. They include Johan Aurick, Trevor Tanchel, Rob Machalek, Kathryn Neal, Bert

Ulrich, Michael Ashford, Scott Wilson, James Upton, Susan Berger, Robert C. McNally, Jr., John Boles, Boris Ruge, Bob Angevine, Mark Milosch, Ben Gold, George Kent, and Cole Frates.

Finally I thank my wife, Maria, agent of my belated conversion from longhand to the world of computers; asker of the always-efficacious question: "When are you going to finish your book?"; and *anima* of the family for Sara, Antonia, and papà.

Introduction

Readers might judge for themselves what share the individual possessed in creating or shaping the nation; but whether it was small or great, the nation could be understood only by studying the individual.

Henry Adams[1]

Every great achievement in every field was a vision before it became a reality.

Henry Kissinger[2]

An old specter has reappeared on the American horizon: conflict and upheaval in the Old World. After a half-century hiatus, history is stirring. Old grievances, ambitions, and neuroses are once again at play. An era of uncertainty lies ahead. Americans cast a wary eye toward post–cold war Europe, East Asia, and their festering internal problems and wonder what kind of contribution they will be called on to make – what kind they can afford to make – to the solution of the European Question. For Americans, by and large, that question has been how to protect the rest of the world – or at least their own political and social experiment – from Europe's destructiveness, if not necessarily to save Europe from itself.

The United States today seems torn between two possible remedies: on the one hand, to try to continue circumscribing the autonomy of the European powers and maintaining the degree of tutelage over European affairs to which it has grown accustomed; on the other, to foster greater European initiative and self-reliance, come what may. American energies are finite and increasingly demanded elsewhere, but a basic doubt remains: left to their own devices, will the Europeans act in their own

1. Henry Adams, *A History of the United States of America During the Administrations of Jefferson and Madison* (Chicago: University of Chicago Press, 1967), 406.
2. Henry Kissinger, "What Kind of Atlantic Partnership?" *Atlantic Community Quarterly*, 7, no. 1 (Spring 1969), 38.

best interests and those of the United States? Despite authoritative disclaimers, America's "historic ambivalence" persists.[3]

The purpose of this book is to unravel the complex skein of American attitudes toward Europe by looking at several of the most important strands. In the process it casts some light on the sources of America's lasting ambivalence and doubt. The method is biographical. This is not because the history of the world is but the biography of great men, but because, as Henry Adams suggests, individual lives illuminate the texture and broader tendencies of the time. It is also because – though here Adams might have disagreed – "at crucial moments, at turning points, when factors appear more or less equally balanced, chance, individuals and their decisions . . . can determine the course of history."[4] More precisely, the method is what might be called partial biography, the investigation of a single, albeit crucial, aspect of several individual lives, in this case the development of their outlooks on the European Question. The book is intended not simply to elucidate what its main characters thought about Europe but to explain how they came to think it. It explores the connection between their experience of Europe and Europeans, on one hand, and their political outlooks, on the other. It is not a general history of transatlantic relations, but a set of essays on the varieties of twentieth century American experience of Europe.

It could be argued that Franklin Roosevelt, George Kennan, and Dean Acheson together constitute a somewhat arbitrary and ultimately subjective choice, and it would be idle to pretend that the roughly equal space devoted to the three reflects their relative historical weight. In the grand scheme of things Roosevelt obviously ranks first, Acheson second, Kennan a distant third. Nor are their lives and achievements readily comparable: Roosevelt was a professional politician, Kennan a diplomat-intellectual-aesthete, Acheson a lawyer-statesman. A study of this kind might have included Carl Schurz, Theodore Roosevelt, Henry Stimson, Woodrow Wilson, Herbert Hoover, Cordell Hull, William Bullitt, Adolf Berle, Sumner Welles, Harry Truman, John Foster Dulles, George Marshall, Robert Taft, Dwight Eisenhower, Paul Hoffman, Charles Bohlen, Averell Harriman, and perhaps many more.

Yet – given the limited space in which to hang them – a triptych

3. George Bush, Commencement Address, Boston University, May 23, 1989, Department of State *Bulletin*, July 1989, 18–19. In this speech the president acknowledged a "historic ambivalence" in the United States with respect to European unity but claimed that his administration was of one mind in supporting the European Community's 1992 initiative and eventual political unity.

4. Isaiah Berlin, quoted in Ramin Jahanbegloo, "Philosophy and Life: An Interview," *New York Review of Books*, 39, no. 10 (May 28, 1992), 51.

of large and detailed portraits may reveal more about the American experience of Europe than a row of smaller sketches. Each of the three subjects displayed a set of deeply rooted and typical American attitudes. Each embodied an alternative approach to Europe, corresponding to a phase of U.S. policy in the 1940s. Each represents a continuing tendency in American thought and behavior. These approaches, or "visions" – a word to be defined presently – were Roosevelt's partial internationalism, aiming to arrange the retirement of Europe from world politics while avoiding direct U.S. entanglement; Kennan's partial isolationism, aspiring to restore Europe's centrality and autonomy through temporary U.S. engagement; and Acheson's accommodating interventionism, establishing the United States as a permanent power in Europe at the behest of European and American interests.

The three lives were interwoven and to a degree interdependent. Roosevelt and his foreign policy exerted a profound influence on the ideas and careers of both Kennan and Acheson. They were his political progeny – Kennan in a negative and Acheson in an ambiguous sense, to be sure. Kennan and Acheson themselves collaborated and clashed in their attempts to give shape to the post-Rooseveltian world in which they lived. Thus the three parts of the book may be read as separate essays; viewed together – with Roosevelt as the central panel – they make up a single story. Needless to say, a different trio – FDR flanked by, say, Welles and Marshall – would have told a different tale.

Part One of the book presents Roosevelt against the background of American "diplomatic culture" in the broadest sense – that is to say, the inheritance from the eighteenth century and the ideas, attitudes, and "tendencies of thought" out of which twentieth century foreign policy has been fashioned. The first chapter on each man deals with the formation of what might be called a personal sensibility, a unique, sometimes contradictory set of feelings and attitudes, bound together by the single personality, persisting throughout life, that inform and condition one's mature political outlook. The early chapters also treat the development of a more formal set of ideas, or worldview, concerning Europe.

Sensibility, in this loose formulation, helps to account for degrees of concern, familiarity, sympathy, empathy, and identification with Europe and is connected to firsthand experience and to family and proximate cultural influence. Worldview constitutes a link to deeper intellectual currents and a more general climate of opinion, including the state of diplomatic culture. The later chapters describe the gradual crystallization of three different visions of Europe under the pressure of world events and of direct responsibility within a particular political milieu. By vision is intended a kind of ideal or ultimate design, representing the inter-mingling of emotional and intellectual influences, never – because of its strongly private and wishful elements – fully realized or realizable, but conditioning thought and action.

The later chapters also trace the fate of the three visions in con-frontation with one another and early postwar reality in the United States and Europe. Accordingly, they analyze the reasons for the decline of Roosevelt's design in 1944–45, for Kennan's isolation after 1947, and for the merely fleeting triumph of Acheson's diplomacy in 1952. Each of the three figures departed from the scene with the taste of defeat in his mouth. At the same time, the legacy of each constitutes a vital part of recent American diplomatic culture. The conclusion of the book briefly takes up the postwar resonance of each of the three approaches as ways of dealing with the seemingly eternal European Question. If, as Kissinger observed, nothing great is achieved without a vision, great designs shattered by events or only imperfectly realized retain their power to influence the collective mind and to condition our future choices.

PART ONE

PART ONE

1

Franklin Roosevelt, Europe, and American diplomatic culture, 1882–1932

"Everybody was going to Europe"

"During that memorable month I basked in the happiness of for once in my life drifting with the tide of a great popular movement. Everybody was going to Europe – I too was going to Europe. . . . If I met a dozen individuals during that month who were not going to Europe shortly, I have no distinct remembrance of it now." The month was June 1867. Mark Twain's maiden trip to the Old World produced the popular travelogue and satire *Innocents Abroad*. The following summer, the young Oliver Wendell Holmes, Jr., was shepherded around London by a "grumblingly generous" Henry Adams. In 1869, it was the turn of ten-year-old Theodore Roosevelt. TR recalled that his "one desire was to get back to America," as he and his siblings – like typical Twain tourists – "regarded Europe with the most ignorant chauvinism and contempt." Twain, Holmes, and TR were part of the post–Civil War resumption of a transatlantic tourism that had taken thirty thousand Americans a year to Europe in the 1850s. James Roosevelt of Hyde Park, New York, his first wife, and son spent much of 1865 and 1866 on the Continent, where Roosevelt had toured extensively in his youth. Sara Delano (born 1854) lived for most of the late sixties in Paris and Dresden – where she attended finishing school – with her father, Warren Delano, a Hudson Valley squire who had made, lost, and regained his fortune as a trader and investor.[1]

What was the magnetic force of Europe? Or rather what was missing

---

1. Mark Twain, *Innocents Abroad* (New York: Harper Bros., 1911), 11; O. W. Holmes to Harold Laski, Mar. 1, 1928, in Mark De Wolfe Howe, ed., *Holmes–Laski Letters, 1916–1935* (Cambridge, Mass.: Harvard University Press, 1953), 1031; Theodore Roosevelt, *Autobiography* (New York: Scribners, 1913), 13. On U.S. tourism and the Roosevelts and Delanos abroad see Geoffrey Ward, *Before the Trumpet: Young Franklin Roosevelt, 1882–1905* (New York: Harper & Row, 1985), chaps. 1 and 2.

7

in the United States? In his biography of Nathaniel Hawthorne, Henry James offered a classic mid-nineteenth century view: America had, according to James,

> no state in the European sense of the word, and indeed barely a specific national name. No sovereign, no court, no personal loyalty, no aristocracy, no church, no clergy, no army, no diplomatic service, no country gentlemen, no palaces, no castles, nor manors, nor country-houses, nor parsonages, nor thatched cottages, nor ivied ruins; no cathedrals, nor abbeys, nor little Norman churches; no great Universities nor public schools – no Oxford, nor Eton, nor Harrow – no literature, no novels, no museums, no pictures, no political society, no sporting class – no Epsom nor Ascot![2]

America, in short, had no past. Its aspiring artists, diplomats, sports enthusiasts, and country gentlemen naturally turned to Europe. Wandering in European museums and visiting European monuments might bring, for those willing to make the effort, new refinement. Even for those who were not, mingling with upper-class Europeans, acquiring European servants and possessions conferred social cachet. For practically anyone, Paris, Pau, and Saint Moritz offered vistas, amusements, and stimulations not to be found in the New World.

England, both part of the Old World and distinct from Europe, exerted its special attraction. There was "the antiquity, the impressiveness, the picturesqueness of England,"[3] the ties of language, culture, and blood. It was as a matter of course that American upper-class society emulated the English aristocracy, that it looked to its politics and culture, and that it adopted its mannerisms and forms. James's Lord Lambeth, hero of *An International Episode* (1878), "was handsome as certain young Englishmen, and certain young Englishmen almost alone, are handsome; with a perfect finish of feature and look of intellectual repose and gentle good temper which seemed somehow to be consequent upon his well-cut nose and chin." The young Bostonian Bessie Alden idealized Lambeth – at least for a time – just as the young Eleanor Roosevelt would find Lambeth's real-life contemporary, Lord Balfour, "charming in the way that a good many Englishmen are and very few of our own men."[4]

2. Henry James, *Hawthorne* (1879) (Ithaca, N.Y.: Great Seal Books, 1963), 34.

3. "He [Lord Lambeth] would be an unconscious part of the antiquity, the impressiveness, the picturesqueness of England, and poor Bessie Alden, like many a Yankee maiden, was terribly at the mercy of picturesqueness." Henry James, *An International Episode* (1879) (Harmondsworth: Penguin, 1985), 62.

4. Ibid., 38. For Eleanor Roosevelt's 1917 remark see Joseph Lash, *Eleanor and Franklin* (New York: New American Library, 1973), 287.

James Roosevelt, corporation lawyer and gentleman farmer, patterned his estate along English country lines.[5] He was an avid collector of British social acquaintances: the Duke and Duchess of Rutland; the Earl of Berkeley; Sir Hugh and Lady Cholmeley of Easton Hall, Lincolnshire; Cecil Foljambe, the fourth Baron Hawkesbury (later Earl of Liverpool) of Osberton-in-Worksop, Nottinghamshire; Richard James Meade, the fourth Earl of Clanwilliam; and Henry George Edwardes, younger son of the third Baron Kensington. Cholmeley and Foljambe were onetime Liberal members of Parliament; Clanwilliam, an admiral of the fleet; Edwardes, a member of the British legation at Washington.

Politically, James Roosevelt was a Whig who had transferred his loyalties to the Democrats during the fifties crisis.[6] His choice of friends suggests that he was attracted by liberal noblemen, though neither he nor his first son (FDR's half brother), the socialite James "Rosy" Roosevelt, was very assiduous in the pursuit of political ideals. Sara Delano (she married James Roosevelt in 1880), FDR's adoring and omnipresent mother, came with her own European connections: her sister Deborah (Dora) Delano Forbes was a lifelong resident of Paris, and her own address book for the nineties included the Comte de Fleury, the Vicomte de Fontenay, and "Cousin" Hortense Howland, whose salon appeared in *À la recherche du temps perdu*.[7]

A closer look suggests, however, that the Roosevelt–Delano links with the Old World were superficial. Neither of Franklin Roosevelt's parents was versed in European history or artistic culture. The majority of their connections in Europe were relatives and other Americans. American society established itself abroad for the social season but

5. On "Mr. James" as English gentleman see Ward, *Before the Trumpet*, 50; Frank Freidel, *Franklin D. Roosevelt: The Apprenticeship* (Boston: Little, Brown, 1952), 14; Nora Ferdon, "FDR: A Psychological Interpretation of His Childhood and Youth," Ph.D. diss. (University of Hawaii, 1971), 120.

6. In 1856 many northern Whigs voted for the Democrat James Buchanan rather than the Whig Millard Fillmore because Buchanan was seen as the candidate who could beat the Republican Fremont. Fremont's victory, it was feared, would provoke the secession of the South. Allan Nevins refers to New York Whigs-turned-Democrats as expressing "conservative union-saving and business-saving sentiment." *Ordeal of the Union* (New York: Scribners, 1947), 2: 506, 511. This seems apt in James Roosevelt's case. In voting to defeat Fremont he was also voting to defeat the candidate of "Know-Nothing" (anti-Irish) sentiment.

7. See Rita Halle Kleeman, *Gracious Lady: The Life of Sara Delano Roosevelt* (New York: Appleton-Century, 1935), chap. 8; address book contained in the Roosevelt Family Papers, Sara Delano Papers, Franklin Delano Roosevelt Library (hereafter FDRL). Howland was a Frenchwoman who had married a brother of James Roosevelt's first wife. See Elliott Roosevelt, ed., *FDR: His Personal Letters, 1905–1928* (hereafter, *PL, 1905–1928*) (New York: Duell, Sloan & Pearce, 1948), 18.

remained largely separate.[8] For most of their lives, transatlantic travel for the Roosevelts and Delanos was recreation; it was also a kind of ritual serving to confirm their place in *American* society vis-à-vis *Americans* like themselves.

In the New York social hierarchy, the Roosevelts stood somewhere between the oldest Hudson Valley families (Roosevelt's great-grandfather moved north from Manhattan in 1818) and more recent – and far richer – arrivals, the Belmonts, Vanderbilts, and Astors. By the eighties, there was no break between feudal-mercantile society – Edith Wharton's "small and slippery pyramid" – on the one hand, and new industrial wealth, on the other. FDR's half brother, for example, had married Helen Astor. Still, old distinctions were dear to people like Wharton's Mrs. Archer, who traced "each new crack in the [pyramid's] surface and all the strange weeds pushing-up between the ordered rows of social vegetables," and to Sara Delano Roosevelt, who disapproved of the frivolity of Rosy Roosevelt and his set.[9] Old New York was convinced that it had upheld a simpler standard of moral conduct and had been more self-satisfied and self-contained.

Self-contained, inter alia, with respect to Europe. Compared with the new late nineteenth century money, the older families were temporally remote from Europe and independent in taste and outlook. Paris dresses were prized, but first laid away for two years to avoid the impression of slavery to foreign fashion.[10] Even if they had had the money, the Roosevelts and Delanos would have been above building baroque revival palaces on the Hudson River. Of Springwood, the Roosevelt's Hyde Park estate, it could be said that there was "wealth without symptoms . . . nothing for show and very little for . . . the senses but a great *aisance*."[11] The house today suggests unpretentious and unabashedly colonial tastes. Except for Sara's Dresden china, there is little trace of imported art or adornment. The dominant motifs are naval and nationalistic, with an emphasis on American exploits in the struggle for autonomy from Europe.

Anti-British nationalism had long been cultivated by both families.

8. Ward, *Before the Trumpet*, 37.
9. On Sara and Rosy see ibid., 197, note 10. The favorite pastime of Rosy's set was carriage driving. Edith Wharton, *The Age of Innocence* (1920) (New York: American Library ed., 1962), 48, 205. On the Roosevelts' place in New York society see Joseph Alsop, *FDR, 1892–1945: A Centenary Remembrance* (New York: Viking Press, 1982), 29–42.
10. Wharton, 207.
11. Felix Young to his sister Eugenia on the home of their Boston cousins, in Henry James's *The Europeans* (1878) (Harmondsworth: Penguin, 1986), 60.

The Roosevelts descended from the Dutchman Claes Martenszen van Rosenvelt, who settled in New Amsterdam more than a decade before its seizure by the English in 1664. A century later, the prosperous merchant and sugar refiner Isaac Roosevelt, whose portrait was hung above the mantel at Springwood, broke ranks with most of the New York elite and supported independence. The Delanos were descended from the Belgian Huguenot Philippe de La Noye, who settled in Plymouth, Massachusetts, in 1621. FDR's great-grandfather, Warren Delano, was a sea captain who had been interned in a British prison ship at the end of the War of 1812. His grandfather, Warren Delano II, was removed to safety when the British threatened to bombard the Delano home at Fairhaven, Massachusetts. He became senior partner in the firm of Russell and Co., the leading American rival of British interests in the Chinese opium trade.[12]

On top of old colonial resentments, Great Britain's prodigious nineteenth century power and smugness gave rise to feelings other than admiration among cultivated American travelers.[13] James Roosevelt was too even-tempered a gentleman to have left evidence of envy or resentment, but it is clear that there were limits to his idealization of England. In March 1894, he wrote the Reverend Endicott Peabody, recent founder of the Groton School, lamenting that his son's English governess had not been a success: "I should prefer a New England man. . . . Have we in this country any men with the culture and training of Englishmen, combined with the high standard and character of the American gentleman?"[14] The distinction between English and American gentlemen was not made casually: the American stood on a higher moral plane. Here was a glimpse of the primordial mistrust and condescension toward Europe embedded in family tradition.[15] The New

---

12. For FDR's own recollections on this theme see Elliott Roosevelt, ed., *FDR: His Personal Letters*, vol. 2: *1928–1945* (hereafter *PL, 1928–1945*, 2) (New York: Duell, Sloan & Pearce, 1948), 942–44. See also Ward, *Before the Trumpet*, chaps. 1 and 2; Freidel, *The Apprenticeship*, chap. 1.

13. Henry Adams remarked on meeting Kipling, "One felt the old conundrum repeat itself. Somehow, somewhere, Kipling and the American were not one, but two, and could not be glued together. The American felt that the defect, if defect it were, was in himself. . . . All through life, one had seen the American on his literary knees to the European. . . . It was in the nature of things." *The Education of Henry Adams: An Autobiography* (Boston: Houghton Mifflin Company, 1918), 319.

14. James Roosevelt to Peabody, Mar. 5, 1894. Copies of Materials from Other Repositories, Endicott Peabody Correspondence with FDR and Eleanor Roosevelt, FDRL.

15. James Roosevelt's own father had nearly forbidden his son to make the Grand Tour of Europe in the late 1840s for fear of the risks he might run. See Ward, *Before the Trumpet*, 30. See also Sara D. Roosevelt, as told to Isabel Leighton and Gabrielle Forbush, *My Boy Franklin* (New York: Long & Smith, 1933), 14.

World country aristocrat was outwardly similar, yet in an essential respect superior to the original Old World model.

The old Europe and the new

For more than fifty years historians and biographers have been fascinated by the quicksilver – if one likes, slippery – quality of Franklin Roosevelt's personality. Frances Perkins called him "the most complicated human being I ever knew"; Ted Morgan, "a chameleon-like creature." For Frederick Marks III, he was "sphinx-like"; for James MacGregor Burns, "a deeply divided man"; for Waldo Heinrichs, "the most elusive and dissembling of Presidents." Kenneth Davis seeks the key to understanding Roosevelt "in the inward certainty that he was a chosen one of the Almighty"; Geoffrey Ward, in the genteel bucolic security of his Hudson Valley youth. No one can really claim to have penetrated his "thickly forested interior" – to use Robert Sherwood's famous phrase.[16]

A persistent view is that FDR did not possess deep-seated principles or ideas and tended to float with the tide of public opinion. Sir Isaiah Berlin contrasts him with statesmen of the de Gaulle or Wilson type, "possessed by [a] bright coherent dream." Unlike them, Roosevelt was not one whose ends were "born within some private world of inner thought or introverted feeling, but [rather] the crystallization, the raising to great intensity and clarity of what a large number of [his] fellow citizens [were] thinking and feeling in some dim, inarticulate, but nevertheless persistent, homely fashion."[17] From this one might derive the favorable conclusion that a lack of systematic views permitted an empirical type of politics and diplomacy and freedom from convention. Supporters of Roosevelt have argued that his approach to governing was marked by brilliant opportunism and experimentalism rather than consistently held opinions. However, from similar premises – the lack

16. Frances Perkins, *The Roosevelt I Knew* (New York: Viking Press, 1946), 3; Ted Morgan, *FDR: A Biography* (New York: Simon & Schuster, 1985), 39; James MacGregor Burns, *Roosevelt: The Soldier of Freedom* (New York: Harcourt Brace Jovanovich, 1970), xii; Frederick W. Marks III, *Wind over Sand: The Diplomacy of Franklin Roosevelt* (Athens: University of Georgia Press, 1988), 1; Kenneth Davis, "FDR as a Biographer's Problem," in *American Scholar*, 53 (Winter 1983–84), 100–8; Waldo H. Heinrichs, *Threshold of War: Frankin D. Roosevelt and American Entry into World War II* (New York: Oxford University Press, 1988), vii; Ward, Prologue to *Before the Trumpet*; Robert Sherwood, *Roosevelt and Hopkins: An Intimate History* (New York: Harper, 1950).

17. Isaiah Berlin, "President Franklin Delano Roosevelt," *Political Quarterly*, 26, no. 4 (October–December 1955), 340–41. For a similar view see Richard Hofstadter, *The American Political Tradition* (New York: Knopf, 1948), 323, 327.

of firmly held or well-developed ideas – critics have arrived at less flattering conclusions. Roosevelt was not simply opportunistic, but shallow, puerile, and fatally haphazard.[18]

The problem with this line of approach is that it tends to confuse flexibility and deception with the absence of clear objectives and beliefs. Roosevelt was in many ways the "multifaceted, mercurial, enigmatic" figure of Davis and others, endowed with Berlin's delicate antennae and gift for communion with his times.[19] But his elusiveness and sensitivity to public opinion should not be made into a fetish.

When Henry Adams met Garibaldi in the 1860s, he was baffled by the great man's almost childlike simplicity. For Adams, Garibaldi proved that "simplicity is complex."[20] Roosevelt, in contrast, would seem to be a case in which complexity is simple. Rexford Tugwell, a discerning observer, suggests that FDR's personality "did seem complex. But that, I think, was because so much of it was hidden. . . . That he was not really more complex than most of us are I am fully convinced: he may well have been less so." Adolf Berle put it more bluntly: "Many found him puzzling; but this, I think, was due more to their own limitations."[21] The question is not really whether Roosevelt *had* definite ideas that gave a logic and consistency to his behavior toward the Old World, but what they were and how he got them.

FDR'S ENCOUNTER WITH EUROPE began during a series of voyages between 1885 and 1896.[22] His earliest recollections are said to be connected

---

18. For a recent example see Marks's *Wind over Sand*. The title aptly evokes the author's view of Roosevelt's character and policies. See also Robert Nisbet, *Roosevelt and Stalin: The Failed Courtship* (New York: Simon & Schuster, 1989). Marks's book is the product of serious scholarship – even if the portrait of FDR seems rather distorted – while Nisbet's relies on the secondary literature in order to present the kind of lurid caricature of FDR that retains its capacity to titillate and outrage the contemporary Right.

19. Davis, "FDR as a Biographer's Problem," 4; Berlin, "President Franklin Delano Roosevelt," 341.

20. Adams, *The Education*, 95.

21. Rexford Tugwell, *The Democratic Roosevelt* (Garden City, N.Y.: Doubleday, 1957), 11; Adolf A. Berle Diary, Apr. 13, 1945, Berle Papers, FDRL. Neither Tugwell nor Berle was exactly an objective observer, but careful students have tended to confirm their basic point. I share Willard Range's view that FDR was "largely guided by a set of assumptions, principles and values which he clung to with remarkable consistency throughout most of his life." See Range, *Franklin D. Roosevelt's World Order* (Athens: University of Georgia Press, 1959), xii; also Warren F. Kimball, *The Juggler: Franklin Roosevelt as Wartime Statesman* (Princeton, N.J.: Princeton University Press, 1991), 8–9. Kimball speaks of "the broader consistency that shaped his policies – his assumptions."

22. The best account of the young FDR and his family in Europe is that by Ward, *Before*

with a violent storm that struck the White Star liner *Germania* en route to New York from Liverpool in the spring of 1885. More substantial memories of Europe probably dated from his second trip, November 1889 to February 1890. After London where he acquired a riding suit and governess, he was shunted to Pau, where Sara noted, "The Borlands of Boston are here and we seem already to know a lot of people."[23]

Beginning in 1891, for five consecutive summers, travel to Europe was associated with his father's failing health.[24] The Roosevelts traveled with their son (and from 1897 to 1899 without him) to the Rhineland spa of Bad Nauheim for treatment of James Roosevelt's ailing heart. He wrote to his cousins, "I go to the public school with a lot of little mickies and we have German reading, German dictation, the history of Siegfried . . . and I like it very much."[25] Roosevelt continued to study German (along with French) with his French–Swiss governess Jeanne Sandoz (between 1891 and 1893) and excelled in it at school.

FDR's most memorable childhood experience of Europe occurred during the summer of 1896, before he entered Groton. He bicycled together with his young American tutor from Frankfurt to Wiesbaden, then Heidelberg (reached by train) to Baden Baden, Strasbourg and St. Blasien, and finally to Freiburg. The trip gave rise to a series of anecdotes involving the petty legalism of Wilhelmine Germany. The two were arrested for entering Strasbourg, "a fortified city of the Empire, on, with, or in a wheeled vehicle after nightfall."[26] Before leaving for Hamburg and thence New York by the steamship *Fürst Bismarck*, FDR attended the Wagner Festival at Bayreuth.

It was natural to connect FDR's adult animus toward Germans with his early experience, and Roosevelt himself encouraged such a link. To King George V, FDR remarked in 1918 that during his school days in Germany he had seen "their preparation for the first stages of the war machine."[27] These included, it seems, preparations tried out on FDR:

the Trumpet, chaps. 3 and 4. See also *PL, The Early Years* and *PL, 1905–1928*; Morgan, chap. 2; Freidel, *The Apprenticeship*, chap. 2. Robert Dallek, *Franklin D. Roosevelt and American Foreign Policy, 1932–1945* (Oxford: Oxford University Press, 1979), 3–20.

23. Sara Roosevelt Diary, Nov. 15, 1889. Roosevelt Family Papers, Sara Delano Roosevelt Papers, FDRL.
24. Ward, *Before the Trumpet*, 148.
25. *PL, The Early Years*, 19–20.
26. See Sara Roosevelt Diary, book 1, Roosevelt Family Papers, Sara Delano Roosevelt Papers, FDRL; see also Ward, *Before the Trumpet*, 176; Freidel, *The Apprenticeship*, 34; Sara Roosevelt, *My Boy Franklin*, 23, 36.
27. *PL, The Early Years*, 391.

He was . . . a bright and lanky boy and as such was always picked out by the heavier German boys for wrestling matches. But he soon learnt how to deal with them; he would let them get him down and then fight like the devil. . . . If he could hold out for five minutes or so they always cracked for some inexplicable reason. There was a yellow streak in the German nature.[28]

FDR wrote his Scottish friend Arthur Murray in early 1940: "I have the distinct impression that education and outlook under the old Kaiser and under Frederick was quickly and almost suddenly changed when Wilhelm II came to the throne." FDR concluded, "The talk among us children became stronger each year towards an objective – the inevitable war with France and the building up of the Reich to the greatest world power."[29]

Historians have also made much of the anti-German prejudice of FDR's family, in particular of his mother.[30] Writing to his son from the Hotel Kurhaus, St. Blasien, in June 1897, James Roosevelt remarked that "Mama [had] struck against feeding in company with German swine so we have a separate table to ourselves at quite the other end of the dining room where we were last year." When FDR returned to the Kurhaus on his honeymoon in 1905, he wrote his mother: "By a show of severity I have secured a table on the veranda – the dining room has four long pig sties where the strange assortment of mortals (swine are mortals, n'est-ce pas?) consume victuals." In effect, FDR's family exhibited what Theodore Roosevelt called the typical American attitude toward Germans: "humorous contempt."[31]

But this is only part of the story. Sara's distaste for her fellow diners probably had something to do with their social class: nouveaux riches

28. Memorandum of Conversation with FDR by Sir Arthur Willert, Apr. 14, 1936, Arthur Willert Papers, folder 59, box 14, Sterling Library, Yale University. See also Sir Arthur Willert, *The Road to Safety: A Study in Anglo-American Relations* (New York: Praeger, 1953), 35.
29. FDR to Arthur Murray, Mar. 4, 1940, President's Secretary's file (PSF) 53, Great Britain, Arthur Murray, FDRL. Murray, later Viscount Elibank, was a Liberal MP (1908–16) and parliamentary private secretary to Sir Edward Grey. After his brief stint as assistant military attaché, he was Sir William Wiseman's liaison at the Foreign Office. Wiseman was the young intelligence officer who befriended Colonel House and President Wilson and became an important go-between for the British and U.S. governments. See Murray, *At Close Quarters* (London: J. Murray, 1946).
30. See Ward, *Before the Trumpet*, 149, n. 4; Morgan, 44; Marks, 130.
31. Theodore Roosevelt to Cecil Spring-Rice, Aug. 18, 1897, in Elting Morison, ed., *The Letters of Theodore Roosevelt* (Cambridge, Mass.: Harvard University Press, 1951), 1: 644. James Roosevelt to FDR, June 9, 1897, Roosevelt Family Papers donated by the children of Franklin D. and Eleanor Roosevelt, 1686–1959, James Roosevelt Papers, FDRL; see also *PL, 1905–1928*, 51.

or common vacationers were unwelcome, regardless of nationality. In fact, Sara had a genuine affection for Germany, including the Black Forest Hotel in question. In June 1899, Sara wrote from the Kurhaus: "I am so thankful that we came here and feel that this is the best place for Papa. We feel much at home." Her cultural interests did not run deep, but while in Germany she continued to study the language, attended German church services (describing them as "simple and hearty"), and saw the Ring cycle several times.[32] When at FDR's urging Sara returned to Europe in July 1901 (the summer after her husband's death), they sailed on the *Deutschland* for Hamburg, cruised to the North Cape aboard the *Prinzessen Victoria Louise*, and toured Berlin, Dresden, and Munich.[33]

In October 1939, Roosevelt composed a famous reply to the columnist Ernest K. Lindley, who had written: "From his earliest years Franklin D. Roosevelt moved in a society which was in a real sense international and which was not conscious of any differentiation between the interests of the U.S. and the interests of Western Europe." The president had "made it plain" that he "did not look upon Germany with the same friendliness that he felt for Great Britain and France." Roosevelt commented:

> This is stated as fact when it is pure invention.... If he would look into the question of "family ties," he would realize that the R family, in the West India sugar business was compelled to contend many years against the British and French interests in those islands.... If he had ever read about the China trade of the Delano family he would have realized that the great fight in those days was between the British and the American firms. And that I was brought up on the story of how the Delano family's principal competitors were the British.

Roosevelt called the assertion about Germany "a deliberate falsification." "As a matter of simple fact," he observed, "I did not know Great Britain and France as a boy, but I did know Germany. If anything I looked upon the Germany that I knew with far more friendliness than I did Great Britain or France."[34]

32. See Sara to FDR, June 7, 1899 (on St. Blasien); May 19, 1899 (on church services); May 27, 1899 (on language lessons, which she "liked"). She attended several Wagner operas the same summer. Roosevelt Family Papers, Sara Delano Roosevelt Papers, FDRL; Kleeman, 165–66.

33. On the 1901 trip see Sara Delano Roosevelt Diary, book 2, July, Aug., Sept. 1901. Roosevelt Family Papers, Sara Delano Roosevelt Papers, FDRL. See also *PL*, *The Early Years*, 457–58.

34. See *PL*, 1928–45, 2: 942–44; Ward, *Before the Trumpet*, 149, n. 4; Freidel, *The Apprenticeship*, 34, fn.; Joseph Lash, *Roosevelt and Churchill, 1939–1941: The Partnership That Saved the West* (New York: Norton, 1976), 38.

One might want to conclude that Roosevelt simply reinvented the past when it was convenient for him to do so. His German school days had been confined to one summer, 1891, and geography does not appear among the subjects reported to his cousins. But again this is only part of the story. Both the reply to Lindley and the letter to Murray expressed Roosevelt's true sentiments. If it was misleading to say that he had not known France and England, he had indeed known Germany better, and there is no reason to doubt that he looked "with far more friendliness" upon the latter. The Germany that Roosevelt remembered fondly was a tranquil and evocative world of thatch-roofed cottages and deep forests, more or less the same Gothic Germany recalled by Henry Adams in 1907. Adams wrote that

> the Germany he loved was the eighteenth-century which the Germans were ashamed of, and were destroying as fast as they could. Of the Germany to come, he knew nothing. Military Germany was his abhorrence. What he liked was the simple character; the good-natured sentiment; the musical and metaphysical abstraction; the blundering incapacity of the German for practical affairs.... Until coal power and railways were created, she was medieval by nature and geography, and this is what Adams, under the teachings of Carlyle and Lowell, liked.[35]

It was the open and amicable Germany visited in 1872–73 by fourteen-year-old Theodore Roosevelt and remembered in 1913: "From that time to this it would have been quite impossible to make me feel that the Germans were really foreigners. The affection, the *Gemütlichkeit*... the more than kind and friendly interest in three strange children – all these manifestations of the German character and of German family life made a substantial impression on me."[36] It was the quaint, romantic, preindustrial Germany that Sara Roosevelt had in mind when she told the German ambassador in the 1930s: "While she knew nothing of the new Germany she had dearly loved the old."[37] No one evoked the sense of loss, tinged with bitterness, associated with the changing German landscape more powerfully than Thomas Wolfe. Wolfe loved the "Albert Durer and Nurnberg style – great delicate gables, cross timbers, and lean-over upper stories." He despised "the Kaiser Wilhelm Deutschland Uber Alles style – great rings and avenues and boulevards filled with these solid ugly masses." Most of the latter dated from the years 1880–1900, "about the time perhaps, it was becoming evident to them that the rest of the world ought to be colonized and given the advantages

35. Adams, *The Education*, 83.
36. Theodore Roosevelt, 21.
37. Kleeman, 73.

of a *real* civilization."[38] It was the semimythic Germany that FDR himself spoke of in 1933, when he expressed hope that "German sanity of the old type that existed in the Bismarck days when I was a boy at school there will come to the front again."[39]

It was the Germany, finally, that coincided with a special moment in Franklin Roosevelt's youth, a time of keen awareness and un-self-conscious openness, before the onrush of adolescent anxieties and inhibitions. His bicycle tour in high summer through the unspoiled German countryside of 1896 was a kind of culmination. As FDR was perhaps aware, it was the swan song of a protected childhood – on the eve of his departure for the new and predatory universe of prep school in the fall. By the late nineties, Roosevelt's boyhood world was fast receding. His school career meant a five-year absence from Europe. The growing difference between the benevolent old and the misguided new Germany was to become another family theme.

Along with the "good Germany," the late nineties saw the ebbing of Roosevelt's father – he died on December 8, 1900 – of his own childhood, and the old century itself. It is hard to imagine a more poignant confluence of events or stronger recipe for nostalgia for a vanished time – with the old Germany as its symbol. By the same token, Roosevelt's return to the United States, adolescent separation from his parents, and formal education coincided with the transformation of America's international position and with the dawn of a century in which Europe's preeminence would be challenged by other areas of the world.

The cosmopolite's return

Writing years later of Roosevelt's reply to Lindley, Rexford Tugwell observed: "It was indeed an elaborate denial. He [FDR] felt strongly about it." FDR, he thought, "had a curiously ambivalent attitude to things British."[40] There is much evidence of this ambivalence in Roosevelt's adolescent and early adult life.

Roosevelt did know England from a tender age and was familiar with the multifaceted "monster" of English upper-class society.[41] He inherited his parents' English connections and acquired others: Sir Cecil Spring-Rice, friend of Theodore Roosevelt and British ambassador to

---

38. Wolfe to Aline Bernstein, Sept. 7, 1928, in Elizabeth Nowell, ed., *The Letters of Thomas Wolfe* (New York: Scribners, 1956), 138.

39. Quoted in Range, 82–83.

40. For reply to Lindley see *PL, 1939–45*, 2: 942–44; Tugwell, 543, n. 7.

41. Henry James, *The Wings of the Dove* (1902) (Harmondsworth: Penguin, 1982), 180.

Washington, 1912–18; Sir Arthur Willert, Washington correspondent of the *Times*, 1910–20; Nigel Law, third secretary of the British Embassy, 1914–17; Arthur Murray, assistant British military attaché in Washington and Liberal MP; and Murray's wife, Faith. His youth coincided with the diplomatic rapprochement of Britain and America and the vogue of transatlantic marriage.[42] Many of FDR's female friends and close relatives had English husbands, and Eleanor Roosevelt had English connections of her own.[43] Roosevelt was fond of English country life (in fair weather) and dressed in English styles.[44] The political dimension of the English aristocratic model also exerted its attraction: the squire stood ready to abandon hearth and home for public service. It was in this respect, a worshipful Nigel Law recalled, that FDR had proved to be a "perfect example of the English Country Gentleman."[45]

Roosevelt, however, lost touch with his parents' English network before the World War and with wartime friends like Law. Faith and Arthur Murray were his only lifelong European correspondents, and this is partly because Murray was politically well informed. Roosevelt crossed the Atlantic twice in 1918–19 as assistant secretary of the Navy, and briefly in 1931, but never returned to Europe for pleasure after his honeymoon in 1905.[46] His distancing from the Old World had

42. Randolph Churchill, Joseph Chamberlain, Lord Curzon, Rudyard Kipling, Sir Michael Herbert, Charles, Duke of Marlborough, and many others found American brides. See Bradford Perkins, *The Great Rapprochement: England and the United States, 1895–1914* (New York: Atheneum, 1968), 111, 151–53.

43. FDR's childhood friend Frances Pell married Sir Martin Arthur Shee, MP. FDR's college-era friend Molly Lowell of Boston married the Earl of Berkeley. FDR's first cousin Muriel Delano Robbins married Cyril Martineau. His first cousin Sara Collier married another Englishman, Charles Fellowes-Gordon. Eleanor Roosevelt studied at Allenswood School near London. James and Irwin Bulloch, the half brothers of her paternal grandmother, had remained in England after their service to the Confederacy during the Civil War. James's daughter, Jesse, married Maxwell H. Maxwell, a high official in the Cunard companies.

44. During his August 1903, stay at the Cholmeleys in Lincolnshire, FDR wrote his mother, "This house is a dream of Nirvana." His London purchases included "1 Dress Suit, 1 Dinner Coat Suit, 1 Winter Suit, 2 Summer Suits, and 1 Frock Coat and Trousers!... Riding Boots and Patent Leather Button Shoes." For letter of Aug. 5, 1903, see *PL, The Early Years*, 496–97. On FDR and the English climate see letter to Ambassador John G. Winant, Oct. 31, 1942: "I love England in the spring, summer and early autumn, but I do dread chillblains." PSF Winant folder, box 53, FDRL.

45. Tugwell and Ward put great emphasis on this point. Law quoted in Jonathan Daniels, *The End of Innocence* (Philadelphia: Lippincott, 1954), 160. See also Nathan Miller, *FDR: An Intimate History* (Garden City, N.Y.: Doubleday, 1983), 153.

46. He made the visit in 1931 to tend to Sara Roosevelt, who had contracted pneumonia in France. On December 8, 1943, FDR landed briefly (en route from Tehran) near Palermo, where he decorated General Mark Clark and General Walter Bedell Smith.

begun at Groton and was connected with his social and intellectual development in those years.

FDR's transition from the relatively serene world of childhood to the regimentation of Groton was not an easy one, and the experience left its mark. A clinging mother delayed his departure for school by two years beyond the normal age of twelve, and by FDR's own account the latecomer remained an "outsider."[47] He was also a late developer physically – 5'3" tall and 100 pounds in his fifteenth year, which heightened his sense of insecurity and inclined others to see him as a lightweight in both senses of the term.[48] Tugwell observes, "Because he was treated with condescension, he made secret resolves, I am quite sure, as any spirited person would, to show the condescender how mistaken he had been." This is a basic insight into FDR's character, as is Harold Ickes's less flattering assessment: "Beneath all his outward charm and cordiality he was cold and calculating, 'not the stuff of which martyrs were made.'"[49]

FDR's adjustment was not eased by the fact that he arrived with an exotic accent and mannerisms, like bowing at the waist. Peabody's Groton, while supposedly modeled on the English public school, was not very hospitable to pampered, Anglicized boys, and Roosevelt was ostracized for his alien refinement.[50] When his parents sent *Punch* and the *Spectator*, he wrote that they were "hardly appreciated by others, as they are 'so English you know.'"[51] But FDR was sensitive and eager to conform. The boy Freidel called a "stripling, almost too high-toned for Groton,"[52] was soon a recognizably American youth who managed the baseball team and disparaged sissies and misfits like his nephew "Taddy" Roosevelt.

This adolescent transition left him permanently hostile to Europeanized Americans and self-conscious about the appearance of "European" effeteness in himself. Aboard the RMS *Oceanic* during her honeymoon, Eleanor Roosevelt wrote FDR's mother, "The stewardess informed me the other morning that my husband must be English, he was so hand-

---

47. See Eleanor Roosevelt, *This I Remember* (New York: Harper, 1949), 43.
48. On his own preoccupation with his small size see letter to his parents, Apr. 28, 1899, *PL, The Early Years*, 297.
49. Tugwell, 36. Ickes's comment was reported by the British ambassador, Lord Halifax, in a letter to Foreign Secretary Anthony Eden, Mar. 30, 1943. FO 954/30, Public Record Office (hereafter, PRO), Kew. Ickes was secretary of the interior.
50. Freidel, *The Apprenticeship*, 34. Freidel's source is an interview with Eleanor Roosevelt. See also Ward, *Before the Trumpet*, 181.
51. *PL, The Early Years*, 315.
52. Freidel, *The Apprenticeship*, 34.

some and had the real English profile! Of course it was a great compliment but you can imagine how Franklin looked when I told him." Roosevelt's son James testified to his father's dislike of American expatriates "even though there were several of these in his own family." In the thirties FDR complained about Americans who spent "their time when visiting Europe in running down or apologizing for their own nation." His disdain for the "white spats boys" – Europeanized professional diplomats – was well known, though he made exceptions for old friends and Grotonians like William Phillips and Sumner Welles.[53]

The Roosevelts and Delanos were "unsnubbable stock" as far as American society was concerned, and FDR inherited his mother's contempt for the American new rich.[54] Although as a graceful youth with Lord Lambeth–like features, Roosevelt moved with apparent ease in English society as well, the Twain-esque persiflage of his letters and conversation contained hints that he had felt the sting of English snobbery. During his 1903 stay at the Cholmeley's, FDR wrote Sara Roosevelt:

> As I knew the uncivilized English custom of never introducing people I had about three fits when we arrived [at a neighbor's house for tea]. . . . I walked up to the best-looking dame in the bunch and said, 'Howdy?' . . . [I] ended up by jawing the hostess herself all by her lonesome for ten minutes while a uniformed Lord stood by and never got in anything except an occasional "Aw" or an "I sy [*sic*]." We stayed about an hour and I made about 15 bosom friends and got on so well with about 10 of these that I found out their names![55]

On a later trip, FDR noted that, thanks to the performance of "Cousin Theodore" in the White House, the English had adopted a more welcome tone toward the United States: "What a change has come over English opinion in the last few years!" As assistant secretary of the Navy, he socialized frequently with British officials in Washington. Of a

53. For Eleanor's letter see *PL, 1905–1928*, 9. James Roosevelt and Sidney Shallet, *Affectionately, FDR: A Son's Story of a Lonely Man* (New York: Harcourt, Brace, 1959), 165. FDR to James Gerard, Sept. 13, 1935, in Edgar Nixon, ed., *Franklin Roosevelt and Foreign Affairs, Sept. 1935–Jan. 1937* (New York: Clearwater, 1969), 7. See also FDR's letter to Mrs. Anthony Biddle, Feb. 26, 1945, PSF-554, FDRL. On FDR and the U.S. Diplomatic Corps see Martin Weil, *A Pretty Good Club: The Founding Fathers of the U.S. Foreign Service* (New York: Norton, 1978), chaps. 1 and 2; Morgan, 369.
54. "Unsnubbable stock" is Freidel's term. *The Apprenticeship*, 14.
55. *PL, The Early Years*, 499–500. Eleanor Roosevelt recounted a similar incident which occurred at the home of FDR's parents' friends, the Foljambes, during her honeymoon in 1905: when no introductions were made at dinner, "I suffered tortures." *This Is My Story* (New York: Harper, 1937), 33.

typical occasion in 1916, he wrote Eleanor: "A nice evening, though thoroughly British!"[56]

Roosevelt concealed his resentment behind the playful philistine mask assumed at the tea party in 1903. Later in life he indulged in a kind of reverse patronage designed to show off his at least equal status – as Hudson Valley patrician and U.S. president – to the most exalted foreigner. The record is full of examples of what Harry Hopkins somewhat misleadingly called FDR's "warm spot for royalty." During the British sovereigns' 1939 visit to the United States, FDR treated them with avuncular condescension, dropping standard protocol requiring that the king be served before FDR and addressing him as "young man," while privately mocking his equerry as "Little Lord Fauntleroy."[57] FDR's imposition of informality was a way of asserting his authority over those whom standard protocol was intended to exalt.

FDR became godfather to Martha, crown princess of Norway, and to Prince Michael of Kent. He exchanged affectionate letters with Crown Prince Louis Ferdinand of Prussia and his brother Friedrich during the thirties and received this typical message from Prince Felix of Luxembourg (whom FDR had recently received in Washington) in September 1939: "Your fatherly kindness has enabled me to support the anguish of the dramatic period through which we are living." FDR considered Peter, king of Yugoslavia, "as a sort of ward" and adopted a similar attitude toward Archduke Otto of Austria. He showed solicitous regard for Queen Wilhelmina and Princess Juliana of the Netherlands, and offered them wartime refuge in the United States. FDR treated the quasi-aristocratic Nigel Law as a kind of page (he was twenty-four when they met, FDR, thirty-two). Law covered for FDR's trysts with Lucy Mercer and recalled that he once caught poison ivy when he "climbed a wild cherry tree in bathing trunks to pick the fruit for Franklin."[58]

---

56. *PL, 1905–1928*, 84, 312.

57. For Hopkins's comment see Henry Morgenthau Presidential Diaries, Nov. 6, 1943, FDRL. On FDR and protocol, Charles Bohlen observed: "He preferred informal relationships which were informal only in structure. He could not stand protocol in the accepted sense of the word but he was quick to resent the slightest departure from the respect normally accorded the President of the United States." *Witness to History, 1929–1969* (New York: Norton, 1973), 210. On FDR and the royal visit, see *PL, 1928–1945*, 2: 8–45. See also J. M. Wheeler-Bennett, *King George VI: His Life and Reign* (New York: St. Martin's Press, 1958), 389. The author describes how, after a long conversation at Hyde Park, FDR placed his hand on the king's knee and said, "Young man, it's time for you to go to bed." See also Eleanor Roosevelt, *This I Remember*, chap. 10. For "Little Lord" comment see FDR to Edwin "Pa" Watson, June 3, 1939, PSF Watson file, box 194, FDRL.

58. See the file of adoring letters from Martha of Norway to FDR during World War

Certainly there were shrewd political reasons for FDR's behavior. Feeding the king of England baked beans and hot dogs played well in Illinois. But there were also personal reasons and these were even stronger. Although FDR saw the European aristocracy as symbols of the kind of traditional, ordered society that he admired, there was an element of scorn as well as admiration. Behind Roosevelt's ostentatious paternalism was the spirit of self-vindication and one-upmanship noted by Tugwell and the mixture of defiance, pride, and sense of moral superiority that characterized his attitude toward Europeans.

In effect, FDR's Groton experience had served to strip away the "European" patina of his childhood and brought his Roosevelt and Delano inheritance into relief. At Groton, FDR also experienced an intellectual awakening of sorts that reinforced the effects of adolescent socialization. The events of 1898 were a powerful stimulant. Freidel observes: "He [FDR] was not of a particularly contemplative nature and there is no evidence that he thought much about what he read, or was influenced a fraction as much by books as by what he heard and saw."[59]

Still, FDR knew Defoe, Francis Parkman, Rudyard Kipling, and the American naval adventure stories of James Russell Soley. At Christmas in 1897 Roosevelt received Alfred Thayer Mahan's *The Influence of Sea Power on History, 1660–1773* and on his sixteenth birthday, January 30, 1898, Mahan's current essays, *The Interest of America in Sea Power, Present and Future.* On January 19, Roosevelt took part in a Groton debate in which he opposed the annexation of Hawaii. In April 1898, the *USS Maine* blew up in Havana harbor and war fever swept the country. That summer brought the "splendid little war" with Spain, U.S. seizure of Cuba and the Philippines, and the annexation of Hawaii. From his rooms at Groton and his parents' home on the Hudson River, Roosevelt followed the rise of his kinsman TR: from assistant secretary of the Navy in April 1898 to "Rough Rider" and

11. Roosevelt Family and Personal Collection, box 21, FDRL; message from FDR to the Duke of Kent, July 11 1942, PSF, Great Britain, 1942 folder, box 49, FDRL; Friedrich to FDR, July 10, 1933, PSF Germany, 1933–38, box 44, FDRL, and numerous exchanges in PPF 110, Prince Louis-Ferdinand file. Prince Felix to FDR, Sept. 4, 1939, PPF 6441, FDRL. Charlotte, Grand Duchess of Luxembourg file, FDRL. On King Peter see FDR to the Secretary of State, PSF Yugoslavia file, 1944, FDRL; on the Dutch royal family see PL, 1938–45, 2: 971–72, and PPF 1382 Queen Wilhelmina file. On the FDR–Law relationship see Daniels, *The End of Innocence*, 158–60, 228, 234.

59. Freidel, *The Apprenticeship*, 32. See also Jonathan Daniels, "Franklin Roosevelt and Books," in Daniels et al., *Three Presidents and Their Books* (Urbana: University of Illinois Press, 1955), 104.

embodiment of the nation's "martial spirit" in July, to Republican governor-elect of New York in November. In 1900, Theodore Roosevelt was elected vice-president and, following the assassination of McKinley in September 1901, became president of the United States.

"The Old World is behind the New in everything"

Turn-of-the-century developments did much to bridge the old ideological divide between Europe and the United States and to hasten Anglo-American rapprochement.[60] Many factors contributed, including British appeasement of the United States. Between 1895 and 1906, Britain abandoned isolation and conducted a retrenchment in the face of German power. A series of Anglo-American disputes – over the Venezuela and Alaska borders and control of the future Isthmus Canal – were settled on U.S. terms, and Britain withdrew its naval forces from the Western Hemisphere. In 1898, the British adopted a position of neutrality favorable to the United States. According to popular myth, a Royal Navy squadron interceded to block German action against Dewey during the Battle of Manila Bay.[61] American public opinion applauded, especially the proponents of Anglo-American racial solidarity and entente.

Well before 1898, social Darwinist doctrine had combined with the fear of Southern European and Asian immigration to produce a heightened feeling of identity among the Anglo-Saxon nations. After 1898, America's entry into the ranks of the imperial powers combined with the sense of Britain's gradual decline to reinforce appeals for Anglo-American friendship. Mahan expressed the anxieties of the early nineties when he called for an Anglo-American "cordial understanding."[62] In 1897, Mahan wrote, "We stand at the opening of a period when the question is to be settled decisively, though the issue may be long delayed, whether Eastern civilization or Western civilization is to dominate throughout the earth." He added significantly, "In unity of heart among the English-speaking races lies the best hope of humanity in the doubtful days ahead."[63] John Hay, Whitelaw Reid, Henry White, Joseph Choate, and Walter Hines Page also promoted the cult of Anglo-

60. Perkins, *The Great Rapprochement*, 15. On the changing American image of England see also Cushing Strout, *The American Image of the Old World* (New York: Harper & Row, 1963), chap. 8.
61. Perkins, *The Great Rapprochement*, 35. See also Robert E. Osgood, *Ideals and Self Interest in American Foreign Policy* (Chicago: University of Chicago Press, 1953), 71.
62. Alfred Thayer Mahan, "The U.S. Looking Outward" (1890), in the collection of essays, *The Interest of America in Sea Power* (New York: Harper Bros., 1897).
63. Ibid., 243, 259.

Saxon kinship, while English counterparts founded the Pilgrim Society and the Rhodes Scholarships to Oxford.

In 1900, Brooks Adams published a brutally frank exposition of Britain's decay, taking as his point of departure the recent South African war. For Adams, Britain's desperate hunger for gold had driven it to provoke a conflict that, while a modest affair, had severely strained its financial position and revealed a loss of national vigor. Britain's future efforts could "hardly be expected to equal those of the past, and society must be prepared to face the loosening of the bond which from beyond the limit of human memory, has been the containing power of the world." Adams was by no means a sentimental Anglophile. Yet he acknowledged:

> On looking back through the history of the century, no one can fail to appreciate the part played by England...it was she who checked the aggressions of Russia and Turkey and the East; it was she who bridled the ambitions of Germany... Americans in particular have relied on her to police the globe and keep distant markets open.

Henceforth, Adams concluded:

> America must fight her own battles.... From the inexorable decree of destiny she cannot escape.... All signs now point to the approaching supremacy of the United States, but supremacy has always entailed its sacrifices as well as its triumphs, and fortune has seldom smiled on those who, besides being energetic and industrious, have not been armed, organized and bold.[64]

Sixteen-year-old Franklin Roosevelt would have agreed. He was too excited by America's debut as a world power to listen to Carl Schurz, Mark Twain, William Graham Sumner, Andrew Carnegie, and others who deplored the jingoism of 1898 and feared its geopolitical, financial, and moral consequences. FDR later embraced what Freidel calls "paternalist imperialism." He supported U.S. military intervention in Mexico in 1914 and Haiti the following year.[65] What bothered him was the suggestion that this had anything to do with European imperialism. Temporary wardship over Cuba and the Philippines was a different matter. The United States had simply acted to sweep away a corrupt and tottering European presence.

In his January 1898 speech at Groton against the annexation of Hawaii, the young Roosevelt had drawn a distinction between the old European and the newer non-European great powers: "The United States

64. Brooks Adams, *America's Economic Supremacy* (1900) (New York: Harper Bros., 1947), 147, 167–70.
65. See Friedel, *The Apprenticeship*, chaps. 13 and 16.

and Russia are the only ones which have no colonies to defend... at present we have no really vulnerable point." "Why," he asked, "should we soil our hands with colonies?... I appeal to your American common sense."[66] FDR later admitted that America and Europe were subject to similar drives for supremacy, but he insisted that the United States had held itself to a higher standard. Panama was "clean and fairly orderly" when he visited the canal under construction in 1912, "a different Panama than under the French." Later he spoke of "the great humanitarian work almost completed... done with our money for the benefit for all mankind." In 1920, when FDR was a vice-presidential candidate, he observed that "Europe [had] laughed cynically at our protestations that we would not annex Cuba, but Europe understands today that we meant what we said."[67]

There is no evidence that turn-of-the-century events engendered greater empathy in FDR toward Europe on the grounds that everyone was now in the same imperialist boat. If anything, 1898 reinforced his sense of the distinctness of the Old and New Worlds – and the decadence of the former. "How cold it must be at Nauheim!" FDR added as a postscript to his parents in April 1898. "You see the Old World is behind the New in everything." This banal remark was an apt summary of his views.[68]

Following the outbreak of the South African war in 1898, Roosevelt wrote his parents, "Hurrah for the Boers! I entirely sympathise with them." Sara Roosevelt, for whom Boer was synonymous with boor, wrote FDR, "I feel very strongly that the Boers are not a race to do good in the world." "I think," he replied, "that you misunderstand my position.... I cannot help feeling convinced that the Boers have the side of right and that for the past ten years they have been *forced* into the war." He was also willing to accommodate his mother: "*However*, undoubtedly, now that the war is actually on, it will be best from the humanitarian standpoint for the British to win speedily and civilization will be hurried on, but I feel that the same result would have been surely obtained without war." It is doubtful whether FDR saw Britain's success as synonymous with the march of civilization, especially with British armies often in retreat. At Harvard, he helped to organize a

66. *PL, The Early Years,* 160, 163–64.
67. FDR wrote in 1916: "The European attitude... is essentially one of national selfishness. I am not at all sure that we are free of this ourselves." Friedel, *The Apprenticeship,* 260. On Panama see ibid., 135, 275; on campaign remark regarding Cuba see speech of Sept. 1, 1920, Papers as Vice-Presidential Candidate (hereafter, PVPC), FDRL.
68. *PL, The Early Years,* 296.

postwar relief fund after news of British mistreatment of the Boers.[69]

The Boer episode coincided with FDR's exploration of his Dutch and American nationalist background. It is easy to dismiss his essay on Roosevelt family history[70] as sophomoric, but it revealed lasting attitudes. After the third generation, the descendants of Claes Martensen Van Rosenvelt had intermingled freely with the English. "But Dutch marriages occurred even then, as the best New York families were still Dutch." Roosevelt remained, according to his eldest son, "extremely proud of his Dutch descent." He was a life member of the Holland Society, but steered clear of the Pilgrim Society. In the Harvard paper, Roosevelt also drew a clear distinction between his own and other elite families of New York: "One reason – perhaps the chief – of the virility of the Roosevelts is their very democratic spirit."[71] Here family lore intermingled with historical fact, but Isaac Roosevelt had stood apart in the Loyalist climate of New York.

Roosevelt's solidarity with the Boers and animus toward European imperialism can be attributed in part to the fact that in a cultural climate exalting racial loyalty he did not really consider himself Anglo-Saxon, and identified himself with a long anticolonialist tradition. Roosevelt the statesman would draw inspiration from primordial and ambivalent feelings toward Europe, just as Roosevelt the domestic politician would draw strength from the new emigrants whose arrival from Europe around the turn of the century filled conservative Anglo-Saxon Americans with dread.

THE TWENTY-THREE-YEAR-OLD FDR who left in June 1905 on a four-month honeymoon voyage carried a well-developed sensibility with regard to the Old World – a thick bundle of memories, feelings, and associations. The trip was a return to Franklin's "boyhood haunts,"[72] the Paris of Aunt Dora and Hortense Howland, the English countryside, and the Germany of his parents. But despite its superficial intactness, FDR's Europe was a changing scene. Ulm remained "a most enchanting old spot," he wrote his mother, but St. Blasien itself was "a good deal changed." The place was "*jammed* with people" and a (military?) band

69. Ibid., 358–59, 378–79; Ward, *Before the Trumpet*, 332, n. 7; Freidel, *The Apprenticeship*, 60.
70. "The Roosevelt Family in New Amsterdam before the Revolution," Sophomore thesis, Harvard University, 1901, Roosevelt Family and Business Papers, box 36, FDRL. For disparaging comments see Morgan, 47.
71. See Roosevelt and Shallet, *Affectionately, FDR*, 107; "The Roosevelt Family."
72. See Lash, *Eleanor and Franklin*, 146–51. For an account of the trip see also *PL, 1905–1928*, 3–85.

played behind the hotel – "quite an innovation." It was on this trip that FDR noted a new respect for the United States. "Even the French were quite enthusiastic but the German tone seemed to hide a certain animosity and jealousy as usual."[73]

In reality, the Europe of his affections had departed along with Bismarck, James Roosevelt, and his own pre-Groton youth. By early manhood the image of a tranquil, unspoiled, quasi–Old Regime Europe had settled in his mind. In effect, FDR was fond of those features of European life least touched by late nineteenth century nationalism and industrialization. He nurtured a disgust for those forces that seemed intent on destroying, or that were unable to protect, the delicate fabric of that world: the radical Left, the grasping industrialists, the Kaiser, the Fascists, the French and English ruling classes.

Europe for the early adult Roosevelt represented the realm of play, of the past, of his lost childhood; America was the terrain of worldly ambition, of progress, of the transition to maturity. The Roosevelt who sailed for New York in September 1905 had had his fill of antiquarians, tailors, saddlemakers, tea parties, country weekends, and expatriate aunts. "I cannot tell you how delighted we shall both be to get home again," he wrote his mother; "we speak of it every day." After 1905, he traveled extensively in the United States, writing his wife in 1908 that "for sheer beauty," Virginia "beat anything that we saw in the Black Forest."[74]

The Roosevelt who entered the New York State Senate in 1910, and arrived in Washington as assistant secretary of the Navy in 1913, had a quasi-chauvinistic side that did not seem to fit the character of such a "cosmopolitan" young man. Certainly there was expedient posturing in his flag waving: he wanted to overcome popular suspicion of his aristocratic roots. But Franklin Roosevelt was something other than cosmopolitan: that term describes someone "free of local, provincial or national ideas, prejudices or attachments."[75] Family history suggests that he came by his "red-blooded Americanism" honestly. What Herbert Croly, describing the Jeffersonian political tradition, called an "optimistic fatalism" about the future role of the United States in world affairs lay at the center of his outlook.[76]

73. *PL, 1905–1928*, 51–52, 83–84.
74. For Sept. 7, 1905, letter, ibid., 85; on countryside, ibid., 141.
75. *The Random House College Dictionary*, 1984 ed.
76. FDR added the following handwritten sentence to a typed copy of his 1920 campaign biography: "His political record has been one of fearless independence and red-blooded Americanism." Papers as Assistant Secretary of the Navy, 1913–1920

On both sides of the divide

"The old isolation is finished," wrote Frank J. Cobb, editor of the *New York World* on April 7, 1917: "We are no longer aloof from Europe, we are no longer aloof from the rest of the world. For weal or woe, whatever happens now concerns us, and from none of it can be withheld the force of our influence."[77] America's entry into World War I marked a turning point in its political relationship to Europe and a milestone along the way to economic and financial supremacy. In 1919 and 1920, U.S. merchandise exports reached a value of $8 billion, more than four times the 1910–14 average; British exports in 1921 averaged half of their 1913 value.[78] In 1914, U.S. assets abroad totaled $3.5 billion compared with $7.2 billion in European investment in the United States. In 1919, private U.S. assets abroad amounted to $6.9 billion, against total foreign assets of $3.9 billion in the United States. The British government – Britain had been America's chief prewar creditor – owed the U.S. government $4.1 billion in 1918.[79]

In the United States, the European war gave rise to a range of positions corresponding to distinct, though overlapping, cultural and political milieus. At one extreme, German- and Irish-Americans and their spokesmen in the Hearst press and Congress poured abuse on the Wilson administration and opposed U.S. entanglement on any terms. Senators O'Gorman (New York), Reed and Stone (Missouri), Smith (Georgia), Norris (Nebraska), and LaFollette (Wisconsin) voted against war in April 1917, as did fifty members of the House. At the other end of the spectrum was the Anglophile coterie that had flourished since 1898. Wilson's adviser, Edward House, and his ambassador to London, Walter Hines Page, "dreamed of a sympathetic alliance between the two

(hereafter, PASN), personal, box 122, FDRL. Herbert Croly, *The Promise of American Life* (1909) (New York: Anchon Books, 1963), 18.

77. *New York World*, Apr. 7, 1917, quoted in Arthur S. Link, *Wilson*, vol. 5: *Campaigns for Progressivism and Peace, 1916–1917* (Princeton, N.J.: Princeton University Press, 1965), 431.
78. Shepard G. Clough, *European Economic History* (New York: McGraw-Hill, 1968), 438; Jim Potter, *The American Economy Between the Wars* (New York: Macmillan, 1974), 18. British exports reached 81.3% of their 1913 volume in 1929 before falling to 50.5% in 1931. In 1938 they stood at 57.1%. See S. N. Broadberry, *The British Economy Between the Wars* (Oxford: Basil Blackwell, 1986), 67; Alan Milward, *The Economic Effects of the World Wars on Britain* (London: Macmillan, 1970), 50–51.
79. Sidney Ratner, James Soltow, and Richard Sylla, *The Evolution of the American Economy* (New York: Basic Books, 1979), 466. Charles Kindleberger, *A Financial History of Western Europe* (London: Allen & Unwin, 1984), 296. See also Kathleen Burk, *Britain, America and the Sinews of War, 1914–1918* (Boston: Allen & Unwin, 1985), app. IV, 266.

countries,"[80] as did the Canadian-born Admiral William Sims. J. P. Morgan, Jr., had personal and business ties to Britain through his father and grandfather; as banker and purchasing agent for the British government, the Morgan Bank had a heavy stake in the success of the Allies. For the most part, the Wilson administration and the Republican Party opposition found themselves somewhere between these two extremes. The administration contained a variety of positions ranging from the backcountry, anti-British populism of Secretary of State William Jennings Bryan and Navy Secretary Josephus Daniels to the more genteel and pro-Ally outlook of Robert Lansing, who succeeded Bryan in 1915, and Secretary of War Newton Baker. Wilson himself initially sympathized with the Allied cause, but he was desperately anxious that war not interfere with his domestic reform program. Gradually he embraced a kind of righteous, "plague on both your houses" outlook. The Allied rejection of his mediation attempt in 1916 was a "crushing disillusionment." British interference with U.S. shipping and scorn for his subsequent peace efforts further hardened this proud and temperamental man. Revelation of the Allies' own predatory war aims in the spring of 1917 filled him with disgust.[81] Although Wilson had no choice but intervention after the colossal German error of resuming unrestricted submarine warfare in early 1917, he went to war not to preserve the balance-of-power system but to destroy it. He told House in July 1917, "When the war is over we can force them to our way of thinking, because by that time they [the Allies] will among other things be financially in our hands."[82] Wilson's "new diplomacy" and internationalism drew its inspiration from an ancient hostility toward European power politics. In the words of his "Peace Without Victory" address of January 22, 1917, "There must be not a balance of power, but a community of power; not organized rivalries, but an organized common peace."[83]

Of Charles Evans Hughes, the Republican candidate in 1916, Arthur Link observes that "it is impossible to say where [he] really stood on foreign policy."[84] The same cannot be said of Senator Henry Cabot

80. See House to Page, Nov. 14, 1913, in Burton J. Hendrick, ed., *The Life and Letters of Walter Hines Page* (London: William Heinemann, 1930), 207.
81. Link, *Campaigns*, 38, 200. See also Lloyd C. Gardner, *A Covenant with Power: America and World Order from Wilson to Reagan* (London: Macmillan, 1984), 17–20; Alexander George and Juliette George, *Woodrow Wilson and Colonel House: A Personality Study* (New York: Dover, 1964), 171.
82. Quoted in Arthur Link, *Woodrow Wilson, Revolution, War and Peace* (Arlington Heights, Ill.: Harlan Davidson, 1979), 80.
83. Quoted in Link, *Campaigns*, 265.
84. Ibid., 100.

Lodge, Elihu Root, and especially Theodore Roosevelt. American politics between 1912 and 1918 was marked by the bitter rivalry of Theodore Roosevelt and Woodrow Wilson, "the warrior and the priest."[85] Roosevelt, in his own words, represented those "who emphatically believe in international morality, in international good faith ... and who no less emphatically believe that it is as wrong to show timidity and weakness as to show brutality and cynicism in international no less than in private dealings."[86] Roosevelt did all he could to provoke a public outcry for the unconditional surrender of the enemy. When Wilson pursued an armistice based on the "Fourteen Points," TR denounced the intention to "double-cross the Allies, appear as an umpire between them and the Central Powers, and get a negotiated peace which would put him [Wilson] personally on a pinnacle of glory in the sight of every sinister pro-German and every vapid and fatuous doctrinaire sentimentalist throughout the world."[87]

Theodore Roosevelt's opposition to Wilson was also grounded in his basic geopolitical views. TR believed that British naval power constituted the Western Hemisphere's outer line of defense and that America and Britain had a common interest in preventing German hegemony in Europe. Homer Lea's popular and dramatic *The Day of the Saxon* (1912) argued that "England and not the United States, guarantees the independence of the American nations, and in the preservation of the British Empire rather than the doctrine of Monroe is to be found the basis of their security." Lea's main thesis was the coming struggle to the death between the Saxon and Teutonic races.[88] Shortly before the outbreak of the war, TR himself had written:

As long as England succeeds in keeping the balance of power in Europe, ... well and good. Should she ... fail in doing so, the United States would be obliged to step in, at least temporarily in order to reestablish the balance of power in Europe, never mind against which country or countries our efforts may have to be directed.[89]

---

85. See John Milton Cooper, Jr., *The Warrior and the Priest: Woodrow Wilson and Theodore Roosevelt* (Cambridge, Mass.: Harvard University Press, 1983). For the original use of Nietzsche's expression "the warrior and the priest" with reference to the two men see Osgood, *Ideals and Self Interest*, 144.

86. TR letter to Bernhard Dernburg, Dec. 4, 1914, in Morison, ed., 8: 860. See also Osgood, *Ideals and Self Interest*, 136–38; Frank Ninkovich, "Theodore Roosevelt: Civilization as Ideology," *Diplomatic History*, 10, no. 3 (Summer 1986), 242.

87. TR letter to Arthur Lee, Nov. 19, 1918, in Morison, ed., 8: 1397.

88. Homer Lea, *The Day of the Saxon* (New York: Harper Bros., 1912), 47.

89. Quoted in Osgood, *Ideals and Self Interest*, 136.

After August 1914, TR made common cause with J. P. Morgan, Jr., and Walter Hines Page. He wrote his English friend Arthur Lee in 1918, "There should be the closest alliance between the British Empire and the United States."[90] But TR held no brief for Wall Street or the "ultra-British party." He had few English friends (Lee, a veteran of the Cuba campaign, and Cecil Spring-Rice, the pro-American diplomat).[91] His support of an Anglo-American alliance was based on the cold geopolitical facts. Even so, he doubted that Britain or the United States could "afford for one moment to rely on the other in a sufficiently tight place." There were simply too many "political tricksters and doctrinaires and sentimental charlatans and base materialists" on both sides.[92]

The most striking thing about Franklin Roosevelt's wartime career is the reckless abandon with which he moved back and forth between the Wilson and Republican camps and their respective social worlds. Obviously he was useful to both sides and therefore the object of cultivation – by the Democrats because of his name and political promise, and by the Republicans because of the help he gave their cause. But FDR had a bona fide claim to membership in both camps – something that made him unique in Washington at the time. His ability to move on both sides of the divide was the key to his intellectual development in these years. He came to see himself, and was seen, as the heir of both Theodore Roosevelt and Wilson and would henceforth try to live on the legacies of both.[93]

Since Groton, FDR had taken Theodore Roosevelt as his mentor, and by 1914 there was a strong similarity of views: they shared an enthusiasm for a big navy and the rise of U.S. power and a disdain for "mollycoddlers" like Bryan and Carnegie.[94] On August 2, 1914, he

90. TR letter to Arthur Lee, Nov. 19, 1918, in Morison, ed., 8: 1397.
91. On these points see Perkins, *The Great Rapprochement*, 16, 106, 108; Osgood, *Ideals and Self Interest*, 72, 74; Strout, 149–50. The phrase "ultra-British party" is Sir William Wiseman's, quoted in W. B. Fowler, *British–American Relations, 1912–1918: The Role of Sir William Wiseman* (Princeton, N.J.: Princeton University Press, 1969), 233.
92. TR letter to Arthur Lee, Nov. 19, 1918, in Morison, ed., 8: 1397. See also Howard Beale, *Theodore Roosevelt and the Rise of America to World Power* (Baltimore: Johns Hopkins University Press, 1956), 150–53.
93. Much has been written about the influence of Wilson and Theodore Roosevelt on FDR. For Tugwell, FDR gave up his "supernationalism" when he embraced the League of Nations, even if "the imperialist instincts did not all die out at once" (118). For F. Marks III, "In practice, it was Wilson, not TR, who made the most enduring impression on FDR" (10). According to Cooper, FDR "always drew his greatest inspiration in foreign affairs from Theodore Roosevelt" (359).
94. Tugwell, 96. See also Friedel, *The Apprenticeship*, 85, and Arthur M. Schlesinger Jr., *The Age of Roosevelt*, vol. 1: *The Crisis of the Old Order* (Boston: Houghton Mifflin, 1957), 330.

expressed hope that England would "join in and with France and Russia force a peace *at Berlin!*"[95] FDR had read Lea's *Day of the Saxon* with keen interest.[96] Mahan wrote on August 3, 1914, to remind him that "both prudence and good faith require Great Britain to declare [war on Germany].... As I see it, all our interests favor British success."[97]

Along with TR's former job, FDR acquired his cousin's N Street residence, his European cronies (Spring-Rice and the French ambassador Jules Jusserand), and his friends Henry Adams, the Cabot Lodges, and their son-in-law, Congressman Augustus Gardner. FDR provided assistance to Gardner, chief Republican spokesman on naval affairs. He met secretly with House to complain about Secretary Daniels's foot dragging on preparedness and attended a famous New York meeting of the "Sanhedrin of the Opposition": TR, J. P. Morgan, Jr., Elihu Root, and others. FDR hailed the appointment of Sims, the pro-British admiral, as commander of U.S. naval forces in Europe. On Christmas Day, 1919, he entertained Sir Edward Grey, who was in Washington to persuade Wilson to compromise on the Versailles Treaty (Wilson had refused to see him). Following Sims, FDR made an extraordinary public attack on the Wilson administration's war record in early 1920. It was no surprise, as Daniels noted in his diary on February 21, 1920, that "FDR [was] persona non grata with W."[98]

Yet FDR leaned toward the Wilson administration after April 1917. His earlier attitude had as much to do with indignation over American pusillanimity as with sentimental attachment to the Allies. The British and French rejection of his bid to study their war efforts firsthand in 1914 did not endear them to him, while his pet project, the North Sea mine barrier, had to be "literally forced on the British Navy."[99] Too much should not be made of FDR's haunting of the British Embassy. That hulking Connecticut Avenue structure was a kind of urban country house and haven from the family life that was not FDR's forte in these years. Cabot Lodge concluded: "He is a pleasant fellow whom I personally liked, but now that the administration is waning to a close

95. *PL, The Early Years*, 238–40.
96. FDR was given a copy of Lea's book in April 1914. Friedel, *The Apprenticeship*, 232. On his interest in it see Daniels et al.
97. Mahan to FDR, Aug. 3, 1914, PASN, personal correspondence, box 137, FDRL.
98. See Jonathan Daniels, *The End of Innocence*, 151, 212, 267, 299, 310. The author was the son of Josephus Daniels. On FDR's wartime trip to Europe see his own account in *PL, 1905–1928*. On the February 1920 speech see Freidel, *Franklin D. Roosevelt: The Ordeal* (Boston: Little, Brown, 1954), 40. See also Josephus Daniels, *The Wilson Era*, vol. 2: *1917–1923* (Chapel Hill: University of North Carolina Press, 1946).
99. Friedel, *The Apprenticeship*, 317. The words are FDR's.

we can see that when it came to the point, he did exactly what Daniels wished him to do. He is a well-meaning, nice young fellow, but light."[100]

There has always been confusion about the extent to which, and the sense in which, FDR was a "Wilsonian." FDR contributed to this confusion by courting Wilson's disciples without embracing Wilson's creed. The personal relationship of the two men was practically non-existent. Daniels tried to smooth over the conflicts that developed – unlike Wilson, he was smitten by FDR's Lord Lambeth looks and charm. Yet FDR was struck, so he avowed, by Wilson's "appeal to the fundamental," his ability "to stir ... the truly profound moral and social convictions" and to speak directly to the masses.[101] FDR espoused the principle of collective security after talking with Wilson aboard the *George Washington* en route from Paris in February 1919, but his conversion to the League of Nations was politically motivated and conditional. The one truly profound conviction that linked Roosevelt to Wilson was that Europe constituted the overriding problem of the twentieth century and that the United States had little choice but to try to solve it. Wilson had also been attached to a pastoral, peaceful pre-1914 Europe, in his case associated with the Lake District, the Romantic poets, and Edmund Burke. He was appalled by the wanton fury with which the Europeans were tearing down their civilization and had an explanation that struck FDR. "Wilson," FDR said, "had an uncanny understanding of the European problem. He understood the moral drives of modern man. He was a Presbyterian ... and he was perfectly sure that all men are sinful by nature. He figured it out that Western civilization would attempt to destroy itself through the natural sinful activities of modern man."[102] Both Wilson and FDR were inclined to believe – the World War tended to confirm – that the New World was morally superior to the Old World and that the future belonged to the dynamic, healthy elements of civilization led by the United States. What linked FDR to Wilson was the notion that the rest of humanity must be saved from Europe, and Europe from itself.

With the end of the war, Wilson engaged TR and his allies in a historic battle over how to organize the peace. For Wilson everything was subordinated to the creation of a collective security system. This required not only self-determination for aggrieved peoples, but a German settlement paving the way for liberal democracy and a solution to the

---

100. Quoted in Daniels, *The End of Innocence*, 316. On FDR's British Embassy connections see by the same author *Washington Quadrille* (Garden City, N.Y.: Doubleday, 1968), chap. 3.
101. FDR quoted in Schlesinger, 1: 482; see also Perkins, *The Roosevelt I Knew*, 15, 46.
102. As recounted to Frances Perkins, *The Roosevelt I Knew*, 15–16.

problem of British naval power, removing what for Wilson had been the chief cause of German animosity leading to the war.[103] Wilson told Sir William Wiseman in October 1918, "If we humiliate the German people and drive them too far, we should destroy all forms of government, and Bolshevism will take its place."[104] He became involved in a bitter controversy over the second of his Fourteen Points, "Freedom of the Seas," seeking to break Britain's traditional ability to wage economic warfare and to invest sole power in the League. For a time, he was prepared to force Britain's hand by building the largest navy in the world.

Theodore Roosevelt had himself suggested (in 1910) a "League of Peace" exercising "international police power" and (in November 1914) an "international posse comitatus."[105] He ridiculed what he saw as the millenarian aspects of Wilson's League but endorsed great-power collaboration with a division of labor along geographical lines.[106] He believed that only a harsh peace would do for Germany, but combined this with a strong awareness of the limits of U.S. power. Logically, it was necessary to back Britain as keeper of the balance. Shortly before his death in January 1919, TR questioned the idea of offering France and Italy an American guarantee "in all future continental wars." At the same time, "America should concede naval supremacy to England... [as] the British Navy is the most potent instrumentality making for world peace."[107]

FDR's emerging worldview combined Wilson's antagonism toward European power politics with Theodore Roosevelt's more traditional and punitive ideas about how to keep the peace. It was toward Wilson that he leaned – though TR had similar ideas – in believing that a group of powers acting in the name of the League could prevent a return to the pattern of intra-European conflict. By virtue of the commercial, financial, and naval might it had acquired during the war, the United States would be the leading member of the group. Also like Wilson, FDR tended to see the League as a mechanism by which the New World

103. On this point see Edward B. Parsons, *Wilsonian Diplomacy: Allied–American Rivalries in War and Peace* (St. Louis, Mo.: Forum Press, 1978), 147.
104. Quoted in Fowler, 284.
105. See Ninkovich, 240, 243; John Morton Blum, *The Republican Roosevelt* (Cambridge, Mass.: Harvard University Press, 1954), 130–33; Osgood, *Ideals and Self Interest*, 96; 147–49; Cooper, 311, 316, 330–33.
106. See TR to W. W. Davies, Nov. 14, 1918, in Morison, ed., 8: 1393. See also Cooper, 333–34.
107. On no guarantee see letter to H. J. Haskell, Dec. 28, 1918, in Morison, ed., 8: 1417; on the British navy see ibid., 1416; also Parsons, 165, quoting a December 1918 speech.

would dictate order to the Old. America's presence in the League was essential lest it become just "a new form of European alliance."[108] But when it came to practical responsibilities, he looked to TR and favored a loose version of "collective security" based on regional blocs. The United States, he said in 1920, was "in a very true sense the big brother of these little [Central American and Caribbean] republics."[109] He favored reservations to the Versailles treaty providing that nothing be "in any way superior to our constitution or in any way interfere with the rights of Congress to declare war or send our soldiers overseas."[110] On Germany, FDR was also closer to TR. In July 1918, he reported to Daniels the view of American soldiers that "a drastic lesson against the Germans themselves on German soil [would] be necessary before any understanding can be hammered into the German mind." This was to be FDR's view of the German problem for the remainder of his life.[111]

On the thorny question of Anglo-American relations, FDR stood somewhere between TR and Wilson. His feelings for Britain were an always fluid mixture of resentment, rivalry, and regard. On the one hand, Britain's staggering sacrifices in the war belied Brooks Adams's and other fin-de-siècle predictions of decline. The same could be said of French aplomb; FDR remarked: "They seem to lose their heads even less than the Anglo-Saxons – very different from what we thought four years ago."[112] During his European trip, FDR was both flattered by the attention of high British officials and angered by their condescension: "I am told it is a very great honor to have had [Admiral] Everett sent down to meet me. Personally I think it is because they wanted to report as to whether I am housebroken or not."[113] Britain's fighting spirit was impressive, but it was also clear that British war aims were selfish and that America had rescued the Allies from stalemate or defeat. The war confirmed the Mahan–TR–Lea thesis that Britain provided an outer line of defense for the United States. On the other hand, FDR had never

108. FDR speech, Mar. 1, 1919. See Basil Rauch, ed., *Franklin D. Roosevelt: Selected Speeches, Messages, Press Conferences, and Letters* (New York: Holt & Rinehart, 1957), 28. See also letter to Robert Mott, Oct. 18, 1920, PVPC, general correspondence, box 18, FDRL.

109. See 1920 campaign speech, quoted in Freidel, *The Ordeal*, 81.

110. *New York Times*, Oct. 12, 1920; on this general topic see Range, chap. 11.

111. See FDR to Daniels, July 29, 1918, PASN, personal correspondence, FDRL. During his inspection tour of the Rhineland in early 1919, Roosevelt insisted that the American flag be raised over the great fortress at Ehrenbreitstein, lest the Germans retain doubts as to who had won the war. See Freidel, *The Ordeal*, 13.

112. *PL, 1905–1928*, 407.

113. Ibid., 384–85. Everett was a high Admiralty official.

idealized the nineteenth century Pax Britannica. From a young age he had welcomed its demise.

FDR supported the Wilson–Daniels effort to bend Britain to America's will. In October 1918, Wilson submitted a three-year program to Congress designed to make the U.S. Navy indisputably number one. Lodge and TR eventually helped to kill the program, but FDR commandeered steel and launched construction.[114] He believed the United States required a fleet large enough to defend its vastly expanded merchant marine and favored the development of a super–battle cruiser despite British reservations. Finally, he blocked the sale of navy radio facilities and patents to the Radio Corporation of America because British (Marconi) interests would indirectly profit.[115]

FDR also supported Wilson's position that Germany's colonies be declared the common property of the League. From contacts with men like the South African leader Jan Smuts – "a fellow Dutchman" – he grasped that "underneath the very unity of the [British] empire ... the pre-war currents of dominion nationalism and separatism were still running deep and strong."[116] In FDR's words, "The tendency for years has been for these dependencies [the white dominions] to assert more and more independence." The United States, not Great Britain, "would be most likely to control the votes of these quasi-independent nations in the League."[117] FDR would henceforth oscillate between TR's view that Britain was America's indispensable partner and Wilson's that British imperialism was a malign force.

TR, FDR, and the origins of containment

A final, central aspect of the European Question emerged after 1917. The issue of Allied intervention in Russia provoked violent disagree-

---

114. See Freidel, *The Apprenticeship*, 227; Parsons, 158, 173, 178; Daniels, *The End of Innocence*, 229, 281; Freidel, *The Ordeal*, 25–26.

115. Freidel, *The Ordeal*, 26–28. In 1920, the total seagoing merchant marine of the United States consisted of 13,789,874 gross tons as compared with 1,871,543 in 1915. Ernest Bogart and Donald Kemmerer, *Economic History of the American People* (New York: Longman Green, 1942), 721–22. By 1920, U.S. ships were carrying 40% of U.S. foreign trade compared with 10% before the war. See Potter, 18. America's merchant marine approached but did not surpass Britain's during the war.

116. TR supported Britain's "right and duty" to retain captured German colonies. See letter to J. M. Clark, Dec. 15, 1918, in Morison, ed., 8: 1416. See also Corelli Barnett, *The Collapse of British Power* (New York: William Morrow, 1972), 119; FDR letter to Smuts, Nov. 24, 1942, *PL, 1928–1945*, 2: 1371.

117. Letter to Nils Goodactive, Oct. 11, 1920, PVPC, FDRL. The latter sentence was not included in the final version of the letter.

ment. Wilson's Fourteen Points message of January 1918 had aimed to derail the Russo-German negotiations that led to the Brest-Litovsk Treaty in March; thereafter Wilson opposed armed intervention on the grounds that it would not succeed in reopening the eastern front, while "trying to stop a revolutionary movement by troops in the field [was] like using a broom to hold back a great ocean."[118] Theodore Roosevelt was closer to the British: "Personally I should be delighted to see us put even a small army together with the Japanese army into Russia and back up some of those Cossack Generals." He added that the United States should "join with *any* faction that would fight the Germans and strive to free Russia."[119] Wilson, after much hesitation, authorized the brief mission of 20,000 U.S. troops to Vladivostok to "keep an eye" on 73,000 Japanese, and 15,000 to Murmansk to guard supplies and prevent the German capture of Archangel.[120] While the distinction was lost on the Bolsheviks, Wilson differed with those who favored a "Grand Crusade" against the Communists and from what can be called a "protocontainment" view.

Such a view was reflected in the turn-of-the-century works of Brooks Adams, Mahan, and the English geographer Halford J. Mackinder. In *America's Economic Supremacy*, Adams had foreseen a Darwinian struggle between Anglo-Saxons and Russians to control the "inexhaustible resources" of China.[121] In *The Problem of Asia* (1900) Mahan pictured a Russia relentlessly encroaching on China, India, and Persia; with Cecil Spring-Rice, he had proposed a counteralliance consisting of the United States, Britain, Germany, and Japan.[122] Mahan favored giving Russia her sought-after warm-water port in Manchuria, "where her efforts would be naturally antagonized by Japan," thus diverting pressure from the more vulnerable Persian Gulf. Anglo-American naval power should always be "at hand and available in the Yangtze valley," the message to Russia being that "trespass as she will in our quarter, a solid core of resistance, invincible, is building up in the decisive field."[123] As for Germany, Mahan wrote an English friend, "I don't know what

118. Link, *Woodrow Wilson: Revolution, War and Peace*, 96.
119. TR letter to William Howard Taft, June 5, 1918, in E. Morison, ed., 8: 1337.
120. Link, *Woodrow Wilson: Revolution, War and Peace*, 96–97.
121. Brooks Adams, chap. 5.
122. See Alfred Thayer Mahan, *The Problem of Asia* (New York: Harper Bros., 1900); Beale, 258.
123. Beale, 250; Mahan to Samuel A. Ashe, Sept. 23, 1899; Mahan to Theodore Roosevelt, Mar. 12, 1901, in Robert Seager III and D. Maguire, eds., *The Letters and Papers of Alfred Thayer Mahan*, vol. 2: *1890–1901* (Annapolis, Md.: Naval Institute Press, 1975), 658, 707.

better conditions there could be for you than to encourage her to stretch *by land* right along the Western border of Russia through Constantinople, to the Euphrates. It would entail enduring friction between her and Russia, and cripple Germany's advance to sea power – by the burden of landward defence etc. entailed."[124]

In 1904, Mahan recommended what he called a "truly remarkable pamphlet" by H. J. Mackinder.[125] In "The Geographical Pivot of History," Mackinder argued that European civilization had been the outcome of a secular struggle between Western sea power and Asiatic land power, the latter arising from the inaccessible (by water) "pivot area" of Siberia and Mongolia.[126] During the "Columbian Age" (1500–1900), the West had reversed its earlier defensive stance by creating a ring of outer, insular bases of sea power and commerce, inaccessible to the land power of Euro-Asia. This was the so-called outer crescent of Britain, North America, South Africa, Australia, and Japan.

Mackinder's message was that this 400-year-old advantage was slipping away. Thanks to the railroad, land power could now tap the resources of the impregnable "pivot area." "A vast economic world . . . will thus develop" while Russian "pressure on Finland, on Scandinavia, on Poland, on Turkey, on Persia, on India, and on China replaces the centrifugal raids of the steppe men." Mackinder warned: "The oversetting of the balance of power in favor of the pivot state resulting in its expansion over the marginal lands of East Asia, would permit the use of vast continental resources for fleet building, and the empire of the world could thus be in sight. This might happen if Germany were to ally herself with Russia."[127]

In *Democratic Ideals and Reality* (1919), written to sway the Paris peacemakers, Mackinder warned: "What if the Great Continent, the Whole World-Island or a large part of it, were at some future time to become a single and united base of sea power?" He renamed the pivot area "Heartland" and extended it westward to include areas where Western "sea power can be refused access," Eastern Europe and the Black and Baltic seas. Indeed, Eastern Europe had now acquired supreme importance as the focal point of struggle for the Heartland between the German and the Slav: "Who rules Eastern Europe commands the

---

124. Alfred Thayer Mahan to Leopold Maxse, Feb. 21, 1902, in Robert Seager III and D. Maguire, eds., *The Letters and Papers of Alfred Thayer Mahan*, vol. 3: 1902–1914, 12.
125. Mahan to Maxse, June 17, 1904, in Seager and Maguire, eds., 3: 99.
126. Halford Mackinder, *Democratic Ideals and Reality: With Additional Papers* (1919) (New York: Norton, 1962), 244.
127. Ibid., 258, 260, 262.

Heartland: who rules the Heartland commands the World-Island: who rules the World-Island commands the world." Mackinder's solution was a "Middle Tier" of states (Czechoslovakia, Poland, Hungary, Yugoslavia, Romania, Bulgaria, Greece) to act as a "complete territorial buffer between Germany and Russia." As high commissioner for South Russia under Foreign Secretary Lord Curzon, Mackinder proposed independent states in White Russia, South Russia, Georgia, Armenia, and the Ukraine.[128]

In sum, from the protocontainment perspective, modern-day Russia was heir to the "cloud of ruthless and idealess horsemen" evoked in Mackinder's essays.[129] Given its location and resources, Russia would pose a greater threat to insular-commercial civilization than Germany or Japan. The task was to use the great energies of the latter in order to keep the bear engaged. The identity of U.S. and British interests was assumed as given, as was the notion that China counted not as a sovereign actor like Japan, but as an anti-Russian glacis and economic asset. The influence of this perspective was clear in Hay's Open Door policy of 1899–1900 and in the Anglo-Japanese Alliance of 1902, permitting Japan to launch war on Russia to general approval in Great Britain and the United States. Protocontainment lost force at a time of Anglo-Russian entente and all-out struggle against Germany, but acquired new life after 1918. Soon it would shape the outlook of diplomats like Robert F. Kelley, Joseph Grew, and their younger colleagues.

What is striking about Franklin Roosevelt's outlook, however, is his relative equanimity, if not indifference, toward Bolshevism and the Russian "threat." FDR, like Wilson, saw Bolshevism as a product of poverty and inequality and therefore preventable through progressive and, if necessary, radical reform. Monied interests manipulated the specter of Bolshevism; skepticism about the existence of a Red menace at home fed doubts about the Russian threat abroad. Roosevelt, moreover, simply did not accept the set of geopolitical notions associated with the protocontainment school.

Once again, FDR was close to Theodore Roosevelt. TR had written in 1897, "I look upon them [the Russians] as a people to whom we can give points, and a beating; a people with a great future as we have; but a people with poisons working in it, as other poisons of similar character on the whole, work in us."[130] On the much-discussed question of

128. Ibid., 70, 150, 160. On Mackinder as adviser to Curzon see G. R. Sloan, *Geopolitics in U.S. Strategic Policy, 1890–1987* (Brighton: Wheatsheaf Books, 1988), 12.
129. Mackinder, 248.
130. TR to Spring-Rice, Aug. 13, 1897, in Morison, ed., 1: 646.

whether Russia or Japan constituted the greater threat, TR shifted for a time toward the anti-Russian, pro-Japanese position of Mahan, Spring-Rice, Hay, and George Kennan, the journalist and anti-czarist crusader. Kennan, author of the celebrated exposé *Siberia and the Exile System*, saw the war between Japan and Russia as a contest between civilization, on the one hand, and barbarism, on the other.[131] In contrast to this group, however, TR was prompted by the outcome of the war in 1905 to readjust his view:

> I have never been able to persuade myself that Russia was going to conquer the world at any time near enough for us to be justified in considering it.... In a dozen years the English, Americans and Germans, who now fear one another as rivals in the trade of the Pacific, will have each to dread the Japanese more than they do any other nation.[132]

Japan's vulture-like descent on German possessions in China, and Russia's collapse during the World War, only reinforced this view.

If Franklin Roosevelt, like TR, took Japan more seriously as a threat to the United States, it was partly because the former was equipped with the kind of naval power exalted by Mahan and Lea that could actually reach the United States.[133] In his belief in the superiority of naval over land power, he may have been more Mahanian than Mahan himself. FDR undoubtedly recognized that protocontainment was essentially a doctrine calling for the defense of a belt of British interests running across the girth of Eurasia from Gibraltar to Hong Kong.[134] The fact that FDR did not see U.S. and British interests as automatically identical, and that he was not concerned about taking British chestnuts out of the fire in India and the Persian Gulf, was additional reason for

---

131. On this point see Beale, 260–64, 311. See also Frederick Travis, Jr., *George Kennan and the American–Russian Relationship, 1865–1924* (Athens: Ohio University Press, 1990), 249–51, 257.

132. TR to Spring-Rice, June 16, 1905, in S. Gwynn, ed., *The Letters and Friendships of Cecil Spring-Rice*, vol. 1: *A Record* (London: Constable, 1929), 472. On September 12, 1905, TR wrote George Otto Trevelyan: "I frankly admire the Russian people and I wish them well. Moreover, I have never been able to make myself afraid of them, because it has always seemed to me that a despotism resting on a corrupt and to a large extent an incapable bureaucracy could not in the long run be dangerous to a virile free people." Morison, ed., 2: 22.

133. On this point see Lea's dramatic account of a Japanese invasion of California in *The Valor of Ignorance* (New York: Harper Bros., 1909). FDR was probably familiar with this book, some of whose themes were developed in *The Day of the Saxon* (1912), which FDR read.

134. Mackinder's term for this belt, including India and China, was the "inner or marginal crescent." There is no evidence that FDR read Mackinder, but it is reasonable to assume that he was familiar with his basic ideas.

his relative indifference to Russia. Moreover – unlike TR, Mahan, Adams, and Hay – FDR took the idea of defending China's "territorial integrity" literally, and not simply as a euphemism for keeping the Russians out and the Anglo-Saxons in. Delano tradition, with its attachment to China and hostility toward Britain, played a role.

Perhaps FDR's skepticism toward protocontainment was also connected to skepticism toward the fatalistic assumptions about countries like Russia that underlay the work of Adams, Mackinder, and Mahan. Theodore Roosevelt wrote: "We are all treading the same path, some slower, some faster; and though the Russian started far behind, yet he has travelled that very path very much farther and faster since the day of Ivan the Terrible than our people have travelled it since the days of Elizabeth."[135] FDR believed this; by 1919, he also believed that the old Europe-centered state system was bankrupt and that doctrines linked to its perpetuation were obsolete. The balance-of-power, turn-of-the-century geopolitics, and protocontainment were part and parcel of a self-serving, self-perpetuating Old World perspective on international relations and therefore were regarded with impatience and contempt.

A Jefferson on the horizon

Leaving Franklin Roosevelt's sickbed at the Lavidia Palace, Yalta, in February 1945, the former Orthodox seminarian Joseph Stalin is said to have remarked, "Why did nature have to punish him so? Is he worse than other people?"[136] It is natural to see FDR's sudden collapse in August 1921 as fate's calling him to account for the selfishness and opportunism of his Washington career. His crippling attack was the culmination of a series of personal calamities: Eleanor's discovery of his affair with Lucy Mercer, his 1920 electoral defeat, and the revelation of his rather sordid role in the Newport vice investigation. For one biographer, "Polio was the dividing point of his life, like Luther's fit in the choir when he fell to the ground raving because he was unable to believe. There were two Franklin D. Roosevelts, before and after polio." Others dispute the "two FDRs" thesis,[137] but it is hard not to see the twenties as a fateful crucible and preparation for Roosevelt's subsequent career.

135. TR to Spring-Rice, Aug. 13, 1897, in Morison, ed., 1: 646.
136. Quoted in Andrei Andreevich Gromyko, *Memories* (London: Hutchinson, 1989), 98.
137. Morgan, 258. Morgan links the polio attack to the weakness of FDR's immunological system, which he in turn links to the highly stressful effects of the Newport investigation scandal. For a sharply different view of the impact of polio on FDR's character, see Daniels, *Washington Quadrille*, 215–16.

FDR's transformation probably should be seen as a result of the *coincidence* of the World War and his own affliction. "The First World War," writes William Pfaff, "put an end to a perception [dear to TR's generation] of individual heroism as a social ideal, as an exemplary proposal of the way a man ought to conduct himself."[138] Physically as well as psychologically, it was almost as if FDR had fought and been gravely wounded in the war. If he had once exalted physical prowess and raw energy, his paralysis led him to emphasize the compensatory virtues of self-control and conciliation. The struggle to recover physical mobility brought greater patience, along with a heightened sense of solidarity toward the outsider and the weak.[139] This is not to say that the twenties were a time of monastic reflection. The years between the 1924 presidential campaign and his election as governor of New York in 1928 were taken up with continuous politicking and self-promotion, as well as physical rehabilitation in Georgia and the Keys. This period did have in store one notable event in FDR's intellectual development: the discovery of Thomas Jefferson.

In his brilliant study *The Jefferson Image in the American Mind*,[140] Merrill Peterson traces the vicissitudes of Jeffersonian thought and iconography in American politics and culture. The generation of Lodge, Mahan, and Theodore Roosevelt venerated Jefferson's historic rival Alexander Hamilton, the champion of centralization, elite rule, and military strength. Turn-of-the-century populists and Democrats, in contrast, "believed that Jefferson, like the Messiah, would rise again."[141] Prominent among them were FDR's wartime boss Josephus Daniels and the editorial writer Claude Bowers, whose partisan recounting of the battle of the two titans appeared in 1925.[142] In a review for the *New York World*, Franklin Roosevelt wrote, "I felt like saying 'At last' as

---

138. William Pfaff, "The Fallen Hero," *New Yorker*, 65, no. 12 (May 8, 1989), 106.
139. An illustration of FDR's frame of mind was the first article he wrote after contracting polio, "Shall We trust Japan?" (*Asia Magazine*, July 1923). FDR's answer – in contrast to earlier and later views – was yes. The article was also an attack on British and Dutch colonialists, who by building up their military power at Singapore and in the East Indies were inviting "the same old vicious circle" (57). For FDR, "The whole trend of the times [was] against wars for colonial expansion. The thought of the world lean[ed] the other way. Populations themselves [had] a say." FDR letter to *Baltimore Sun*, Aug. 13, 1923, quoted in Freidel, *The Ordeal*, 134–35.
140. Merrill Peterson, *The Jefferson Image in the American Mind* (New York: Oxford University Press, 1960).
141. Ibid., 254.
142. *Jefferson and Hamilton* (Boston: Houghton Mifflin, 1925). All quotes are from the 1953 edition.

I read Mr. Claude G. Bowers' thrilling 'Hamilton and Jefferson.'"
Jefferson, "eclipsed in the cabinet by Hamilton," had nonetheless con-
ducted a "mobilization of the masses against the autocracy of the few."
"I have a breathless feeling," FDR concluded, "as I wonder if, a century
and a quarter later, the same contending forces are not again mobilizing.
Hamiltons we have today. Is a Jefferson on the horizon?"[143]

Bowers's Jefferson was a glittering protean bundle of contradictory
elements. He was fundamentally a gentleman farmer and firm believer
in the superiority of country civilization over the corrupt and crowded
city. He was also "the first consummate practical politician of the
Republic," an opportunist, organizer, and manipulator of men. He was
"the lord of the domain," also leveler, radical, and "traitor to his
class." In FDR's own words, "He was a great gentleman. He was a
great commoner. The two are not incompatible."[144] He was a model
more compelling than either TR or Wilson, and someone whose political
saga prefigured with uncanny accuracy the one Roosevelt had by now
imagined as his own.

Roosevelt's interest in Jefferson was not a passing fancy. Peterson has
shown how as president he systematically attempted to drape Jefferson's
mantle over the policies of the New Deal, in the process completing
Jefferson's canonization while transforming his original message.[145] It is
easy to see why Bowers's Jefferson left Roosevelt impressed. Jefferson
was a connoisseur of European culture and science; as American
minister at Paris he displayed a taste for fine claret and aristocratic
women. He also wrote, "I find the general fate of humanity here
most deplorable."[146] Bowers's Jefferson had seen "the wantonness of
Versailles, the drunkedness [sic] of the King, the profligacy of the
Queen." In short, he had seen European society firsthand and had
found it "rotten to the core."[147]

If Jefferson prayed for the collapse of Old Regime Europe, Hamilton's
aristocratic-plutocratic faction looked upon the French Revolution as
the great catastrophe of the age. Hamilton's faction was also the original
"ultra-British party." Supine before England's "arrogant and impu-
dent" Orders in Council and impressment of American seamen, the
Hamiltonians sought to entangle the United States in war with

143. "Is There a Jefferson on the Horizon?" *New York World*, Dec. 3, 1925. Copy in
     FDR Family and Business Papers, box 109, FDRL.
144. Bowers, 92–115, passim; FDR address at Monticello, Virginia, July 4, 1936,
     in Samuel L. Rosenman, ed., *The Public Papers and Addresses of Franklin D.
     Roosevelt*, vol. 5: *1936* (New York: Russell & Russell, 1938), 241.
145. Peterson, chap. 7, pt. 3.
146. Jefferson quoted in Bowers, 99.
147. Ibid., 210. The words are Bowers's.

France.[148] The victory of the Jeffersonians guaranteed the survival of democracy and the avoidance of American military adventurism in league with Britain.

Jefferson's sensibility and outlook with respect to Europe emerge in bold colors from *Hamilton and Jefferson*; Bowers's description is basically confirmed in Jefferson's own writings and the secondary accounts that FDR read.[149] Jefferson's Europe, foreshadowing Wilson's, was essentially depraved. Its "every charm [was] the vicious opposite of an American virtue."[150] But it was also a storehouse of accumulated knowledge from which one could usefully return "charged like a bee, with the honey gathered on it."[151] The honey consisted of standards of beauty and practical scientific information. As a social and political model, Europe was as decadent and corrupt as the United States was youthful and unspoiled. Europe's system of international relations revolved around the most brutal and cynical of human drives and was something to be avoided like the plague. Jefferson held out some hope – before the degeneration of the French Revolution into tyranny and imperialism – that the peoples of the Old World might escape perdition by following the example of the New.

Jefferson's mature vision of Europe emerged only from the experience of his presidency, beginning in 1801. As president his basic objective – as Henry Adams writes, "the essence and genius" of his statesmanship – was peace.[152] Peace – it was practically equivalent to the absence of entanglement with Europe – was necessary in order to avoid the oppressive garrison state of the Hamiltonians and to allow a new system of peace-loving republics to flourish in the Western Hemisphere. He was hardly indifferent to the need for a balance of power between France and Britain, lest one become strong enough to menace American independence, but sought to rely not on armed force but on "peaceable coercion." For Jefferson, "non-intervention was the substitute for war – the weapons of defense and coercion which saved the cost and danger of supporting army or navy and spared America the brutalities of the Old World."[153]

---

148. Ibid., 224.
149. FDR's Thomas Jefferson file, PPF 259, FDRL, contains extensive notes by George Marvin on *The Relation of Thomas Jefferson to American Foreign Policy, 1783–93* by W. K. Wollery; see also a nineteen-page, single-spaced compilation of information on "Jefferson's attitude toward Foreign Affairs," including numerous passages from Jefferson's speeches and letters.
150. Strout, 28.
151. Ibid., 29, quoting Jefferson himself.
152. Adams, quoted in Peterson, 287.
153. Ibid., 289.

The story of Jefferson's presidency is one of achievement laced with irony and disappointment. Once in office, the anti-Federalist and democrat "could no more resist the temptation to stretch his powers than he could abstain from using his mind on any object merely because he might be drawn upon ground supposed to be dangerous."[154] In foreign affairs, Jefferson stretched the power of the executive in order to acquire the Louisiana Territory and later to enforce the capstone of his policy of "peaceable coercion," the total embargo on trade with France and Britain. But Jefferson's attempt to influence Europe from afar with nonviolent methods was a miserable failure. The embargo caused more hardship and dissension at home than abroad and was repealed shortly before Jefferson left office in 1809. The collapse of this experiment in the nonviolent defense of U.S. neutral rights made war all the more likely. It came in 1812.

Jefferson's splenetic outbursts against Europe reflected years of practical experience: "That Bonaparte is an unprincipled tyrant, who is deluging the continent with blood, there is not a human being, not even the wife of his bosom, who does not see."[155] The British government, meanwhile, was "totally without morality, insolent beyond bearing, inflated with vanity and ambition, aiming at the exclusive domination of the sea, lost in corruption, of deep-rooted hatred towards us, hostile to liberty wherever it endeavors to show its head, and the eternal disturber of the peace of the world."[156]

One hundred years before Wilson, Jefferson discovered to his chagrin that isolation did not work. The innate perfidy and predatory instincts of Europe made it impossible for America to cultivate its garden without outside interference. Out of this conviction grew Jefferson's mature vision of Europe and of the relationship between the Old and New Worlds. The vision's force and finality derived from personal disillusionment but also from confidence that matters would be put right in the end: "Not in our day, but at no distant one, we may shake a rod over the heads of all [the Europeans], which may make the stoutest of them tremble. But I hope our wisdom will grow with our power, and teach us, that the less we use our power, the greater it will be."[157] Here was the vision of a Europe not necessarily remade in the American image, but rendered harmless by an America acting for essentially selfish reasons: to be able to pursue its domestic and hemispheric experiments in peace.

154. Ibid., 286.
155. Letter to Thomas Leiper, Jan. 1, 1814, in Norman Graebner, ed., *Ideas and Diplomacy* (New York: Oxford University Press, 1964), 122.
156. Letter to Thomas Leiper, June 12, 1815, in ibid., 123.
157. Ibid., 124.

However he imagined it, Jefferson's rod was something to be wielded sparingly and from a distance. There was no suggestion of American physical or political entanglement in Europe. Jefferson abhorred the thought.

Franklin Roosevelt's discovery of the Sage of Monticello, his identification of himself with the enemy of "Anglomania" at home and autocracy abroad, was an important stage in the development of his European sensibility and outlook. As in the case of Roosevelt's collapse from polio, the discovery of Jefferson did not trigger a Saul-like conversion; rather, it accentuated certain existing attitudes and left him even more conscious of the moral and political gulf between the New World and the Old. Like Jefferson's and Wilson's, FDR's mature vision of Europe would grow out of the experience of his own presidency, specifically out of the dilemma of how to pursue policies of improvement at home and in the Western Hemisphere, with the rest of the world – thanks to Europe's unresolved conflicts – sliding into war.

Bowers's story ended with Jefferson's triumph over the conservative monied interests in the election of 1800. But Jefferson's true measure, complexity, and tragedy emerged only after 1800, the year in which Henry Adams opens his classic narrative account. Roosevelt's analogous triumph came in 1932, the year in which the Bowers period of his career closes and the Adams period begins.

2

The Roosevelt administration and the European Question, 1933–1941

A welter of rivalries

"At the heart of the New Deal," according to Richard Hofstadter, "there was not a philosophy but a temperament," experimental, improvisational, and reactive to events.[1] At the heart of New Deal foreign policy, it often seems, there was not a program but a syndrome: fear of reentanglement in Europe, abhorrence of war, the supremacy of home affairs. Contemporaries had the frequent impression of discontinuity and disinterest in foreign policy; historians have seen the administration's diplomacy as parochial and inept.[2] Both sympathetic and critical observers have complained of the impossibility of penetrating beyond the level of generalities to "determine or demonstrate the President's outlook, reasoning and attitude on specific questions or policies."[3] Any attempt to understand FDR's diplomacy must reckon with the "happy go lucky" methods,[4] the administrative chaos, and the welter of personal and political rivalries that characterized the realm of foreign as well as domestic policy. To elucidate Roosevelt's foreign policy one must turn first to the diplomatic culture of the 1930s, and to his courtiers and advisers.

1. Hofstadter, 311.
2. For critical treatments see, e.g., F. Marks III; Robert A. Divine, *The Reluctant Belligerent: American Entry into World War II* (New York: Wiley, 1965); Donald Offner, *American Appeasement: U.S. Foreign Policy and Germany, 1933–38* (Cambridge, Mass.: Harvard University Press, 1969); David Schmitz, *The United States and Fascist Italy, 1922–1940* (Chapel Hill: University of North Carolina Press, 1988).
3. See William L. Langer and S. Everett Gleason, *The Challenge to Isolation, 1937–1940* (New York: Harper Bros., 1952), 2. See also D. Cameron Watt, "Britain and the Historiography of the Yalta Conference and the Cold War," *Diplomatic History*, 13 no. 1 (Winter 1989), 75.
4. The expression is Henry Stimson's, quoted in Langer and Gleason, *Challenge*, 10.

The world crisis of the thirties gave rise to a range of positions resembling that of the 1914–17 period[5] but complicated by the Bolshevik Revolution and the Wilsonian crusade. The hyphenate communities of the Middle West continued to oppose European entanglement, but pacifist-isolationist sentiment was now far more widespread and respectable:

> Having waged a war to make the world safe for democracy, the country watched with bitter disillusionment the rise of dictatorships. . . . On all sides it was felt again that the European system was basically rotten, that war was endemic on that continent, and that the Europeans had only themselves to blame for their plight.[6]

At the other end of the spectrum, the Anglophile business and cultural elites who had spearheaded intervention found themselves weakened and discredited by the Wall Street crash and by charges of war profiteering – a theme of the famous mid-decade Nye committee hearings.

The political and ideological composition of the Roosevelt administration itself was fluid and complex. Its foreign policy apparatus was a kind of carnival of cliques whose internal balance shifted according to the preference of the president, the settling of personal scores, and the pressure of events. Some people changed their position over time; others defy easy categorization. Nonetheless, it is possible to identify four basic tendencies of thought with respect to the problem of Europe, two of which struck a responsive chord in Roosevelt's own makeup and two of which he identified with more sporadically, or for reasons of domestic political expediency, if at all. Those tendencies were Hullian liberalism, protocontainment, Europhobic hemispherism, and finally activism of a Progressive Republican stamp.

"I have seen war"

When asked to explain the presence of Cordell Hull in his government, Roosevelt said that his secretary of state was "the only member of the cabinet who brings me any political strength that I don't have in my own right."[7] Hull, in other words, represented something distinct from Roosevelt: the southern, evangelical, free-trade, and purist strain of Wilsonian internationalism that continued to have an important constituency in the country and in Congress. FDR needed the Wilsonians and wished to seem sufficiently orthodox, despite his lapses, to be

5. See Chapter 1, this volume.
6. Langer and Gleason, *Challenge*, 14.
7. Quoted in Morgan, 371.

accepted as their champion. There were features of Hull's outlook that held genuine appeal to FDR: the necessity of disarmament, the animus toward European imperialism, the importance of exports for domestic recovery. But unlike Hull,[8] Roosevelt saw the international crisis of the thirties as only partially, and not essentially, economic and commercial in origin. Nor did Roosevelt believe in the universalistic version of collective security with its vision of a Parliament of Mankind associated with Hull, his fellow Tennessean Norman H. Davis, and Leo Pasvolsky of the State Department. FDR's rejection of U.S. membership in the existing League of Nations in 1932 was a case where conviction and short-term political considerations happened to coincide.[9]

The second tendency of thought within the administration was proto-containment, the intellectual legacy of Brooks Adams, Halford Mackinder, and Alfred Thayer Mahan.[10] The strength of this outlook within the Democratic Party of the thirties was considerable. It conditioned the views of a number of FDR's crony-ambassadors, Breckinridge Long, John Cudahy, and Joseph P. Kennedy, as well as the professional diplomatic corps. A protocontainment outlook was systematically cultivated within the Division of Eastern European Affairs of the State Department, founded in 1924, and directed by the scholar-diplomat Robert F. Kelley. The esprit de corps and intellectual prowess of the Russian specialists set them apart from their colleagues, as did the sensation that they "took Russia too seriously" and were out of step with the administration. They were frequently at odds with Roosevelt himself; as a firsthand observer recalled, "There was strong evidence that pressure was brought to bear from the White House" when the division was summarily disbanded in 1937, its members scattered to the four winds (Kelley to Ankara) and its fine library and special files dispersed.[11]

As has been seen, Roosevelt discounted the geopolitical assumptions

---

8. For a precise summary of Hull's views on the economic causes and solutions to the interwar crisis, see *The Memoirs of Cordell Hull* (London: Hodder & Stoughton, 1948), 1: 364.

9. For FDR's Feb. 2, 1932, statement, see Edgar Nixon, ed., *Franklin D. Roosevelt and Foreign Affairs* (New York: Clearwater, 1969), 1: 23–24 (hereafter, *FFA*).

10. On the origins of "protocontainment" see Chapter 1, this volume.

11. George F. Kennan, *Memoirs*, vol. 1: *1925–1950* (Boston: Little, Brown, 1967), 84–85. The division was integrated with the Division of Western European Affairs to form the new Division of European Affairs (EUR). Kennan served one year, in his words "on the so-called Russian desk" of EUR. The expression "took Russia too seriously" is also Kennan's. See also Thomas Maddux, *Years of Estrangement: American Relations with the Soviet Union, 1933–41* (Tallahassee: University Press of Florida, 1980), 89.

connected with protocontainment, its tendency to seek common cause
with Germany and British imperialism, its denigration of China, and its
deterministic view of Russia.[12] He dismissed Kelley's objections and
extended diplomatic recognition to the Soviet Union in 1933. He had
no direct experience of Russia to dampen his native optimism; nor did
he take domestic communism seriously, and he distrusted those who
did. He believed that Wilson and the Allies bore a share of responsibility
for embittering relations after 1917, and he had TR's sense that the two
countries were fundamentally similar and growing more alike. The
United States and the Soviet Union after all were continental, federal,
essentially non-European, and noncolonial (recall FDR's 1898 debate);[13]
their peoples were forward-looking, experimental, and religiously inclined. Not only did history indicate, as Walter Lippmann later put
it, that Russia and America had "usually, each in its own interest,
supported one another in the critical moments of their history [e.g., the
American Civil War and World War I],"[14] geography and national
temperament suggested the likelihood of collaboration rather than
conflict – so long as reactionaries on both sides could be contained.

At first glance, then, it seems odd that two of FDR's closest advisers
were among the most articulate spokesmen of the protocontainment
view. Adolf Berle, assistant secretary of state, 1938–44, and William C.
Bullitt, ambassador to Moscow, 1933–36, and Paris, 1936–40, had
been advisers on Russia at Versailles. Both were part of the self-styled
jeunesse radicale, the Ivy League idealists who, like the slightly older
British Treasury official John Maynard Keynes, had quit Paris in shock
and disgust over the "Carthaginian peace."[15] Bullitt nursed a hatred of
Wilson and the British who had rejected the plan of reconciliation he
had personally obtained from Lenin in early 1919. In 1933, Roosevelt
had thought Bullitt seemed an ideal diplomatic choice, but the mercurial,
Francophile ambassador was disenchanted again, this time by the controversy over Russian war debts and Comintern activities in the United
States. Departing from Moscow, Bullitt offered a piece of advice-cum-
personal-confession: "We should not cherish for a moment the illusion

12. See Chapter 1, this volume.
13. *PL, The Early Years*, 160; see also Chapter 1, this volume.
14. Walter Lippmann, *U.S. Foreign Policy: Shield of the Republic* (Boston: Little, Brown,
    1943), 140.
15. See Jordan Schwarz, *Liberal: Adolf A. Berle and the Vision of an American Era*
    (New York: Free Press, 1987), 33; see also Max Ascoli, Introduction to Beatrice Berle
    and Travis Beal Jacobs, eds., *Navigating the Rapids, 1918–1971: The Papers of
    Adolf A. Berle* (New York: Harcourt Brace Jovanovich, 1973), xv. For Berle's
    recollection see letter to Upton Sinclair, Dec. 27, 1939, Berle Papers, box 211, FDRL.

that it is possible to establish really friendly relations with the Soviet Government or with any Communist party or communist individuals."[16] Berle's post-1919 disillusion with Europe was even more radical; his anti-Bolshevism was reinforced by political battles in New York. Berle and Bullitt were separated by State Department infighting,[17] but they approached the European crisis along strikingly similar lines. Both saw the Versailles settlement as a strategic and moral travesty. Both wanted to foster a territorially self-satisfied unit in Central Europe of sufficient stability, cohesion, and economic scale to ensure peace and to stem the tide of Bolshevism – without outside help. This was the goal of Bullitt's insistent efforts in 1936–38. "The root of the problem," he told FDR in November 1936, "is still – as it has been for so long – reconciliation of France and Germany." He felt sure that "the essential thing the Germans must have is the development of their economic relations with Central Europe and the Balkans," something that French leaders did not object to and that would happen even if they did.[18]

Bullitt urged Roosevelt to change ambassadors in Berlin because William E. Dodd was not on speaking terms with high Nazi officials. German control over Austria and Czechoslovakia might not be

> a promising picture but there is one element in it that is not altogether dreadful. The Russians have now apparently retired behind their swamps, and the fact is beginning to be recognized even in France that the eastern boundary of Europe is not the Ural Mountains but the swamps which extend from Finland, past Poland, to Romania.... The only way that I can see that the growth of German strength, which I regard as inevitable, can be used for constructive instead of destructive purposes is by a general effort to make the giving of these concessions to Germany a part of a general plan of unification for Europe.[19]

When war seemed imminent in May 1938, Bullitt advised Roosevelt to call an emergency meeting at The Hague "to attempt to work out a peaceful settlement of the dispute between Germany and Czechoslovakia." War could "only end in the establishment of Bolshevism from one end of the Continent to the other." During the Munich crisis he had a similar suggestion incorporated into FDR's September 27, 1938, message to Hitler.[20]

16. William Bullitt (hereafter, WB) to Secretary of State, Apr. 20, 1936, in Orville H. Bullitt, ed., *For the President, Personal and Secret: Correspondence Between Franklin D. Roosevelt and William C. Bullitt* (Boston: Houghton Mifflin, 1972), 155.
17. Bullitt was a friend of Judge R. Walton Moore, counselor of the department after 1937; Berle of Moore's department rival, Under Secretary Sumner Welles.
18. WB to FDR, Nov. 8, 1936, in Bullitt, ed., 180.
19. WB to FDR, Nov. 23, 1937, in ibid., 235–37.
20. WB to FDR, May 20, 1938, in ibid., 262–63; WB telephone conversation with

Berle, for his part, wrote in late 1937: "Anglo-French discussion about a political solution which includes ceding colonies to Germany is going forward. This is all to the good." But colonies alone were not the solution; "great free trade areas of middle Europe" were.[21] On the eve of the *Anchluss* in early 1938, he noted: "I think this is all to the good. Whatever can be done by diplomacy does not have to be done later by war."[22] Hitler, like Napoleon III, was transitory. The economic and political logic of a united Central Europe was not.[23]

Berle returned to this theme during the Munich crisis, telling Roosevelt that the breakup of the Austro-Hungarian Empire had been "more dictated by French military considerations than trained political men." As for the assumption that

> a reconsolidation of that area would create a power which would invariably move westward: this is emotion rather than analysis. Actually that unit of sovereignty existed in Europe for some centuries after the death of the Emperor Charles V.... Instead of swallowing West Europe, it was principally occupied in maintaining its own organization and putting off the Turks.

This time the "eastern march [would] meet the Russians" and the new empire would find itself "occupied by the Slavs." Hitler was quite possibly "the only instrument capable of reestablishing a race and economic unit which can survive and leave Europe in balance."[24]

Needless to say, it was something other than the ardent anti-Bolshevism of Bullitt and Berle that accounted for their intimacy with FDR. Both eventually repudiated Roosevelt's Soviet policy and this figured in their political demise.[25] Berle was a domestic adviser par excellence valued for his intellect and troubleshooting skills. Bullitt,

Sumner Welles, Sept. 27, 1938, in ibid., 294–95; Roosevelt to Hitler, Sept. 27, 1938, *FFA*, 2: 226–28.

21. Berle Diary, Nov. 30, 1937, FDRL.
22. Ibid., Feb. 16, 1938.
23. Memorandum to the Under Secretary and Secretary of State, Mar. 16, 1938. Berle Papers, box 210, FDRL.
24. Berle, personal memo to the president, Sept. 1, 1938. PSF, State Dept.–Berle, box 94, FDRL. Berle made a similar argument in a memo dated Aug. 29, 1938, concluding: "At the moment what is needed is clear and cold heads, rather than soft hearts." Berle Papers, box 210, FDRL.
25. Berle was sent to Brazil as ambassador after the November 1944 reorganization of the State Department and after two blunt memos warning of Soviet expansionism. See Jordan Schwarz, 241–42. Bullitt's fall was connected to his role in the Sumner Welles affair, but it is certain that he would have turned against Roosevelt and his Russian policy in any event. See his memos to the president of Jan. 29 and May 12, 1943, in Bullitt, ed., 575–600.

the insouciant spirit and "fellow Huguenot," knew how to amuse Roosevelt, telling him, for example, that the upper classes were "just as dumb" in Paris "as their opposite numbers" at home.[26] But there was also a fundamental feature of their outlooks that matched them with FDR, even as he filtered out their message about the Russians. It is misleading to call it "isolationism"; rather, it was a particularly Europhobic strain of Wilsonianism, combined, especially in Berle's case, with an underlying "hemispherism," which should not be confused with the "Fortress America" of Charles Lindbergh and his supporters.

The message that FDR took from Berle and Bullitt was the folly of fighting a war to uphold a political-territorial settlement that reflected the triumph of European selfishness and stupidity — in Berle's words, "to maintain a situation which was untenable from the time it was created by the treaties of Versailles and Saint-Germain."[27] Both were especially suspicious and contemptuous of the British. Bullitt maintained that London stood in the way of Franco-German reconciliation while at the same time lacking the spine to stand up to the Nazis. Berle rarely concluded a memorandum or diary entry without warning against the type of Anglophile emotionalism and intrigue that, he believed, had led to American entanglement in 1917. He told the president, "We have not yet developed a Walter Hines Page or a Colonel House who will secretly start us on the road to war behind your back and that of the State Department; but there are probably three or four candidates for these roles in the offing."[28]

All of this struck a responsive chord in Roosevelt, as did the visceral fear of destruction from the air and entrapment in Europe that pervaded Bullitt's outlook. FDR probably pronounced few words with more conviction than those — written for him by Bullitt — of August 14, 1936: "I have seen war, I have seen war on land and sea. I have seen blood running from the wounded. I have seen men coughing out their gassed

26. See WB to FDR, Oct. 24, 1936, in Bullitt, ed., 173; on the Huguenot connection, see FDR to WB, Nov. 11, 1937, in ibid., 230.
27. See Berle memo of Sept. 1, 1938, cited in note 24.
28. For Bullitt on Britain see letter to FDR, Nov. 23, 1937, in Bullitt, ed., 236–37. Bullitt's brother Orville comments, "Bill had a distinct bias against the British that went back to his childhood, when England was engaged in the Boer War in South Africa. His sympathies were all with the Boers." Ibid., xli. See also Berle to FDR, Sept. 1, 1938, cited in note 24. Berle agreed to enter the State Department in late 1937 on the grounds that "I would rather do it myself than leave it to some second rate intriguer picked from the political basket who will get us in a British alliance and a European–Atlantic war." Berle Diary, Nov. 29, 1937, FDRL.

lungs.... I hate war."[29] Biographers have noted Roosevelt's acute phobia of fire. Whether acquired during his tour of the western front in 1918 or during his forced immobility in the twenties, he had a morbid aversion to mud and the modern battlefield, with its swamplike landscape, trenches, and barbed wire. This terror of paralysis on the ground, combined with the exaltation of sea and increasingly of air power, was always inherent in his foreign policy.[30] During the war FDR told the British ambassador that he thought "history would judge Neville Chamberlain on Munich more kindly than he was judged at present." One of the reasons for Roosevelt's endorsement of the Munich agreement at the time was the mistaken belief that the Western powers were hopelessly outclassed in the air.[31]

In September 1938, Berle and Bullitt believed that the United States should not enter a war whose "result would be such a devastation of Europe that it would make small difference which side should emerge the ostensible victor." For Bullitt, "We should attempt to stay out and be ready to reconstruct whatever pieces may be left of European civilization." After Munich, Bullitt's Francophile instincts came to the fore, while Berle argued that "we should be developing a North–South axis, and not be swung off base by either diplomacy or emotion."[32] Berle was now closer than ever to his best friend in the department, Under Secretary of State Sumner Welles.

Welles was, and remains, the mystery man of the Roosevelt State Department and the focal point of its endemic personal feuding. There were many reasons for his unpopularity, starting with his "portentous gravity" and "cold, Curzonian manner." The main reason was his

---

29. Speech at Chautauqua, N.Y., Aug. 14, 1936, *FFA*, 3: 377, 380; on Bullitt's authorship see 383, n. 3, 384, n. 13.
30. On FDR and fire, see Ward, *Before the Trumpet*, 117–19.
31. Bullitt was particularly insistent on this point. WB to FDR, Sept. 20, 1938, in Bullitt, ed., 288. Ambassador Joseph Kennedy and Charles Lindbergh also encouraged the impression of overwhelming German superiority. See Telford Taylor, *Munich: The Price of Peace* (Garden City, N.Y.: Doubleday, 1979), 650, 865. For FDR's view as reported by Harold Ickes, see entry for Sept. 24, 1938, in *The Secret Diary of Harold L. Ickes*, vol. 2: *The Inside Struggle, 1936–39* (London: Weidenfeld & Nicholson, 1955), 474. Josephus Daniels reported similar remarks by FDR in January 1939. See Carroll Kirkpatrick, ed., *Roosevelt and Daniels* (Chapel Hill: University of North Carolina Press, 1952), 181. For FDR on Chamberlain, see Halifax to Eden, May 21, 1943, FO 954/30, PRO. See also Henry Morgenthau's account of the White House meeting of November 14, 1938. John Morton Blum, ed., *From the Morgenthau Diaries* (Boston: Houghton Mifflin, 1965), 2: 48.
32. Bullitt to FDR, Aug. 31, 1938, in O. Bullitt, ed., 283; Berle memo of Sept. 1, 1938, cited in note 24.

privileged relationship with the White House, based on family and
political ties and on the fact that Welles faithfully and effectively
interpreted the Europhobic-cum-hemispheric tendency in FDR's own
makeup.[33] The man whom Roosevelt kept as his most intimate foreign
policy adviser had obtained his diplomatic education in Buenos Aires,
Santo Domingo, and Havana. Like Berle, Welles had deeper sympathy
for Latin American than for European civilization. He wrote of American
foreign policy in 1927, "In the Western Hemisphere lies its strength and
its support."[34]

The "Good Neighbor policy" absorbed much of the attention of U.S.
diplomacy in the thirties. At its heart was the original defensive and
anti-European conception of the Monroe Doctrine, given new credibility
by the renunciation of unilateral intervention in the internal affairs of
Latin American states. The system of hemispheric consultation and
solidarity hammered out at Montevideo (1933), Buenos Aires (1936),
and Lima (1938) was designed to serve as a "salutary example to
the world" and to protect the region from Old World subversion or
aggression.[35] There was no question in the minds of Welles, Berle,
and Josephus Daniels, now ambassador to Mexico, where the main
commitment of U.S. energies belonged. The future of Western civilization in the thirties depended on the survival of the Americas. Welles's
late-thirties foray into the European snake pit reflected this fundamental
view.

Like other Wilsonians of his generation, Welles viewed Europe with
a jaded eye and saw little to choose between the new imperialism

33. The expression "portentous gravity" is Ickes's, 351. The expression "cold, Curzonian
    manner" is contained in the British Embassy document "Supplement to Weekly
    Political Report," Dec. 2, 1944, FO 371/38551, PRO. Welles, scion of a rich New
    York family, had attended FDR's wedding as a boy of twelve and graduated from
    Groton and Harvard. He was a prominent figure in the Maryland Democratic
    Party and contributed heavily to FDR's campaign in 1932. See Irwin F. Gellman,
    Good Neighbor Diplomacy: United States Policies in Latin America, 1933–1945
    (Baltimore: Johns Hopkins University Press, 1979), 13–14. See also Berle's letter
    to FDR recommending Welles's appointment as under secretary and stressing his
    domestic political prestige. Berle to FDR ("My Dear Caesar"), June 30, 1936, PSF,
    State Department, Berle, box 94, FDRL.
34. Sumner Welles, *Naboth's Vineyard*, 2 vols. (New York: Payson & Clarke, 1928),
    quoted in Irwin Gellman, 14. This was Welles's history of the Dominican Republic.
    Berle was also tied emotionally to the Dominican Republic. His first contact there
    with Latin America in the early twenties was according to his biographer "a turning
    point in Berle's life." Schwarz, 19.
35. For the expression "salutary example" see FDR speech to the Buenos Aires con-
    ference, Dec. 1, 1936. FFA, 9: 519. On this point see also Irwin Gellman, chaps. 2
    and 3; Kimball, *The Juggler*, chap. 6.

(German and Italian) and the old (British and French). Welles's "memoirs" are notable for their self-serving obfuscation, also for the ill-will and bitterness they reveal toward the British and French. The "fictitious 'national government' of Ramsay McDonald was chiefly to blame" for German rearmament, while France in the thirties was "a maze of gross corruption, of political scandal, of petty partisan chicanery."[36] Welles promoted a "general settlement" of European differences – the term was synonymous with appeasement – on the grounds that Versailles was untenable and unjust, that legitimate economic grievances fueled Nazi demands, and that conciliation might strengthen the hand of reasonable people in Germany at the expense of Hitler and his cohorts. Before one rushes to pillory Welles, it should be remembered that Winston Churchill claimed that he would have sought a similar settlement – had he been in the cabinet – and when Foreign Secretary Anthony Eden resigned in early 1938, he did so over the side issue of how and whether to detach Mussolini from Hitler and not the main issue of a deal with the latter.[37] Even the strongly anti-Nazi William Dodd blamed France for the rise of the "Hitler–Goring–Goebbels triumvirate" and believed that Germany was entitled to some colonies.[38]

The so-called Welles Plan continued in fits and starts after October 1937 and ended with Welles's famous trip to Europe in early 1940.[39] Welles envisioned a United States–led group of neutrals laying down rules of international behavior according to which the necessary "practical agreements," including concessions to Germany, were to

---

36. Sumner Welles, *Seven Decisions That Shaped History* (New York: Harper Bros., 1950), 2, 4.

37. See Gerhard L. Weinberg, *The Foreign Policy of Hitler's Germany: Starting World War II, 1937–1939* (Chicago: University of Chicago Press, 1980), 670. David Reynolds writes, "Even Churchill advocated not war but negotiation from a position of strength." *The Creation of the Anglo-American Alliance: A Study in Competitive Cooperation* (London: Europa Publications, 1981), 9.

38. Dodd wrote that the German people had been inclined to democracy in 1919, but "40 billion of indemnity demanded by France plus the refusal of France to disarm slowly brought the [German] population back to their faith in militarism and the Hitler–Goering–Goebbels triumvirate is the result." Dodd to FDR, May 9, 1935. *FFA*, 2: 500–1. On German colonies, see diary entry for Dec. 11, 1937, in William E. Dodd, Jr., and Martha Dodd, eds., *Ambassador Dodd's Diary, 1933–1938* (New York: Harcourt, Brace, 1941), 437.

39. For a running account, free of moralizing, see Callum A. MacDonald, *The United States, Britain and Appeasement, 1936–1939* (New York: St. Martin's Press, 1981); see also Langer and Gleason, *Challenge*, 20–32. The most acute interpretation of the Welles mission is Reynolds's, 69–72.

be made.[40] This initiative foundered on Hull's insistence that Britain and France give prior approval, something Welles felt would rob the proposal of impartiality and dramatic impact. Welles revived the idea in January 1938, but this time Prime Minister Chamberlain was consulted. Chamberlain first rejected, then, after Eden's well-founded advice not to snub Roosevelt, agreed to consider the plan. FDR himself suspended it, pending the outcome of the political crisis in Germany during which Hitler purged moderates from the government and the army. Throughout, Welles insisted that the United States did not endorse Chamberlain's policy per se, nor could it participate directly in any "political appeasement."[41]

Supported by Berle and Jay Pierrepont Moffat, a senior colleague, Welles stuck to the idea of a "general settlement" and, once war began, of a compromise peace. The "Welles Plan" reemerged in the presidential request of April 15, 1939, to the dictators that they pledge not to attack a list of thirty-one nations for at least ten years.[42] At the height of the "phony war" in February–March 1940, Welles spent several weeks sounding out Mussolini, Hitler, Daladier, and Chamberlain on the possibility of action by the United States in the role, presumably, of "umpire" or "moderator." Welles came home confirmed in his belief that the Europeans were utterly bereft of "the kind of visionary statesmanship required to stave off destruction."[43]

The striking thing about this initiative is the cynicism it reflected about European motives, along with its hemispheric preoccupations. Despite the signing of an Anglo-American trade agreement in 1938, the United States feared as late as August 1939 the conclusion of an Anglo-German deal that would act as a fillip to German penetration of Latin

---

40. For documentation see U.S. Department of State, *Foreign Relations of the United States* (Washington: U.S. Government Printing Office, 1954) (hereafter, *FRUS*), 1937, 1: 665.

41. See *FRUS*, 1938, 1: 116, 128; MacDonald, 70. On the concern of British officials to avoid the appearance of snubbing FDR, see David Dilkes, ed., *The Diaries of Sir Alexander Cadogan, O.M., 1938–1945* (London: Cassell, 1971), 36–39.

42. In return the United States would arrange and take part in a conference promising disarmament and trade liberalization. See Dallek, 185–86.

43. The term "umpire" was used by FDR in a January 1940 conversation with Lord Lothian, the British ambassador. See Reynolds, 71. "Moderator" was used in the parallel (to Welles's) conversations conducted with Hitler and others by U.S. businessman James Moody, acting on behalf of FDR. See Moody's report to FDR, Mar. 15, 1940, PSF Italy, box 4, FDRL. For documentation of the Welles mission, see *FRUS*, 1940, 1: 1–117. The otherwise interesting diaries of Jay Pierrepont Moffat, who accompanied Welles, are of little use on the trip. See N. H. Hooker, ed., *The Moffat Papers* (Cambridge, Mass.: Harvard University Press, 1956).

America.[44] The outbreak of war did not allay these fears. Berle noted in March 1940: "There has always been a strong opinion in Great Britain for making peace with the Germans on the best terms.... It would be just like some bright Englishman to concede them a sphere of influence in South America leaving it up to us to meet the ensuing situation."[45] Certainly there was little reason to "count on a military victory of Britain, France and Poland,"[46] and in the performance of that alliance as of June 1940, noted Langer and Gleason, "will be found the principal justification for Mr. Roosevelt's belief that a peace negotiated with Hitler was at least preferable to a peace dictated by him."[47]

The timing of the U.S. initiatives reflected their mainly defensive and hemispheric rationale. In late 1937, the Americans feared a Rome–Berlin–Tokyo alliance. Since, or so Welles assumed, the Germans would attend a conference leading to concessions while the Italians and Japanese would probably refuse, the plan would split the Axis and counter the encirclement of the Western Hemisphere.[48] With the collapse of Poland in September 1939, Roosevelt told Berle:

> The real objective would be to get into the Atlantic. He [FDR] had been thinking that this would be done by a Mediterranean drive, with the ultimate design of getting a strong foothold on the Atlantic coast or in some of the Atlantic islands: the Azores, Cape Verde, or the like; possibly through pressure on Portugal. This involved having a land line, and therefore Italy's action became singularly important.

Welles attached special importance to keeping Italy out of the war, realizing that a successful German offensive would pull Mussolini in its wake. In fact, Hitler and the German navy did seriously contemplate taking the Azores; Roosevelt's fears of an Atlantic drive faded only with the invasion of Russia in June 1941.[49]

Finally, Berle and Welles did not rejoice at the prospect, however remote it may have seemed, of a decisive Allied victory in 1939–40.[50]

44. See MacDonald, 116, 165, 174.
45. Berle Diary, Mar. 29, 1940.
46. See Berle memo, undated but sometime in Sept. 1939. Berle Papers, FDRL.
47. Langer and Gleason, *Challenge*, 375.
48. See *FRUS*, 1937, 1: 668.
49. Memorandum, Sept. 22, 1939, Berle Papers, box 211, FDRL. See conclusion to his report, *FRUS*, 1940, 1: 116–17. On the Atlantic islands see Heinrichs, 64, 78, 82.
50. The British themselves were surprisingly optimistic about the outcome of the war in early 1940. On this point see William R. Rock, *Chamberlain and Roosevelt: British Foreign Policy and the United States, 1937–1940* (Columbus: Ohio State University Press, 1988), 247. For Rock's discussion of the motive behind the Welles mission, see 262–63. See also Stanley E. Hilton, "The Welles Mission to Europe, February–March 1940: Illusion or Realism?" *Journal of American History*, 58 (1971), 93–120.

Should Germany suddenly collapse through economic strangulation, the Americans would have no reason, in view of the Versailles precedent, to be optimistic about the kind of peace settlement that would ensue – and from which this time they might be excluded. Thus Welles's diplomacy was inspired in part by Wilson's "peace without victory" formula of 1917 – by the hope of bringing American leverage to bear during the military stalemate in order to settle European matters definitively and in a manner favorable to the United States. Essentially this meant preventing Europe's internecine quarrels from engulfing the New World. A British Foreign Office official accurately characterized Welles (on a later occasion) as "another Wilson only 20 years out-of-date."[51]

A fighting edge

"Europhobic-hemispherism" (if more ponderous, this term is more descriptive than "appeasement," a word that now carries connotations it did not in the thirties) was the dominant tendency within the administration from the time the president denounced the "so-called statesmen" and the "so-called peace" of 1919 and renounced unilateral intervention in Latin America.[52] The record is full of presidential expressions of the anxiety, suspicion, and disgust that animated this tendency, and Welles remained the president's confidant and able lieutenant until his downfall in 1943.[53]

51. Reynolds, 20, is convincing on the "underlying Wilsonianism of U.S. policy" during this phase. For the Foreign Office opinion of Welles, see Steven Merritt Miner, *Between Churchill and Stalin: The Soviet Union, Great Britain, and the Origins of the Grand Alliance* (Chapel Hill: University of North Carolina Press, 1988), 217.
52. Speech to the Woodrow Wilson Foundation, Dec. 29, 1933, *FFA*, 1: 560–63.
53. Pressed by Hull and Bullitt to fire Welles, lest his homosexuality become public, FDR reluctantly accepted his friend's resignation in September 1943. The incident provoked Roosevelt's final break with Bullitt, whose conduct infuriated him. On the president's feelings toward Europe, see his letter to W. Dodd of Aug. 27, 1934: "I am too downhearted about Europe but I watch for any ray of hope or opening to give me an opportunity to lend a helping hand." *FFA*, 1: 187; to Hull, Mar. 9, 1935, referring to British unwillingness to accept international armament inspection, "At some future time it may be advisable to pull this rabbit out of our hat as proof that the present British Government is not sincere [about disarmament]....I am much discouraged." PSF, Disarmament Conference, box 144, FDRL; to Dodd, Jan. 6, 1936, "Your letter confirmed my feeling of supreme disgust in regard to European and Atlantic affairs." PSF Germany, Dodd 1936–38, box 45, FDRL; to William Phillips, Mar. 16, 1936, commenting on the occupation of the Rhineland, "What a thoroughly disgusting spectacle so-called civilized man in Europe can make himself!" PSF, Russia, 1935–36, FDRL; to Phillips, May 17, 1937, on peace efforts, "The progress of the disease is slowed up but the disease remains – and will probably prove fatal in the next few years." *PL, 1928–1945*, 1: 681.

Needless to say, there was an opposed tendency of thought within the administration, one associated with Ambassador Dodd, the professional diplomat George Messersmith, Treasury Secretary Henry Morgenthau, Interior Secretary Harold L. Ickes, Agricultural Secretary Henry Wallace, and later Navy Secretary Frank Knox, War Secretary Henry L. Stimson, the ambassador to Great Britain John Winant, and the editor William Allen White.[54] Of Chamberlain's – and implicitly Welles's – policy, Messersmith wrote, "No concession has yet satisfied Germany and never will satisfy her."[55] Morgenthau overrode the State Department and imposed countervailing duties on Germany in 1936 and 1939, while Ickes blocked the sale of helium to Germany and made scathing anti-Nazi speeches.[56]

Many of the men who gave the administration its "fighting edge" were linked to the Progressive Republican tradition, as was FDR himself. Stimson, Winant, and White fell into this category. Ickes had been Theodore Roosevelt's Chicago campaign manager in 1912, Knox his Rough Rider comrade in 1898, Henry Wallace a Progressive Republican before 1919. With the exception of Wallace, they had not believed in notions like "peace without victory" or the "war to end wars." They were more inclined to think that the problem with the 1919 settlement was that it had never been carried out. They tended to see Germany as Clemenceau, Henry Cabot Lodge, and Theodore Roosevelt had seen it: as a dangerous beast of prey. Their domestic progressivism prompted them to favor cooperation with the Russians, whom, following Theodore Roosevelt, they could not really take seriously as a threat.[57]

While lacking the fixation with Russia that characterized turn-of-the-century geopolitics, the activists embraced the idea of strategic partnership with Britain. In preserving the Continental balance of power, Britain acted in the American interest, and the security of the Western Hemisphere depended on friendly control of the Atlantic. But they were not sentimental Anglophiles. "This catastrophe which is overhanging the world today could have been averted," wrote Ickes in January 1939,

54. White, the Emporia, Kansas, editor was not a member of the administration, but became a trusted informal adviser of FDR.

55. Memos to the Secretary of State, Feb. 18 and Sept. 29, 1938. *FRUS*, 1938, 1: 21, 705.

56. See Dallek, 124; Blum, ed., *Morgenthau Diaries*, 2: 88; Ickes, 533.

57. On Theodore Roosevelt's view of Russia see Chapter 1, this volume. For the views of Dodd, Ickes, and Messersmith favorable to cooperation with Russia see Dodd to FDR, Dec. 15, 1935, *FFA*, 3: 122; Dodd, *Diary*, Nov. 18, 1937, 433; Ickes, 670–75. On Messersmith see MacDonald, 61; Jesse Stiller, *George Messersmith: Diplomat of Democracy* (New York: New York University Press, 1987), 78–79; 135. Messersmith's domestic political views were progressive. See ibid., 6.

"if England had supported the Stimson Doctrine in China and taken a stand against Italian and German aggression." After the Nazi–Soviet pact, Ickes wrote: "I entertain no doubt that England could have concluded a satisfactory treaty with Russia months ago or even years ago. . . . The situation today is the perfect flower of a course of British diplomacy that traces from Sir John Simon through Baldwin to Chamberlain."[58] Such sentiments were a precursor of the anger felt by Stimson and General George Marshall when the British refused to be drawn into a second front in Europe in 1942–43.

Of Roosevelt himself, Tugwell observes, "The indignation he [FDR] had felt when the Germans escaped the penalties of their crimes had lain dormant for a long time; it was roused again by the Hitlerian political victories of 1933."[59] Roosevelt's propensity to use Russia to contain Japan and Germany, rather than vice versa, has already been pointed out. He renewed these efforts in 1937–38, sending Joseph Davies to Moscow, and always kept his eye on what he saw as the "fundamental congruity" of U.S. and Soviet interests.[60] As for Britain, Roosevelt felt, as undoubtedly many other people did, *both* Welles's indignation and bitterness over its responsibility for the injustice and stupidity of Versailles, and Ickes's incredulity and anger at its failure to enforce the terms.

By the late thirties, Roosevelt was increasingly preoccupied with Britain's failure to play the role assigned to it by American statesmen from John Quincy Adams to TR. "I do wish our British friends would see the situation as it seems to be," he wrote in August 1938; in November: "The dictator threat from Europe is a good deal closer to the United States and the American continent than it was before." After talks with Lord Lothian, who was soon to be appointed British ambassador, he wrote in early 1939, "I wish the British would stop this 'we who are about to die salute thee' attitude," according to which "the scepter or the sword or something like that had dropped from their palsied fingers – [and] that the U.S.A. must snatch it up." FDR concluded: "What the British need today is a good stiff grog, inducing not only the desire to save civilization but the confirmed belief that they can do it. In such an event they will have a lot more support from their American cousins." He told Ickes, "The wealthy class of England is so afraid of communism, which has constituted no threat at all to England, that they have thrown themselves into the arms of Naziism and now

58. Ickes, 569, 703–4.
59. Tugwell, 437.
60. For his 1937–38 and 1939–40 efforts see Maddux, chaps. 7–10; the expression "fundamental congruity" is Heinrichs's, 54.

they don't know which way to turn."[61] These words suggest the contempt and incomprehension of someone who had always taken for granted, and grudgingly respected, Britain's ability to advance its own interests, as if an erstwhile athletic rival had inexplicably gone to seed. By the same token, a stiffening of British resolve was bound to arouse Roosevelt's old fighting instincts and suspicions, lest America's virility suffer by comparison with Britain's and British selfishness go unchecked.

A peaceful equivalent to war

It is not difficult to see why Roosevelt's foreign policy was so often accused of incoherence and confusion. A prospective ally could be forgiven for regarding the president with a mixture of doubt, hope, and fear: doubt that he would ever intervene effectively, hope that he would in the end, and fear of the price to be paid if he did. "Doubts, hopes and fears" is how a leading British historian describes the attitude of his country's leaders toward Roosevelt's foreign policy.[62]

Much of the doubt arose from the impression that Roosevelt was a prisoner of isolationist opinion, also that he was inclined to save his political capital for domestic battles, culminating in the quixotic Supreme Court and governmental reorganization showdown of 1937–38. The latter impression was undoubtedly true. One irony of Roosevelt's presidency is that by the time the European crisis demanded his attention in the late thirties, his commanding self-confidence had given way to gun-shyness, and his ability to manipulate public opinion had considerably eroded. After the Depression resumed in late 1937, Vice-President John Nance Garner described Roosevelt as "scared and tired"; to Ickes, the president seemed "a beaten man" in early 1938.[63] It was the foreign policy crisis of the end of the decade that allowed for the recovery of both the U.S. economy and Roosevelt's old "touch."

But it is a mistake to argue that Roosevelt's foreign policy in the thirties was essentially the product of equivocation and drift.[64] Tugwell's is a useful reminder: "There never was a prominent leader who was more determined about his objectives and never one who was more flexible about his means." Berle adds that FDR "developed community" with a variety of groups but "made himself at all times the principal

61. See FDR to Claude Bowers, Aug. 31, 1938, PSF Spain 1938, box 69, FDRL; FDR to Herbert Pell, Nov. 12, 1938, PSF Portugal, FDRL; FDR to Roger Merriman, Feb. 15, 1939, PSF Great Britain 1939, FDRL; Ickes, 571.
62. See Reynolds, chap. 1.
63. Quoted in Morgan, 485; Ickes, 340.
64. Such tends to be the recent view of Frederick Marks III.

unifying element."[65] Both suggest that he was not only a broker but an architect, a searcher for harmony and synthesis among the conflicting political and cultural tendencies present in his own makeup, the administration, and the country.

Roosevelt sought a basis for harmony and synthesis in the example of Thomas Jefferson. Roosevelt's conscious identification with Jefferson grew as he came face to face with a Jeffersonian landscape in foreign as well as domestic affairs, marked by an Old World threat to the peace and autonomy of the New. Roosevelt's Jeffersonianism did not imply mechanical imitation but a common sensibility and set of attitudes, a search for similar solutions to the problem of Europe, and a shared vision of its future. If he frequently did not succeed in harmonizing the conflicting tendencies of his foreign policy, the muse he harkened to was usually Jeffersonian, and this endows his diplomacy with a unity and purpose over time.

Like Jefferson, Roosevelt based his foreign policy on a belief in the virtue and special destiny of America, and held out occasional hope that American behavior might "set an example which the Christian world should be led by interest to respect and at length to imitate." There was an enduring tension in both men "between the desire to reform the international system and the desire to remain separate from it." Like Jefferson's, Roosevelt's was a *partial* internationalism, whose purpose was not universal salvation for its own sake but the safeguarding of democracy in the United States. For both presidents, the Western Hemisphere was "a separate system of interests" and sanctuary of civilized values; the relationship among its parts should constitute a defensive system as well as an example to the world.[66] Both recognized that, if morally superior, America – alas – was not geopolitically separate from the Old World. Means had to be found to deter Europe, and if necessary to coerce it.

As presidents, both wished to exhaust the possibilities of instruments other than military force. This is partly because they eschewed direct

65. Tugwell, 332; Berle Diary, Apr. 13, 1945, FDRL.
66. On Jefferson and the power of example see Henry Adams, *History of the United States*, 108; on the reform-withdrawal tension see Robert W. Tucker and David C. Hendrickson, "Thomas Jefferson and American Foreign Policy," *Foreign Affairs*, 69, no. 2 (Spring 1990), 149. On U.S.–Canadian relations see FDR speech, Nov. 11, 1935, *FFA*; on Latin America Jefferson wrote (Oct. 18, 1808), "We consider our interests and theirs as the same and that the object of both must be to exclude all European influences from this hemisphere"; also, "America has a hemisphere to itself. It must have its separate system of interests; which must not be subordinated to those of Europe" (Dec. 6, 1813). From "Jefferson's Attitude toward Foreign Affairs," 19, typed notes found in PPF 259, Jefferson file, FDRL.

intervention in or political contact of any kind with Europe. Jefferson's belief that the Old World might be redeemed had been severely tested by the outcome of the French Revolution, FDR's by the World War and Wilson's failure. Both presidents feared that war, or large-scale military preparations, would destroy their progressive domestic policies and transfer wealth and power to reactionaries at home. Jefferson loathed the Hamiltonian party; Roosevelt, its modern-day equivalent, the "economic royalists." For both, the sacrifice of private gain from commerce with belligerents was a small price to pay to avoid the risk of war and the internal economic and political distortions it would bring.[67]

The essence of the resulting statecraft was the attempt to manipulate European conduct from afar. Both the Good Neighbor policy – to which Welles's European diplomacy was essentially an adjunct – and the neutrality policy of the mid-thirties had Jeffersonian roots. Jefferson, secretary of state during the Anglo-French war that began in 1793, had helped to devise the traditional U.S. notion of neutrality based on impartiality and freedom of the seas, including the right of U.S. citizens to trade in contraband with belligerents. During his presidency, Jefferson embraced a radically different concept of neutrality. In 1807, his administration replied to systematic French and British interference with U.S. shipping by imposing an embargo on American trade. According to the official explanation:

> The ocean presents a field of danger where no harvest is to be reaped but that of danger, of spoilation and of disgrace. Under such circumstances the best to be done is what has been done; a significant retirement within ourselves; a watchful preservation of our resources; and a demonstration to the world that we possess a virtue and a patriotism which can take any shape that will best suit the occasion. It is singularly fortunate that an embargo whilst it guards our essential resources will have the collective effect of making it to the interest of all nations to change the system which has driven our commerce from the ocean.[68]

The statement suggested a threefold rationale: to avoid incidents involving U.S. ships that might lead to war, to buy time as the United

---

67. On Jefferson and Hamilton see Chapter 1, this volume; see also Tugwell, 479, n. 2. For Jefferson's views see Donald F. Drummond, *The Passing of American Neutrality, 1937–1941* (Ann Arbor: University of Michigan Press, 1955), 8–9. On Jefferson's abhorrence of war because of its domestic consequences see Tucker and Hendrickson, 140.

68. Official spokesman quoted in Dumas Malone, *Jefferson the President: Second Term, 1805–1809* (Boston: Little, Brown, 1974), 488.

States grew in strength, and to *compel* those responsible to change their behavior by denying them U.S. resources. Similar considerations, prompted by the bitter World War experience, lay behind the neutrality laws of the thirties, which embargoed U.S. exports of arms and munitions to belligerents (later extended to restrict loans, export of war-related goods except on a cash-and-carry basis in non-U.S. ships, the use of U.S. ports by belligerent parties, and U.S. travel in areas of risk). There were also common domestic political considerations, spelled out by FDR at Chautauqua, New York, in 1936: "Industrial and agricultural production for a war market may give immense fortune to a few men; for the nation as a whole it produces disaster.... If we face the choice of profits or peace, the nation will answer – must answer – 'we choose peace.'"[69]

There are striking differences between the two policies – Jefferson's was a far more extreme experiment – but they were similar in spirit and purpose. It was Congress that determined the final shape of the neutrality laws and consistently denied Roosevelt the discretion he preferred in order to apply them selectively in favor of one belligerent party against another, but from the moment he asked Congress for action on an embargo in 1933 (the McReynolds resolution), FDR was among the inspirers of the New Neutrality. In 1934, he invited Senator Gerald Nye's committee to prepare neutrality legislation. Even if he retained some discretion through his powers to invoke the laws (he did so in the Ethiopian war, penalizing Italy; he did not in the Sino-Japanese case in order to avoid hurting China), to determine a list of war materials, and to declare partial "moral embargoes,"[70] FDR disliked limitations on his freedom of action and eventually lost patience with legal restrictions. "Anything," he wrote shortly after the extension of the Neutrality Act in May 1937, "that postpones war is that much to

---

69. Chautauqua speech, cited in note 29.
70. Drummond observes that FDR's "opposition to the various neutrality acts never ripened into a veto; his occasional requests for impartial embargo legislation, and his use of such laws as were passed, tended to make it appear that he did not find them altogether without merit" (47). Robert Divine's account suggests that Roosevelt, at least until 1936–37, was certainly not averse to a nondiscriminatory embargo. To the shock of Hull and Norman Davis, who saw a U.S. discretionary embargo as a means of supporting League of Nations collective security efforts, Roosevelt did not hesitate to accept the Johnson amendment to the embargo resolution (May 1933) removing executive discretion. In March 1935, he told the Nye committee that William Jennings Bryan had been correct to favor an embargo in 1915, and, according to Divine, FDR was pressured into supporting an internationalist position by the State Department in 1935. Divine, *Illusion*, 86, 102–3, 170. See also Jurg Martin Gabriel, *The American Conception of Neutrality after 1941* (London: Macmillan, 1988), 14–15, 29.

the good." By March 1939, he believed that the act "should be repealed *in toto* without any substitute."[71]

Jefferson had hoped to develop a peaceful equivalent to war; in the end, according to Dumas Malone, he "created an impression of ambivalence while keeping his options open and did not infuse his countrymen with ardor in his effort to prepare them for a war that he probably regarded as ultimately unavoidable but sought to postpone as long as possible."[72] The same words might have been written about Roosevelt in the thirties. Jefferson left the task of devising a new policy to his successor. FDR's doubts led him to a more activist policy in 1938–39. But his shift represented less a change in philosophy than a groping forward along the continuum of "peaceable coercion."

At Chicago on October 5, 1937, Roosevelt warned: "Let no one imagine that America will escape, that America may expect mercy, that this Western Hemisphere will not be attacked.... When an epidemic of physical disease starts to spread, the community approves and joins in a quarantine of the patients in order to protect the health of the community against the spread of the disease."[73] He now wished to develop an international naval blockade-embargo of the type Jefferson had conceived in the 1780s to deal with the Barbary pirates and later executed – unilaterally – to bring Tripoli to terms.[74] Public reaction to FDR's speech was hostile, and even after the Japanese deliberately sank the gunboat *U.S.S. Panay* (December 1937), Congress only narrowly defeated the so-called Ludlow amendment, which would have required a popular referendum to commit the country to war. Public opinion was an obvious factor encouraging FDR to try methods of coercion short of declared war. But on principle he preferred to develop "a technique which [would] not lead to war," or one that would produce "the same result" as war but without having "to go to war to get it."[75]

71. FDR to William Phillips, May 17, 1937, *PL, 1928–1945*, 1: 681; FDR memo to Hull and Welles, Mar. 28, 1939, *PL, 1928–1945*, 2: 873.
72. Malone, 523.
73. Franklin Delano Roosevelt, *Development of U.S. Foreign Policy, Addresses and Messages of FDR* (Washington, D.C.: U.S. Government Printing Office, 1942), 22, 23.
74. On Jefferson and the Barbary pirates see "Jefferson's Attitude toward Foreign Affairs," 3, 7, PPF 259, FDRL. On the explicit link FDR made between the two cases see Heinrichs, 37.
75. FDR discussed the problem of public opinion and the idea of a blockade with his English friend Arthur Willert. See memo of Apr. 14, 1936, A. Willert Papers, box 14, fd. 59, Sterling Library, Yale University. The referendum was defeated in January 1938 in the House by a vote of 209 to 188. On FDR's search for a new method see his comment to Morgenthau, in Blum, ed., *Morgenthau Diaries*, 1: 409; Ickes, 275; Reynolds, 30–33.

Roosevelt's subsequent steps involved measures ever more coercive and less peaceable, but falling short of conventional war. During the Munich crisis, Roosevelt expounded on a kind of long-range defensive war, combining a naval blockade with air attacks. If war came, he told the British ambassador, it should be fought "with minimum of suffering and the least possible loss of life and property. . . . In this connection . . . bombing from the air was not the method of hostilities which caused really great losses of life." To his cabinet he observed that war waged principally from the air "would cost less money, would mean comparatively few casualties and would be more likely to succeed than a traditional war." He soon called for a huge buildup of American air power, though his requests were met with skepticism by Congress and the military.[76]

In November 1938, FDR told his cabinet that "for the first time since the Holy Alliance in 1818 the United States now faced the possibility of an attack on the Atlantic side in both the Northern and Southern Hemispheres." His emphasis on the threat to the Western Hemisphere was not a rationalization for intervention to defend Britain. Securing Britain and the Atlantic was necessary for hemispheric defense. Those close to Roosevelt understood that this was his visceral concern. In lobbying for reinforcement of the Atlantic fleet from Pearl Harbor in June 1941, Secretary of War Stimson used rumors of a German attack on Brazil.[77] The British later fabricated a set of German plans for the conquest of South America and passed them to the president. Calling public attention to the peril to the Western Hemisphere represented by Axis air power, Roosevelt took further steps along the continuum from peaceable coercion toward war. "There are many methods short of war," he said in January 1939, "but stronger and more effective than mere words," foreshadowing his "Arsenal of Democracy" speech of December 1940.[78]

Roosevelt's famous speech of September 21, 1939, reflected his chagrin and disillusionment with the failed neutrality experiment of the thirties. He now called for a return to the "historic and traditional American policy," appropriately comparing the neutrality laws to Jefferson's em-

76. See Sir Ronald Lindsay to Foreign Secretary Lord Halifax, Sept. 20, 1938, in *Documents on British Foreign Policy*, 3d ser., 7: 627; Ickes, 469, 474.

77. For November 1938 statement see Blum, ed., *Morgenthau Diaries*, 2: 48. Heinrichs's description of FDR's motives in May 1941, "The President focused on threats to the safety of the United States in a most direct and visceral sense" (82), applies *throughout* his presidency. On rumors see Henry Stimson Diary, June 18–19, 1941, microfilm version, vol. 6, Sterling Library, Yale University.

78. Speech of Jan. 4, 1939, *Development of U.S. Foreign Policy*, 33.

bargo. Nonetheless, his proposal to allow belligerents to buy arms on a cash-and-carry basis was a far cry from a return to the policy upheld by Wilson in 1914–17. FDR's explicit purpose – like Jefferson's in the 1790s – was now to favor one side in the European contest, but also to avoid "incidents and controversies which tend to draw us into conflict." In accordance with the new law, passed in November, the president declared combat zones where U.S. ships and citizens were forbidden to enter. Private interests would continue to be sacrificed to avoid incidents that might lead to war.[79] Another characteristic action was the Declaration of Panama (October 1939) on collective American neutrality, creating a 300-mile zone off the mainland of the Western Hemisphere (excluding Canada) in which hostile acts by belligerents were forbidden. The difficulty in enforcing this policy was obvious (e.g., the *Graf Spee* incident off Montevideo in December 1939), but the declaration spoke eloquently of FDR's concern with the integrity of the hemisphere and his willingness to resort to novel types of neutrality to preserve it. Once again FDR consciously took an idea from Jefferson, who had proposed a similar zone – a kind of proto–Monroe Doctrine – in the late 1790s.[80]

Roosevelt and the "ultra-British party"

In April 1940 the blitzkrieg overran Scandinavia; the collapse of France two months later meant the "shattering of many illusions."[81] On June 10, "the hand that held the dagger struck it into the back of its neighbor," and Italy was at war. May–June 1940 marked the beginning of serious rearmament and, with the appointment of Knox and Stimson, a decisive shift of the balance of power in Roosevelt's government in favor of the activist camp.

The summer of 1940 saw the crystallization, to use Sir William Wiseman's First World War expression, of an "ultra-British party." At its core were the lawyers, businessmen, clergymen, and journalists

---

79. Ibid., 47–53; on speech see also Samuel Rosenman, *Working with Roosevelt* (New York: Harper Bros., 1952), 188–91; Hull, 1: 682–84. Cash and carry favored Britain and France, which had the ships and cash to pay. Otherwise, according to Langer and Gleason, *Challenge*, the new law "largely continued the provision of the Act of 1937" with the United States "abdicating its neutral rights and deserting the principle of freedom of the seas" (232–33).

80. See Langer and Gleason, *Challenge*, 206–18; Irwin Gellman, 90–92. On FDR's reference to Jefferson see Berle and Jacobs, 245, 252.

81. Fireside chat quoted in Langer and Gleason, *Challenge*, 479.

who met occasionally at the Century Association in New York. The members of this loosely organized but well-connected group were linked to Britain by reasons of education, family, or personal self-interest. Some, like Lewis Douglas, the future ambassador to Britain, opposed the New Deal. Others, like William Clayton (founder of Anderson, Clayton and Co., the world's largest cotton exporter), had supported the president because of the trade policies of Hull. Like their predecessors since the 1890s, they were driven by broad geopolitical and economic convictions – that the defeat of the British Empire would fatally weaken the United States and that the two countries must reconstruct a world system along the lines of the nineteenth century Pax Britannica whose breakdown, in the final analysis, was the cause of the present war.[82]

The group's strategist and animator in Washington was the Harvard Law School professor and later Supreme Court justice Felix Frankfurter. Vienna-born, of remarkable versatility and talent for ingratiation – his friend Oliver Wendell Holmes spoke of his "unimaginable gift of wiggling in wherever he wants to be" – Frankfurter was in regular contact with the White House and operated in Washington through his famous network of former students. The "Frankfurter gang" – Benjamin Cohen, Thomas Corcoran, James Landis, and Herbert Feis, among others – were the obsession of Adolf Berle. In contrast to Berle's penchant for planning and business–government partnership, they espoused the Louis Brandeis philosophy of antitrust and free competition that had inspired the "Second New Deal" (e.g., the passage of the Securities Exchange Act and the Public Utility Holding Company Act) and had supplanted the influence of the original Brain Trust.[83] By the late thirties Berle saw Frankfurter as the Colonel House of the Roosevelt administration or, as he called him in March 1940, "the spear-head of the war party." According to Frankfurter, Berle was "almost pathologi-

---

82. There were twenty-eight more or less regular members of the "Century Group." In addition to Douglas and Clayton, among the most important were Admiral William Standley, Francis Miller, Allen Dulles, James Warburg, Herbert Agar, Joe Alsop, James Conant, Robert Sherwood, and Henry Luce. See Mark C. Chadwin, *The Hawks of World War II* (Chapel Hill: University of North Carolina Press, 1968), chaps. 3 and 4.

83. For Holmes on Frankfurter see Howe, ed., *Holmes–Laski Letters*, 272. Holmes made the remark in his letter to Laski of July 30, 1920. On the Roosevelt administration's shift to the Second New Deal, see Tugwell, 324–26, and Arthur M. Schlesinger, Jr., *The Age of Roosevelt*, vol. 2: *The Coming of the New Deal* (Boston: Houghton Mifflin, 1958), pt. 7.

cally anti-British and anti-Russian, and his anti-Semitism is thrown in, as it were, for good measure."[84]

Frankfurter fitted naturally into the Republican-activist camp. He had backed TR in 1912 and had made his name as a trust-busting lawyer under Henry Stimson when the latter was U.S. attorney for the Southern District of New York. He was a strong supporter of FDR's opening to Moscow and an early denouncer of the Nazis. But there was a devoutness and uncritical partisanship in Frankfurter's feelings for England that set him apart. It was the same quality of feeling that Holmes had discerned in his friend Brandeis – England was what Brandeis "admired beyond everything else." Isaiah Berlin, an Anglicized Jew and friend of Frankfurter, described it as "the touching and enjoyable Anglomania – the childlike passion for England, English institutions, Englishmen – for all that was sane, refined, not shoddy, civilized, moderate, peaceful, the opposite of brutal, decent – for the liberal and constitutional traditions that before 1914 were so dear to the hearts and imaginations especially of those brought up in eastern or central Europe, more particularly to members of oppressed minorities, who felt the lack of them to an agonizing degree."[85]

Frankfurter and the "Century Group" were the driving force behind the campaign to transfer U.S. destroyers to Britain, and henceforth the "ultra-British party" was a force to be reckoned with in shaping U.S. policy. In early 1941, Frankfurter helped to draft the lend-lease bill and placed his protégé Cohen as an assistant to the new ambassador to Britain, John Winant. It was Frankfurter who told Prime Minister Winston Churchill that he must "sell himself" to the visiting Harry Hopkins in order to win FDR's confidence. Churchill did his job well and Hopkins became the prime minister's enthusiastic friend.[86]

Nineteen forty was a presidential election year, and it is natural to assume that Roosevelt's extreme caution and emphasis on hemispheric

---

84. For Berle on Frankfurter see Berle Diary, Mar. 18, 1940, FDRL. For Frankfurter on Berle see Joseph Lash, ed., *From the Diaries of Felix Frankfurter* (New York: Norton, 1974), 168.

85. On Frankfurter's early career and ideas see the article from *Fortune*, Jan. 1937, reprinted in Max Freedman, ed., *Roosevelt and Frankfurter: Their Correspondence, 1928–1945* (Boston: Little, Brown, 1976), 303–10. On Frankfurter's support of FDR's Soviet policy see his letter to FDR, Oct. 29, 1933, in ibid., 165. For Frankfurter's efforts to convince FDR of Britain's fast friendship see, e.g., letters of Oct. 17, 1933, and July 11, 1936, in ibid., 164, 346. For Holmes's remark on Brandeis see Howe, ed., 272. For Berlin on Frankfurter see "Felix Frankfurter," in Berlin, *Personal Impressions* (New York: Penguin, 1982), 89.

86. Reynolds, 181.

defense, even after the fall of France, were calculated to avoid an isolationist backlash while quietly aiding Britain. However, there is little evidence that Roosevelt would have proceeded much differently had there been no election or that his publicly stated motives differed from his real ones. Roosevelt's concern – as well as General George C. Marshall's – was now more than ever the security of the hemisphere. The State Department warned the new Vichy government not to surrender its fleet to the Nazis; FDR was consulted, and he fully approved the British attack on the French squadron at Mers-el-Kebir on July 3.[87] Roosevelt was not confident about Britain's chances and accepted the warnings of his army and navy chiefs (Marshall and Admiral Harold Stark, respectively) against transferring B-17 bombers and other equipment. He signed into law (July 2) the Walsh amendment to the Navy Expansion Act of 1940 forbidding disposal of material unless certified by the chiefs as "not essential to the defense of the United States."[88]

The "destroyers for bases" deal suggests that while Roosevelt and the "ultra-British party" pursued the same policy of aiding Britain, their priorities and outlook did not exactly coincide. The Century Group maintained that "it was futile to talk of hemispheric defense and highly desirable to recognize that America's prime interest lay with Britain." When the group persuaded Ben Cohen to argue in favor of the transfer of World War I–era destroyers, FDR demurred, telling Knox to consider "trying to get Congressional action to allow sale of these destroyers to Canada on condition that they be used solely in American Hemispheric defense." On July 21, 1940, a full-scale Pan-American conference convened at Havana to reaffirm the Monroe Doctrine's implicit ban on the transfer of possessions in the Western Hemisphere from one European power to another. It was in this context that the Century Group proposed (July 25) and presented to FDR (August 1) the trade of one hundred destroyers in return for naval and air bases on British territory in the Western Hemisphere and a guarantee that the British fleet would "never be scuttled nor surrendered."[89]

Most of its members favored sending the destroyers without a quid pro quo, but the Century Group was shrewd enough to link their aim to FDR's hemispheric anxieties. Members of the group also helped to overcome his fear of Congress with a legal argument (August 11) to the effect that no new legislative action was required for the transfer. It would be a mistake to underestimate the psychological significance of

87. Langer and Gleason, *Challenge*, 565, 573.
88. Ibid., 520–23; Reynolds, 112–13.
89. See *PL, 1928–45*, 2: 1048–49; Langer and Gleason, *Challenge*, 745–51.

the departure from neutrality implied in the deal, yet the final terms were so one-sided that they offered Britain little concrete aid. In return for fifty antiquated destroyers and other materiel, the United States received a pledge on the British fleet and the right to build and lease bases on Newfoundland, Bermuda, British Guiana, and a half-dozen locations in the British West Indies. On August 17, the United States concluded a separate agreement with Canada, creating a Permanent Joint Defense Board to plan the defense of northeast Canada, where, FDR believed, "sudden attack was very likely."[90] His comparison of the "destroyers for bases" coup with Jefferson's acquisition of the Louisiana Territory has been dismissed as "one of his typically loose historical analogies."[91] But the similarity of the arc of Atlantic bases to the defensive glacis provided by the 1803 purchase seemed obvious to FDR.[92]

To "shake a rod"

It will never be known for sure when – or even if – before December 7, 1941, Roosevelt became convinced that America's formal participation in the war was necessary and inevitable. The evidence is mixed. On one hand, FDR shared the view, expressed in Admiral Stark's (November 12, 1940) "Plan Dog" memorandum, that "the continued existence of the British Empire combined with building up a strong protection in our home areas, will do most to assure the status quo in the Western Hemisphere, and to promote our principal national interests."[93] He was certainly sensitive to the argument – he had made it himself after 1914 – that the Americans could not stand idly by while the British proved their mettle. His visceral instinctive desire to "measure up" to Britain created the impression, especially to Englishmen, that "he would not be sorry to see the United States in the war."[94] There is considerable

---

90. See Stimson's account of the Roosevelt–MacKenzie King meeting at Ogdensburg, New York. Stimson Diaries, Aug. 17, 1940, microfilm version, vol. 6, Sterling Library, Yale University.

91. This is Reynolds's view, 161. For FDR comparison, see letter to Senator David Walsh, Aug. 22, 1940, *PL, 1928–1945*, 2: 1056–57; off-the-record press conference, Sept. 3, 1940, in Rosenman, ed., 8: 380–81; Langer and Gleason, *Challenge*, 770.

92. During the campaign his emphasis on hemispheric defense was pointed and relentless. See his speech at Dayton, Ohio, Oct. 12, 1940, and at Cleveland, Nov. 2, 1940. Rosenman, ed., 8: 460–67, 544–47.

93. Plan Dog, quoted in William L. Langer and S. Everett Gleason, *The Undeclared War*, 1940–41 (New York: Harper Bros., 1953), 222. See also Heinrichs, 38.

94. See memo of conversation with FDR, Mar. 25–26, 1939, by Sir Arthur Willert. Wil-

evidence, especially after May 1941, when the British disaster in Crete coincided with a critical point in the Battle of the Atlantic, that he was awaiting the kind of incident that would unite the country behind war.[95]

On the other hand, Roosevelt could have done more to hasten such incidents and before September 1941 did not really try to exploit the ones that occurred – for example, the sinking of the U.S. merchantman *Robin Moor* in April. Those who hoped for formal U.S. entry into the war after the 1940 elections, at the time of FDR's declaration of "unlimited national emergency" in May 1941, or on the eve of the Anglo-American conference at Placentia Bay in August 1941, were disappointed. His important actions, including the conception of lend-lease (December 1940), did not aim to involve the United States in war. The official military historians point out that Roosevelt "in no way committed himself to the theory of strategy" outlined in Stark's memo,[96] arguably because it contemplated a major land offensive in Europe involving U.S. troops. Nor did he officially endorse the conclusion of the December 16, 1940, meeting of Stark, Marshall, Knox, and Stimson, that "this emergency could hardly be passed over without the country being drawn into the war."[97] Roosevelt feared the possibility of a British defeat or compromise peace in late spring 1941, but Hitler's providential attack on Russia – arguably – gave new life to a war by proxy strategy.[98]

There are many reasons, if one wants to pursue this line of argument, why Roosevelt might have wished to avoid war until the very end. A formal declaration, even in late 1941, would have encountered serious resistance in Congress.[99] Expert opinion held as late as September 1941

lert Papers, box 14, Sterling Library, Yale University. FDR gave a similar impression to King George VI in June 1939 (see Wheeler-Bennett, 391) and to his friend Arthur Murray (see Rock, 288).

95. For a list of FDR's remarks (to Ickes, Bullitt, Morgenthau, and Halifax) implying that he was waiting for an incident see Reynolds, 347, n. 38.

96. See Maurice Matloff and Edwin M. Snell, *Strategic Planning for Coalition Warfare*, vol. 1: *1941–1942* (Washington, D.C.: Office of the Chief of Military History, 1953), 27, 28.

97. See Stimson Diary, Dec. 16, 1940, microfilm version, vol. 6, Sterling Library, Yale University.

98. Heinrichs notes that keeping the Russian front open was "the centerpiece of his world strategy" (159).

99. At least this seemed evident from the debate over revision of the neutrality laws to allow U.S. ships into war zones, passed after much debate in mid-November. The renewal of selective service had been passed in August by a vote of 203 to 202 in the House.

that the United States would "be more effective for some time as a neutral, furnishing aid to Britain, rather than as a belligerent."[100] More fundamentally, Roosevelt's entire thirties policy, his keep-them-at-arm's-length posture toward the Old World, suggested that if peaceable coercion had been a failure, he was still inclined to grasp at practically any available alternative to conventional, declared war until the bitter end.[101]

But, ask two students of Jefferson: "What of the day that he was sure would come, a day when America might 'shake a rod over the heads of all ...'? Why should it not do so then, if doing so might contribute to America's security and well-being while also striking a blow for the cause of liberty?"[102] It is highly likely that by mid-1941 Roosevelt had seen the day coming when America would not only be able but as a question of self-preservation would have to "shake a rod" over the heads of the European powers. He also saw that in order to do so with full effect America would have at some point to be physically present *in* Europe, as Stark, Stimson, and Marshall had insisted.[103]

The turning point in FDR's mind was probably the German invasion of the Soviet Union on June 22, 1941. After that date, formal U.S. entry into the war probably seemed more rather than less likely to Roosevelt than before. If Germany were to conquer the Soviet Union and turn its vast resources against the West – a distinct possibility – direct U.S. participation would become all the more necessary and inevitable. FDR also realized that the kind of American–Soviet entente that he had envisioned since 1933 could not be built on the basis of Russian blood and American materiel alone – some American blood would have to be added to the mixture. Finally, after the advent of all-out war in the spring of 1940, it was hard to see how the United States could secure a say in the postwar political settlement unless it played an important role on the battlefield, and that could not be done without placing an American army in Europe. The alternative was a peace settlement once

---

100. American entry would divert materiel to U.S. forces, which were in no position to employ it. See the September 1941 War Department memo, quoted in Matloff and Snell, 55. General Marshall's chief adviser on strategy, Lieutenant General Stanley D. Embick, had stated in April that entering the war "would be wrong in a military and naval sense" as well as "unjust to the American people." Ibid., 53. See also Eric Larrabee, *Commander in Chief: Franklin Delano Roosevelt, His Lieutenants, and Their War* (New York: Harper & Row, 1987), 47.
101. Reynolds (212) suggests that FDR sought to avoid involvement until the very end. See also Sherwood, 272.
102. Tucker and Hendrickson, 155.
103. Here I disagree with Kimball's argument. See *The Juggler*, 34, 207, n. 34. On this point see also Larrabee, 49.

again dominated by the Europeans themselves: if not a German victory, an Anglo-Russian division of Europe setting the stage for a new round of conflict, this time between the old antagonists, the British and the Russians.[104]

Despite, or rather *because of,* his deep-seated hemispherism and cynicism about the Old World, Roosevelt believed that the only calamity worse than entanglement in Europe was the one likely to ensue from leaving the Europeans to their proverbial own devices. The declaration of war aims at the Placentia Bay conference in August 1941 came after signs that the British and Russians would attempt to settle the future of Europe on a secret and bilateral basis. FDR's order to the Atlantic Fleet (September 13, 1941) to shoot German raiders on sight was tantamount to an American declaration of war.[105] It is revealing that this order was given at a moment when the British seemed to have "fairly well mastered the submarine menace in the North Atlantic" and after an incident involving the U.S. destroyer *Greer* in which the American ship had been the clear aggressor.[106] Thus, along with the immediate possibility of Soviet defeat, it was the prospect of an eventual Allied victory, the preoccupation about what kind of Europe would ensue, and the determination to shape the peace that prompted Roosevelt to enter World War II in the late summer of 1941.[107]

---

104. James Roosevelt records his father's conviction that, left to their own devices, Britain and the Soviet Union would go to war with each other. See *My Parents: A Different View* (Chicago: Playboy Press, 1976), 167. See also William Roger Louis, *Imperialism at Bay: The United States and the Decolonization of the British Empire, 1941–45* (Oxford: Oxford University Press, 1977), 21.

105. There is no reason to doubt the accuracy of Churchill's account of FDR's views at Placentia Bay. According to Churchill, Roosevelt was "obviously determined that they should come in." See Lash, *Roosevelt and Churchill,* 401–2.

106. Langer and Gleason, *The Undeclared War,* 742.

107. There was an additional, less intentional reason the German invasion of the Soviet Union hastened U.S. entry into the war. When the United States decided to freeze Japanese assets at the end of July, which had the effect of cutting off U.S. petroleum exports to Japan, one of the reasons was to deter a Japanese attack on the Soviet Union from the rear. The Japanese were in fact contemplating such an attack, but the U.S. move led them to change their plans, leading to the events of December 7, 1941. See Akira Iriye, *The Origins of the Second World War in Asia and the Pacific* (London: Longmans, 1987), 149.

3

The Roosevelt solution,
1941–1945

A Palladian Europe

According to an old myth, Franklin Roosevelt subordinated postwar political objectives to the pursuit of a cheap and rapid victory.[1] In fact, Roosevelt's "interventions in the *hows* and *wheres* and *whens* of strategy arose principally from a desire to protect and advance his political objectives."[2] When Roosevelt told his son, "War is too political a thing. Depending on how desperate are a country's straits, she is likely to wage war only in such a way as will benefit her politically in the long run, rather than fighting to end the war as swiftly as possible,"[3] he was attributing to others behavior that was similar to his own.

Roosevelt's personal political objectives in Europe were too brutal to be proclaimed. They had to be dressed up as universal war aims and worked toward gradually, using a combination of military and diplomatic means. If not everyone grasped Roosevelt's intentions, many shared his basic assumptions. Walter Lippmann summarized them in 1943:

Our grand objective must be a settlement which does not call for a permanent American military intervention in Europe to maintain it. . . . Thus if we think as clearly and exactly about American interests as Jefferson . . .

1. See Range, 57; Winston S. Churchill, *The Second World War*, 6 vols. (Boston: Houghton Mifflin, 1948–53), 64; Hull, 2: 1109–11.
2. William Emerson, "Franklin Roosevelt as Commander-in-Chief in World War II," in Ernest May, ed., *The Ultimate Decision: The President as Commander-in-Chief* (New York, G. Braziller, 1960), 175–76. See also Mark A. Stoler, *The Politics of the Second Front* (Westport, Conn.: Greenwood Press, 1977), 165–67. Marshall's view of this question is also of interest. See Larry Bland, ed., *George C. Marshall Interviews and Reminiscences for Forrest C. Pogue* (Lexington, Va.: George C. Marshall Research Foundation, 1991), 415.
3. Elliott Roosevelt, *As He Saw It* (New York: Duell, Sloan & Pearce, 1946), 129.

was able to think, we shall see that the traditional American policy against being involved in European affairs is not in the last analysis inconsistent with the consolidation of America's vital interest in the world.[4]

Roosevelt's solution – his mature vision of Europe – was Jeffersonian in its Europhobic spirit and Palladian design. Like the Jefferson Memorial, which rose during the war at FDR's behest within view of the White House, the vision took definite shape over several years. Like Jefferson's, FDR's vision was inspired by a fundamental cynicism, compounded by the vexation of his failure to insulate America from Europe or to influence it from a distance. FDR sketched in the details, calling up concepts and sentiments that had accumulated over a lifetime and now became the brick and mortar of a culminating structure. To pursue the metaphor, FDR's eventual design for Europe consisted of three

4. Lippmann, *U.S. Foreign Policy*, 146, 163.

mutually reinforcing levels or components: a new political and territorial groundwork, two regional pillars bearing direct responsibility for peace, and an overarching structure in which the United States would occupy the position of keystone or *primus inter pares*. The purpose of these arrangements was to bring about a radical reduction in the weight of Europe, in effect to preside over its indefinite retirement from the international scene. As such, it was conceived as a set of arrangements drastic and definitive enough to allow the United States to return to its natural Western Hemisphere and Pacific habitat and preoccupations – but with one eye cocked toward Europe and able to exercise long-range striking power. The trick, which had been beyond America's power in Jefferson's time, was to be able to arbitrate from afar.

"His particular preserve"

In December 1939, Roosevelt wrote: "I do not entertain the thought of some of the statesmen of 1918 that the world can make, or we can help the world to achieve, a permanently lasting peace.... On the other hand I do not want this country to take part in a patched up temporary peace which would blow up in our faces in a year or two." Let us "secure peace for fifty years," he said on another occasion, "and leave the rest to posterity."[5] The Welles mission of 1940 had aimed to prevent a "patched up" settlement by the Europeans themselves. Roosevelt made a formal statement of American aims in January 1941. The world of the Four Freedoms (freedom of speech, of religion, from want, and from fear) was "no vision of a distant millennium but a definite basis for the kind of world attainable in our own time and generation."[6]

Roosevelt's wish to have his way at the peace table grew more imperious over the course of 1941. In January 1941, Harry Hopkins told the British that FDR "regarded the postwar settlement...as being his particular preserve."[7] In May, FDR told the British ambassador Lord Halifax and the visiting John Maynard Keynes to change the text of a speech by Foreign Secretary Eden on British postwar aims because it did not mention a U.S. contribution. FDR's "decision to postpone political and territorial decisions" arose from both short- and long-term

5. Letter to William Allen White, Dec. 14, 1939, *PL*, 1928–1945, 2: 967; FDR conversation with Eduard Beneš, June 7, 1943, *The Memoirs of Dr. Eduard Beneš* (New York: Arno Press, 1972), 196.
6. *Development of U.S. Foreign Policy*, 86–87.
7. Quoted in Reynolds, 254.

considerations.[8] But this "decision" was not rigid and applied only early in the war. On July 8, 1941, Berle warned Roosevelt about possible "preliminary commitments" being made in London and Moscow. FDR warned the British not to limit his margin of maneuver or create domestic problems for him. Such considerations lay behind the Atlantic Charter of August 1941. When the Russians insisted on recognition of their June 21, 1941, borders as part of an Anglo-Soviet treaty, FDR delivered the same message to them in December 1941.[9] During the summer of 1941, Roosevelt also sketched out the ground level of his vision. Peace would be ensured "by disarming all the troublemakers and considering the possibility of reviving small states." He told Halifax and Keynes that "the Europeans ... are to be told just where they get off."[10] The Atlantic Charter reiterated the call for disarmament "pending the establishment of a wider and permanent system of general security." Reviving small states amounted to the "further fractionization" of Europe.[11]

When FDR spoke in May 1941[12] of the Anglo-Americans policing the Continent, the Soviet Union was not yet at war with Germany. After Hitler's attack on June 22, 1941, he foresaw a situation in which Britain and the Soviet Union would be the only major European powers. FDR's wish that Britain act on America's behalf in Europe is clear from his position on decolonization and the postwar economic order. He saw British rule of India as an untenable burden and began to press Churchill to unload it. At the same time his stand on the quid pro quo to be extracted from Britain in consideration of lend-lease was more conciliatory than Hull's. He did not like the imperial preference system but

8. See FDR memo to General Edwin Watson (with draft of the speech attached), May 26, 1941, POF 2, OF 48 England, 1940–41, FDRL. See also FDR to Berle, June 26, 1941, *PL, 1928–1945*, 2: 1175; Roy Harrod, *The Life of John Maynard Keynes* (New York: St. Martin's Press, 1963), 509; Reynolds, 256. See also Welles, *Seven Decisions*, chap. 5; Robert A. Divine, *Roosevelt and World War II* (Baltimore: Johns Hopkins University Press, 1969), "Roosevelt the Pragmatist." Berle memo to FDR, July 8, 1941, Berle Papers, box 213, FDRL.

9. See FDR to Churchill, July 14, 1941, in Warren F. Kimball, ed., *Roosevelt and Churchill: Their Complete Correspondence* (Princeton, N.J.: Princeton University Press, 1984), 1: 221–22. On the U.S. message to Eden for use during his Moscow talks see Sherwood, 401–2. See also Herbert Feis, *Churchill–Roosevelt–Stalin: The War They Waged and the Peace They Sought* (Princeton, N.J.: Princeton University Press, 1957), 25–26.

10. Kimball ed., *Correspondence*, 1: 221; FDR quoted by Halifax, in Reynolds, 262.

11. For the text of the charter, see *FRUS*, 1941, 1: 367–69. The expression "further fractionization" is Welles's (*Seven Decisions*, 136).

12. During his conversation with Keynes and Halifax on May 28, as well as on other occasions. See Reynolds, 262.

was more anxious that Britain have the strength to help the United States in Europe than that it be hustled into a multilateral trading system that would cripple its economy.[13]

The future Anglo-Soviet relationship across a prostrate Europe was a vital concern; as suggested in Chapter 2, it was a basic factor in Roosevelt's decision to go to war. FDR hoped, in effect, to exorcise the protocontainment tendency that had conditioned Anglo-Saxon behavior toward Russia and to transform the historical antagonists into co-operating gendarmes. His 1941–42 intervention in Anglo-Soviet relations aimed to influence the nature of their relationship to each other and to their respective European spheres.[14] Personally, FDR was inclined to go along with British recognition of the Soviet Union's June 21, 1941, borders. Berle wrote that Roosevelt "would not particularly mind about the Russians taking quite a chunk of territory." FDR himself reportedly said in 1943, "Yes I really think those 1941 frontiers are just as good as any . . . and all those Baltic republics are as good as Russian."[15] It was the prospect of domestic controversy that prompted him to try to stop the emergence of formally defined Soviet and British spheres of influence implied in the draft Anglo-Soviet treaty of 1942. Ideally, the special roles of Britain and the Soviet Union in their respective areas of Europe would follow the lines of U.S.–Latin American policy.[16] It is doubtful, however, that Roosevelt really believed the "Good Neighbor" model could be applied to Europe. The essential point was that troublemakers, bullies, and "loose cannons" be rendered harmless, using whatever methods might avail.

Untainted by Russophobia and controlling vast war supplies, FDR believed he had high cards and was always prepared to gamble in

13. On India see, e.g., FDR to Churchill, Mar. 10, 1942, Kimball, ed., *Correspondence*, I: 402–4. On FDR's economic diplomacy see Reynolds, 222–27; Sherwood, 507; Elliot Roosevelt, 36–37; Kimball, *The Juggler*, 51, 58, 128.

14. On "protocontainment" see Chapter 1, this volume. On Churchill's view of Russia see Fraser Harbutt, *The Iron Curtain: Churchill, America and the Origins of the Cold War* (New York: Oxford University Press, 1986), chap. 2.

15. Berle Diary, Apr. 28, 1942; Berle later remarked that FDR "was tolerant of many things that shocked me: the crude and bitter intrigue of the European powers." Diary, Apr. 12, 1945, quoted in Schwarz, 264. See also the account of a conversation with FDR by Lieutenant Miles of the British army, who spent the weekend of October 31 to November 2, 1943, as a guest of Eleanor Roosevelt at Hyde Park. FO 371/38516, PRO; and Miner, chap. 6, esp. 214.

16. See Berle memo to Welles, Apr. 3, 1942, Berle Papers, box 214, FDRL. See also memo of Feb. 5, 1942, Berle Papers, box 213, FDRL. On this general subject see Eduard Mark, "American Policy Toward Eastern Europe and the Origins of the Cold War, 1941–46: An Alternative Interpretation," *Journal of American History*, 68, no. 2 (Sept. 1981).

dealing with the Russians. This was another reason to keep political and territorial questions open early in the war: Roosevelt "proposed to negotiate these matters with Stalin personally."[17] In effect, *he* would be the one to bless the extension of Russian influence into Europe. Roosevelt gave the Russians a glimpse of his vision when Foreign Minister Molotov visited Washington in May 1942. Rather than a new League of Nations – he had already rejected this idea during the Placentia Bay conference[18] – the United States, Britain, the Soviet Union, and China ("provided the last achieves a unified central government") would be "the policemen of the world." The first step was general disarmament including not only Germany, Japan, and Italy, but France, Spain, Belgium, the Netherlands, Scandinavia, Turkey, Romania, Hungary, Poland, and Czechoslovakia as well. "If any nation menaced the peace, it could be blockaded and then if still recalcitrant, bombed."[19] Molotov soon reported that Stalin "was in complete accord ... on disarmament, inspection, and policing with the participation of at least Great Britain, the United States, the Soviet Union, and possibly China." FDR invited the Russians to consider setting up "international trusteeships" in Japanese-occupied islands. "The Japanese should of course be removed, but we did not want these islands and neither the British or the French ought to have them."[20]

Molotov's purpose was to obtain a second front on the European continent that would draw off forty German divisions in 1942. When he requested "a straight answer," Roosevelt turned to General Marshall to ask whether "we could say ... that we are preparing a second front." Marshall replied yes, and FDR authorized Molotov to inform Stalin: "We expect the formation of a second front this year."[21] Six months later, however, the Allies landed not in northwestern France but in North Africa; at Casablanca in January 1943, they made decisions that delayed a second front until 1944.

---

17. "I know you won't mind my being brutally frank when I tell you," FDR cabled Churchill in early 1942, "that I think that I can personally handle Stalin better than either your Foreign Office or my State Department. Stalin hates the guts of all your top people [including you?]. He thinks he likes me better and I hope he will continue to do so." Kimball, ed., *Correspondence*, 1: 421. FDR made the remark about handling things personally to Averell Harriman. See the account of Harriman's conversation with FDR in September 1943 in W. Averell Harriman and Elie Abel, *Special Envoy to Churchill and Stalin, 1941–1946* (New York: Random House, 1975), 227.
18. See *FRUS*, 1941, 3: 363–66.
19. *FRUS*, 1942, 3: 568–69, 573.
20. Ibid., 580–81.
21. Ibid., 576–77.

Eating his cake and having it

In the caustic debate between the British, who feared an early cross-channel operation, and Marshall and Stimson, who fought to avoid what they saw as wasteful diversions, Roosevelt appeared until 1943 to adopt a mediating or, less charitably, a vacillating position. Like the British, Roosevelt believed that Germany's defeat would doom Japan and that the European war should take precedence. He was determined to commit U.S. troops against the Germans *somewhere* in 1942, in order to relieve pressure on the Red Army and to create a "going concern" that would counteract pressure within the United States for a wholesale shift to the Pacific. He had long ago decided that U.S. forces would have to occupy Germany: "It was well known," he said at one point, "that both General Foch and General Pershing wanted to occupy Germany but that this was denied for political considerations, and that the unwisdom of this policy had long ago become apparent."[22] He probably wished to be able to make even a temporary landing in France if the Russians faced defeat in 1942. In April 1942, FDR endorsed the "Marshall memorandum" calling for the buildup of U.S. forces in Britain (code-named Bolero), a possible emergency Continental landing (Sledgehammer) later in the year, followed by a major cross-channel operation (Round-up) by March 1943.[23] In May, Roosevelt told Marshall that he "regarded it as essential that active [European theater] operations be conducted in 1942."[24]

Shortly after Molotov left Washington, however, Roosevelt told Churchill's envoy Lord Louis Mountbatten how much he "had been struck by [Churchill's] remark in a recent telegram 'Do not lose sight of GYMNAST!' "[25] "Gymnast" was the plan for an invasion of North Africa. The meeting with Mountbatten occurred before Rommel's offensive leading to the British defeat at Tobruk on June 21, 1942. Mountbatten, with his Lord Lambeth looks and naval background, had been chosen to persuade FDR to drop Sledgehammer in favor of North Africa, but little persuasion was required.

---

22. *FRUS, Conferences at Washington and Casablanca*, 611.
23. On Marshall's plan, see Matloff and Snell, 185–89; Feis, *Churchill–Roosevelt–Stalin*, 49.
24. See FDR memo to Marshall, May 6, 1942, PSF 5 Marshall, FDRL; see also memo to the Secretary of War et al., May 6, 1942, PSF 106 Marshall, FDRL.
25. See Mountbatten to FDR, June 15, 1942, Map Room files (MR) 164, general correspondence, FDRL, in which Mountbatten discussed his report to Churchill of his June 9 conversation with Roosevelt. See also Philip Ziegler, *Mountbatten: The Official Biography* (London: Collins, 1985), 183–84.

British "acceptance" of the Marshall strategy in April 1942 had been essentially a ploy to head off demands in the United States for a shift to the Pacific on the grounds that the British were dragging their feet in the European theater. The same considerations figured in FDR's "acceptance" of Marshall's plan.[26] A case can also be made that FDR saw the offer of Sledgehammer to Molotov as a way to relieve Stalin's pressure on the British to recognize the Soviet Union's June 1941 frontiers.[27] In any event, though he feared that an emergency cross-channel operation might prove necessary, he strongly preferred something else: a peripheral landing of the sort discussed at the Arcadia conference in January 1942. Stimson was essentially right when he said that North Africa was FDR's "great secret baby" all along.[28]

The seizure of French North-West Africa was the logical continuation of FDR's hemispheric strategy. Since June 1940, he had worried about the French fleet, Casablanca, and Dakar. He personally orchestrated a French policy – the mission of Admiral William Leahy (January 1941 to May 1942) to Vichy, the attempt to woo Vichy's North African delegate general, Maxime Weygand (early 1942), the deal with Admiral Jean Darlan (November 1942) – whose purpose was to prevent German use of French ships and bases against the Western Hemisphere.[29] West Africa, he later said, "was of such vital importance to us, that it would never be let go."[30] A more immediate reason for preferring North

26. See Kimball, ed., Correspondence, 1: 458; Stoler, Second Front, 41; William McNeill, America, Britain and Russia: Their Cooperation and Conflict, 1941–46 (London: Oxford University Press, 1953), 175.

27. This case is made most convincingly by Feis, Churchill–Roosevelt–Stalin, 58–61. See also Sherwood, 526; Stoler, Second Front, 43; Gaddis Smith, American Diplomacy During World War II (New York: Wiley, 1965), 44–45; Victor Rothwell, Britain and the Cold War, 1941–1947 (London: Cape, 1982), 95. FDR's message to Stalin inviting him to send Molotov to Washington to discuss a "very important military proposal" (April 11, 1942) came during a deadlock in the Anglo-Russian talks. There is evidence, however, that FDR had already resigned himself to the conclusion of a treaty including British recognition of the Soviet Union's June 21, 1941, frontiers. See FRUS, 1942, 3: 538, 541.

28. On Stimson's point see Kent Roberts Greenfield, American Strategy in World War II: A Reconsideration (Baltimore: Johns Hopkins University Press, 1963), 59; Emerson, 157.

29. See FDR's instructions to Leahy, Dec. 20, 1940, printed in Leahy, I Was There (New York: Whittlesey House, 1950), 443–46. These were composed by the State Department for FDR's signature on the basis of Leahy's oral rendering of the president's wishes to him. See Julian Hurstfield, America and the French Nation, 1939–1945 (Chapel Hill: University of North Carolina Press, 1986), 29.

30. See FRUS, Conferences at Washington and Casablanca, 72, 162; Berle, Memo of conversation with the president, June 10, 1943, Berle Papers, box 215, FDRL.

Africa was that a 1942 cross-channel operation would have been largely British. FDR undoubtedly shared Leahy's view that a 1942 invasion of France "would have failed and we still would have been safe, but England would have been lost."[31] In short, it would have been relatively modest in size, overwhelmingly British in composition, and a probable disaster.

Delaying the decisive action of the war until an American-dominated and -commanded army could be put on the Continent under conditions less risky than those of 1942 would tend both to shorten America's stay in Europe and maximize its prestige and leverage at the peace. An early victory in the West, however unlikely, would have been a mainly British affair, and a European settlement heavily conditioned by British interests was something Roosevelt had tried to avoid since the thirties. Similar considerations of timing were probably not absent from Wilson's mind in 1918. The North African invasion had hardly begun in November 1942 before Roosevelt suggested the possibility of further Mediterranean operations.[32] He also wished to continue Bolero, but it was obvious that the decision to invade Sicily, made at Casablanca in January, eliminated the possibility of a cross-channel operation in 1943.[33] At Casablanca, an additional argument was available: German resistance could be worn down from the air. FDR's faith in air power would be put to the test by Operation Pointblank, the around-the-clock bombing of Germany, in 1943.[34]

Why did Roosevelt think he could reconcile delay of the cross-channel invasion with his courtship of the Russians? It is necessary to look at the circumstances surrounding his May 30 commitment. If FDR's advocacy of a European landing was partly designed to relieve Russian

31. Leahy, 110. When FDR heard that Montgomery's El Alamein offensive was scheduled just before the North African landing, he said, according to Marshall, "not to let him do that because they always got licked." Bland, 594.

32. See FDR to Churchill, Nov. 11, 1942, Kimball, ed., *Correspondence*, 1: 668–69; FDR to Churchill, Nov. 19, 1942, Kimball, ed., *Correspondence*, 2: 20; Minutes of Meeting between FDR, Hopkins, and the Joint Chiefs of Staff, Dec. 10, 1942, MR files, box 29, FDRL.

33. See FDR to Churchill, Nov. 25, 1942, Kimball, ed., *Correspondence*, 2: 41. At Casablanca Marshall told FDR that by mid-1943 there would be six to nine U.S. divisions in Britain, along with thirteen British. Thus, it could be assumed, a 1943 cross-channel operation would still be mainly British. See *FRUS, Conferences at Washington and Casablanca*, 583.

34. See Maurice Matloff, *Strategic Planning for Coalition Warfare*, vol. 2: *1943–1944* (Washington, D.C.: U.S. Government Printing Office, 1959), 28–29. On FDR's interest in the strategy, see Michael Howard, *Grand Strategy*, vol. 4: *August 1942–September 1943* (London: HMSO, 1970), 297–98; FDR to Churchill, Kimball, ed., *Correspondence*, 2: 156.

diplomatic pressure on the British, that result had been achieved when Molotov suddenly signed a treaty in London with no territorial strings attached on May 26. The Russians were expecting a U.S. quid pro quo, but FDR was hardly forthcoming. When Molotov raised the second-front question on May 29, FDR countered with the problem of allied shipping: "It all came down to transportation."[35] The next day Molotov was reminded that an early cross-channel operation would be mainly British. When at this point Molotov called the second front a "predominantly political" issue and "requested a straight answer," FDR got Marshall to reply.[36] On June 1, FDR was prepared to say that he "hoped and expected to open a second front in 1942," but that consequently the Russians would have to consider halving their lend-lease requirements. "The Soviets," he said, "could not eat their cake and have it too." Roosevelt was probably hoping that Molotov would see the advantages of a later, American-dominated second front. When confronted once more with "the direct question," he had little choice but to say yes.[37]

Still, FDR was gambling that this was the kind of "promise" he could afford to break. Fear of a Russo-German separate peace had abated after Stalin's May Day speech calling for the overthrow of the "Hitler–Goering adventurist clique." The Soviet military situation was serious but not desperate.[38] Certainly the situation Molotov painted was less dramatic than Hopkins's rendering of it when he heavily edited a Roosevelt message to Churchill on May 31. This message may be explained by the fact that Hopkins, unlike Roosevelt, was a sincere proponent of Sledgehammer, while the latter wished to remain on record as favoring a 1942 second front.[39] Maybe he reckoned that "the second front in Europe" (the language of the official communique) could be stretched to include North Africa or that Stalin might even see the advantages of such a landing.[40] Undoubtedly, FDR calculated that blame for delay of the cross-channel operation would fall mainly on the British. He knew perfectly well that the British opposed Sledgehammer

35. *FRUS*, 1942, 1: 570.
36. Ibid., 575–77.
37. Ibid., 582–83.
38. On the speech, see McNeill, 170. See also Sherwood, 565–68; *FRUS*, 1942, 2: 570, 576. On May 30, Molotov noted that the balance was "slightly" in Hitler's favor. In fact, the Red Army was now on the defensive after the failure of its Kharkov offensive in late May.
39. See *FRUS*, 1942, 2: 570; see also Kimball, ed., *Correspondence*, 1: 502–4.
40. Stoler argues that the Russians were perfectly aware that FDR could not keep his promise. Stoler, *Second Front*, 51. Feis says, "Actually there is reason to believe that both Stalin and Molotov appreciated that no firm pledge had been given of a second front in the West in 1942" (*Churchill–Roosevelt–Stalin*, 71).

and were in a position to stop it when he gave his "straight answer" to the Russians.[41] Since the British would veto Sledgehammer, he had nothing to lose by urging Hopkins and Marshall to continue to push for it when they went to London in July. At the same time, he rejected Marshall's bid to blackmail the British into accepting Sledgehammer by threatening to shift American efforts to the Pacific. After the decision in favor of Gymnast, it was Churchill who trekked to Moscow to break the news to Stalin. Sending Averell Harriman with him was certainly not Roosevelt's idea.[42]

On May 14, 1942, FDR had told a group of advisers: "You know I am a juggler, and I never let my right hand know what my left hand does. . . . I may be entirely inconsistent, and furthermore I am perfectly willing to mislead and tell untruths if it will help win the war." Sometimes the right hand found out anyway, but this was an apt description of Roosevelt's handling of the second front. The affair demonstrated his "natural gifts for useful deceit" – not that this was his exclusive province at the time.[43] He sought to reap the benefits with Stalin of his ostensible support of Sledgehammer, while pursuing the British alternative, Gymnast (later renamed Torch), to American advantage. Characteristically, it was Roosevelt who wished to eat his cake and have it. There were risks, but he told Churchill in October, "I feel sure the Russians are going to hold this winter."[44] FDR was also playing a hunch similar to Wilson's in March 1918, when the latter had declined to commit American troops to counter the German breakthrough at the juncture of the French and British lines. FDR believed that Wilson had been correct to gamble that the Allies would recover on their own.[45] Like

41. See Churchill to FDR, May 28, 1942, containing a May 22 memo setting forth the British objections. Kimball, ed., *Correspondence*, 1: 495–500. The purpose of Mountbatten's trip was to press these objections personally on FDR.

42. For FDR's instructions to Hopkins and Marshall, see Sherwood, 603–5. When the British held their ground against Sledgehammer, FDR cabled the U.S. delegation that the news did "not wholly take me by surprise" and urged them to decide quickly on an operation for 1942, i.e., Gymnast. See FDR to Hopkins et al., July 22, 1942, PSF 4 Hopkins, FDRL. On Harriman's inclusion, see Feis, *Churchill–Roosevelt–Stalin*, 73.

43. The "juggler" remark came during a discussion of Argentina. See Blum, ed., *Morgenthau Diaries*, 3: 197. An example of the right hand learning what the left was doing was Marshall's learning the contents of FDR's messages to Churchill and of Churchill's replies through Sir John Dill, representative of the British Chiefs of Staff in Washington. See Bland, ed., 413–14. The expression "useful deceit" is Gary Wills's. See "The Power of Impotence," *New York Review of Books*, 36, no. 18 (Nov. 23, 1989), 4.

44. See Kimball, ed., *Correspondence*, 2: 616, 643.

45. FDR recounted this incident to William Bullitt in 1943. See Bullitt, "How We Won the War and Lost the Peace," *Life*, Aug. 30, 1948, 91. FDR said he had discussed the matter personally with Wilson.

Wilson, Roosevelt wished to delay his main thrust until the enemy had been further weakened and until the weight of American arms would leave no doubt as to their contribution to the final outcome. Like Wilson, it did not bother him excessively that in the meantime America's allies would themselves grow relatively weaker and less able to resist American demands.

Along with a further delay in the cross-channel operation, Casablanca produced the call for the unconditional surrender of the Axis. "Of course it's just the thing for the Russians," said FDR. "They couldn't want anything better."[46] FDR realized that words were no substitute for a second front, and Stalin angrily demanded a cross-channel operation in 1943.[47] But the deeper meaning of FDR's remark is that he was proposing to the Russians that they take part in the construction of a new political order in Europe. It was by no means certain that the Red Army would pursue the Germans beyond their 1941 frontiers.[48] There is evidence that Stalin considered a separate peace between the end of the battle of Stalingrad in February and the German offensive at Kursk in July 1943. At Casablanca, Roosevelt not only renewed his stated aim of destroying German militarism, but formally invited Russian power into the heart of Europe. As he told Elliott Roosevelt in late 1943, whether Russian power in Europe was a bad thing depended on many factors. A Russia aggrandized, therefore satisfied, might be a constructive force.[49]

In September 1943, FDR had his famous conversation with Cardinal Spellman of New York. According to Spellman's account, Roosevelt foresaw Russian domination of Germany, Austria, Hungary, and Croatia, though in time – ten or twenty years – he hoped "European influence would bring the Russians to become less barbarian." Spellman attributes more fatalism to Roosevelt than most contemporary witnesses and suggests that he expected Russian treatment of East Central Europe to be very harsh. The conversation also indicates that FDR saw the

---

46. Elliott Roosevelt, 117. On unconditional surrender, see also Axel Gietz, *Die neue Alte Welt: Roosevelt, Churchill und die europaische Nachkriegsordnung* (Munich: Wilhelm Fink, 1986), 73–74.

47. In his February 16, 1943, message, Stalin expressed "outrage" over the slowness of the Allied campaign in Tunisia. See Kimball, ed., *Correspondence*, 2: 151.

48. On this point see Leahy, 147; Kimball, ed., *Correspondence*, 2: 119; Joseph Davies memo to FDR, May 29, 1943, PSF Russia 1942–43, box 68, FDRL.

49. On the possible separate peace, see Vojtech Mastny, *Russia's Road to the Cold War* (New York: Columbia University Press, 1979), 73–85. FDR had stated that unconditional surrender was his objective in his January 6, 1942, speech to Congress and on other occasions. See FDR, *Development of Foreign Policy*, 136–42. Elliott Roosevelt, 185. The remark about Russian power in Europe was made at Tehran.

installation of Russia deep in Europe as a less than tragic prospect. Indeed, it provides a rare look at the "let them go to the devil" streak in his European vision. His message to the cardinal was that, while he did not like what the Russians would do, the Nazis and their smaller allies were not undeserving of their fate. In any event, he did not intend to risk World War III in order to prevent the inevitable from taking place. With Harriman, FDR was franker still. Harriman remarked in November 1944, "The President consistently shows very little interest in Eastern European matters except as they affect sentiment in America." On another occasion, Roosevelt told Harriman "that he didn't care whether the countries bordering Russia became communized" or not. [50]

Divide et impera

Roosevelt's conception of the new European groundwork went beyond the conventional Mazzinian–Wilsonian belief in national self-determination dear to liberal internationalists like Hull. FDR wanted to encourage the breakup and recomposition of existing national units. FDR was not clear about the ideal size of the new units – to questions of economic viability he seemed indifferent – but one of his aims was presumably to release provincial energy and initiative in a world that had become overcentralized and unbalanced. Such a vision drew on images of the peaceful, partly fanciful pre-1890 Europe as recounted to FDR by his parents and the picturesque, postage-stamp Europe that Roosevelt had seen fading away in 1896. It also drew on the Jeffersonian strain in Roosevelt's outlook – the opposition of rural civilization to urban-industrial blight.

Like Jefferson, FDR was less interested in saving Europe from itself than in rescuing the rest of the world from Europe. "Fractionization" was the path to a weak and harmless Europe, and one subject to outside manipulation. Decentralization and renewal from below meant removal of the old forces that had pursued destructive foreign policies. The new political forces would be in no position to resist the restructuring of Europe's world position through disarmament and decolonization. FDR's ideal was an Indian Raj writ in European terms: a fragmented

---

50. See Robert Gannon, *The Cardinal Spellman Story* (Garden City, N.Y.: Doubleday, 1962), 222–24. See also Averell Harriman, "Memorandum of Conversations with the President During Trip to Washington, October 21–November 19, 1944," Averell Harriman Papers, Public Service, World War II, Moscow files, chronological file, Nov. 19–24, 1944, box 175, Library of Congress.

continent over which the two remaining powers, Britain and the Soviet Union, could conduct a game of *divide et impera* without depending on the United States.

The logic of decentralization and territorial rearrangement pervades FDR's discussion of postwar problems. To Eden in March 1943 he expressed his "opinion that the Croats and Serbs had nothing in common" and that it was "ridiculous to try to force them to live together." Belgium was another "artificial bilingual state" that might share the fate of Yugoslavia. The same argument applied to the chief troublemakers, Germany and France. He considered detaching Alsace and Lorraine from both, perhaps incorporating the contested areas into a new entity including Belgium and Luxembourg. He also asked, "After Germany is disarmed, what is the reason for France having a big military establishment?"[51]

Roosevelt's often-expressed wish to allow the French people to determine their postwar institutions reflected the legal arguments of Alexis Léger, former secretary general of the Quai d'Orsay and one of the most influential French exiles in the United States. To Harriman, Roosevelt laid out Léger's "elaborate theory that as the Allies liberated areas of France, the local people should be encouraged to select their own representatives." In other words, "the French people ought to have the opportunity to develop their government from the grass roots up."[52] In the meantime, Roosevelt told General Charles de Gaulle, the Allies held the sovereignty of France in "trusteeship." France was "in the position of a little child unable to look out and fend for itself."[53] Perhaps Léger's argument appealed to FDR's sense of the *bonté* and vitality of provincial political life, but his main aim was to prevent the recrystallization of the prewar French elites.[54]

---

51. *FRUS, 1943*, 3: 13, 16. On Belgium see FDR conversation with State Department officials, Oct. 5, 1943, *FRUS, 1943*, 1: 543. On Alsace and Lorraine see ibid., 543; *FRUS, 1943*, 3: 17.

52. Harriman and Abel, 228. See also Elliott Roosevelt, 113–14. In a January 31, 1944, memo to FDR, Léger wrote, "Whatever decisions the Allies might make, they must respect the Treveneuc Law, the Constitutional Law of 1872." This law laid down a procedure to be followed after a period of occupation in order to create a new constitutional regime. The *conseils généraux* would meet and elect two delegates to a special provisional assembly charged with the task of preparing a general election. See Raoul Aglion, *Roosevelt and De Gaulle: Allies in Conflict – A Personal Memoir* (New York: Free Press, 1988), 189.

53. *FRUS, Conferences at Washington and Casablanca*, 1694–96.

54. *FRUS, Conferences at Cairo and Tehran*, 484, 509. His abhorrence of the Third Republic political class was reminiscent of Jefferson's for the *ancien régime* as described in Bowers's *Jefferson and Hamilton*.

Roosevelt admittedly found it hard to imagine a world in which America's historic friend would no longer play a part,[55] while the prospect of siring a new France appealed to a sort of Wilsonian vanity in his makeup. He took boyish pride in his radio message delivered in French on the eve of the North African landing and was encouraged to see himself as the savior of France by French admirers and advisers. But France's was to be a long penance – "Many years of honest labor would be necessary before France would be reestablished" – tantamount to its indefinite retirement from the world of the great powers.[56] FDR had his fingers crossed when he told Vichy that the empire would be restored in return for collaboration with the United States. France's ignominious colonial and military record had stripped it of any moral title.[57]

On the main postwar problem, FDR wrote, "There are two schools of thought – those who would be altruistic in regard to the Germans . . . and those who would adopt a much 'tougher' attitude." In effect, the two schools were the liberal, Versailles revisionist school inspired by Keynes's *The Economic Consequences of the Peace*, on the one hand, and the Theodore Roosevelt–Clemenceau school, on the other. FDR continued, "Most decidedly I belong to the latter school."[58] There was to be no nonsense this time about broken armistice "contracts" or doubts about who had won the war.

FDR's solution to the German problem was dismemberment of a kind that went well beyond the detachment of East Prussia and the restoration of Austria. He was encouraged by Welles, Morgenthau, Hopkins, and former ambassadors James Gerard and Hugh Wilson, but

---

55. See his comment in Elliott Roosevelt, 75.
56. See, e.g., letter of Eve Curie to FDR, Nov. 26, 1942, PSF France 1942, FDRL. "I wish – oh, so much – that you could address my compatriots again, in the same straightforward way that you used on the first day [of the invasion] in your own, sincere French words. . . . Your voice can be a guide, a rallying point. . . . You can show them the way." For the text of FDR's November 7, 1942, message, see OF 203 France 1941–42, FDRL. According to Alexis Léger, FDR "should be trusted and considered as the sole guarantee of French interests in the world." Quoted in Aglion, 188. On "reestablishment" see *FRUS, Conferences at Cairo and Tehran*, 485. Just before Tehran, he told the Joint Chiefs of Staff, "France would certainly not again become a first class power for at least 25 years." Ibid., 194.
57. See Elliott Roosevelt, 75–76. On Indochina see memo to Hull, Jan. 24, 1944, *PL, 1928–1945*, 2: 1489. For message to Pétain on the French Empire see FDR to Leahy, Jan. 20, 1942, ibid., 1275–76. On French strong points see FDR conversation with Joint Chiefs of Staff, Nov. 15, 1943, in Matloff, 339; Memo to Secretary of State, Aug. 4, 1943, MR Naval Aide President's File, FDRL.
58. FDR to Queen Wilhelmina, Aug. 26, 1944, *PL, 1928–1945*, 2: 1535.

the notion was very much his own.[59] In March 1943, he told Eden, "We should encourage the differences and ambitions that will spring up within Germany." Even if "that spontaneous desire [should] not spring up ... Germany must be divided into several states."[60] At Tehran, FDR suggested a five-state Germany, with the Kiel Canal–Hamburg area, the Ruhr, and the Saar under international control.[61] He privately accepted the cession to Poland of German territory up to the Oder River to compensate for Polish territory lost to the Soviet Union.[62] FDR agreed with Stalin that most of the differences among the Germans had been eliminated by the experience of unity, but thought religious, dynastic, linguistic, and cultural divisions could be revived.[63] According to Ickes, he toyed with the idea of a Roman Catholic southern German state under Archduke Otto of Austria. He believed the German people themselves were redeemable within a looser, pre-1870 political framework and did not lose sleep over the possibility that they would go communist "in the Russian manner."[64] The important thing was "not to leave in

59. See Sumner Welles, *The Time for Decision* (New York: Harper Bros., 1944), chap. 9. On Gerard see Don Whitehead, "Split Up Reich, Gerard Proposes," *Chicago Daily Times*, June 16, 1942, copy forwarded to FDR by Gerard, PPF 977, James W. Gerard 1941–42, FDRL. On Wilson see his letter to Will Clayton, July 3, 1944, copy in PSF 16, William Donovan, FDRL. Around the time of the second Quebec conference, FDR set up a cabinet committee on the German issue. Hopkins wrote FDR on September 9, 1944, "Could we not agree *today that we are going to dismember* Germany without determining exact details which would be left to the committee?" (emphasis in original). Harry Hopkins Papers, Treatment of Germany F (1), FDRL. See also letter by Gerard Swope to the *New York Times* calling for dismemberment, Sept. 3, 1943. On FDR's interest in the letter, see John H. Backer, *The Decision to Divide Germany* (Durham, N.C.: Duke University Press, 1978), 21–22.

60. See *FRUS*, 1943, 3: 16, 21–22; Welles, *The Time for Decision*, chap. 9. On State Department planning see Backer, chap. 2. In October, Roosevelt said "categorically that he favor[ed] partition of Germany into three or more states, completely sovereign but joined by a network of common services." In November, he told the Joint Chiefs of Staff that Germany should be split into three states, or possibly five. On this occasion FDR used a map to pencil in his conception of postwar occupation zones. See Matloff, 341.

61. *FRUS, Conference at Tehran*, 611–12.

62. FDR mentioned the Oder line but did not consent specifically to the Curzon line claimed by the Russians. Ibid., 594.

63. See ibid., 510.

64. See the March 30, 1943, memo from Halifax to Eden in which the British ambassador reported on a conversation with Ickes. FO 954/30, PRO. See also FDR to William Donovan, Nov. 7, 1941, *PL, 1928–1945*, 2: 1234; FDR to Joseph Kennedy, Oct. 31, 1939, ibid., 949. He wrote, "The German upbringing for centuries, their insistence on independence of family life, and the right to hold property in a small way" made them resistant to communism.

the German mind the concept of the Reich." The word itself "should be stricken from the language."[65]

When Stalin spoke at Tehran of the danger of creating "large frameworks within which the Germans could operate," Churchill asked whether he contemplated "a Europe composed of little states, disjoined, separated and weak." Churchill's remark was a fair description of Roosevelt's own intentions. Isolated on this, as on most questions at Tehran, Churchill observed that "he hoped for larger units."[66] Charles Bohlen's appraisal of Soviet aims around the time of Tehran was also an apt rendering of what FDR himself envisioned:

> Germany is to be broken up and kept broken up. The states of eastern, southeastern and central Europe will not be permitted to group themselves into any federations or associations. France is to be stripped of her colonies and strategic bases beyond her borders and will not be permitted to maintain any appreciable military establishment. Poland and Italy will remain approximately their present territorial size, but it is doubtful if either will be permitted to maintain any appreciable armed force. The result will be that the Soviet Union will be the only important political and military force on the continent of Europe. The rest of Europe will be reduced to political and military impotence.[67]

IN 1943, William Bullitt wrote Roosevelt several letters on the subject of Russia. They are of considerable interest because they are links in a chain connecting the turn-of-the-century protocontainment outlook with the post–World War II strategy of the United States. According to Bullitt, Stalin aimed to dominate all of Europe, but he put "out pseudopodia like an amoeba rather than leaping like a tiger. If the pseudopodia meet no obstacle, the Soviet Union flows in." What he tactfully referred to as British policy – it was actually FDR's – Bullitt called the "Balance of Impotence." "Europe cannot be made a military vacuum for the Soviet Union to flow into." FDR should try personal diplomacy with Stalin, but the best way to deal with him was the "prior arrival of American and British Armies in the Eastern Frontiers of Europe ... by way of Salonika and Constantinople." In August, he repeated that "the first step toward preventing Soviet domination of Europe is the creation of a British–American line in Eastern Europe."[68]

FDR's subsequent actions suggest that he was not converted by

---

65. *FRUS, Conference at Tehran*, 510.
66. Ibid., 603.
67. Bohlen, 153.
68. Bullitt to FDR, Jan. 29, 1943, in Bullitt, ed., 579, 585, 588; Bullitt to FDR, Aug. 10, 1943, in ibid., 598.

Bullitt's thesis but was alarmed by its appearance.[69] In May, he tried to arrange a tête-à-tête with Stalin in Alaska (Stalin declined) and pledged his support – this time definite – to the plan for a cross-channel invasion in the spring of 1944. In August, he won a commitment to plan "Overlord" from the British. Roosevelt said, "We could if necessary carry out the operation ourselves." He was "anxious to have American preponderance . . . starting from the first day of the assault." A second plan ("Rankin") was developed in case of sudden German collapse, reflecting Roosevelt's desire "to be ready to get to Berlin as soon as did the Russians" (and the British).[70] These decisions indicate a sense of urgency about forging a direct relationship with Stalin while harnessing the British to his will.

Since mid-1941, Roosevelt had been on guard against arrangements that might be construed as an Anglo-American bloc directed against Moscow.[71] The tireless – for others tiresome – advocate of European unity, Count Richard Coudenhove-Kalergi, talked to Berle, Welles, and Hull, but got nowhere at the White House. Roosevelt dismissed the count's design, similar to Bullitt's, for a federal bloc including Germany.[72] British plans for a European regional organization were a

69. Roosevelt asked Eden about Bullitt's view and sent Hopkins to talk to Soviet Ambassador Maxim Litvinov. See *FRUS*, 1943, 3: 22. Eden said he did not believe the Bullitt thesis "but that in any event a wise and expedient thing to do was to cultivate to the utmost possible extent the friendship and confidence of the Soviet Government." See also Dallek, 399–401.

70. For FDR's letter to Stalin, May 5, 1943, see *PL, 1928–1945*, 2: 1422–23. For the report of Joseph Davies, who carried the letter, see Davies to FDR, May 29, 1943, PSF Russia, 1942–43, FDRL. On the cross-channel decision, see Matloff, 125. On Overlord, see ibid., 168. For FDR on U.S. "preponderance," see Minutes of meeting with Joint Chiefs of Staff, Aug. 10, 1943, MR, FDR–JCS, FDRL. On FDR and Rankin, see Matloff, 226.

71. See Elliott Roosevelt, 207.

72. A copy of Coudenhove-Kalergi's July 4, 1941, speech, "The Future of Europe and America," is located in OF 5207 Coudenhove-Kalergi, 1933–43, FDRL. FDR's secretary, Edwin Watson, wrote the count to refuse an appointment on December 9, 1940. See OF 5207 CK 1933–43, FDRL. In late 1942 he tried again. See unsigned memo of December 17, 1942, to Watson informing him that the State Department had recommended against an appointment and asking whether Watson himself cared to receive him. OF 5207 CK 1933–44, FDRL. Watson's reply was, "NO if I can avoid it." On Berle's conversations with Coudenhove-Kalergi, see Berle Diary, Dec. 7, 1940, FDRL; memo of July 19, 1941, Berle Papers, FDRL. See also Arnold Zurcher, *The Struggle to Unite Europe, 1940–1958* (New York: New York University Press, 1958), 16; David Weigall, "British Ideas of European Unity and Regional Confederation," in M. L. Smith and Peter M. R. Stirk, eds., *Making the New Europe: European Unity and the Second World War* (New York: Pinter Publishers, 1990), 61–63.

more serious concern. In early 1943, Churchill proposed "an instrument of European Government" including Scandinavian, Danubian, and Balkan blocs or confederations. Churchill warned, "None can predict with certainty that the victors will never quarrel amongst themselves."[73]

In May, he proposed a "Supreme World Council" including the United States, Russia, Britain (and, if the United States insisted, China) and regional councils for Europe, the Western Hemisphere, and Pacific. Members of the Supreme Council would "sit on the Regional Councils in which they were directly interested." Thus "in addition to being represented on the American Regional Council the United States would be represented on the European Regional Council."[74] Churchill also wanted a strong France and thought Coudenhove-Kalergi's ideas "had much to recommend them."[75] In November 1943, Jan Smuts called for a close alignment of Western Europe with Britain, including possible Commonwealth membership for France, Belgium, Holland, Denmark, and Norway.[76]

Such proposals created a basic dilemma for Roosevelt. On one hand, Theodore Roosevelt's notion of great-power regional hegemony was central to his vision.[77] FDR said: "Russia would be charged with keeping peace in Europe. The United States would be charged with

73. Churchill to FDR, Feb. 2, 1943, Kimball, ed., *Correspondence*, 2: 129–32. On Churchill's private view see Weigall, 160.

74. Churchill to FDR, via Halifax, summarizing the prime minister's luncheon conversation of May 22, 1943, with Henry Wallace, Senator Tom Connally, Welles, Ickes, and Stimson. Kimball, ed., *Correspondence*, 2: 130. See also John Morton Blum, ed., *The Price of Vision: The Diary of Henry Wallace, 1942–1946* (Boston: Houghton Mifflin, 1973), 201–10.

75. On the same occasion, he proposed an Anglo-American "fraternal association" including the closest military cooperation, even "some common form of citizenship." Kimball, ed., *Correspondence*, 2: 130.

76. For Smuts speech of November 25, 1943, see Jan Van Der Poel, ed., *Selections from the Smuts Papers* (Cambridge: Cambridge University Press, 1973), 4: 456–69. See also the memo "British Plans for a Western European bloc," Feb. 1945, MR Naval Aide A/16, FDRL. On the Smuts–Churchill relationship see Lord Moran, *Churchill: Taken From the Diaries of Lord Moran* (Boston: Houghton Mifflin, 1965), chap. 6. See also Ernest Llewellyn Woodward, *British Foreign Policy in the Second World War*, abridged ed. (London: HMSO, 1962), 463–64; Terry H. Anderson, *The United States, Great Britain, and the Cold War, 1944–47* (Columbia, Mo.: University of Missouri Press, 1981), 16.

77. FDR also hoped Britain (as an American friend of Smuts put it) would be seen in Europe after the war "as a greater, a wiser, and a more steadfast leader." See the excerpt from an article on Smuts by Thomas Lamont in the *Saturday Review*, May 6, 1944, sent by Lamont to FDR. PPF 70 Lamont, FDRL.

keeping peace in the Western Hemisphere."[78] Pan-American and
European councils might facilitate the regional policemen's work. In the
first public airing of the four-policeman concept, Forrest Davis's April
1943 article in the *Saturday Evening Post*, FDR let it be known that his
basic approach to foreign policy was closer to Theodore Roosevelt's
than to Wilson's. He floated the idea of "a security commission" of
Britain, the United States, and Russia "to police the peace of Europe . . .
until the political reorganization of the Continent is completed."[79] At
the same time, Roosevelt feared Churchill's council as a device for tying
the United States down in Europe. FDR did not foresee "the U.S.
forever embroiled in foreign quarrels and required to keep large military
forces abroad."[80] He was "very emphatic" that the United States could
not join "any independent regional body such as a European Council."
America's military assets were to be committed elsewhere; FDR had
commissioned elaborate studies for an expanded chain of postwar U.S.
bases in the Atlantic and Pacific.[81] But a European council to which the
United States did not belong presented a different set of problems: it
might resist U.S. influence or evolve into an anti-Soviet combination.
On balance, regional bodies were not a good idea.

FDR's shift away from regionalism, embodied in the Moscow Conference Four Power Declaration of October 1943, was also a victory for
Hull and his advisers. They had argued, with regrettable accuracy from
FDR's standpoint, that domestic and world opinion would support
only a "general international organization based on the principle of
sovereign equality" – as opposed to a cabal of the big powers.[82] Public

78. Memo of conversation between FDR, Grace Tully, and Clark Eichelberger, Nov. 13,
    1942, PSF 188 UN, FDRL. FDR continued, "The U.S. and China would be charged
    with keeping peace in the Far East." The published version of the memo contains the
    curious transcription "Russia would be charged with keeping peace in the Western
    Hemisphere." See *PL, 1928–1945*, 2: 1366–67.
79. Forrest Davis, "Roosevelt's World Blueprint," *Saturday Evening Post*, 115 (Apr. 10,
    1943), 20–21, 109–11. This article was an officially sponsored trial balloon based
    on an interview with FDR.
80. Ibid., 109.
81. *FRUS*, 1943, 3: 39. At Tehran, FDR said he "doubted if the United States Congress
    would agree to the United States' participation in an exclusively European Committee
    which might be able to force the dispatch of American troops to Europe." At most he
    "envisaged the sending of American planes and ships to Europe" with Britain and
    Russia providing the land armies "in the event of any future threat to the peace."
    FRUS, Conferences at Cairo and Tehran, 531. On the chain of bases see Louis,
    270–72.
82. For the Four Power Declaration see *FRUS*, 1943, 3: 756. On Hull's lobbying efforts
    and arguments against the regional principle see his *Memoirs*, 2: 1642–47. For Isaiah
    Bowman's arguments see his memos of June 5 and 12, 1943, Postwar Problems, Berle
    Papers, 1942–43, FDRL.

reaction to the Davis article had not been enthusiastic and FDR was obliged to juggle once again. If in his frank secret dealings with Churchill and Stalin he continued to think in terms of great-power regional hegemony,[83] he henceforth had to cater to public and congressional support for an egalitarian United Nations. Such an organization, hatched by Hull's inner circle, would prove to be the secretary's fitting, if unintended, revenge for years of humiliation by the White House.

The invasion and occupation of southern Italy in mid-1943 put another thorny question on the table: as the Soviet ambassador to London put it, whether the Soviet Union and the Allies should each "have a sphere of influence" or "admit the right of the other to an interest in all parts of Europe."[84] Roosevelt's answer, for all practical purposes, was the former. FDR was sympathetic to Russian demands for reparations from Italy and a portion of its fleet, but the Russians were excluded from the occupation authority, the Allied Control Commission. FDR also wished to limit the powers of tripartite, European-wide political commissions suggested by the British and Russians. The "European Advisory Commission" set up at Tehran to prepare occupation zones and armistice terms for Germany was, as its name suggests, an advisory affair. Much has been made of Stalin's use in Eastern Europe of the "Italian precedent." From Roosevelt's standpoint the precedent was not an unhappy one: while Italy had no international autonomy, a degree of democratic political life was reestablished, and the fate of the monarchy was reserved for a decision by the people.[85]

For FDR the counterpart of the "Italian precedent," in any case the best that could be hoped for in Eastern Europe, was the "Czech model." The Soviet–Czech Treaty of December 1943 foresaw a Czechoslovakia whose foreign policy was dictated by Moscow, but internally pluralistic. FDR encouraged the president of the Czech exile government, Eduard Beneš, to pursue his special relationship with Moscow.[86] Needless to say, comparing Czechoslovakia to Poland was like comparing Costa

83. On the "Good Neighbor" model for the USSR see Forrest Davis, "What Really Happened at Teheran," *Saturday Evening Post*, 216 (May 13, 1944), 12–13+; 217 (May 20, 1944), 22–3+.
84. Quoted in Mastny, 107.
85. On this point see Geir Lundestad, *The American Non-Policy towards Eastern Europe, 1943–1947: Universalism in an Area Not of Essential Interest to the United States* (Oslo: Universitetsforlaget, 1978), 81. See also James E. Miller, *The United States and Italy, 1940–1950: The Politics and Diplomacy of Stabilization* (Chapel Hill: University of North Carolina Press, 1986), 68–76.
86. On the "Czech model" see E. Beneš, "Czechoslovakia Plans for Peace," *Foreign Affairs*, 23, no. 1 (Oct. 1944), 26–38. See also Beneš, *Memoirs*, 181–96; Mastny, 133–44; Lundestad, 150–51; Joseph Korbel, *Twentieth Century Czechoslovakia*

Rica to Mexico. Even before the discovery of the Katyn Forest massacres and break with Moscow in April 1943, the Polish exile government in London had adopted a defiant, demanding posture in contrast to the Czechs. Still, the Russians had every interest in achieving Stalin's professed aim of a Poland strong enough to help defend the Soviet Union against Germany. Such a Poland, Stalin said, could not be built exclusively or even primarily on communist foundations.[87] Both Stalin and Roosevelt were hoping – even if not really expecting – to find a Polish Beneš.

Putting the pillars in their place

Roosevelt's purpose at Tehran, and throughout 1944, was to put himself in an intermediary position between Great Britain and the Soviet Union.[88] At Tehran, FDR played the card of the second front to the embarrassment of the British, who wanted to delay it once more in favor of Mediterranean operations.[89] "The trip was *almost* a complete success," he wrote, "specially the Russians." He referred to the personal relationship established with Stalin, as well as the latter's pledge to enter the war against Japan.[90]

Roosevelt was always on guard against what he saw as British efforts to entangle the United States in Europe. He flatly rejected the U.S. occupation zone – southern Germany, France, and Austria – contained in a plan that gave the British northwest Germany, Belgium, Holland, and Denmark. Since, according to the invasion plans, U.S. forces would occupy the right (south) side of the line and the British the left (north), FDR insisted that there would have to be a "cross-over" of U.S. and British armies after they entered Germany to allow the United States to

(New York: Columbia University Press, 1977), 175–77. On the State Department's view of the treaty as a model see Eduard Mark, "American Policy Toward Eastern Europe," 323.

87. Mastny, 168–73.
88. This involved deliberately distancing himself from Churchill by refusing to meet him alone before the conference. See Kimball, ed., *Correspondence*, 1, Introduction.
89. FDR did so after having ascertained that the cross-channel invasion was still Stalin's preference. There had been some doubts as to whether the Russians still placed importance on the northwestern France operation or might prefer Balkan or eastern Mediterranean operations. See General Deane to Joint Chiefs of Staff, Nov. 9, 1943, MR 167 A/16 Overlord, FDRL.
90. Undated entry in FDR diary kept during the Tehran conference, OF 200-3-N Wartime Conferences, Nov. 11–Dec. 17, 1943, FDRL.

occupy the northwest zone and channel ports.[91] He cabled Churchill, "I am absolutely unwilling to police France and possibly Italy and the Balkans as well."[92] He dismissed Churchill's answer that "the question of policing" France did not arise:

> "Do please don't" ask me to keep any American forces in France. I just cannot do it! ... As I suggested before, I denounce and protest the paternity of Belgium, France and Italy. You really ought to bring up and discipline your own children. In view of the fact that they may be your bulwark in future days, you should at least pay for their schooling now.[93]

Roosevelt accepted an Anglo-Soviet proposal to settle the boundary between the Soviet occupation zone and the western zones in Germany, but he was adamant that the United States would take the northern zone.[94]

There is little need to emphasize that 1944 was a presidential election year; "political considerations in the United States" made his decision final.[95] But Roosevelt's aversion to entrapment in Europe went beyond electoral politics, as did his intention to force the British to accept the consequences of a rapid U.S. pullout. They would have no choice, as Churchill himself put it, except "to make friends with Stalin," and this was one of the purposes of forcing Churchill to face the nakedness of the British position at Tehran.[96] FDR's reservations about Britain's 1944 approach to the Russians on Eastern Europe had to do with the possible domestic fallout and with his abiding suspicion of the British. Though the two were supposedly "95 percent together," FDR knew perfectly well that Eden opposed his plans for the weakening and

---

91. See FDR meeting with the Joint Chiefs of Staff, Nov. 19, 1943 *FRUS, Conferences at Cairo and Tehran*, 253–54. FDR said, "We should not get roped into accepting any European sphere of influence. We do not want to be compelled, for instance, to maintain US troops in Yugoslavia." For a running account of the controversy see Memo from George Elsey to Admiral Brown, Aug. 31, 1944, MR 167 Naval Aide Germany and German Occupied Territories, FDRL.
92. FDR to Churchill, Feb. 7, 1944, Kimball, ed., *Correspondence*, 2: 709.
93. See Churchill to FDR, Feb. 23, 1944, Kimball, ed., *Correspondence*, 2: 745–47; FDR to Churchill, Feb. 29, 1944, ibid., 766–67.
94. The U.S. representative to the European Advisory Commission was Ambassador John Winant. On the east–west zonal agreement see Elsey memo, 10–11, cited in note 91. For FDR's acceptance of the line proposed by the British and Russians to the EAC see Memo to Hull Mar. 30, 1944, MR 35, German Zones of Occupation, FDRL.
95. FDR to Stettinius, Feb. 21, 1944, MR 167 Naval Aide German and German Occupied Countries, FDRL.
96. Quoted in David Carlton, *Anthony Eden* (London: Allen & Lane, 1981), 243. Of Churchill after Tehran, Moran wrote, "He is appalled by his own impotence." Quoted in ibid., 231.

fragmentation of Europe.[97] Eden, in any case, was far too stereotypical a Tory creature to be trusted by FDR.

Roosevelt's relationship with Churchill himself has been "much romanticized."[98] When Churchill took power in 1940, FDR reportedly considered him a "playboy and a drunkard."[99] Churchill the nationalist, imperialist, Russophobe, and purveyor of Anglo-American brotherhood deeply irritated Roosevelt, even if the prime minister was too much of a "museum piece, a rare relic,"[100] to be taken altogether seriously. It is also true that Churchill's "un-English" exuberance – he was after all half-American – allowed for a kind of informality and companionship that FDR found impossible with most Britons. The only precedent was the young Nigel Law, whose rapt courtship of FDR during the First World War had won him a similar condescending warmth. Roosevelt remarked, "I have a feeling when I am with Winston that I am twenty years older than he is." Churchill recalled, "I always looked up to him as an older man, though he was eight years my junior."[101] If there was a basic element of trust in the relationship, it was based on a tacit acceptance of Roosevelt's dominant position: in effect, FDR trusted Churchill as long as he thought he could control him.

In April 1944, Churchill began to explore an arrangement whereby the Russians would "take the lead" in Romania and the British in Greece. He asked FDR's "blessing" on May 31.[102] Ostensibly temporary, the arrangement was supposed to formalize what FDR himself favored: the predominance of the British on the Mediterranean littoral and of the Russians in Eastern Europe. When Hull objected, FDR allowed the State Department to draft a disapproving cable, but the

97. See FDR's remarks at press conference, Mar. 30, 1943, on the occasion of Eden's departure from the United States. *FRUS*, 1943, 3: 43. For Eden's view, see *The Reckoning* (London: Cassell, 1965), 377, 380. Eden unburdened his doubts in a private converation with Hopkins.

98. Kimball, ed., *Correspondence*, 1, Introduction. On the personal relationship see also Warren F. Kimball, "Wheel Within a Wheel: Churchill, Roosevelt and the Special Relationship" (typescript, courtesy of the author); Francis L. Loewenheim, Harold D. Langley, and Manfred Jonas, eds., *Roosevelt and Churchill: Their Secret Wartime Correspondence* (New York: Dutton, 1975), 3–13.

99. See account of the conversation between William Chenery and FDR in Chenery letter to Dean Acheson, July 8, 1970, Dean Acheson Papers, Sterling Library, Yale University. Chenery believed the impression had come from Bullitt.

100. The expression is Halifax's, quoted in Moran, 791. On Churchill's view of Russia see Harbutt, chap. 2; Berlin, *Personal Impressions*, 8.

101. Lash, ed., *Diaries of Felix Frankfurter*, 245; Moran, 447.

102. See Carlton, 236–39; Churchill to FDR, May 31, 1944, Kimball, ed., *Correspondence*, 3: 153–54.

next day he unilaterally approved Churchill's suggestion that the arrangement be tried for three months. FDR complained that the Foreign Office had decided to tell the United States about its Balkan negotiations only after the Russians had broached the subject with the State Department, but he did not oppose the idea.[103] FDR accepted Hopkins's suggestion that Stalin and Churchill be told that any decisions made during Churchill's visit to Moscow in October 1944 were subject to his approval, but his intuition told him that the mission was worthwhile. He soon knew the gist of the sphere-of-influence arrangements and there is little evidence that he objected.[104]

Much had changed, needless to say, by October 1944. The opening of the second front in June prompted Stalin's decision to launch his armies beyond the June 1941 borders.[105] Churchill had lost a bitter dispute when FDR insisted on a landing in southern France rather than a drive into Central Europe. Churchill claimed that Stalin wanted the Anglo-Americans "to do their share in France." Meanwhile, "east, middle and southern Europe should fall naturally into his control." Lord Moran's patient dreamed "of the Red Army spreading like a cancer from one country to another." In early September, the Russians stood before Warsaw, where the Home Army uprising neared its bloody end. By early October, Finland, Romania, and Bulgaria had left the war, the Red Army had entered Hungary and Yugoslavia and was poised on the borders of Turkey and Greece. On September 29, Eden proposed that Britain draw Western Europe into close association with the Commonwealth, along lines suggested by Smuts in November 1943.[106]

103. See FDR to Churchill (drafted by Hull), June 11, 1944, Kimball, ed., *Correspondence*, 3: 178; Churchill to FDR, June 11, 1944, ibid., 178–80; FDR to Churchill, June 12, 1944, ibid., 182; FDR to Churchill, June 22, 1944, ibid., 201–2.
104. See FDR's message to Churchill and Stalin, *FRUS, Conferences at Malta and Yalta*, 6–7. On Hopkins's intervention see Sherwood, 832–33. See also Warren Kimball, "Naked Reverse Right: Roosevelt, Churchill and Eastern Europe from Tolstoy to Yalta – and a Little Beyond," *Diplomatic History*, 9, no. 1 (Winter 1985), 2–7; Albert Resis, "The Churchill–Stalin 'Percentages' Agreement on the Balkans, Moscow October, 1944," *American Historical Review*, 83, no. 2 (April 1978), 368–87.
105. See Mastny 156–57, 182.
106. Churchill to FDR, July 1, 1944, Kimball, *Correspondence*, 3: 227–29. On the French landing controversy see also Matloff, 470–79. On Churchill's fear of Communism see Moran, 185. On Eden's initiative see "British Plans for a Western European Bloc," MR Naval Aide A/16, FDRL. For revealing figures on American predominance in manpower and supplies over Britain by mid-1944 see Randall Bennett Woods, *A Changing of the Guard: Anglo-American Relations, 1941–1946* (Chapel Hill: University of North Carolina Press, 1990), 250.

A number of historians insist that FDR's own position toward the Soviet Union hardened at this point, anticipating the general shift of 1945–46. According to Robert Dallek, FDR decided to take the southern German occupation zone because it would "considerably increase the possibility of a long term role for American ground forces in Europe." Others cite the Anglo-American agreement on atomic power of September 1944, rejecting the idea "that the world should be informed regarding tube alloys [the atomic bomb project] with a view to an international agreement." The "Hyde Park *aide-memoire*" called for an investigation of the Danish physicist Niels Bohr to ensure that he was not leaking information, "especially to the Russians."[107] Otto of Austria, who spoke to him at Quebec, said that Roosevelt "want[ed] to do everything to contain Russia's power – naturally *short of war*." His "main concern" was how to keep the Communists out of Austria and Hungary, and he was "particularly disgusted" by Moscow's handling of Bulgaria.[108] The Russians had first refused to help the British arrange an armistice with Bulgaria, at war with the Anglo-Americans but not the Soviet Union. On September 5, they gave the Allies two hours' notice before declaring war. On the 9th they engineered – or so it appeared – a coup by the Communist-dominated Fatherland Front.[109] Soviet troops entered Sofia on September 15, the day of Roosevelt's talk with Otto. There were other signs of Roosevelt's bad temper – and physical decline. He had suffered congestive heart failure by early 1944; a physician described him as "irascible" and "very irritable if he had to concentrate his mind for long." He was now engaged in the most bitterly fought campaign of his life against a candidate, Governor Thomas Dewey of New York, whom he despised. The Republicans were eager to exploit Soviet policy in Eastern Europe and the Democratic hold on ethnic voters was in doubt.[110]

107. Dallek, 476. Dallek is particularly concerned to refute the view that FDR was either soft or naive with respect to Russia. For the Hyde Park agreement see *FRUS, Conference at Quebec, 1944*, 492–93. For an argument similar to Dallek's on this general point see Harbutt, 72.
108. See *FRUS, Conference at Quebec, 1944*, 367–69.
109. On the Fatherland Front coup Mastny observes, "As in Rumania, the Russians may not have wanted the government to be overthrown from within, for on September 8 they surprisingly agreed to an armistice request from the very regime the Communists were planning to topple the next day. It is also possible that Stalin doubted whether the Communists were strong enough to carry out the job. In any case, while Moscow seemed to falter at the last minute, the conspirators demonstrated their competence by masterminding on September 9 a classic palace revolt, if not any popular insurrection" (202).
110. On FDR's health see letter of Dr. Roger Lee to Lord Moran, in Moran, 242–43;

But the evidence that Roosevelt was changing his Soviet policy does not add up. The Allies subsequently obtained seats on the Allied Control Commission for Bulgaria and the withdrawal of Bulgarian troops from Yugoslavia and Grecian Thrace. As for Hungary, it seems that FDR and Stalin saw Admiral Horthy as their Beneš, but he would not play the part. In the event, the provisional government set up by the Russians in December 1944 "proved a rather respectable body.... Stalin did not seem intent on treating the Hungarians much more harshly than their Finnish 'cousins.' "[111]

If anything might have been expected to harden Roosevelt's attitude, it was Stalin's failure to help the Polish Home Army. On the contrary, Roosevelt's view was that Polish folly had created an ugly dilemma for Stalin and himself. When the Polish premier Stanislaw Mikolajczyk and General Stanislaw Tabor of the Home Army visited Washington in June, FDR insisted on close liaison between the underground and Red armies and that several notoriously anti-Soviet members of the London Polish government be dismissed.[112] One was Defense Minister Kazimierz Sosnkowski, who authorized the uprising without consulting either the Soviet Union or the United States. Stalin knew that failing to help the Poles would create serious problems with the Allies and discredit those Poles who were disposed to work with Moscow. The latter included the local Communists (the National Council of the Homeland, or KRN), who had more or less foisted themselves on him, and gained his (reluctant) support for the cession of German territory up to the western Neisse River and a provisional Polish administration at Lublin in mid-1944.[113] But a Home Army victory was a victory for the anti-Soviet element of the underground and would set the stage for a future conflict. Roosevelt's passivity during the agony of Warsaw indicated his understanding of Stalin's dilemma and his bilious displeasure with the Poles.[114] Roosevelt had seen the London Poles all along as more or less

Morgan, 710–11, 732, 737, 758; Kimball, *The Juggler*, 205–6. On FDR's view of Dewey and the New York political situation see Blum, ed., *The Price of Vision*, 217, 320.

111. Mastny, 205–9. For FDR's view of Horthy see conversation with Otto von Habsburg, cited in note 108. On Soviet policy see also Lundestad, 117.

112. On the Mikolajczyk visit see Thomas Campbell and George Herring, eds., *The Diaries of Edward Stettinius, Jr., 1943–1946* (New York: New Viewpoints, 1975), chap. 3; *FRUS, 1944*, 3: 1285–89.

113. On the uprising see Mastny, 183–90. On the complex relationship between Lublin and Moscow see ibid., 168–81.

114. Stalin waited from August 1, when the uprising began, until early September before giving landing rights to Allied aircraft and launching an attack on Warsaw. On

the same gang of troublemakers who had "kicked Czechoslovakia in the stomach" in 1938.[115] Now they risked creating a major crisis in U.S.–Soviet relations on the eve of the elections. On balance, he may well have shared Stalin's view that it was better for the Germans to eliminate the Home Army than to face the likely prospect of a Polish–Soviet war.

There is no evidence that Roosevelt's acceptance of the southern occupation zone portended a long-term military presence. The zonal accord was part of a broader set of agreements reached at the Quebec conference and Hyde Park whose purpose was to put the British pillar in its appointed European place and to appease the British lest they be tempted to take action that might eventually wreck Allied–Soviet entente. FDR's architectural efforts had reached a critical juncture. The basic outlines of his Palladian Europe were becoming apparent. After Quebec and the Dumbarton Oaks conference, juggling, postponing, and dissimulating were of little use. FDR would spend the last six months of his life trying to hold together a semicompleted structure whose radical purpose and implications could no longer be concealed.

OF HENRY MORGENTHAU, Tugwell writes, "The secret of the curious relationship between the political genius and the inarticulate and un-original co-worker is not one that is easily penetrated." Part of it was the Treasury secretary's "sheer dog-like devotion." Indeed, there was something of the aroused canine in Morgenthau's late-1944 foray into the realm of high policy, whence – overshadowed by more dashing courtiers like Hopkins and Harriman – he had been banished years before.[116] But the Dutchess County apple farmer was also the senior member of Roosevelt's entourage, "a Jeffersonian, a devotee of agricultural society." His vision of Germany was radically so: "The only thing

---

August 25 FDR told Winant that it would not be good "for our long range general war prospects" to press Stalin on landing rights for Western aircraft to aid Warsaw. FDR to Winant, Aug. 25, 1944, MR Russia-Political (1) Section 2, FDRL. The next day he declined to join in a message to Stalin from Churchill on the airfield issue, citing the reasons given to Winant. See FDR to Churchill, Aug. 26, 1944, Kimball, *Correspondence*, 3: 269. FDR's "ill humor" about the Poles was noted by Archduke Otto. See memo cited in note 108.

115. See FDR's message to Colonel Josef Beck, head of the Polish government, Sept. 29, 1938, following the Polish annexation of the Teschen district during the Munich crisis. FDR compared Polish behavior to that of a boy who sees a smaller boy at the mercy of a bully and nonetheless kicks the defenseless boy in the stomach. *PL, 1928–1945*, 2: 812–13.

116. See Tugwell, 442.

you can sell me is the complete shutdown of the Ruhr. . . . I would take every mine, every mill and factory and wreck it. . . . Steel, coal, everything. Just close it down."[117]

For years contemporaries debated FDR's connection with Morgenthau's "Program to Prevent Germany from Starting World War III." Hull, Stimson, and Sherwood said that FDR carelessly endorsed the plan but then abandoned it; Morgenthau and Eleanor Roosevelt insisted that he stuck to it to the end.[118] In fact, FDR never endorsed the Morgenthau Plan per se. He initialed a brief memorandum dictated by Churchill calling for the closing down of the metallurgical, chemical, and electrical industries of the Ruhr and Saar, to be placed under international control as part of a program "looking forward to converting Germany into a country primarily agricultural and pastoral in its character."[119] This memo was milder and vaguer than the Morgenthau Plan. It said nothing about mining or other industries and areas. FDR told Hull on September 29: "No one wants to make Germany a wholly agricultural nation again. . . . Also, it must not be forgotten that outside the Ruhr and the Saar, Germany has many other areas and facilities for turning out large exports." After press stories and an explosive controversy, FDR retreated but did not repudiate the memo.[120]

---

117. Blum, ed., *Morgenthau Diaries*, 3: 377, 354.
118. For the Plan, see *FRUS, Conference at Quebec, 1944*, 128–43; for a somewhat milder version of the plan prepared by Harry White but rejected by Morgenthau see ibid., 86–90. For Hull's recollection see Hull, 2: 1621; Stimson quoted in Blum, ed., *Morgenthau Diaries*, 3: 380–81. See also Sherwood, 832, Eleanor Roosevelt, *This I Remember*, 330–35. See also Warren F. Kimball, *Swords into Ploughshares: The Morgenthau Plan for Defeated Germany, 1943–1946* (Philadelphia: Lippincott, 1976), chaps. 4 and 5.
119. Memo, Sept. 15, 1944, *FRUS, Conference at Quebec, 1944*, 466–67.
120. See FDR to Hull, Sept. 29, 1944, PFS Hull folder 1944, FDRL. See also "Morgenthau Plan: Say Program Cannot Work Because of Interlocking Economy of Europe," *New York Times*, Sept. 24, 1944, 1. The closest FDR came to repudiating the plan was in a conversation in October with Stimson. According to Stimson FDR expressed disbelief at having signed the memo. But the substance of what he said is that of his September 29 memo to Hull, qualifying his position but not reversing it. Stimson Diary, Oct. 3, 1944, microfilm version, Sterling Library, Yale University. See also Stettinius–FDR conversation, Nov. 10, 1944, in Campbell and Herring, eds., 171. Stettinius's account suggests that FDR regretted the "agrarian" concept mainly for the domestic storm that it had provoked. On November 26, Stettinius recorded Keynes's account of the latter's conversation earlier in the day with FDR. Keynes had asked FDR whether the Quebec decisions "meant a complete agrarian economy and he [FDR] stated not quite but it goes pretty far in deindustrializing the Ruhr and eliminating many of Germany's basic industries." Ibid., 179. Keynes wrote, after talking to FDR, "As regards the postwar treatment of Germany, he

The revival, within the limits of practicality, of the "Old Germany" was central to his vision. On September 9, he began a conversation with an account of his boyhood studies in Germany, "when . . . he grew fond of the German people as they were in the 1890s." The same day he quoted from a Treasury Department memorandum, "It is a fallacy that Europe needs a strong industrial Germany." FDR noted, "I agree with this idea."[121] In effect, it was the old ambition of Clemenceau (and perhaps TR)

> to set the clock back and undo what, since 1870, the progress of Germany had accomplished. By loss of territory and other measures her population was to be curtailed; but chiefly the economic system, upon which she depended for new strength, the vast fabric built upon iron coal and transport, must be destroyed.

For Keynes it was "the policy of an old man, whose most vivid impressions and most lively imagination are of the past and not of the future."[122]

By taking an extreme position, FDR undoubtedly reasoned that the ultimate compromise would still represent a hard policy, despite the pressure of the State and War departments and pro-German business interests. The added beauty of the Quebec policy was that it would give Britain Germany's export markets. FDR linked British agreement to the September 15 memo to the continuation of lend-lease after the defeat of Germany and promised terms that would allow Britain to restore its civilian export trade. The State Department was outraged when FDR failed to press for further concessions, but his concern at the time was to build up Britain's self-confidence and strength.[123] With the

---

seemed to be in very much the same state of mind as he had been in Quebec." FDR also left the impression that his mind was "extremely fluid over the whole question." Donald Moggridge, ed., *The Collected Writings of John Maynard Keynes*, vol. 24, *Activities, 1944–1946* (London: Macmillan, 1981), 183–84. On December 22, FDR attacked Morgenthau for having stirred up controversy during the campaign and, in Stettinius's words, said that the "agrarian thing was absurd." Campbell and Herring, eds., 203. He was essentially repeating what he had said earlier to Hull and Stimson.

121. Memo of conversation with FDR by Robert Murphy, political adviser on Germany, Sept. 9, 1944, *FRUS, Conference at Quebec, 1944*, 144; Blum, *Morgenthau Diaries*, 3: 367. See also his conversation with Morgenthau on September 9, HM Presidential Diary, book 6 1422, FDRL.

122. J. M. Keynes, *The Economic Consequences of the Peace* (1919) (London: Macmillan, 1921), 22–23.

123. On his return from London in August 1944, Henry Morgenthau told FDR that Britain was simply "broke." Blum, ed., *Morgenthau Diaries*, 3: 301–5. See also

Ruhr–Saar and lend-lease questions decided, FDR conceded Britain the northern occupation zone and thus direct responsibility for German industrial policy.

Together, the Quebec agreements represented Roosevelt's supreme effort to install the British pillar of his design. At Dumbarton Oaks, meanwhile, he tried to erect an overarching structure that would permit America to remain aloof from Europe while retaining a decisive voice in the determination of its fate. FDR's reluctant acceptance of a universal world organization had to do with the development of wide support for such a body in 1943.[124] In deference to the claims of smaller countries, FDR also agreed that the organization's executive council would have three or more revolving as well as four permanent members.[125] Still, FDR stuck to his conviction that only the "four policemen" would be armed and would enforce peace on the basis of regional assignments.[126] The real problem was how to ensure collaboration among the great powers themselves. FDR had said, "The United States will have to *lead*" and use its "good offices always to conciliate, to help solve the differences which will arise between the others."[127]

Roosevelt envisioned that each of the permanent members of the executive council would be in some way dependent on the United States. China would line up with the United States – thus Churchill's sneering remark that Chungking was but a "faggot vote" for Washington – as would Britain.[128] In a sense, it was a four-party balance-of-

Isador Lublin to Hopkins, Aug. 4, 1944, Harry Hopkins Papers, book 9, England Phase II, FDRL. FDR later told Hull, "The real nub of the situation is to keep Britain from going into complete bankruptcy at the end of the war." Sept. 29 memo, cited in note 120. Hull recalled, "This whole development at Quebec, I believe, angered me as much as anything that had happened during my career as Secretary of State." Hull, 2: 1614.

124. He was sensitive to the charge that his design amounted to a great-power directorate, something "only remotely connected with the generalities of the Atlantic Charter and the Four Freedoms." See Robert Divine, *Second Chance: The Triumph of Internationalism in America During World War II* (New York: Atheneum, 1967), esp. chaps. 4–8.

125. On UN plans see *FRUS, 1944*, 1: 621, n. 10; Ruth B. Russell, *A History of the United Nations Charter* (Washington, D.C.: Brookings Institution, 1958), 250.

126. See Divine, *Roosevelt and World War II*, 61; Range, 188–89; Russell, 97–98; Louis, 148, 160, 284, 295; Kimball, *The Juggler*, 46, 103.

127. Elliott Roosevelt, 129–30. He went on to say that the United States alone could play this role because "we're big, and we're strong, and we're self-sufficient. Britain is on the decline, China – still in the eighteenth century. Russia – suspicious of us and making us suspicious of her. America is the only great power that can make peace in the world stick."

128. Churchill, quoted in Dallek, 389.

power system, no longer Euro-centered – Europe's demotion was the system's chief virtue – but with the United States as balancer and coalition maker. Roosevelt once remarked, "When there were four people sitting in a poker game and three of them were against the fourth, it is a little hard on the fourth." Hopkins used a similar analogy to describe how the Ameri ans and Russians would gain British agreement at Tehran.[129]

The crucial problem at Dumbarton Oaks was whether the four policemen could veto decisions in cases where they were directly involved. If the big powers possessed an absolute veto, the kind of United States–led coalitions suggested by FDR's poker allusion could not materialize within the council. The organization would become a mere debating society, and "a poor one at that."[130] There were obvious counterarguments: no country would accept restrictions when its vital interests were involved. The United States and Britain decided to support the principle that the big four should not vote on questions involving the peaceful settlement of a dispute to which they were a party, while retaining the right to veto enforcement measures. Soviet insistence on an absolute veto was another reason for FDR's ill humor at Quebec.[131]

How should one interpret Roosevelt's decision in this same context to initial the secret aide-mémoire on atomic energy at Hyde Park? The agreement is the chief exhibit in the case that far from being naive or too optimistic, FDR was now preparing to contain the Russians.[132] According to Martin Sherwin, FDR saw an atomic-armed Britain as "America's outpost on the European frontier." Sherwin and Barton Bernstein emphasize the importance that the weapon had acquired: FDR was "reserving the option of using it in the future as a bargaining

---

129. Blum, ed., *The Price of Vision*, entry for Dec. 16, 1942, 145–46. Hopkins to Churchill, quoted in Carlton, 230. See also John Lewis Gaddis, *Strategies of Containment* (New York: Oxford University Press, 1982), Prologue.

130. This was FDR's view of the League of Nations, quoted in Divine, *Roosevelt and World War II*, 57.

131. For a detailed explanation of the U.S. position see Russell, 402–8, 445–46. This was despite FDR's personal plea to the Soviet delegate Andrei Gromyko at the White House and cable to Stalin. See *FRUS*, 1944, 1: 786–89. Another explosive issue was the so-called x matter, Moscow's demand for membership for all fifteen republics of the USSR.

132. For examples of this general line of argument see Martin Sherwin, *A World Destroyed: The Atomic Bomb and the Grand Alliance* (New York: Random House, 1977); see also his "The Atomic Bomb and the Origins of the Cold War: U.S. Atomic Energy Policy and Diplomacy, 1941–45," *American Historical Review*, 78, no. 4 (Oct. 1973), 945–68; Barton Bernstein, "Roosevelt, Truman and the Atomic Bomb: A Reinterpretation," *Political Science Quarterly*, 90, no. 1 (Spring 1973), 23–40; Dallek; Gaddis, Prologue; Harbutt.

lever, threat, military counter-weight, or even as a weapon against the Soviets."[133]

It was natural to invest the bomb with extraordinary attributes – even before it existed – if one's traditional military power was in obvious decline.[134] Churchill's reaction to the news of the Alamogordo test was: "It's the Second Coming. . . . If the Russians had got it, it would have been the end of civilization. . . . It has just come in time to save the world."[135] It is not so easy to reconstruct Roosevelt's thoughts. Everything about his view of air power, the postwar policing mechanism, and the future U.S. relationship to Europe suggests that he saw the bomb as a matter of paramount importance, but he did not embrace the Churchill thesis unconditionally, as Sherwin and Bernstein suggest.

In all likelihood, FDR's real preference was an American monopoly. As someone concerned to allay Soviet suspicion of Britain and of Anglo-American collusion, he probably saw exclusive American control as more palatable to Moscow than independent British possession of the bomb. In a more visceral way, he no doubt coveted the bomb as the symbol and instrument of American supremacy and independence. At this level, the bomb was the rod of yore that someday "we may shake . . . over the heads of all [the Europeans],"[136] the means by which America could remain remote and secure from Europe, as well as the arbiter of its fate. The air-delivered atomic bomb was the ultimate Jeffersonian weapon.

FDR initially tried to reconcile the need to obtain the bomb before the Germans did with the desire for American control. Anglo-American cooperation was "a hasty marriage of convenience between British research and American resources."[137] In 1942, once the Manhattan Project had achieved a certain autonomy, FDR accepted the recommendation that the flow of information to the British be restricted. Faced with "a policy based on a wartime and postwar partnership in order to develop an atomic bomb as quickly as possible, versus a policy of ensuring a postwar American monopoly of the weapon at the possible cost of delaying the bomb's production," Roosevelt chose the latter.[138]

---

133. Sherwin, *A World Destroyed*, 113–14; Bernstein, 31.
134. On this point, and especially on the impact of Roosevelt's death on U.S. perceptions of the bomb, see John L. Harper, "Henry Stimson and the Origin of America's Attachment to Atomic Weapons," *SAIS Review*, 5, no. 2 (Summer–Fall 1985), 17–28.
135. Quoted in Moran, 301.
136. Jefferson to Thomas Leiper, June 12, 1815, in Graebner, ed., 123.
137. Sherwin, "The Atomic Bomb," 948.
138. Sherwin, *A World Destroyed*, 76. Sherwin emphasizes the concern of James Conant

This policy changed after the first Quebec conference in August 1943. The Quebec agreement restored a full exchange of information and pledged the parties not to use the bomb or transfer information to third parties without the other's consent. This agreement did not come at a time of deteriorating relations with the Russians. The period from middle to late 1943 was one in which FDR was preoccupied with establishing his bona fides and distinguishing himself from Churchill in the mind of Stalin. The Quebec agreement, to which the Hyde Park aide-mémoire was essentially a codicil, came about after Churchill threatened to pursue the bomb on his own and in a way that might have negative consequences for the United States.[139] FDR's choice was now a possibly serious delay in the Manhattan Project and crisis with Britain versus an agreement restoring a flow of information that would allow the British to build a bomb at some point in the future. Anglo-American atomic diplomacy is another instance in which FDR made a valiant effort to eat his cake and have it. The Quebec agreement served, in any event, both to appease Churchill and to give the United States leverage over British atomic policy. It came in the context not of an impending showdown with the Russians but of a brewing Anglo-American confrontation related to FDR's decision to force the British to accept Overlord and to develop his privileged ties to Stalin.

During the last eighteen months of his life, FDR tried to face up to the implications of the bomb. By September 1943, if not before, FDR knew that the Russians were receiving information on the Manhattan Project.[140] In April 1944, Felix Frankfurter related to FDR Neils Bohr's opinion that the Russians not only knew about the project but were capable of producing a bomb. Bohr and Frankfurter thought that the Russians should be approached immediately with a view to arranging international control. It was now obvious that an American or Anglo-

that the British were interested in gaining commercial advantages from U.S. research. FDR would have been inclined to share such misgivings and perhaps, as Bernstein argues, the worry that the British might pass information to the Russians, according to some secret accord. See also Bertrand Goldschmidt, *The Atomic Complex: A Worldwide Political History of Nuclear Energy* (La Grange Park, Ill.: American Nuclear Society, 1982), 48.

139. On this point, see Sherwood, 704; Sherwin, *A World Destroyed*, 73–75, 84. As Sherwin points out, Conant's original recommendation had played down the possible losses to the United States if the British decided to end their collaboration, including the cutoff of uranium supplies from Canada and of production from the Trail Heavy Water Plant.

140. See Sherwin, "The Atomic Bomb," 956; John Lewis Gaddis, "Intelligence, Espionage and Cold War Origins," *Diplomatic History*, 13, no. 2 (Spring 1989), 196–97, 206.

American monopoly would be short-lived and that, given advances in aircraft, the United States would be vulnerable to attack. FDR predicted: "Before too long it might be possible to drop this bomb in New York City at 42nd Street and Broadway. The resulting explosion . . . would lay New York low." Roosevelt told Frankfurter that the bomb "worried him to death" and asked him to have Bohr make his case in London. Churchill spurned Bohr, but FDR received the physicist with apparent sympathy in August 1944. According to Bohr, FDR said the Russians must be approached and that Churchill "would eventually share these views."[141]

Once again, however, Churchill intervened. Once again, FDR opted to give him what he wanted – and continued to keep a harness on British policy. The Hyde Park agreement (composed by Churchill) was the result. The atomic agreement came soon after the Quebec memo on Germany – something the British had been forced to swallow – and helped to sweeten the liberalization of the occupation regime in Italy, another unpleasant pill.[142] According to the aide-mémoire, "Full collaboration between the United States and British Governments in developing tube alloys for military and commercial purposes should continue after the defeat of Japan and until terminated by joint agreement." This did not mean that the United States might not decide, again, and unilaterally, to change the rules – as was later to be the case. The agreement also stated, "The suggestion that the world should be informed regarding tube alloys with a view to an international agreement regarding its control and use is not accepted. The matter should continue to be regarded as of the utmost secrecy."[143] This did not rule

---

141. On Frankfurter meeting and FDR's reaction see Sherwin, "The Atomic Bomb," 955. See also Richard Rhodes, *The Making of the Atomic Bomb* (New York: Simon & Schuster, 1986), 526. On FDR's knowledge of the increase in the range of aircraft see Louis, 268. On FDR's prediction of U.S. vulnerabilty see E. Stettinius, *Roosevelt and the Russians: The Yalta Conference* (Garden City, N.Y.: Doubleday, 1949), 33. Sherwin, "The Atomic Bomb," 958. For the memorandum prepared by Bohr and delivered to FDR by Frankfurter see Freedman, ed., 728–35.

142. One of FDR's closest advisers, Leahy, who attended the Churchill–FDR discussion on atomic energy on September 19 and the FDR–Bush–Lord Cherwell discussion on September 22, believed that "the President's attitude was that the atomic military secrets should not be divulged even to an ally, but since the British had contributed to the atomic experiments and had been working on it, Roosevelt thought they should share equally with us in its industrial use." This suggests that the Hyde Park aide-mémoire was a personal arrangement between Churchill and FDR, and that one of FDR's concerns at the time was the postwar British economy. Leahy, 265–69. See also Rhodes, 537.

143. For the full text see Sherwin, *A World Destroyed*, 284.

out a private approach to the Russians, to whom the matter was not exactly secret. When Stimson later expressed the opinion that the secret could not be kept indefinitely, but that the Russians should not be taken into "our confidence until we were sure to get a real quid pro quo for our frankness," FDR agreed.[144] Perhaps he wanted to wait until the bomb had been tested, or to be in a position to propose something concrete in the way of international sharing,[145] rather than simply telling the Russians of the existence of the project – something they already knew.

FDR shocked Churchill at Yalta by raising the possibility of talking about the bomb with Stalin. Obstensibly this was because "de Gaulle if he heard of it, would certainly double cross us with Russia."[146] Not for the first time one senses that FDR wanted to get the issue out in the open so the Russians would not feel double-crossed. Once more, however, he allowed Churchill to overrule him. On March 9, 1945, FDR told the Canadian premier MacKenzie King that "the time had come to tell them [the Russians] how far the developments had gone" but that Churchill was still opposed.[147] In the end Roosevelt kept silent because he was not prepared to double-cross the British. He was tempted but not persuaded by the argument that the bomb would bestow "the power to mould the world."[148] Indeed, the notion of the bomb as "ace card" and diplomatic panacea took hold within the U.S. government only after April 12, 1945, when people grasped for something concrete to fill the sudden void of charismatic leadership and persuasiveness created by his death.[149]

Power politics at bay

William Roger Louis writes of Roosevelt's anticolonialism: "[His] ideas did not progress. His enthusiasm for trusteeship reached its peak in the winter and spring of 1944, after which time he began to retreat. His large ideas began to crack on the necessity for precise solutions."[150]

144. The conversation took place on December 31, 1944. Ibid., 134.
145. Ibid., 127. For example, of the kind being urged at the time by Bush and Conant and later supported by Stimson. Presumably he also feared a negative domestic reaction to a disclosure to the Russians.
146. See Churchill memo to Eden, Mar. 25, 1945, quoted in Sherwin, *A World Destroyed*, 290.
147. King quoted in Bernstein, 31, n. 23.
148. Churchill remarked on June 23, 1945, "It gives the Americans the power to mould the world." Moran, 301.
149. For a fuller exposition of this point see Harper, "Henry Stimson."
150. Louis, 356.

Much the same can be said of his vision of a fragmented and disarmed metropole. In the case of his program for the European continent, however, there was not so much a loss of enthusiasm as a gradual entropy of intellectual and physical force. FDR wielded greater power than Wilson and was more flexible and ruthless. But his plan for Europe was also more brutal and ambitious than Wilson's, and no one was more aware of this by late 1944 than the Europeans. FDR's vision began to crack on the necessity for concrete solutions. It was also worn down by the obstacles raised against it and was deliberately undermined. The moment of truth for Roosevelt's Europe arrived when the will to power of the New World collided head on with the instinct for survival of the Old.

FDR's relations with de Gaulle were only slightly colder than Churchill's, but there was a fundamental difference. FDR worked to eliminate de Gaulle's influence; Churchill, having pledged support to him in 1940, tried to promote his fortunes and through him those of France. If de Gaulle had proved more useful early in the war, say by capturing Dakar in 1940, relations might have been smoother. "I am not a Wilsonian idealist," FDR told the general's envoys in November 1942; "I have problems to resolve."[151] (It was Admiral Darlan, not de Gaulle, who could deliver Algiers.) But FDR's hostility toward de Gaulle only increased as the latter proved his mettle as a leader. One should not discount the suave pleading of Alexis Léger, for whom de Gaulle was an extremist and usurper.[152] Certainly FDR saw de Gaulle as co-imperialist and tool of the British. The British, he allowed, owned de Gaulle "body, soul and britches."[153] Even so, there was a "confounding" element in FDR's anti-Gaullism, something "primordial, elementary, visceral." The "prima donna," "jackenape," and "fanatic" was no ordinary villain.[154]

FDR's animus for de Gaulle boiled down to two basic ingredients. One was something akin to pure and simple jealousy. At one level, FDR, like Jefferson, fancied himself France's truest friend. Léger, Jean

151. FDR conversation with André Philip and Adrien Tixier, as recounted by Jean Lacouture, *De Gaulle*, vol. 1: *Le Rebelle, 1890–1944* (Paris: Editions du Seuil, 1984), 545.
152. See Welles to FDR, Aug. 13, 1942, transmitting the memo of a conversation with Léger. PSF Welles 1–42, FDRL. See also Aglion, chap. 21.
153. Elliott Roosevelt, 74.
154. Lacouture, 546–47. For Alexander Codogan, Roosevelt was "simply not normal on this subject [de Gaulle]." Dilkes, ed., 633. For use of the epithets see FDR to Churchill, Aug. 7, 1943, Kimball, ed., *Correspondence*, 2: 441; FDR to Henry Stimson, quoted in Blum, ed., *Morgenthau Diaries*, 3: 174; FDR to Eleanor Roosevelt, quoted in Aglion, 154.

Monnet, and other French flatterers cast him as France's patron and liberator, and thus de Gaulle was his uncompromising rival. That the general was a particularly unattractive – rigid, solemn, authoritarian – but also charismatic and effective rival added greatly to the chagrin. The other ingredient was the combination of hostility and uneasiness that Roosevelt felt in the presence of someone who seemed impervious to his personality, who saw through his dissimulation and successfully fought back.[155]

De Gaulle's resumé of his conversations at the White House in July 1944 indicates that he grasped the essence of Roosevelt's vision – "an imposing one although disquieting for Europe and for France." A "four-power directory – America, Soviet Russia, China and˙ Great Britain – would settle the world's problems." Meanwhile,

> the questions relative to Europe, notably the fate of Germany, the destiny of the states along the Vistula and the Danube, as well as of the Balkans, and Italy's destiny, seemed to him quite subordinate. In order to find a satisfactory solution for them, he would certainly not go to the lengths of sacrificing the monumental conception that he dreamed of turning into a reality.[156]

In fact, de Gaulle did feel the force of Roosevelt's personality, fueled as it was by the conspicuous military and industrial might of the United States: "As was only human, his will to power cloaked itself in idealism." FDR "did not explain things as a professor setting down principles, nor as a politician who flatters passions and interests. It was by light touches that he sketched in his notions, and so skillfully that it was difficult to contradict this artist, this seducer, in any categorical way." Still, de Gaulle warned Roosevelt that

> his plan risked endangering the Western world. By considering Western Europe a secondary matter, was he not going to weaken the very cause he meant to serve – that of civilization? In order to obtain Soviet approval, would he not have to yield them, to the detriment of Poland and the Baltic, Danubian and Balkan states, certain advantages that threatened the general equilibrium? ... Now, Western Europe, despite its dissensions and its

155. In domestic life this would have included Robert Moses and John Nance Garner. On de Gaulle's imperviousness to FDR's charm, see Claude Fohlen, "De Gaulle and Franklin Roosevelt," in Cornellis A. Van Minnen and John F. Sears, eds., *FDR and His Contemporaries: Foreign Perceptions of an American President* (New York: St. Martin's Press, 1992).

156. Charles de Gaulle, *The Complete War Memoirs of Charles de Gaulle, 1940–46,* vol. 2: *Unity* (New York: Simon & Schuster, 1964), 573. This passage, in effect, summarizes three separate conversations de Gaulle had with FDR during the visit. There are no U.S. records of these talks.

distress, is essential to the West. Nothing can replace the value, the power, the shining example of these ancient peoples. This is true of France above all, which of all the great nations of Europe is the only one which was is and always will be your ally.[157]

Perhaps FDR in turn was not unaffected by the mystique of "this strange man," as Harold Macmillan called him. But de Gaulle's vision of the centrality and greatness of Europe was the very opposite of his own. FDR wrote: "He and I skated pretty roughly on current subjects. . . . He is very touchy about the honor of France but I think he is essentially selfish." De Gaulle returned to France with the impression that the United States was "already trying to rule the world." Roosevelt's remarks proved to him that, "in foreign affairs, logic and sentiment do not weigh heavily in comparison with the realities of power; that what matters is what one takes and what one can hold onto; that to regain her place, France must count only on herself."[158]

FDR continued to slight de Gaulle, the symbol of France's continuity as a great power, until the very end.[159] But Roosevelt had to reckon with the "realities of power" that de Gaulle, thanks to his skill and tenacity as a leader, came to represent. No one – China did not want to – could replace France in Indochina, and FDR had to fall back on the idea that France itself would be trustee over an area where he had declared it would never be allowed to return. No one – Britain was unable to – could replace France on the Continent; FDR found himself calling France a possible "bulwark" and referring to its "postwar responsibilities" with regard to Germany.[160] No one – certainly not General Henri Giraud, Léger, or Monnet – could replace de Gaulle's authority. On October 23, 1944, the United States, Britain, and the Soviet Union recognized a cabinet headed by de Gaulle as the Provisional Government of France. In December, de Gaulle signed a twenty-year treaty with Stalin. The Franco-Soviet pact had little practi-

---

157. Ibid., 574.
158. Macmillan quoted in Lacouture, 674; de Gaulle, 271; FDR to Congressman J. C. Baldwin, July 19, 1944, OF 203 France 1944–45, FDRL. This letter was somehow obtained by de Gaulle. De Gaulle made the remark about the United States to Raoul Aglion on July 10, 1944, in New York. Aglion, 181. De Gaulle, 575.
159. FDR refused to have de Gaulle at Yalta or, until the last minute, to allow France onto the Allied Control Commission for Germany. See J. W. Young, *France: the Cold War and the Western Alliance, 1944–49* (Leicester: University of Leicester Press, 1990), 40–43.
160. Louis, 356, 551; *PL, 1928–1945*, 2: 1489. On France as "bulwark" see FDR to Churchill, Feb. 29, 1944, Kimball, ed., *Correspondence*, 2: 766–67. See also FDR to Churchill, Nov. 18, 1944, ibid., 3: 394.

cal meaning, but indicated that old patterns were reemerging. Another sign was Churchill's visit to Paris in November, where the British agreed to a German occupation zone for France and urged the French to rebuild a large army. Churchill affirmed the "fundamental principle of British policy that the alliance with France should be unshakable, constant and effective."[161]

De Gaulle – the "rebel," his biographer aptly calls him – struggled throughout his adult life against what he saw as the Anglo-Saxon tendency to dominate the world. The leitmotiv of Churchill's long career, by contrast, was Anglo-American unity. His support for an Anglo-French alliance did not extend to its logical corollary, Eden's Western European bloc. One reason was that France did not yet have a large army and Britain could not assume the burden of defending Holland, Belgium, and Norway. Another reason was that the Americans were opposed to the bloc notion because it was provocative to Moscow. The "only real safeguard," Churchill told the cabinet on November 27, 1944, was agreement between the "three Great Powers" within the United Nations Organization.[162] The "percentages deal" of October 1944 had arisen from fear of Russian encroachment and U.S. abandonment of Europe, as well as from continuing deference to Roosevelt's message that Britain had no choice but to get along with Russia. Churchill's plan was that his meeting with Stalin would be followed almost immediately by a Big Three conference to consolidate the progress and cordial atmosphere of Moscow. Churchill's diplomacy continued to incorporate the American point of view and reflected his basic concern: to preserve his relationship with Roosevelt.

Anthony Eden commented on that relationship: "FDR was a 'charming country gentleman' but business methods were almost non-existent, so W had to play the role of courtier and seize opportunities as and when they arose. I am amazed at [the] patience with which he does this." "Three bad messages from FDR," Eden wrote in November. Roosevelt's attitude was "generally arrogant and aloof."[163] After telling Churchill before his departure for Moscow, "I am prepared for a meeting of the three of us anytime after the elections here for which your meeting with Uncle Joe should be a useful prelude," FDR now

---

161. Churchill in Paris quoted in Martin Gilbert, *Winston S. Churchill*, vol. 7: *The Road to Victory, 1941–1945* (Boston: Houghton Mifflin, 1986), 1059–60.
162. For British discussion of the bloc idea, including Churchill's position, see ibid., 1069–71. For the U.S. position see the State Department memo, "British Plans for a Western European Bloc," Feb. 1945, MR Naval Aide A-16, FDRL.
163. Eden quoted in Gilbert, 564. Moran remarked that, with FDR, Churchill's patience, "not his most obvious virtue – never seemed to give out" (837). Eden, 496.

dismissed the prime minister's proposal for a prompt tripartite session, as well as for French participation and for U.S. equipment to arm an eight-division French army. As if to add insult to injury, FDR reminded the British, "You know, of course, that after Germany's collapse I must bring American troops home as rapidly as transportation problems will permit."[164] Churchill's forbearance was indeed amazing, but not without its limits. Developments in the fall of 1944 precipitated a crisis in the Churchill–FDR relationship from which it did not recover. Churchill's retrospective comment is revealing, if not completely accurate. He had had "great influence over the President until about three months before Yalta [early November 1944]; then he ceased to answer my letters."[165]

FDR's decision to postpone a conference until after the inauguration suited his personal schedule but badly undercut Churchill's plans for a rapid agreement on the Polish question.[166] Roosevelt also began to behave "as though he had never heard" of the Quebec agreement on lend-lease. This was due partly to State Department pressure to extract British concessions, including civil aviation matters where Berle was in charge of negotiations. Churchill's private secretary called the lend-lease–aviation linkage "pure blackmail." Other disagreements smoldered: Britain's alleged friendliness toward the pro-Axis Argentine government and coolness toward China. Roosevelt had decided to give a sharp pull on the reins and warning to the British. His earlier, less than wholehearted appeasement of Britain gave way to a suspicion that was always near the surface. The stress of the campaign played a part. There was a widespread impression in the United States that British interests were dictating Allied policy. In mid-November, Morgenthau remarked that Churchill's recent statements had "ruffled [FDR] tremendously." In an October 22 speech, Churchill had predicted that France would "resume her rightful and historic role upon the world stage." On November 9, he praised Governor Dewey's "sportsmanlike

---

164. See FDR to Churchill, Oct. 4, 1944, offering to meet anytime after the elections; also Nov. 14, 1944, Nov. 18, 1944, Nov. 18, 1944 (no. 650), Kimball, ed., *Correspondence*, 3: 389–90, 395–96.
165. Moran, 371.
166. His strategy received another blow when Premier Mikolajczyk, having failed to sell the Curzon line to his cabinet, resigned on November 24. The London government was now composed of anti-Soviet ultras, and Stalin replied by recognizing the "Lublin Poles" as the Provisional Government of Poland. In a speech on December 15, 1944, Churchill accused the United States of delaying agreement on the Polish issue. See George McJimsey, *Harry Hopkins* (Cambridge, Mass.: Harvard University Press, 1987), 359.

manner" upon losing the election and declared that it was "high time" for a Big Three meeting.[167]

Matters precipitated when the British vetoed the inclusion of Count Carlo Sforza, an antimonarchist, in the Italian cabinet (December 1), then intervened in Greece (December 6). American outrage over the bloody repression of the Communist revolt in Athens left Churchill, according to Sherwood, in an "extremely dangerous and explosive mood." Churchill was trying to salvage something from the shambles of his Moscow strategy – he was not about to lose Greece, now that his "50–50" arrangement in Yugoslavia had collapsed.[168] But Churchill's behavior had the hallmarks of a deliberate message to the United States. In effect: "We will do as we see fit to protect our vital interests. Don't push us too far."[169] Churchill's cable to Roosevelt on civil aviation was laced with irony:

> You will have the greatest navy in the world. You will have, I hope, the greatest airforce. You will have the greatest trade. You have all the gold. But these things do not oppress my mind with fear because I am sure the American people under your reclaimed leadership will not give themselves over to vainglorious ambitions, and that justice and fair play will be the lights that guide them.[170]

167. On lend-lease, see Blum, ed., *Morgenthau Diaries*, 3: 319–20. On aviation, FDR to Churchill, Nov. 21, 1944, Kimball, *Correspondence*, 3: 402–3. Churchill to FDR, Nov. 28, 1944, ibid., 419–22; FDR to Churchill, Nov. 30, 1944, in ibid., 424–25; John Colville quoted in Gilbert, 1074. On Argentina and China, see Campbell and Herring, eds., 172, 210. On the Anglophobe mood in the United States, ibid., 172; Sherwood, 836–37; Woods, 248–49. For Morgenthau's comment on speeches, see Blum, ed., *Morgenthau Diaries*, 3: 319. For text of Churchill's speeches, see *New York Times*, Oct. 28, 1944, 4; Nov. 10, 1944, 4. In early 1944, Hopkins had warned the British that FDR "was going to run doing things we should not like too much – lend lease, dollar balances, trade, palling up with Uncle Joe, partly in order to dispel any damaging impression that he was in our or your pocket, and partly because he will be getting a good deal of not always good advice. But we should not take all this too seriously." Halifax to Eden, Feb. 13, 1944, FO 954/30, PRO. This indicates that there was an element of election-time posturing in FDR's anti-British attitude, but the point is that his attitude grew harder after the election than before.

168. Sherwood, 839. Tito had ordered the evacuation of British forces from the coastal area of Yugoslavia, where, according to Churchill's view of the Moscow deal, they were entitled to stay. See Churchill's December 3 message to Smuts on this point in Gilbert, 1082.

169. U.S. reporters got the point. Edwin James observed: "The British do not believe that we will maintain an active issue in European politics even during the period of post-war adjustments. So doubtless Mr. Churchill feels certain obligations to look out for Britain's interests." "Washington and London Have Unhappy Collision," *New York Times*, Dec. 10, 1944.

170. Churchill to FDR, Nov. 28, 1944, Kimball, ed., *Correspondence*, 3: 419–21.

As he dictated orders to the army in Athens, Churchill was reportedly "in a bloodthirsty mood and did not take kindly to suggestions that we should avoid bloodshed if possible." British gunboat methods seemed to provide a precedent for Stalin while mocking U.S. calls for a "good neighborly" brand of great-power behavior in Europe.[171]

The final meeting of Roosevelt and Churchill, though it gave rise to a brief euphoria, did not reestablish trust. At the center of the negotiations were the questions of the future Polish regime and the United Nations voting formula. The Americans agreed to the mere broadening of the Lublin cabinet, through the inclusion of additional democratic elements, rather than a genuinely new government. FDR's earlier resistance on this point melted away once Stalin had accepted the U.S. voting formula for the United Nations and dropped a demand for membership for all fifteen Soviet republics. The British, who held out for more concrete guarantees on Poland, had no choice but to go along. FDR approached the question, in his words, as the inhabitant "of another hemisphere" and once again reminded those present that U.S. troops would leave Europe within two years after the war. Stalin and FDR reiterated the Tehran decision to proceed with the dismemberment of Germany; the British were reluctant. On the question of German reparations, the U.S. and Soviet sides agreed to the figure of $20 billion as a basis of discussion, with the Russians to receive half. Churchill was appalled. FDR and Stalin conducted secret talks resulting in territorial gains by the Soviet Union in the Far East. FDR's haste to conclude business was anything but reassuring. "The President is behaving very badly," Churchill said near the end of the conference. "He won't take any interest in what we are trying to do."[172]

Churchill later said of the president at Yalta, "He was a tragic figure."[173] He was referring to FDR's shrunken, world-weary appearance, but the remark conveys the regret that he felt over the fading of a relationship based, at least for Churchill, on affection as well as self-

---

171. Sir Pierson Dixon Diary, quoted in Carlton, 249. The orders read, in part: "Naturally ELAS [the Communist partisans] will try to put women and children in the van where shooting may occur. You must be clever about this and avoid mistakes. Do not however hesitate to act as if you were in a conquered city where a local rebellion is in progress." An unusual slip allowed these orders to fall into American hands and they appeared in Drew Pearson's column. See Gilbert, 1085–86, 1098. For FDR's angry reaction to the Greek affair see Elliott Roosevelt, 222–24. See also on this point Kimball, ed., *Correspondence*, 1, Introduction, 16–20; Moran, 836–37.

172. For Yalta as seen by the British see Gilbert, chaps. 61 and 62; Moran, chap. 24; Dilkes, 716–17. Cadogan was more upbeat than other British participants.

173. Quoted in Gilbert, 1171.

interest. When it came in April, FDR's was "an enviable death." He "had brought his country through the worst of its perils and the heaviest of its toils."[174] But it was enviable also because it prevented further estrangement and more violent disagreement. Churchill, with his sense of the drama of history, was suggesting that Roosevelt's decline had been tragic in the deeper, classical meaning of the term – a great figure brought down by a fatal flaw of character. Roosevelt's vision of America's relationship to the Old World was animated by a combination of animosity and hubris. Both impulses, along with a dose of sadism, were present in his personal relationships with Churchill and de Gaulle.[175] At bay in 1944, the two exponents of old-fashioned European power politics turned and defied the New World. Their resistance opened cracks in Roosevelt's "monumental conception," even as the Soviet pillar seemed to be rising in its place.

The juggler's last act

After 1943, Roosevelt was gradually hemmed in by the two tendencies that, while marginal to his own outlook, had deep roots in public opinion: the idealistic Wilsonianism of Hull and the anti-Soviet perspective of the State Department Russian specialists, of Berle and Bullitt, and after September 1944 of Harriman and many others. FDR had tried to accommodate the Wilsonians at Dumbarton Oaks while preserving the substance of great-power domination. During and after the 1944 campaign, he had to reckon with anti-Soviet and isolationist Republicans who were eager to exploit growing public anxiety about the postwar situation.[176]

A warning signal, evoking memories of Wilson's bitter 1919 struggle, was the famous speech by Arthur Vandenberg, Republican senator from Michigan, on January 10, 1945. Vandenberg's name had been synonymous with conservative isolationist opposition to Roosevelt. When

174. For Churchill's eulogy see ibid., 1301; on this point see also Kimball, ed., *Correspondence*, 1: 19. Churchill wrote Hopkins, "I feel a very personal loss quite apart from the ties of public action which bound us so closely together. I had a true affection for Franklin." Churchill to Hopkins, Apr. 13, 1945, FO 954/30, PRO.

175. Harriman observed that FDR "undoubtedly took pleasure in the prime minister's difficulties; he unquestionably had a sadistic streak." Harriman is referring specifically to Churchill's difficult voyage to Moscow in August 1942. "Recollections of Mr. Harriman, after the Moscow 1942 Trip," Averell Harriman Papers, Writings file, Feis file, Subject file, Harriman recollections, 1953–54, box 972.

176. On public opinion in late 1944 and early 1945 see James MacGregor Burns, *Roosevelt: The Soldier of Freedom* (New York: Harcourt, Brace, 1970), 559; Campbell and Herring, eds., 178, 208.

he announced his conversion to collective security, Vandenberg created a national sensation. It could not have escaped Roosevelt's notice, however, that Vandenberg's "conversion," like Henry Cabot Lodge's, was on his own conditions:

> If Dumbarton Oaks should specifically authorize the ultimate international organization to review protested injustices in the peace itself, it would at least partially nullify the argument that we are to be asked to put a blank check warrant behind a future status quo which is unknown to us and which we might be unwilling to defend.

Vandenberg, who had thousands of Polish-American constituents, was saying in effect that he would support the United Nations if it could be used to challenge the Soviet conquest of Poland and the iniquitous Curzon line.[177] At a meeting the day after the speech, FDR was brutally frank with Vandenberg and other members of the Senate Foreign Relations Committee: "The Russians had the power in Eastern Europe . . . it was impossible to break with them, and . . . therefore, the only practicable course was to use what influence we had to ameliorate the situation."[178] Roosevelt must have realized that such advice fell on deaf ears and that the Republicans, by attaching strings to their support of the United Nations that would result in a confrontation with Moscow, were setting a trap for him on the eve of Yalta. The domestic political success of the United Nations would depend more than ever on liberal Wilsonian support. Such support depended in turn on an understanding with Stalin that satisfied, or appeared to satisfy, liberal expectations.

FEW SOURCES HAVE AFFECTED OUR VIEW of the Soviet dictator like Milovan Djilas's *Conversations with Stalin*. The author concluded that his former idol had been "the greatest criminal in history." Several of Djilas's anecdotes have achieved immortal status: "Churchill is the kind who, if you don't watch him, will slip a kopeck out of your pocket. . . .

---

177. For excerpts see Arthur H. Vandenberg, Jr., ed., *The Private Papers of Senator Vandenberg* (Boston: Houghton Mifflin, 1952), 136–38. Vandenberg's son and editor observes, "The attitude of Moscow towards the small states of Europe had raised grave concerns about the peace settlement and the basic importance of Vandenberg's speech was directed toward a showdown on this issue" (136; see also 152). On the role of Walter Lippmann in advising Vandenberg see Ronald Steel, *Walter Lippmann and the American Century* (Boston: Atlantic Monthly Press, 1980), 418–19. Liberals hailed portions of the speech, particularly Vandenberg's support for the notion that U.S. military action under the auspices of the United Nations would not automatically require a congressional declaration of war.

178. This is Stettinius's account. Herring and Campbell, eds., 214. See also Blum, ed., *The Price of Vision*, 424–25.

Roosevelt is not like that. He dips in his hand only for bigger coins."
Stalin told Tito and Djilas: "This war is not as in the past; whoever
occupies a territory also imposes on it his own social system. Everyone
imposes his own system as far as his army can reach. It cannot be
otherwise."[179] Out of such statements, and actions that tended to
confirm them, developed several axioms about Soviet behavior: Stalin
was incapable of trusting the West, and therefore a policy based on the
attempt to win his confidence was a delusion; Stalin's determination to
communize Eastern Europe was not subject to negotiation and the final
responsibility for the division of Europe was his alone.[180] It is not hard
to make the case that, far from being "charmed" by Roosevelt, Stalin
was prevented by his *Weltanschauung* from seeing FDR as anything but
a class enemy and a trickster: Stalin took FDR's "attempts at friendship
as deception or debility or both."[181]

Yet if Stalin saw the self-described "juggler" as a confidence man and
manipulator, he was not so different from countless Englishmen and
Americans.[182] A reasonable person might have interpreted FDR's behavior with respect to the second front in 1942–43 as an attempt to
have the Russians pay while putting the United States in a position to
take advantage of their sacrifices. Presumably Roosevelt did not consider
it a bad thing if the Soviet Union emerged from the war in an exhausted
condition, preferring America's friendship and material help to its
wrath. It is no coincidence that Stalin portrayed FDR as a thief literally
on the eve of the cross-channel invasion and amid remarks to the effect
that reports of D-Day were "just promises as usual." By the same
token, Stalin was grateful for Overlord when it came and impressed
by its enormous scale.[183] Stalin was not a slave of Marxist–Leninist
categories and made distinctions among his "class enemies" depending
on their actions. According to Khrushchev, Stalin esteemed Eisenhower,
who had allowed the Russians to take Berlin. He considered Churchill
dangerous, and Truman "worthless." Khrushchev attests to Stalin's

179. Milovan Djilas, *Conversations with Stalin* (New York: Harcourt, Brace, & World,
   1962), 187, 73, 81.
180. See, among many examples, Ronald Hingley, *Joseph Stalin: Man and Legend*
   (London: Hutchinson, 1974); William Taubman, *Stalin's American Policy* (New
   York: Norton, 1982); Lloyd Gardner, Arthur M. Schlesinger, Jr., and Hans J.
   Morgenthau, *The Origins of the Cold War* (Waltham, Mass.: Ginn-Blaisdell, 1970),
   chap. by Schlesinger.
181. Taubman, 9. See also McNeill, 1564–65; Smith, *American Diplomacy*, 11;
   F. Marks, 169–70.
182. For example, Ickes, Eden, or Halifax. See Moran, 791.
183. See Djilas, 81; Harriman and Abel, 314.

sympathy for Roosevelt, as does Gromyko, to whom Stalin remarked that Roosevelt was the "personification of rationality and concision." This resembles FDR's remark about Stalin: "He really gets things done... that man. He really keeps his eye on the ball he's aiming at."[184] Litvinov believed that only direct talks between FDR and Stalin could improve Soviet relations with the West in late 1944. *"That's absolutely the only way, in fact, to improve matters."* According to his personal interpreter, Stalin did not believe Roosevelt when the latter referred to his difficulties with Congress, but he welcomed the possibility of postwar cooperation with the United States. For a deeply skeptical American expert, it was impossible to deny "that useful things have been accomplished in [the] past and can be accomplished in the [the] future by direct contact with Stalin." The so-called Novikov telegram (September 1946 – inspired by Molotov) would later lament the fact that "the foreign policy of the United States is not determined at present by the circles in the Democratic Party that (as was the case during Roosevelt's lifetime) strive to strengthen the cooperation of the three great powers."[185]

It is safe to assume that sentiment, charm, and "power of personality" had a limited effect on Stalin's attitude toward Roosevelt or Roosevelt's toward Stalin. The genuine, if highly tenuous, understanding they achieved was based on their belief in the congruity of U.S. and Soviet

184. Arthur M. Schlesinger, Jr., "FDR's Vision Is Vindicated by History," *Wall Street Journal*, June 22–23, 1990. The author observes: "Stalin was not the helpless prisoner of Marxist–Leninist ideology. The Soviet dictator, not a man given to undue modesty, saw himself less as the disciple of Marx and Lenin than as their fellow prophet." See also Edward Crankshaw and Strobe Talbott, eds., *Khrushchev Remembers* (London: Book Club Associates, 1971), 221; on Churchill, see Djilas, 115. Khrushchev observed, "Stalin could never be accused of liking someone without reason, particularly a class enemy" (222). This suggests that he was not totally incapable of liking some of them. Gromyko, 98; Elliott Roosevelt, 183.

185. Litvinov conversation with Edgar Snow in Moscow, Oct. 6, 1944. Transcript sent by Snow to FDR, Jan. 2 1945, PSF Russia 1945, FDRL. Emphasis in original. Stalin's interpreter at Tehran and Yalta affirms: "It seems to me that the Yalta experience, and the certain degree of trust between Stalin and Roosevelt that was revealed then, could have led to a new era in international affairs, and most important in relations between the Soviet Union and the United States.... At least this feeling existed in Moscow." See Valentin Berezhkov, "Stalin and Franklin D. Roosevelt," in Van Minnen and Sears, eds., 58–59. The American expert was George F. Kennan. See Kennan to Secretary of State, Mar. 20, 1946, *FRUS*, 1946, 6: 722. For text of the Novikov telegram, along with commentary by historians (including Kennan), see John Lewis Gaddis, ed., "The Soviet Side of the Cold War: A Symposium," *Diplomatic History*, 15, no. 4 (Fall 1991), 523–63.

national interests.[186] This is what FDR meant when he said that Stalin was "getatable," as opposed, say, to the London Poles, Eden, or de Gaulle. The fact is that Stalin's European aims – Soviet hegemony in Eastern Europe, a dismembered Germany, a weakened Western Europe, friendly relations with Britain – coincided with Roosevelt's. Stalin favored a *Dreikaiserbundnis* – an American–British–Russian alliance; his first preference was probably not to communize Eastern, let alone Western, Europe; and he was prepared to go to some lengths to prevent what he did not want – an anti-Soviet alliance and new war.[187]

John Erickson writes:

> The underlying issue [at Yalta] was the degree to which the Soviet Union would or would not pursue a path of cooperation. Within very strict or formally prescribed conditions Stalin indicated that he had chosen the path of collaboration . . . to this end, he engineered compromises and offered concessions of a minimum order, but concessions nevertheless.[188]

Stalin's biggest concession at Yalta was on the issue of greatest concern to Roosevelt, the UN voting formula. Stalin allowed Roosevelt to return home with a prize for his Wilsonian supporters. Roosevelt insisted on free elections and the broadening of the Lublin (now Warsaw) government, but with the realization that these were largely matters of form. Form was important for domestic opinion, but did not affect the substance of Soviet control of Poland, just as the much-publicized "Declaration on Liberated Europe" had no enforcement mechanism.[189]

---

186. According to Cardinal Spellman, FDR said in September 1943: "Churchill is too idealistic, he [FDR] is a realist. So is Stalin. Therefore an understanding between them on a realistic basis is possible." Gannon, 223. For all his anticommunism, Churchill had the tendency to be taken, on occasion, by Stalin at a personal level far more than FDR. See Moran, 303.

187. On the *Dreikaiserbundnis* see Mastny, 221. Alexander George says, "Stalin in fact *was* disposed to cooperate." See "Domestic Constraints on Regime Change in U.S. Foreign Policy: The Need for Legitimacy," in Ole R. Holsti, Randolph M. Silverson, and Alexander L. George, eds., *Change in the International System* (Boulder, Colo.: Westview, 1980), 247. See also John Lewis Gaddis, "Intelligence, Espionage, and Cold War Origins," 209; Lundestad observes, "One, probably *the* most important objective for the Soviet rulers must have been to avoid any new war, particularly with the United States" (453). See also Melvyn P. Leffler, "Was the Cold War Necessary?" *Diplomatic History*, 15, no. 2 (Spring 1991), 269.

188. John Erickson, *Stalin's War with Germany*, vol. 2: *The Road to Berlin* (London: Grafton Books, 1983), 680. Erickson's (638–80) is a magisterial treatment of the Yalta conference.

189. On the importance of the United Nations to FDR at Yalta see Burns, *Roosevelt: The Soldier of Freedom*, 566. On the declaration see Stettinius, 36–37. According to the voting formula adopted at Yalta, permanent members of the Security Council

The conference record suggests that if not for the British and other members of the U.S. delegation, FDR would have concluded business with Stalin in far fewer than eight days of tense debate.

The unexpected controversy occurred during the two months between Yalta and Roosevelt's death. Stalin's mid-April remark ("Everyone imposes his own system. . . . It cannot be otherwise") was not a declaration of strategy but a reflection on what, willy-nilly, was actually taking place. It rings like an epitaph for Roosevelt and the Rooseveltian vision of Europe. What Stalin meant was, "From now on, it cannot be otherwise."[190] Without Roosevelt, Rooseveltian policies were certainly doomed.

What went wrong? Who was responsible? Robert Messer makes a convincing case that initial post-Yalta troubles had to do with the manner in which the agreements were presented to the public in the United States. James Byrnes, FDR's "Yalta salesman," returned from the conference, where, thanks to FDR, he had received a selective impression of what had happened and proceeded to portray the Declaration on Liberated Europe and the Polish settlement as the triumph of self-determination. FDR was pleased by the performance, at least by the positive public reaction to Yalta that resulted.[191] In private remarks immediately after Yalta, Roosevelt denounced the U.S. Senate as incompetent and obstructionist, affirming that the only way to accomplish anything was to circumvent it.[192] But the Russians were bound to take a dim view of the Wilsonian love feast being staged by FDR. Vice Foreign Minister Vishinsky's brutal ultimatum to the Romanian government on February 27 was a reminder that the Declaration on Liberated Europe was something less than an instrument to foster

agreed to forgo a veto in matters involving the peaceful settlement of disputes, while retaining it when sanctions or military measures were involved. This was a clear departure from the Russians' Dumbarton Oaks position.

190. Djilas does not provide a precise date for Stalin's remark. He refers to the Soviet–Yugoslav treaty signed on April 11, to a formal dinner a day or two later (102–3), and to a second dinner (107), during which Stalin made the observation. Thus it appears that it was made in the immediate aftermath of FDR's death.

191. FDR excluded Byrnes from some of the more controversial meetings at Yalta, the Far Eastern discussions, for example. See Robert Messer, *The End of an Alliance: James Byrnes, Roosevelt, Truman and the Origins of the Cold War* (Chapel Hill: University of North Carolina Press, 1982), 10, chaps. 3 and 4. For accounts that draw on Messer's, see Harbutt, 92–93, and Melvyn Leffler, "Adherence to Agreements: Yalta and the Experience of the Early Cold War," *International Security*, 11, no. 1 (Summer 1986), 92–94.

192. FDR made his remarks about the Senate to his adviser and interpreter, Charles Bohlen. See *Witness to History*, 210, fn.

bourgeois democracy in Eastern Europe. Other historians argue that FDR was naive to assume that the Russians would behave in a way that would not create undue embarrassment for him at home, while his own vagueness at Yalta had only encouraged Stalin to make new demands.[193] But if Soviet behavior after Yalta was partly a reaction to distorted public claims arising from FDR's domestic requirements, Roosevelt's responsibility appears in a somewhat different light. It is hard to avoid the conclusion that Roosevelt had been sincere with Stalin (with whom he had tended to deal as if he himself were a kind of absolute monarch) and was trying to deceive his Wilsonian public. The Russians appear not to have understood this and believed somebody was trying to deceive them.

FDR's, arguably, was another case of "useful deceit" and in any event unavoidable given his ambiguous, instrumental relationship to Wilson and the Wilsonians all along. By 1945, William McNeill notes, "Roosevelt embodied a myth." Partly through his own doing, the myth was essentially Wilsonian. To be sure, FDR had occasionally tried to explain to the public – through the Forrest Davis articles, for example – that his was a hardheaded and "partial internationalism," closer to Theodore Roosevelt than to Wilson. Privately he had said, "You can't invoke high moral principles when high moral principles don't exist." But since the twenties – and never more so than in 1944 – he had prospered as a politician by wrapping himself in Wilson's mantle.[194] While he shared Wilson's dream of abolishing the centrality of Europe, his postwar plans had little to do with the self-determination of nations. As the gap between right hand and left, between public expectations and the Eastern European reality, plainly widened after Yalta, the helpless juggler was hoist aloft on his Wilsonian petard.

Controversy erupted after the February 23 meeting of the "Moscow Commission" set up to consult the various Polish groups with a view to reorganizing the Polish government.[195] While disturbed, Roosevelt

---

193. Mastny, 283, 309–10. See also Taubman, 38–39.
194. McNeill, 760. Forrest Davis, "Roosevelt's World Blueprint" and "What Really Happened at Teheran." For FDR on "moral principles" see memo by Lieutenant Miles to the Foreign Office, giving an account of his conversations with FDR in Nov. 1943, FO 371/38516, PRO.
195. The commission included Molotov, Harriman, and the British ambassador to Moscow Archibald Clark Kerr. According to the Yalta agreement, the three were "authorized as a commission to consult in the first instance in Moscow with members of the present Provisional Government and with other Polish democratic leaders from within Poland and from abroad, with a view to the reorganization of the present Government along the above lines," that is, "on a broader democratic basis." *FRUS, Conferences at Malta and Yalta*, 973. Unexpectedly, Molotov asked

recognized the predominance of the Communist Poles and was determined not to allow a secondary issue to destroy his foreign policy.[196] For his part, however, Churchill asked Parliament on February 27:

> Are they [the Poles] to be free, as we in Britain and the United States or France are free? Are their sovereignty and independence to be untrammelled, or are they to become a mere projection of the Soviet State, forced against their will by an armed minority to adopt a command or totalitarian system. I am putting the case in all its bluntness.

Privately he said, "I have not the slightest intention of being cheated over Poland, not even if we go to the verge of war with Russia."[197] Churchill was now in revolt against FDR's foreign policy.

The Russian interpretation of the agreement, Deborah Larson argues, was "neither arbitrary nor without textual justification."[198] After a statement like Churchill's, Moscow could reasonably conclude that the British were either trying to gain through the Moscow Commission what they had failed to gain at Yalta or else seeking the pretext for a major confrontation.[199] Marshal G. K. Zhukov found Stalin "tired, dispirited and far from well" in early March. A careful reconstruction indicates Soviet confusion over the Polish issue by late March and signs of "growing panic."[200] The military situation had by then given rise to fear that the Soviet Union might be denied the capture of Berlin. The Red Army's January drive from the Vistula to the Oder had provided respite to the Allies, who were licking their wounds from the German Ardennes offensive; at Yalta, however, the Russians got "no firm assurances" that German troop movements to the East "would be effec-

that the Communist Poles be called first and be allowed to "express an opinion" on the other Poles to be invited. The Lublinites refused to deal with the London ultras or even Mikolajczyk, who had not yet endorsed the Yalta agreement.

196. FDR to Churchill, Mar. 29, 1945, Kimball, ed., *Correspondence*, 3: 593–95.
197. Speech quoted in Harriman and Abel, 418–19. Churchill remark quoted by John Colville in *The Fringes of Power: Downing Street Diaries, 1939–1953* (London: Hodder & Stoughton, 1976), 566. See also Churchill to FDR, Mar. 8, 1945, Kimball, ed., *Correspondence*, 3: 547–51.
198. Deborah Welch Larson, *Origins of Containment: A Psychological Explanation* (Princeton, N.J.: Princeton University Press, 1985), 117.
199. See Stalin to FDR, Apr. 7, 1945, in *Correspondence between the Chairman of the Council of Ministers of the U.S.S.R. and the Presidents of the U.S.A. and the Prime Ministers of Great Britain during the Great Patriotic War of 1941–1945* (hereafter, *Stalin's Correspondence*) (Moscow: FLPH, 1957), 2: 211–13. On this point see Leffler, "Adherence to Agreements," 95–96. On Churchill's intentions, see Harbutt, 97–99; Gilbert, chap. 64.
200. Erickson, 703; Mastny, 258–60.

tively hampered, much less inhibited" by Anglo-American action.[201] In fact, the spearhead of the Ardennes offensive, Sixth SS Panzer Army, turned up in Hungary to take part in the savage German counter-offensive in March.[202]

At this point, the Berne affair – Allied–German contacts on the possible surrender of German forces in Italy – appeared to herald a long-dreaded separate peace. Why, Stalin asked in one of several emotional messages to Roosevelt, were the Germans "fighting desperately against the Russians for Zemlenice, an obscure station in Czechoslovakia, which they need just as much as a dead man needs a poultice, but they surrender without any resistance such important towns in the heart of Germany as Osnabruck, Mannheim, and Kassel?" On March 26, the Soviet government suddenly indicated a marked coolness toward the dismemberment of Germany. Maybe Moscow reckoned that the prospect of dismemberment would encourage the Nazis to deal with the West, while if carried out, it might produce a Germany divided into two camps with the lion's share in Western hands.[203] On the same day (April 1) that he told Eisenhower that Berlin had "lost its former strategic importance" and that the Russian offensive would not begin before mid-May, Stalin ordered a massive attack on the German capital to begin by April 16.[204] He now seemed sure of an Allied double-cross. At the end of March he said that Roosevelt would not violate the Yalta agreements, "but as for that Churchill . . . he can be up to anything."[205] Stalin was not wrong. Churchill was infuriated by the U.S. decision not to go for Berlin, pleading with Roosevelt and Eisenhower to "march as far east into Germany as possible" and, "if open to us," into Poland.[206]

201. See Erickson's account of the meeting at Yalta of the Allied and Soviet military chiefs (650–51).

202. Matters were not improved by the fact that in late February Marshall had forwarded what turned out to be faulty information to the Soviets as to the eastern destination of Sixth Panzer. Ibid., 690–91; Soviet Chief of Staff Antonov to Marshall, Mar. 30 1945, in *Stalin's Correspondence*, 2: 210–11.

203. For the FDR–Stalin exchanges on the Berne affair, see *Stalin's Correspondence*, 2: 204–14; Mastny, 258; Harriman and Abel, 432. On the Soviet shift on dismemberment see Philip Mosley, "Dismemberment of Germany: The Allied Negotiations from Yalta to Potsdam," *Foreign Affairs*, 28, no. 3 (Apr. 1950), 493; Winant to Secretary of State, Mar. 29, 1945, PSF Germany 1944–45, FDRL.

204. Erickson, 708–9; Mastny, 269.

205. Stalin quoted by Zhukov, in Erickson, 721.

206. Churchill to FDR, Apr. 1, 1945, Kimball, ed., *Correspondence*, 3: 603–6; Churchill to Eisenhower, Apr. 2, 1945, quoted in Gilbert, 1276. On March 28, Eisenhower had informed Stalin that the Allies would not attempt to take Berlin. For Eisenhower's reasoning in shifting the axis of the Allied attack toward the Dresden–Leipzig area see Eisenhower to Marshall, Apr. 7, 1945, MR Western Front Offensive, FDRL.

According to Erickson, "At the beginning of April, in one momentous week, Stalin sieved the whole of his strategy through his fingers."[207] If so, it was the strategy that had been based on his personal understanding with Roosevelt. That Roosevelt was a frail reed on which to lean a departure from isolation must have been obvious to Stalin for some time. Hopkins, who also sat at the table at Yalta, doubted that FDR "had heard more than half of what went on."[208] After that effort, FDR was no more than a fading symbol of his earlier hopes and plans. Even if they discounted Byrnes's performance as arising from domestic exigencies, the Russians could see by March that Roosevelt was losing control of the British and of American public opinion. In March and April, Leahy, Marshall, and the State Department handled Roosevelt's correspondence. In a rare message he wrote himself to Churchill (April 11), FDR urged forbearance. FDR's conciliatory message to the Russians on the Berne affair arrived in Moscow on April 13, the day after he died.[209]

The weight of the temple

Measure and physics had their revenge on Roosevelt's Palladian concept in the end. By early 1945, it was less a serious political program than a personal conceit. The revenge of measure came in the form of a domestic reaction against the grand deception inherent in Roosevelt's policies, as well as de Gaulle's defiance, Churchill's rebellion, and Stalin's loss of nerve.[210] The laws of physics decreed that FDR's structure would not stand: his two telemones, Russia and Britain, emerged from the war profoundly inimical and disproportionate in stature. Britain and Russia did not believe that, even acting together, they had the strength to keep Europe in the reduced and fragmented condition that Roosevelt envisioned. "Give them [the Germans] twelve to fifteen years and they'll be on their feet again," Stalin told Djilas in April 1945. "We shall recover in fifteen or twenty years, and then we'll have another go at

207. Erickson, 723.
208. Hopkins's remark was reported by Halifax to Churchill, Apr. 16, 1945, FO 954/30 PRO. See also Gromyko's comment on FDR's failing health and absent gaze at Yalta (98).
209. FDR's April 6 message to Churchill suggesting the time would arrive to "become 'tougher'" was drafted by Leahy. See Kimball, ed., *Correspondence*, 3: 617. The harshly worded April 5 reply to Stalin on the Berne incident was drafted by Marshall. Ibid., 614. See also Erickson, 722; FDR to Churchill, Apr. 11, 1945, Kimball, ed., *Correspondence*, 3: 630. For FDR's last message to Stalin see *Stalin's Correspondence*, 2: 214.
210. For "nerve" one could substitute "faith."

it."[211] The prospect of the American withdrawal, brutally reiterated by Roosevelt at Yalta, the absence of an American pillar in Europe, weighed heavily in the calculations of both Churchill and Stalin in 1945. Every instinct drove Churchill to try to force the Americans to confront the dominant Continental power and re-create the Anglo-American intimacy of 1940–41. As for the Russians, Eden had predicted in 1943 that they had two courses in mind, "one based on British–American cooperation with Russia and the other on the assumption that the U.S. would withdraw all interest in European affairs after the war." According to Eden, "Russia preferred and hoped for the former because Stalin was not prepared to face the implications of Russia's control over European affairs." Lippmann wrote of Stalin later the same year: "You do not invite in an [Allied] army of a million men if you do not wish to cooperate with the Governments which sent in the army."[212]

Eden and Lippmann were overly optimistic but not wrong. The prospect of a helpless Europe stretched at his feet was doubtless enticing to Stalin, but only as long as he could count on American restraint of Britain. He did not want to contend with a hostile Britain, exercising influence over the American elites and probably in league with a resurgent Germany. In the end he could not afford to gamble on the flimsy, untested structure of the United Nations and on a distant and unpredictable post-Rooseveltian America. He had deceived himself in 1939–41 with nearly fatal results. The shift in American opinion during the 1944 campaign must have raised serious questions in his mind as to whether Roosevelt's policies would survive the man. Roosevelt's imminent death confirmed the decision to begin to fall back on a defensive strategy, the extension of the Soviet system, and the "unity of the Slavs."[213]

The progressive hardening of the British and Soviet positions in Europe weighed heavily on Roosevelt in the last days of his life. There

---

211. Djilas, 114–15. Stalin had said essentially the same thing to FDR at Tehran, *FRUS, Conferences at Cairo and Tehran*, 532.

212. *FRUS*, 1943, 3: 13; Lippmann quoted in Stoler, *Second Front*, 159.

213. On Hitler's "outsmarting" of Stalin, see Robert C. Tucker, *Stalin in Power: The Revolution from Above, 1928–1941* (New York: Norton, 1990), 619. On "unity of the slavs," see Djilas, 114. Earl Browder, the American Communist, later said, "Stalin needed the Cold War to keep up the sharp international tensions by which he alone could maintain such a regime in Russia." Quoted in Arthur M. Schlesinger, Jr., "Some Lessons from the Cold War," *Diplomatic History*, 16, no. 1 (Winter 1992), 49. If, indeed, Stalin's internal control depended on the existence of a Western threat, it was not unreasonable for him to think, by the spring of 1945, that he would have one.

could have been no more eloquent signal of the collapse of his design. Stalin's behavior was a bitter cup to swallow. Like Churchill in Greece, he reverted in the end to the atavistic European type.[214] It is impossible to say whether with approaching death came self-knowledge, whether, in other words, Roosevelt recognized the Jeffersonian hubris and fatal ambivalence about entanglement in Europe that lay at the heart of his monumental failure. He had tried to concoct the transformation and retirement of Europe – a solution to the European Question – without American responsibility and entanglement. Only someone of Roosevelt's profoundly solipsistic nationalism and sense of American superiority – incorporating a turn-of-the-century certainty of the Old World's moral bankruptcy – could have seriously entertained the idea. "We're going to make this the twentieth century after all!" had always been his credo. It was equally true to say that Roosevelt's vision was that of a late nineteenth century man whose "most vivid impressions and most lively imagination" harked back to the semimythical Europe of Sara Delano and Mr. James.[215]

FDR wore a brave face to the end. His last public message was on the occasion of Thomas Jefferson Day: "The only limit to our realization of tomorrow will be our doubts of today. Let us move forward with strong and active faith."[216] But it must have been Roosevelt's stark sense of futility, that nothing fundamental had changed in the Old World – the weight of his collapsing temple – that someone close to him felt when he said that it "finally crushed him. He couldn't stand up under it any longer."[217]

---

214. There is a sense of injury and disbelief in some of his April 1945 observations on Stalin – for example, the one reported by Anne O'Hare McCormick, quoted in Harriman and Abel, 444. See also Frank Freidel, *Franklin D. Roosevelt: A Rendezvous with Destiny* (Boston: Little, Brown, 1990), 601–2.

215. Remark made to Elliott Roosevelt, in December 1944, in Elliott Roosevelt, 224. See also Keynes, 23.

216. Quoted in Burns, *Roosevelt: The Soldier of Freedom*, 597.

217. Sherwood, 880.

PART TWO

4

George F. Kennan: the sources of estrangement, 1904–1944

A historical chasm

In 1900, the year Brooks Adams published his prophetic fin-de-siècle declamations on the decline of England, the world's "containing power," and the inexorable rise of the United States in its place, his elder brother haunted the Gallery of Machines of the Great Exposition in Paris, an experience that produced the musings and broodings of *The Education*'s Chapter 25.[1] As Henry Adams stood before the forty-foot electric dynamo, he began to feel the huge revolving wheel "as a moral force.... Before the end one began to pray to it; inherited instinct taught the natural expression of man before silent and infinite force." The dynamo generated the invisible energy that would animate, and dominate, America's "twenty-million horse power society," just as the Virgin – and Venus – had supplied the mysterious force behind the achievements of Chartres and the Louvre. "The Woman had once been supreme... not merely as a sentiment but as a force." But what of America? "This energy was unknown to the American mind. An American Virgin would never dare command; an American Venus would never dare exist." He felt helpless before the "historical chasm" between the Dynamo and the Virgin.[2]

Adams returned frequently to the link between the blind thralldom of the American man to the Dynamo and the fate of the American woman:

> The typical American man had his hand on a lever and his eye on a curve in the road; his living depended on keeping an up average speed of forty miles an hour, tending always to become sixty, eighty, or a hundred, and

---

1. See discussion of Brooks Adams in Chapter 1. Henceforth, he wrote, "America must fight her own battles whether she wills or no. From the inexorable decree of destiny she cannot escape" (147, 167–70). "The Dynamo and the Virgin" is the title of chap. 25 of Henry Adams, *The Education*.
2. Henry Adams, *The Education*, 259, 380, 383–84, 416.

he could not admit emotions or anxiety or subconscious distractions, more than he could admit whiskey or drugs, without breaking his neck. He could not run his machine and a woman too; he must leave her, even though his wife, to find her own way, and all the world saw her trying to find her way by imitating him.

For Adams, the twentieth century meant a headlong plunge down a benighted path toward sterility and flatness, of which the transformation of the American woman was a sad reflection. Adams sought refuge on the European side of the chasm – "He did not want to Americanize Europe" – and in his historical quest into the twelfth century, the century of the Virgin.[3]

In 1905, or thereabouts, a lone college coed, the orphaned daughter of a New England–born lawyer, stood on a hill near the Mississippi where Chippewas had camped two generations before. "The days of pioneering, of lassies in sunbonnets, and bears killed with axes in piney clearings, [were] deader now than Camelot; and a rebellious girl [was] the spirit of that bewildered empire called the American Middle-West."[4] The girl was Carol Milford, soon to be the wife of Will Kennicott, a leading citizen of Gopher Prairie. The setting of Sinclair Lewis's *Main Street* is an obscure Minnesota hamlet, but it could have been any small town or urban neighborhood in middle western America. In Carol, Lewis chronicled the fate of a vital, ingenuous, provincial woman. She represents sensitive youth of either sex, tested by the forces of shallowness and uniformity foreseen by Henry Adams.

Gopher Prairie is a place where independent New England farmers have been transformed into softer, superficially genteel middle men and professionals. The passing of the frontier and the beginnings of urban life reveal the pathetic cultural inheritance of these recently poor and deeply Puritan pioneers. For Lewis, like Adams, the effect on women wrought by the transformation is both emblematic and tragic. With the end of frontier life, the "kind and ample bosomed pioneer woman" degenerates into the catty clubwoman. Norwegian farm women with their "scarlet jackets embroidered with gold thread and colored beads, in black skirts with a line of blue," still provided a touch of color. But they too would be "zealously exchanging their spiced puddings and red jackets for fried pork chops and congealed white blouses, trading the

3. The American woman "must, like the man, marry machinery. Already the American man sometimes felt surprise at finding himself regarded as sexless; the American woman was oftener surprised at finding herself regarded as sexual." Ibid., 445–47, 285.
4. Sinclair Lewis, *Main Street* (1920) (New York: Signet, 1980), 1–2.

ancient Christmas hymns of the fjords for 'She's My Jazzland Cutie,' being Americanized into uniformity." College-educated and idealistic, Carol rebels against the "unsparing ugliness" and "distrust of beauty" of the town. She is attracted by the pioneer sangfroid of her physician-husband but repelled by his intellectual complacency and childish fascination with automobiles and guns. Carol's effort to reform and beautify are a failure and she is driven to escape from the agonizing dullness of the town. Her destination is Washington, D.C.[5]

The ebb tide of Carol's rebellion constitutes Lewis's prognosis for the coming decade (the book appeared in 1920). Lewis himself was headed for the European side of the chasm, where he spent much of his later life. But whether the Atlantic Ocean itself could contain Main Street only time would tell. Lewis had his doubts:

> A village in a country which is making pains to become altogether standardized and pure, which aspires to succeed Victorian England as the chief mediocrity of the world, is no longer purely provincial, no longer downy and restful in its leaf-shadowed ignorance. It is a force seeking to dominate the earth, to drain the hills and sea of color, to set Dante at boosting Gopher Prairie.... Sure of itself, it bullies other civilizations.[6]

Around 1920, an adolescent boy raised in a leaf-shadowed middle western neighborhood, the motherless offspring of Puritan-farmers-turned-lawyers, discovered Sinclair Lewis. *Main Street*, George F. Kennan wrote forty years later, was the "first native aesthetic impulse" to come his way. It hit him, he said, "like a hammer blow."[7]

An escapist urge

George F. Kennan's leaf-shadowed street was Cambridge Avenue in central Milwaukee, Wisconsin, not far from Juneau Park, where as a small boy he imagined the existence of fairies, or from Prospect Avenue, where his grandfather, Thomas Lathrop Kennan, had built an imposing stone residence with plunging gables and lofty mansard-roofed towers crowned by ornamental widow's walks with ornate wrought iron railings. The latter feature was a tribute to the high-Victorian convention that dictated the tastes of Thomas Kennan, and a reminder of the family's New England roots. Thomas Lathrop Kennan, who arrived as

5. Ibid., 41, 111, 134, 258.
6. Ibid., 259.
7. George F. Kennan (hereafter, GFK), "Notes for Russian Seminar," Harvard University, Apr. 25, 1960, George F. Kennan Papers (hereafter, GKP), Seeley G. Mudd Library, Princeton University, box 20.

a pioneer in Wisconsin in 1849, was the grandson of the Presbyterian minister Thomas Kennan and of Sally Lathrop, a descendant of Elder Brewster of the *Mayflower*.[8] Thomas Lathrop married Loa Brown, of old Connecticut stock, who gave birth to Kossuth Kent Kennan, George F. Kennan's father, in 1851. The career of the nouveau riche Thomas Lathrop Kennan was a watershed in the history of the family. The poor Oshkosh farmer ended his life as a successful lawyer, member of the Wisconsin Society of Mayflower descendants and Sons of the American Revolution, trustee of the Presbyterian Church, and 32nd-degree mason. If his break with the soil was proof of the self-reliance and ambition connected to his Puritan and frontier origins, his fortune was consumed by a perhaps too literal preoccupation with the outward signs of grace. When he died in 1920, he left a legacy not much more substantial than the hollow towers of his Prospect Avenue house.

George F. Kennan described Cambridge Avenue as possessing a kind of "Booth Tarkington provincial innocence."[9] Tarkington was the Indiana-born idealizer of a pre-1914 middle western, middle-brow America of friendly neighborhoods whose main residential street was

> amply broad for family carriages, bicycles, phaetons, buggies, and light delivery wagons; and was shadowed by maples, by sycamores and old elms, hickory and black walnut trees, relics of the original forest. . . . Life was slower, but that means there was time to enjoy it a little capaciously. There was a tremendous universal respect for respectability.[10]

Such a neighborhood seemed the natural habitat of Kossuth Kent Kennan, like his father a farm boy who settled in Milwaukee, far from the ambience of his youth. He attained fame as a tax expert and was a leading member of the Wisconsin legal establishment. His life suggests the effort to fulfill the expectations of a demanding father, yet he departed in basic ways from the pattern of Thomas Kennan. Kent

8. For a photograph of the house see T. L. Kennan, *Genealogy of the Kennan Family* (Milwaukee, Wis.: Cannon Printing Co., 1907), facing page 57. On the history of the family see also GFK, "Letter to the Kennan Children on Genealogy," Apr. 15, 1961, GKP, box 20. See also GFK, *Memoirs*, vol. 1: *1925–1950* (hereafter, *Memoirs*, 1) (Boston: Little, Brown, 1967), 1–9; Walter Issacson and Evan Thomas, *The Wise Men: Six Friends and the World They Made* (New York: Simon & Schuster, 1986), chap. 2. On Kennan's family and early life see also David Mayers, *George Kennan and the Dilemmas of U.S. Foreign Policy* (New York: Oxford University Press, 1988), 15–23.

9. See GFK, "Notes for Russian Seminar"; GFK speech, "Where Do We Stand?" Dec. 21, 1949, GKP, box 17; GFK quoted in the *Milwaukee Journal*, Apr. 2, 1961.

10. Booth Tarkington, from his autobiography, *The World Does Move*, quoted in J. Beecroft, ed., *The Gentleman from Indianapolis: A Treasury of Booth Tarkington* (Garden City, N.Y.: Doubleday, 1957), 3.

Kennan had to work his way through Ripon College, but a four-year classical course was a relative luxury nonetheless. With the transition from country to city accomplished by his father, Kent could afford less mundane and mercenary pursuits. He was, George Kennan tells us, a reflective and cultivated man; his life (1851–1933) spanned the transition from the Victorian era to twentieth century industrial modernity. As for the habits and verities of the former age, Kent Kennan assumed them "but they sat poorly upon him." He became aware, "increasingly as the years went by, of their tawdriness, their artificiality, their inadequacy as a guide to life." At the same time, "the outlines of the new century...were disturbing, forbidding, partly incomprehensible to his eyes."[11] George Kennan's father believed, in other words, that the Victorian world of Thomas Lathrop Kennan and Booth Tarkington was a glorified version of Main Street, while the Dynamo-driven society of the future was a bleaker prospect still.

A character in *Main Street* tells Carol, "Your Middle-West is double Puritan – prairie Puritan on top of New England Puritan."[12] To this must be added a third layer – Thomas Kennan's High Presbyterian Prospect Avenue Respectability – in order to glimpse the conflict of his son Kent, unlike Carol not much of a rebel, but like her bedeviled by the problem of aesthetic experience within a religious and cultural tradition that tended to equate beauty with sin. This outwardly conventional man was the first of the family, his own son later believed, to achieve a "breakthrough" from the inheritance of "total unaestheticism." The Puritan distrust of beauty was a "form of self-denial, of self-starvation," perhaps breeding strength and discipline but leaving "an *inner thirst for beauty,* and vulnerabilty to it, beyond the normal." Kent Kennan's breakthrough opened new vistas to his children, leaving them "richer in the possible range of [their] own experience and self-fulfillment but also bearing a greater spiritual and intellectual burden – more endowed and more endangered."[13] The occasion, and agent, of Kent Kennan's breakthrough was his discovery of Europe.

The elder Kennan spent five years after 1878 in Germany, Sweden, Norway, Denmark, and Switzerland recruiting emigrants to settle the lands of the Wisconsin Central Railroad and skilled laborers for a rapidly industrializing state. He learned French, German, and Danish; he acquired a library of French and German literature; he attended the

11. *Memoirs,* 1: 7–8.
12. Lewis, *Main Street,* 423.
13. GFK, "Letter to the Kennan Children." See also GFK's poignant sketch of his father written on the occasion of his stay at Ripon College in February 1965. *Sketches from a Life* (New York: Pantheon, 1989), esp. 214.

passion play at Oberammergau, where, according to his son, he "was so moved by what he saw that he could not bear it, left the hall and fled down the road, weeping for the sheer unendurable beauty." His sister, Loa Brown Kennan, married Paul Heinrich Louis Mausolff, a Silesian employed by one of the great German chemical concerns.[14] In 1912, Kennan took his family for six months to Kassel, where he worked on his second book on income taxation. In Milwaukee, he patronized German-speaking cultural life, the richest of its kind in North America.[15]

Beyond the confines of Cambridge Avenue was a bustling, cosmo-politan Milwaukee of cafés, *Biergartens*, theaters, and music societies that helped to define the style of the Gay Nineties in the American imagination. German immigrants had laid the foundations for the late nineteenth century prosperity of the city, based on tanning, brewing, creameries, and merchandising; they built its first opera house and ran many of its newspapers. In 1870, one-third of Milwaukeeans were native-born Germans; by 1910, the figure had fallen to 17 percent, but more than half of the population was still of German origin.[16] It is easy to imagine that Thomas Lathrop Kennan remained aloof from German Milwaukee. It is equally easy to imagine that his son moved with a certain ease across the boundary between Anglo-Saxon and German society – at the higher levels they mixed freely by 1900. Here was an experience of Germany and Germans in striking contrast to the more typical experience of ritual travelers like James and Sara Roosevelt, who were enamored of mythic medieval Germany but who had only superficial contact with the flesh-and-blood reality and looked on German-Americans with the same good-natured disdain reserved for middle westerners in general.

If European, especially German, music and literature were a window of escape from the colorless decorum of Prospect Avenue, George Kennan's father did not find serenity in later life. He was afflicted with tragedy: his first wife died after four years of marriage in 1889, his second, George Kennan's mother, after nine years in 1904. Toward the end of the century, Milwaukee was engulfed by successive waves

---

14. See GFK, "Letter to the Kennan Children"; on Kossuth Kennan's European experi-ence, see also T. L. Kennan, *Genealogy*; Gerd Korman, *Industrialists, Immigrants and Americanizers: The View From Milwaukee* (Madison: State Historical Society of Wisconsin, 1967), 24, n. 24.

15. *Memoirs*, 1: 19; Issacson and Thomas, 75.

16. On German Milwaukee see Harry Anderson, ed., *German-American Pioneers in Wisconsin and Michigan: The Frank Kerber Letters, 1849–1864* (Milwaukee, Wis.: Milwaukee County Historical Society, 1971); Bayard Still, *Milwaukee: The History of a City* (Madison: State Historical Society of Wisconsin, 1965), 259–67.

of immigrants – Roman Catholic Poles, Italians, and Slovaks – who menaced the self-confidence and entrenched power of the German and Anglo-Saxon elites. The city's population increased fivefold between 1870 and 1910. The city's historian observes, "If it was the Europeanism of Milwaukee that lent the city distinction in the nineteenth century, industrialism was its prevailing feature in the twentieth."[17] In his novel *The Autocrats,* set in turn-of-the-century Milwaukee, Charles Lush captured the transformation: "From the liberty of the country swarm men and women to a new bondage, to be warped and twisted by the fierce heat of competition – competition for all things, for the air they breathe ... the City is the Dark Continent of this century."[18] Kent Kennan was enough of a farm boy to know that rural life was itself a form of bondage, but infinitely preferable to proletarianization.

The decade of George Kennan's birth saw the growth of slums, of urban political machines, of a strong social democratic movement – the specter of class conflict loomed over stately Prospect Avenue. This transformation helps to explain Kent Kennan's ambivalence toward the new Milwaukee and the new century, why he tried to shelter his children within the precincts of Cambridge Avenue and at a summer home on Lake Nagawicka, where he tended a large flower and vegetable garden. George Kennan later suggested that his family could not identify with either the capitalist exploiter or the exploited.[19] Perhaps it would be truer to say that they were able to recognize the grievances of both. In any event, they were bemused by the arrival of urban-industrial society and its gritty, lacerating politics. They felt a desire to escape. The same is presumably true of the great trauma and turning point in Milwaukee history: World War I. German-Americans naturally sympathized with the Central Powers; Wilson, the "keep us out of war" – and antiprohibitionist – candidate, carried Milwaukee in 1916, and Wisconsin's congressional delegation voted against the declaration of war, almost to a man. American entry, the "Americanization" campaign and anti-German demagoguery that accompanied it, was the final catastrophe of *Gemütlichkeit* Milwaukee.[20] For someone with Kent Kennan's attachment to German culture and understanding of the qualities of German farmers and laborers, the cant and self-serving anti-Germanism of the war years must have been an additional source

17. Still, 476.
18. C. Lush, *The Autocrats: A Novel* (New York: Doubleday, Page, 1904).
19. *Memoirs*, 1: 7.
20. On this subject see Clifton J. Child, *The German-Americans in Politics, 1914–1917* (Madison: University of Wisconsin Press, 1939), 151–62.

of estrangement and dismay. "Of course, since we're at war with Germany," Carol Kennicott told the Gopher Prairie worthies, "anything that anyone of us doesn't like is 'pro-German,' whether it's business competition or bad music.... How we do sanctify our efforts to keep them from getting the holy dollars we want for ourselves!"[21]

A romantic egotist abroad

The destiny of exceptional men is sometimes to pursue the frustrated dreams of their fathers, to continue a quest spanning several generations, even if the nature of the quest may not be fully understood. Kent Kennan was a remote, inhibited man – he was more than fifty when George Kennan was born – but this did not prevent him from indicating the path of aesthetic awakening cum rebellion cum escape from the "blind alley"[22] of Victorianized Puritan Respectability, on one hand, and the dead end of Dynamo-driven industrial civilization, on the other. The original, fundamental legacy of Kent Kennan to his son was an attachment to the land. The young Kennan learned to handle the implements of farm life and gained a feeling for its rhythm and routine. At the same time, through disjointed conversations and "bashful sidelong glances," he received from his father the message that Carol gave an aspiring artist-farm boy: "Young man, go East."[23]

An early milestone on this path was Germany, its language and its culture. Thanks to his father, German was George Kennan's first foreign language and Germany was the first foreign country he knew. Kennan later wrote, "It was a country with which I was never able to identify extensively in a personal sense." This meant that it did not satisfy some deep appetite or longing. "But," he added, "intellectually and aesthetically, Germany [had] made a deep impression on me."[24] Kennan learned German at Kassel in 1912. His father chose the Kaiser's summer residence because of the purity of the language spoken there. When Kennan joined the Foreign Service in 1926, it was German that he chose to perfect. At twenty-two, he immersed himself in Goethe's *Faust* and Spengler's *The Decline of the West* in the setting of Heidelberg, Berlin, and the Baltic coast. He met his Uncle Paul again, "a lovely, civilized man from the old Frankfurt," who made "a lasting impression... by

21. Lewis, *Main Street*, 403.
22. This is Kennan's expression; see "Notes for Russian Seminar." On his relationship with his father see also Melvin Lasky, "A Conversation with George Kennan," *Encounter*, 14, no. 3 (March 1960), 50.
23. Lewis, *Main Street*, 331. See also Issacson and Thomas, 73.
24. *Memoirs*, 1: 415.

remarking enviously in French, as we inspected the ruins of Heidelberg castle (destroyed by the French in the late seventeenth century): '*Ce ne sont que les français qui puissent faire une si belle ruine.*'"[25]

In his uncle's remark Kennan presumably understood the sense of inferiority and resentment felt by Germans vis-à-vis the universalist pretensions of French culture, as well as the fact that Franco-German conflict had not begun in 1914 or 1870 and that the question of historical responsibility was more complicated than wartime propagandists and Versailles peacemakers ordained. Kennan's fluency in German presumably led to the choice of a German city, Hamburg, as his first regular posting. There, through the poems of Franz Werfel, he became aware of "the whole tragic pathos of postwar Germany" and sensed the fragility of Weimar. In spite of his hostility toward Marxism, he felt compassion for the ragged masses demonstrating under red flags and drizzling rain at the Dammtor Station, and he was at home at Zillertal, the great beer hall: "There was a magnificent camaraderie about it."[26] Kennan's German meant, finally, that when he chose to undertake the deep study of Russia, he did so, alone among his colleagues, in Berlin. There he was to find "more intellectual inspiration and education than in any other city in Europe." In 1931, Berlin was "the nearest thing [he] had known to an adult home."[27] Thus his father's legacy included a deep knowledge of Germany, an empathy for its people, and an angle of vision that contrasted with the more conventional outlook of someone formed not in Cambridge Avenue and Berlin, but in, say, Cambridge, Massachusetts, and Paris. A Milwaukee–Berlin perspective was more objective and critically knowledgeable but also more emotional; it was intellectually more sophisticated but more sentimental with respect to the problem and plight of Germany.

A second milestone was Princeton University. An Ivy League education meant distinction unattained by Kent Kennan, escape from Milwaukee, a linking of oneself more or less consciously to the broader cultural migration from the provincial heartland to the East. Sinclair Lewis had entered Yale in 1903; ten years later his fellow Minnesotan, F. Scott Fitzgerald, arrived at Princeton, an experience that produced his first novel, *This Side of Paradise*, in 1920. Kennan read *Main Street* – also published in 1920 – and *This Side of Paradise* in his senior year of high school, 1920–21. His reaction to Lewis's book has

25. Ibid., 18–19.
26. Ibid., 22; GFK, *Sketches*, 3–5.
27. GFK, "Ernst Reuter Memorial Lecture," Oct. 12, 1955, GKP, box 19; *Memoirs*, 1: 35.

already been noted; Fitzgerald's awed him and provided a kind of late-adolescent cultural model.[28]

Kennan later referred to an "excitement and sense of revelation" connected with Fitzgerald's book. One can surmise its impact on the seventeen-year-old youth, like his father introspective, moody, restless in his surroundings (at the time, the St. John's Military Academy), prone to catharsis, conscious of a special destiny – Kennan called it an "intimation of immortality" – but uncertain of its nature.[29] *This Side of Paradise* is the story of Amory Blaine, a kind of middle western Rupert Brooke, scion of a rich though declining family, handsome, narcissistic, talented, and ambitious. The first part is set at Princeton, where Amory is drawn by the mystique of Gothic towers and idling aristocrats; it chronicles a series of poses and infatuations under the heading of the "Romantic Egotist." Toward the end of college comes disillusionment with the social rat race, a shedding of superciliousness, and an intellectual awakening. The end of the first part coincides with American entry into the World War – Amory, like Fitzgerald, leaves Princeton for the army in 1917.

The second part is the far starker story of Amory's loss of innocence. In 1919 he and his generation stand between the wrecked Victorian world, on one hand – for him the war is the "Victorian war" – and the spiritual desert of an America whose "business is business," on the other. Amory's crisis is across the board and existential: the loss of love, of his parents, of his mentor-alter ego, of all certainties and models. Out of suffering, he constructs a new identity; "Amory was alone – he had escaped from a small enclosure into a great labyrinth. . . . He began for the first time in his life to have a strong distrust of all generalities and epigrams. . . . In self-reproach and loneliness and disillusion he came to the entrance to the labyrinth." Amory has nothing left except self-knowledge, but thus armed he is ready to face the 1920s as a "spiritually unmarried man."[30]

George Kennan did not have the self-assurance or money to participate in club life at Princeton; his description of his isolation there suggests that it was the "spiritually unmarried man" who broke with inherited categories that attracted him, at least in retrospect, rather than the slick and blasé clubman. "It finally dawned on me," Kennan re-

28. On GFK's reaction to *Main Street* see "Notes for Russian Seminar"; on *This Side of Paradise* see *Memoirs*, 1: 9.
29. *Memoirs*, 1: 4, 9.
30. F. Scott Fitzgerald, *This Side of Paradise* (1920) (New York: Collier Books, 1986), esp. 263–65, 271, 280.

called, "pondering this unhappy situation, that to be fair to oneself, one had to make one's own standards, one could not just accept those of other people."[31] This was the voice of the later Amory, the middle westerner who had suffered at the hands of eastern society – in Amory's case the crowning indignity of rejection by his great love, a New York debutante, because he had no money. In a sense, the "spiritually un-married man" is itself a new pose, very middle western, designed to steel him against the wounding pretensions of the East, and to allow him a sort of revenge through high skepticism and cultivation. The later Amory has escaped from the enclosure, but he is not without a chip on his shoulder.[32]

Kennan describes his decision to join the Foreign Service after Prince-ton as the result of a process of elimination: "I made the decision largely because I didn't know what else to do, and was afraid of getting into a rut of some sort if I remained at home."[33] There was little appeal in law or business (Amory had briefly tried advertising), and Milwaukee "held no charms."[34] In effect, all roads were blocked – they were the well-known dead ends – except the one leading farther east. Like Amory's, Kennan's intellectual appetite had been whetted but hardly satisfied at Princeton. The Foreign Service was a way to continue his education. Kennan described his intellect as "reasonably lucid and open . . . lazy and passive when left to itself, but capable of vigorous reaction when challenged . . . what I had most keenly missed to that point was the stimulus and steadying effect, of association with older and wiser men."[35] Thus the Foreign Service satisfied a desire for father figures and mentors; it provided a "protective paternalism," a structure, a "welcome mask" behind which Kennan felt a "hitherto unknown strength."[36] The Foreign Service was also "a pretty good club." Its leading lights were patrician figures like Joseph Grew, his brother-in-law Pierpont Moffat, Theodore Marriner, and Alexander Kirk.[37] The

---

31. *Memoirs*, 1: 12. See also Oliver Pilat, "Close-up of Diplomatic Chief of Staff," *New York Post*, June 4, 1947, copy in GKP, box 21.
32. This is particularly evident during his car ride with "the big man" at the end of the novel.
33. GFK, "Problems and Opportunities of the Foreign Service," Talk at the Lawrenceville School, Apr. 30, 1953, GKP, box 18.
34. *Memoirs*, 1: 17.
35. Ibid., 16–17.
36. Ibid., 20–21.
37. These were men whom Kennan later called "the strength of the service" in the thirties. See GFK to Charles Thayer, Apr. 20, 1959, Charles Thayer Papers, Harry S. Truman Library (hereafter, CTP, HSTL). The expression "a pretty good club" is Hugh Wilson's. See also Weil.

Foreign Service was an answer of sorts to the middle westerner's social predicament and outlet for the romantic egotism that Princeton had failed to slake. Kennan described what amounted to his own romantic egotism in a lecture given in 1947 on the diplomatic profession:

> There still existed after all an international society which was considered to have smartness and glamor. . . . In short there was still the faint gleam of the romanticism of the 19th century, that fell on all of us like the beams of a setting sun, and we were preoccupied, like all romantics with the shadows which our individual figures might cast in that mellow and seductive light.[38]

There was also the gleam of the slightly older wartime, and after 1918 "lost," generation – of men like Fitzgerald, Hemingway, Cole Porter, and William Bullitt – who migrated eastward in the twenties.

Kennan's first, brief assignment was Geneva, where he drank port and read French novels along the Quai de Mont Blanc.[39] Except for Lisbon, this was as close as he came to a Latin setting in his professional career. For France he did not have much affinity. There was a deep-rooted Yankee-Puritan reserve about the French; probably he shared his uncle's mixed feelings about the pretensions of French classicism; maybe the clamor and spectacle of everyday Latin life did not suit his nervous system. (Italy left him literally ill when he visited in 1924 and 1940, and years later cold – the rain-swept Capri he described as an older man has all the warmth and humanity of a De Chirico cityscape.) Latin Europe was also crowded with Americans. Sinclair Lewis's Sam Dodsworth found Paris "the pleasantest of modern American cities." Paris, as Kennan himself later put it, was the home of "the emigré crowd" who made "such a fuss about themselves" – superficial and socially forbidding. The Germans, by contrast, were the pariahs of the interwar period, another reason for Kennan, the middle westerner and outsider, to identify with their fate.[40] In its hospitable German setting Kennan's life-style was far from stuffy: amid serious duties it was, if anything, Fitzgeraldian. The pursuit of women played a part, along with cham-

---

38. GFK, "The Problems of the Foreign Service," Lecture to the Foreign Service Institute, Aug. 1, 1947, GKP, box 17. He added that the Foreign Service in 1947 was "no longer a refuge for escapists, for introverts, for romantics."
39. Ibid.
40. On his illness in Genoa in 1924, see *Memoirs*, 1: 13; on the same in 1940, see 116; for his description of Capri, see GFK, *Sketches*, 328–29. For the reference to the "emigré crowd," see letter to Thayer, May 22, 1935, CTP, HSTL. See also Sinclair Lewis, *Dodsworth* (New York: Signet, 1929), 113. For the point about Kennan's identification with the Germans as outsiders I am indebted to Thomas Hughes.

pagne, an "elegant Nash roadster," dinner clothes at breakfast, writing, traveling, and jazz.[41] Fun, freedom, and fraternity, after all, were what he had missed at Princeton. Certainly he was a long way from Milwaukee. At the same time, the anti-Victorian, anti-Puritan figure of this moment was one to which the inchoate rebel Kent Kennan might also have aspired.

Romantic egotism, by definition, is destined for its comeuppance. Perhaps a turning point in Kennan's case was early 1928 when he returned home, apparently planning to quit the Foreign Service and to marry a woman (the daughter of a prominent writer and radio commentator) by the wonderfully Fitzgeraldian name of Eleanor Hard. Like Amory Blaine, Kennan had looks and talent, but not money or evidently a great deal of promise, and the engagement was broken off.[42] It was in the immediate aftermath of this incident that Kennan made the decision to stay in the Foreign Service and study Russian, and was assigned to do so in Berlin. For a while he lived the Fitzgeraldian part – the Berlin of Brecht and Sally Bowles was a fair stage – but something fundamental had changed.

In March 1931, Kennan lounged in a fashionable Alpine resort. His diary recorded: "The evenings were long, as only such evenings can be when one feels one's youth sliding gently but firmly away without the compensation of either vice or virtue.... In the music which droned across the dancefloor, the notes of a Negro cornetist danced and played and ran circles around the conscientious rhythms of his less imaginative European colleagues." The diarist reproaches himself for his self-pity:

> Don't you see that you really don't want a woman at all, as a woman. That you only want a mother, who will let you hold your head on her shoulder and will dry your dancing tears and flatter your delicate little egotism and tend to your little physical necessities for you? ... You had better go out in the open air and realize that Mother is far away.[43]

A few months later Kennan met, and almost immediately became engaged to marry, a twenty-one-year-old Norwegian woman living in Berlin.

41. For references to these various activities see *Memoirs*, 1: 34–37; on Kennan's love of jazz see the interview with his sister Jeanette conducted by C. Ben Wright, Sept. 26, 1970. C. Ben Wright Kennan Biography Project, box 8 ff 16, George C. Marshall Foundation Library, Lexington, Va. (hereafter, CBW KBP, GCML).

42. Eleanor Hard recalled years later that, while genuinely fond of each other, she and Kennan were "very different and in the end...quite incompatible." Eleanor Hard (Mrs. Gerald K. Lake) letter to the author, July 12, 1990. For a brief account of this incident, see also Issacson and Thomas, 145–46.

43. GFK, *Sketches*, entry for Mar. 8, 1931, 18–21.

The call of the North

Germany in a literal sense was Kennan's "father-land," a country associated with Kent Kennan, and Kennan's relationship with Germany contained some of the reserve that characterized his relationship with his father. But Germany was not the real horizon of Kent Kennan's parental aspirations. If in naming children parents wish to confer their destiny, Kent Kennan's eye was not on Germany but on Russia. He named his first son for the first cousin of his own father, George Kennan (1845–1923), author of *Siberia and the Exile System*, the famous exposé of the czarist prison system, and other works on pre-1917 Russia. The sense of an uncanny link between the two George Kennans was reinforced in the younger man's mind by the fact that they had the same birthday, February 16, and that the elder Kennan had lost a son, also named George, in infancy. Needless to say, this was known to Kent Kennan at the time of his son's birth. One can only wonder what significance he attached to his own first name, that of the great Hungarian patriot. Certainly there were liberal sympathies running in the family with respect to Eastern Europe. Kent Kennan encouraged his son's identification with his namesake, and they visited the elder Kennan and his wife when young George was a teenager. Kennan wrote his father that in going to Russia, he "would be more or less in the family tradition." In his *Memoirs* he said, "What I have tried to do in life is, I suspect, just the sort of thing the latter would have liked a son of his to try to do, had he had one."[44] The 1928 decision to become a Russian specialist could also be seen as a kind of early manhood coming to terms with his father, an embrace of the destiny Kossuth Kent Kennan had in a sense decreed.

That the decision to immerse himself in Russian language and culture had a deeper meaning is suggested by the fact that it was, in a way, connected to Kennan's break under painful circumstances with a woman. On the first page of his *Memoirs*, Kennan writes, "I have found myself tempted to relate that this child was deeply affected, and in a certain sense scarred for life, by the loss of his mother shortly after his birth."[45] It would be foolish to place too much weight on the loss or to try to construct a clinical interpretation for which the writer has neither the tools nor raw materials. But it is too fundamental and eloquent a fact to

---

44. See Issacson and Thomas, 75–76, 145. See also *Memoirs*, 1: 8–9, 23; GFK, Introduction to George Kennan, *Siberia and the Exile System* (1891) (Chicago: University of Chicago Press, 1958).

45. *Memoirs*, 1: 3, 4.

be ignored. Needless to say, each case is different, but observers of motherless children have noted common tendencies connected with prolonged, unresolved mourning – feelings of guilt, self-pity, hostility, and uniqueness, gastrointestinal troubles, a powerful fantasy life. Also, "An interesting skill is developed by some few of the most able mother-less children whose growth has not been seriously altered by the separation, writing ability apparently serving as a way to abstract, perhaps to recreate the mother in fantasy in order to please her with gifts, and as an attempt to master the hurt."[46] It is well to be wary of such generalizations, yet in Kennan's case, they all would seem to apply. It appears, moreover, that the loss of his mother, combined with the particular experience of women that resulted, inclined him toward a state of mind – melancholy – that in turn influenced his strong aesthetic and geographical preferences. The loss also helped to incline him toward a posture of estrangement with respect to modern America, which informed his political views. In other words, Kennan's very personal experience linked him with a broader native critique of modernity – that of Adams, Lewis, and, to an extent, Fitzgerald[47] – in which the quality of *women* was a recurrent theme and touchstone.

At the risk of oversimplification, one might venture that the women in Kennan's childhood and early adult life fall into two sharply different categories. Of his own mother he wrote years later, "We have all held you, in retrospect, in a sort of awed adoration – our ever-young, dead mother, beautiful, unworldly, full only of love and grace for us, like a saint."[48] Kennan also idealized the women who actually nurtured and protected him – one can imagine their assiduity – like the youngest of his three elder sisters.[49] But there were also the women who did not nurture, like his schoolteacher-stepmother, who was perhaps partly responsible for his dispatch to a tough military school, or the childless wife of the elder George Kennan, who did not take kindly to the

46. Besse Lee Alnutt, "The Motherless Child," in Joseph Noshpitz, ed., *Basic Handbook of Child Psychiatry* (New York: Basic Books, 1979), 1: 376.

47. Amory Blaine thinks while riding the New York subway during the evening rush hour: "It was not so bad where there were only men or else only women; it was when they were vilely herded that it all seemed so rotten. It was some shame that women gave off at having men see them tired and poor. It was some disgust that men had for women who were tired and poor. It was dirtier than any battlefield he had seen." Fitzgerald, *This Side of Paradise*, 256.

48. On another occasion, he wrote of her "as the woman without whose sacrifice and agony I would not have existed," as if he were unintentionally responsibile for her death. See GFK, *Sketches*, 165, 305.

49. Of Jeanette he wrote, "Buoyant sociability, optimism, and conciliatoriness are the essence of her being." GFK, *Sketches*, 206.

aspiring surrogate son.[50] Those in the first category were a reminder of the day when "women were still women," of a fertile pioneer and seafaring tradition.[51] The second represented twentieth century American womanhood, still Puritan, but not so fertile or maternal.

It is hard to avoid the conclusion that the persistent melancholy that suffuses Kennan's writings and outlook on the modern world arises ultimately from the sense of loss connected with his mother and of the precariousness of all maternal love. It is possible to imagine that these are feelings attached to an unrelinquished "object," to borrow from the psychoanalysts,[52] feelings so unrequited and precious that they are melded to the personality itself. There is, needless to say, a powerful drive to overcome melancholy through human relationships and, as has been suggested, creativity. In this deeply affective sense, Kennan's way pointed once again to Europe, especially to Norway and to Russia, Kennan's "mother-countries."

In his description of Norway and the Baltic region one sees the deeper reasons for his preference for the North over Latin Europe. There was something familiar and stimulating about the northern climate and environment. What kind of intense familiarity is suggested by Fitzgerald through Nick Carraway, the narrator of *The Great Gatsby*, who describes his trips home from college in the East: "When we pulled out into the winter night and the real snow ... and the dim lights of small Wisconsin stations moved by, a sharp wild brace came suddenly into the air. We drew in deep breaths ... unutterably aware of our identity."[53] Perhaps Kennan also felt a connection to Norway at a kind of archaic, racial level, as had Henry Adams.[54] The most revealing of Kennan's statements about his attachment to the North is the following:

> It is in this series of rigorous contrasts – the length of winter, the brevity of summer; a soul-trying sternness and longevity of all that is grim, the intensity and fleetingness of all that is beautiful; the brief moments of

50. On the elder George Kennan's wife see Issacson and Thomas, 76.
51. On this association see GFK, "Letter to the Kennan Children."
52. See, e.g., Melanie Klein, "A Contribution to the Psychogenesis of Manic-Depressive States," in Peter Buckley, ed., *Essential Papers on Object Relations* (New York: New York University Press, 1986), 40–45.
53. On climate and the intellect see GFK, *Sketches*, 213; see also F. Scott Fitzgerald, *The Great Gatsby* (New York: Scribners, 1925), 177.
54. Adams "felt at least the emotion of his Norwegian fishermen ancestors, doubtless numbering hundreds of thousands, jammed with their faces to the sea, the ice on the north, the ice-cap of Russian inertia pressing from behind, and the ice a trifling danger compared to the inertia." *The Education*, 415. Kennan admired the political achievements of the modern Norwegians. See GFK, "The Appointment of the New State Council in Norway," Feb.–Apr., 1940, GKP, box 23.

magic loveliness all the more exquisite for the long ordeal of denial by which they are preceded – it is these that are the essence of Norway.[55]

The North was the natural theater of Kennan's melancholy disposition – a setting suited to a person for whom the experience of beauty was inseparable from the sense of loss. Not surprisingly he was attracted by the warm, phlegmatic women of the North – the ones Lewis had evoked – women with a natural grace and luster that had faded in the America of Main Street and the Dynamo. Through his parents-in-law, Kennan found a second family, and in Norway, "a second country."[56]

Of his fiancée he wrote his father: "She has the true Scandinavian simplicity and doesn't waste many words. She has the rare capacity for keeping silent gracefully. I have never seen her disposition ruffled by anything resembling a mood, and even I don't make her nervous."[57] There was an additional element in his attraction to the North, suggested in Kennan's recollection of the seashore near Riga where he bathed, "in the nocturnal hours, in the magic, and to me, commandingly erotic twilight of the Northern world in the weeks of the summer solstice.... It was a marvellous, diffuse half-light, marking the unbroken transition of the glow of the Northern sky from sunset to sunrise – a condition of nature under the spell of which all human emotions and situations seemed to take on a heightened poignancy, mystery, and promise."[58] That element was sensual awakening and awareness.

Perhaps Kennan's experience can be illuminated once again by fiction, in this case Lewis's autobiographical *Dodsworth*, published in 1929.[59] Dodsworth is a prematurely retired automobile maker from Zenith, a larger Gopher Prairie, whose handcrafted line is bought up by a Detroit company and who follows his wife to Europe. He is an indifferently educated – at Yale – somewhat clumsy, but also sensitive figure; Mrs. Dodsworth – one of Lewis's most vitriolic portraits of the well-heeled female – is beautiful, spoiled, and frigid, a social climber and a snob.

55. GFK, "Unused Material Written for Possible Inclusion in *Memoirs, 1950–1967*," GKP, box 27.
56. He described his wife's mother in terms reserved for his closest sister, "a warm open-hearted person, capable at times of a childlike gaiety, but always against the background of a great maternal dignity and purity, a woman from whose lips I never heard an ungenerous or spiteful word." *Memoirs*, 1: 39.
57. Quoted in Issacson and Thomas, 150.
58. *Memoirs*, 1: 31.
59. Lewis wrote *Dodsworth* during his courtship of his second wife, Dorothy Thompson, whom he met in Berlin in 1927.

After he is left by his wife for more dashing companions, Dodsworth wanders in aimless solitude. Having seen "Fordized America" through the prism of Europe, he hesitates to go back. Gradually he experiences an awakening of unknown sexual feelings and a new awareness of nature that heal the wounds of abandonment and loss of vocation and give him serenity and depth. The catalyst of Dodsworth's breakthrough is a Russo-Portuguese woman; the setting of his rediscovery of nature is the Neapolitan coast. Eventually he finds an American woman, but one softened and refined by Europe, who tells him, "That's the strength of Europe – not its so-called 'culture' . . . but its nearness to earth. . . . And that's the weakness of America," the postfrontier urban civilization that insulates it from "the good vulgarity of earth."[60] There is nothing subtle about Lewis's allegory, but it is a classic illustration of what Europe represented to a certain kind of middle western sensibility – a kind of romantic primitivism – that was akin to Kennan's own. Europe meant self-knowledge, rejuvenation, and refuge from the spiritually parched America of the twenties.

The emotional disposition and posture toward contemporary America that attracted Kennan to Norway also help to account for his more momentous attraction to Russia. His description of the study of Russian during the years 1928–33 indicates that he derived from it something more than the intellectual rewards involved in learning a new language: "I conceived then and there a love for the great Russian language . . . that was not only never to leave me but was to constitute in some curious way an unfailing source of strength and reassurance. . . . Russian seemed to me, from the start a natural language."[61] It was not only a refuge and sustenance but a vehicle for the more intense and open expression of affection, delight, sadness – of a register of feelings that the normal Puritan American tends to keep bottled up inside. Russian gave him the broader emotional repertoire, the new medium of expression, the new persona that a foreign language can provide. Naturally all of this was inseparable from his ready embrace of Russian people – his White Russian emigré tutors and especially the Russian family, an impoverished mother and her two children, who seem to have adopted him in Berlin: "I was embarrassed by the reckless spontaneity of their devotion. . . . But I was grateful and reciprocated the affection in my way. I was pleased that they accepted me as a Russian, as one of them, not as a foreigner. Sharing their woes and crises, I felt like a Russian

60. Lewis, *Dodsworth*, 335.
61. *Memoirs*, 1: 28.

myself."[62] By the time he first went to Russia in 1933, Kennan had developed "a consuming curiosity to know it in the flesh."[63]

Kennan revealed the appeal of Russia when describing a visit to Yasnaya Polyana, Tolstoy's estate, around 1935: "The atmosphere... reminded me of my uncle's country home in Wisconsin where I used to seek refuge as a little boy from the rigors of a military academy." Of his return to the house in 1952 as U.S. ambassador to the Soviet Union he said, "Once more I was permitted to feel close to a world to which, I always thought, I could really have belonged... much more naturally and wholeheartedly than to the world of politics and diplomacy."[64] Of Russian country life he wrote:

> The magic of this atmosphere was derived not just from the fact that this was Russia but also from the fact that it was a preindustrial life... in which people were doing things with their hands, with animals and with nature, a life little touched by any form of modernization, a pre-World War I and pre-revolutionary life.[65]

Sustaining, symbolizing this wholesome refuge from modernity was the Russian woman. Kennan was moved by the fact that Yasnaya Polyana had an "air of having been tended for years by the hands of kind women – women who had intelligence and character and had suffered" – women like his mother and sister. On another occasion, Kennan described farm women with the "broad faces, brown muscular arms, and the powerful maternal thighs of the female Slav. They laughed and joked as they worked; and it was clear that they enjoyed the feeling of the sun on their bodies and the dark earth cool and sandy, under their bare feet."[66] Here indeed was the "good vulgarity of earth."

Kennan's wistful travelogues frequently dealt with visits to Russian Orthodox churches and monasteries. The visits were more than touristic exercises. The lapsed Presbyterian perhaps took from them a kind of

---

62. Ibid., 34.
63. From Kennan's seventy-six-page typed diary, covering the years 1933–38, "Fair Day Adieu!" 3, GKP, box 25. At some later date, Kennan attached the following statement to this document: "All this is autobiographical material written in 1938, and never published. Should anyone else make use of it for publication, he should point out the early date of its composition, as well as the fact that it was blanketed by the *Memoirs*, published 30 years later."
64. Ibid., 37; GFK, *Memoirs*, vol. 2: *1950–1963* (Boston: Little, Brown, 1972) (hereafter, *Memoirs*, 2), 130.
65. Ibid., 128, referring to the atmosphere of the dacha he frequented in 1952.
66. GFK, "Fair Day Adieu!" 37; GFK, *Sketches*, 90, passage written in July 1944.

comfort and sustenance.[67] Probably he was attracted by the ritual, music, and iconography of a religion in which the female, the Mother of God, still occupied an exalted position, a religion reflecting the values and moral vision of a traditional society in which the creative power of the female was everywhere palpable – witness Yasnaya Polyana or the peasants in the fields. The achievements of Russian art and architecture, the ritual of the church, were in part animated by the mysterious premodern spirit that Henry Adams, suffering the tragic loss of his wife, had sought at Mont St. Michel and Chartres. Perhaps Kennan sought something similar: communion with the compassionate, restorative power of the Virgin. Adams had remarked – presumably he was referring to both the Reformation and Nietzsche's more recent declaration of the "Death of God" – "At times the historian would have been willing to maintain that man had overthrown the Church chiefly because it was feminine." Adams suggested that to prove his worth before a sterner deity, one stripped of its feminine attributes, urban Protestant man had created the modern world, trampling mother nature under foot. Women, having lost their religious mystique, were freed, but freed to be proletarianized – to "marry the machine."[68] Kennan was following in Adams's footsteps. But the kind of communion he sought was rarely available even in Russia – there the traditional order had been overthrown by a new religion and form of progress more violently corrosive than anything in the West.

A Chekhovian detachment

Kennan's lifelong relationship with Russia recalls his description of Norway: the "soul trying sternness and longevity of all that is grim; the intensity and fleetingness of all that is beautiful."[69] His search for intimacy was, except for brief moments, unrequited; throughout his

---

67. See, e.g., the accounts of his visit to an Estonian monastery near the Soviet border where he spent Christmas 1928 (*Memoirs*, 1: 28) and of his Easter 1929 visit to a Russian church at Riga Dorpat (GFK, *Sketches*, 14–15). On his visit to the New Jerusalem monastery at Voskresensk in 1936 see ibid., 23; see also the account of a similar outing in 1944 (ibid., 85–90). Particularly striking is his mid-thirties description of the Church of the Holy Shroud on an island at the confluence of the Nerl and Klyazma rivers – "the most beautiful building in Russia." See GFK, "Fair Day Adieu!" Kennan at this point does not seem to have been a practicing Presbyterian, though he followed his father's advice that he "should not cease entirely . . . to go to Church." *Memoirs*, 1: 17. On this point see also GFK, *Around the Cragged Hill: A Personal and Political Philosophy* (New York: Norton, 1992), 39, 49.
68. Henry Adams, *The Education*, 446–47.
69. GFK, "Unused Material."

career circumstances conspired to keep him isolated from the object of his longing. In 1932, he considered quitting the Foreign Service when he was denied permission from his own government to visit Russia to research a biography of Anton Chekhov. With U.S. recognition of the USSR in 1933, Kennan and his colleagues spent an exciting, euphoric year setting up the new embassy and satisfying their hunger for Russia. Perhaps they came with preconceptions – the so-called Riga axioms – but also with considerable hope for the evolution of Russia and the improvement of relations with the United States. The initial period ended with the murder of Kirov and the beginning of the purges in late 1934. Kennan lived what his colleague Charles Thayer called the "madness of '34" at high intensity. The result was a physical break-down (duodenal ulcers) and a transfer to Vienna to recuperate in 1935. He wrote Thayer: "Moscow had me somewhat on the run. I was too fascinated by Russia to take the restrictions of diplomatic status with equanimity and was inclined to feel bitter about things. It was always a little incredible to me that in a world as interesting as the USSR we should have to reconcile ourselves to anything as boring and out of date as life in the Moscow diplomatic corps."[70]

After 1934, Kennan and the others experienced an emotional letdown and were gradually cut off from their Russian friends and contacts. His yearning for the world of Yasnaya Polyana becomes more comprehensible in the new climate. He wrote, "The intellectual discipline of Soviet reality was always cruel, always relentless, and only one who has lived in Russia can understand how powerful was the yearning for escape."[71] In 1937, Kennan was removed from Russia – this time by a politically appointed ambassador – to return only in 1944. His description of the second tenure (until 1946) indicates his eagerness for human contact – he called himself "a thirsting man on a clear stream of water" – and his inability to tolerate restrictions: "We were sincerely moved by the suffering of the Russian people as well as by the heroism and patience they were showing in the face of wartime adversity.... It was doubly hard, in these circumstances, to find ourselves treated as though we were the bearers of some species of the plague."[72] His sense of embittered isolation reached its breaking point in 1952:

70. For Thayer's description see Thayer to GFK, Apr. 10, 1940, CTP, HSTL. See also GFK to CT, May 22, 1935, CTP, HSTL. On the "Riga axioms" see Daniel Yergin, *The Shattered Peace: The Origins of the Cold War and the National Security State* (Boston: Houghton Mifflin, 1977). On this point see also Mayers, 25.
71. GFK, "Fair Day Adieu!"
72. *Memoirs*, 1: 191, 195. In February 1945, he wrote: "There are perhaps 20 to 25 officials, at the most, with whom this Mission comes into contact in its work. There

For more than two decades now, Russia had been in my blood. There was some mysterious affinity which I could not explain even to myself; and nothing could have given me deeper satisfaction than to indulge it. But this was not to be. My guards strode relentlessly at my heels. Even if they had not done so, I knew myself to be the bearer of a species of the plague. I dared not touch anyone, for fear of bringing him infection and perdition.[73]

There were many reasons for Kennan's hostility toward the Bolsheviks; he refers to his own social background, his "sheer intellectual distaste" for the "pseudo science" of Marxism, his time spent in the interwar Baltic countries, his Russian exile friends. He identified with his namesake George Kennan, "who had profoundly deplored the Bolshevik seizure of power."[74] To these reasons must be added that the Bolsheviks were in the process of destroying the nurturing, maternal Russia of his affections while denying him the emotional outlet that speaking, *being*, Russian provided. Whatever else it was, Bolshevism seems to have been seen by Kennan as a virulent form of modernity, the uprooter and leveler of a more natural order, the analogue of "Fordizing" tendencies in the United States. Collectivization of agriculture had left the countryside "generally a scene of neglect, exhaustion, and discouragement." He found the sight of proletarianized peasants idling in vacation hotels repellent. A sounder form of recreation would have been "a return to the village for a few weeks." The Bolsheviks had even tampered with the language – Kennan "admired and cherished" his early school books with "their beautiful unreformed Cyrillic script." In Kennan's reaction to the Bolsheviks there is a filial possessiveness, also the helpless anger of someone who sees the object of his affections debauched. Few statements reveal more about Kennan's deep feelings than his comparison of the Russian people to "a beautiful lady guarded by a jealous [Communist] lover."[75]

Kennan's youthful sensibility is summed up in his attraction to Chekhov. His study of Chekhov was partly an intellectual exercise:

> are practically none who are permitted to have sufficiently close social contact with foreign representatives in the Soviet Union so that it would be possible to know anything much of their personal lives or characters." GFK memo to Secretary of State, Feb. 2, 1945, Averell Harriman Papers, Public Service, WW II, Moscow files, box 176.

73. *Memoirs*, 2: 116.
74. Ibid., 1: 68–69. GFK letter to Joe Wershba, Jan. 9, 1956, GKP, box 31; on the same point, see GFK, "Draft of an Unsent Letter to William F. Buckley, Jr.," Apr. 11, 1960, GKP, box 27.
75. GFK, *Sketches*, 34; GFK, "Fair Day Adieu!"; *Memoirs*, 1: 28; see also GFK, "Draft of Information Policy on Relations with Russia," July 22, 1946, Department of State, Under Secretary, 1945–1947, Correspondence, Dean Acheson Papers, box 27, HSTL.

there could have been "no finer grounding in the atmosphere of pre-revolutionary Russia."[76] But there was also an admiration and identification of the kind that tied him to the elder Kennan. Chekhov's life, Kennan no doubt discovered, contained a series of parallels to his own. Chekhov grew up in an unappealing provincial port city, Taganrog on the Sea of Azov, from which he eventually escaped thanks to his writing talent and a traditional profession, medicine. His grandfather was a serf who bought the family's freedom from the soil through hard work and shrewdness; his merchant father, a recent biographer suggests, "had much in common with the classic self-made Victorian puritan." Their urban household was stuffy and patriarchal. Chekhov carried a feeling for the music and ritual of the church but lost his youthful faith. He loved the steppe, gardening, farming, and country houses – the latter despite frequent financial problems. He suffered a rather severe trauma during his adolesence involving separation from his family. He was beset by intestinal troubles; he depended on the care of an especially devoted sister.[77]

The most singular feature of Chekhov's fiction is its evocation of mood, more often than not nostalgic, melancholic, autumnal. The sources of Chekhov's mood were manifold, but probably chief among them was the fact that he suffered from consumption – the most romantic of maladies – and was thus aware from the depths of his being of the precariousness and fleeting quality of what he loved. His most poignant works were written shortly before his death, at forty-four, in 1904. In "The Bishop" he describes the Palm Sunday encounter of a bishop with his peasant mother, who has come, unannounced, to visit for the first time in many years. The meeting evokes wonderful memories of a distant childhood, yet his mother now treats him with a deference that marks his changed status and the loss of intimacy between them. Only when he falls suddenly, mortally ill of typhoid the day before Easter does she embrace him "as if he had been a little child whom she dearly, dearly loved." But he has already drifted off.[78] In *The Cherry Orchard*, Chekhov recounts the calamity of a sympathetic, genteel, but feckless family whose beautiful estate is to be sold off to an enterprising peasant who will cut down the treasured cherry orchard and subdivide the property. Chekhov does not moralize or sentimentalize in these pieces – V. S. Pritchett tell us that he admired the boorish peasant

76. *Memoirs*, 1: 49.

77. These biographical details are contained in V. S. Pritchett, *Chekhov: A Spirit Set Free* (New York: Random House, 1988). Quote on Chekhov's father, 3–4.

78. "The Bishop," in Ralph E. Matlaw, ed., *Anton Chekhov's Short Stories* (New York: Norton, 1979), 246; the story was written in 1902.

Lopahin;[79] rather, he suggests the irretrievability of lost attachments, the inescapable nature of life's predicaments, the equal distribution of vice and virtue across the social spectrum.

Chekhov was a man of liberal political instincts. He read George Kennan's exposé and explored the Sakhalin prison colony firsthand.[80] At the same time he was detached from the main political and social currents of his day. His basic predicament was strikingly like the one Kennan identified as his father's and his own. His stories are full of the dullness and vulgarity of provincial bourgeois life. No one was more conscious that the Russian version of Victorian Respectability was a moral-aesthetic dead end. There was a strong antipuritan, bohemian streak in Chekhov. He frequented elegant French resorts. He died with the taste of champagne on his lips. He was deeply attached to women, whose educational equality he favored while at the same time trying to show in a celebrated story that "it is the law of [woman's] being to love someone or something."[81]

Chekhov looked with disquiet on the consequences of industrialization; Adams's forty-foot Dynamos were also looming over Russia. This was the theme of several of his short stories, especially "The Doctor's Visit" (1898). A doctor – Chekhov himself – treats the daughter of a factory owner (there is nothing physically wrong with her) and sees the inside of a factory compound for the first time. He is perplexed:

> Fifteen hundred or two thousand people are working without rest in unhealthy surroundings, making bad cotton goods, living on the verge of starvation, and waking from this nightmare only at bare intervals in the tavern; a hundred people act as overseers and the whole life of that hundred is spent imposing fines, in abuse, in injustice, and only two or three so-called owners enjoy the profits, though they don't work at all, and despise the wretched cotton. But what are the profits and how do they enjoy them? Madame Lyalikov and her daughter [the patient] are unhappy – it makes one wretched to look at them.

The doctor feels that workers, overseers, and owners alike are moving to the tune of some larger, sinister force, which he identifies simply as the Devil. It was the Devil "that had created the mutual relation of the strong and the weak, that coarse blunder which one could never correct ...the strong and the weak were both equally victims of their mutual relations."[82] Chekhov's Devil is a close relative of Adams's Dynamo, the

---

79. Pritchett, 221.
80. On this point see ibid., 85.
81. See Ernest J. Simmons, *Chekhov: A Biography* (Chicago: University of Chicago Press, 1962), 438. The author is referring specifically to "The Darling."
82. "The Doctor's Visit," in Matlaw, ed., 206–8.

animating spirit of modernity, of runaway technology, of humanity's Faustian drive to transform nature and build useless monuments to itself. But is redemption to be found in a return to rural life? This was Chekhov's occasional escape, along with his liberal-artistic friends. But he was too critical and secular a figure – like Chaadaev, the disenchanted intellectual of the 1830s, or Gogol, the author of *Dead Souls* – too aware of the *poshlost*, the meretriciousness and backwardness of Russian rural life, to place his hopes in the masses or a return to religious values. Besides, the cherry orchards were beginning to fall, foreshadowing a more general catastrophe.

In Chekhov, Kennan found another reference point along the lines of the "spiritually unmarried man," one whose life was more faithful to that model than was Amory Blaine's creator. The discovery of Chekhov, of the striking resemblance to his own life, reinforced Kennan's natural posture of "Chekhovian" detachment. Chekhov's pessimism, his melancholic and at times misanthropic side were highly appealing to Kennan. But mixed with the fatalism was a finesse, a lightness, a lack of cynicism that counseled something other than despair.[83] The optimism that Kennan always nursed for Russia's future could be traced in part to the flowering of a figure like Chekhov in the soil of the pre-1917 regime, one that by Russian standards had been extraordinarily open to the West.[84] Perhaps, as has been suggested, Kennan imagined himself a kind of American Chekhov[85] or, rather, heir to the master's legacy.

83. On this point see Maxim Gorky, "Anton Chekhov," in Matlaw, ed., 286. I have also relied on George P. Kent, "Towards Containment: The Impact of George Kennan's Views of the Russian National Character and the Soviet Regime on His Policy Formulation, 1944–47," Masters' thesis (Johns Hopkins University, 1992).

84. On this point see GFK lecture, "Russia and the U.S.," May 27, 1950, GKP, box 2. "There was," said Kennan, "no purer example of liberal humanism and honest literary workmanship than Anton Chekov." He also said, "I am sure that the organic development of moral feeling so closely linked with the great figures of Russia's cultural past, must someday take its place in the creation of new political forms." See also GFK lecture at the National Defense College, May 31, 1948, GKP, box 17. Here he stressed the importance of leaving the way open for "that renewed evolution of the Russian state in the direction of greater liberalism which I believe to be entirely possible . . . but which must be a spontaneous Russian process organically connected with those deep, strange groundswells of Russian development that are so hard for the Western mind to fathom." After the arrival of Gorbachev, he spoke of the "unfinished business of the old czarist regime, whose not inconsiderable positive efforts – to introduce into Russian political life the elements of a proper parliamentary system, to restructure Russian agriculture, and to modernize Russian society generally – were so rudely put to an end by war and revolution in 1917." "The Gorbachev Prospect," *New York Review of Books*, 34, nos. 21–22 (Jan. 21, 1988), 6.

85. See Anders Stephanson, *Kennan and the Art of Foreign Policy* (Cambridge, Mass.: Harvard University Press, 1989), 251.

After all, Kennan was born in the year of his death and was the product of a set of historical circumstances not dissimilar to those that shaped Chekhov. Their lives, in any event, were witness to the parallel development of Russia and the United States, two great outlying pioneer nations impinging more and more on Europe.

An exile in time

Political ideas and opinions, no matter how rationalized and elaborate, are ultimately connected to an underlying disposition, a substratum of experience, a personal sensibility. Such a connection becomes evident in George Kennan's intellectual development during the decade of the thirties. For reasons that were deeply personal and affective in origin, Kennan had come to view the American scene from a position of melancholy disaffection and critical detachment. He felt the longing for a more nourishing society, a longing partially satisfied by his relationship with Europe. Around this emotional trellis grew a set of convictions, a worldview, with respect to American domestic and foreign affairs. Kennan's more systematic ordering of his ideas in the thirties was not unrelated to those events that marked, in a patent and inescapable way, the beginning of adulthood. These included his marriage (1931), the birth of his first child (1932), and the death of his father (1933), which coincided almost exactly with his assumption of important professional responsibilities. Needless to say, the beginning of the decade was a watershed in a more general sense; the collapse of prosperity ushered in a new economic and cultural climate, new political experiments, new questions for debate.

Kennan has been linked with an essentially European current of "organicist conservatism," including Spengler, Ortega y Gasset, T. S. Eliot, Ezra Pound, D. H. Lawrence, and Wyndam Lewis, whose common preoccupation was mass culture and "mass man" associated with the machine age and democracy. The nominal Americans in this group, Eliot and Pound, embraced doctrines that permanently cut them off from their native context, Anglo-Catholicism and fascism, respectively. There is much to be said for this view as far as Spengler is concerned. Kennan read him and found much that was congenial. Spengler saw the great historical cultures – classical, Arabian, Chinese, Indian, modern Western – as living organisms, arising from the soil of a "mother region" and passing through the life cycle of spring, summer, autumn, and winter. "These Cultures, sublimated life-essences, grow with the same superb aimlessness as the flowers of the field." The great statesman was but "the gardener of a people." Like the Adamses, like Chekhov,

Spengler was deeply concerned with the fate of the European West, which he believed had experienced the fatal transition from culture to "economic-megalopolitan" (*großstädtisch*) civilization. At this stage, "technics," the machine, "became tired of being life's servant and makes itself tyrant." The machine "forces the entrepreneur not less than the workman to obedience. *Both* become slaves, and not masters of the machine, which now develops its devilish and occult power." Thus, like Chekhov, Spengler believed that Marxism was based on a misunderstanding of the nature of modern industrial civilization – and here is a source of Kennan's own view of the matter. The machine, in turn, is in danger of being subdued by an even stronger power, money or high finance. Money achieves political domination through democracy, like all political forms a historically contingent and passing phase. At this point, wrote Spengler,

> men are tired to disgust of money-economy. They hope for salvation from somewhere or other, for some true ideal of honor and chivalry, of inward nobility, of unselfishness and duty. And now dawns the time when the form filled powers of the blood, which the rationalism of the Megalopolis has suppressed, reawaken in the depths.[86]

Practical experience – for example, observation of the Schuschnigg government during Kennan's Austrian service in 1935 – prompted questions about the supposed vices of authoritarian government and the virtues of democracy. The Austrian regime was not democratic, yet its approach to the problem of social insurance, Kennan argued, was a "masterpiece of clarity, brevity, and adherence to fact." He "could not pass over the implications of this example. There seemed to be little doubt that if malicious despotism had greater possibilities for evil than democracy, benevolent despotism likewise had greater possibilities for good."[87]

A basic preoccupation with blind individualism, the loss of community, the inability of the American political system to contain the forces of economic change was reinforced by visits home.[88] In June

---

86. On "organicist conservatism" see Stephanson, 230–31. Spengler's advice to statesmen was that "political forms are living forms whose changes inexorably follow a definite direction, and to attempt to prevent this course or to divert it towards some ideal is to confess oneself 'out of condition.'" Oswald Spengler, *The Decline of the West*, ed. Helmut Werner (New York: Modern Library Edition, 1962), 17, 23, 396, 401, 412–13.

87. GFK, "Fair Day Adieu!" chap. 2.

88. In 1936, in Wisconsin, he was "overwhelmed by that complex of feelings that has found its classic description in the novels of Thomas Wolfe: nostalgia, the yearning for roots, a sense of the mystery of time, yet also – alienation and the realization that you can never go back." *Memoirs*, 1: 75.

1938, Kennan took a solitary bicycle trip through rural Wisconsin. In a town, "there was no place where strangers would come together freely – as in a Bavarian beer hall or a Russian amusement park – for the mere purpose of being together and enjoying new acquaintances." Above all, there were automobiles: "the sad climax of industrialism, the blind alley of a generation which had forgotten how to think or live collectively, of a people whose private lives were so brittle, so insecure, that they dared not subject them to the slightest social contact with casual strangers."[89]

With each return from the United States to Europe, the invidious comparisons were more sharply etched. Sailing up the Elbe in 1936 with the U.S. Olympic team aboard, Kennan wrote, "It was one of those mellow, windless evenings peculiar to Europe when the foliage of the chestnut trees stands motionless as if on stage, and the mysteries of a deep dramatic past seem to float up to mould the dreams and winding streets all over the continent." Kennan saw that his fellow Americans had "failed to notice that the country before their eyes was a country different – excitingly, provocatively different from their own. To myself, for whom these transitions from one world to another had never ceased to be a momentous, awe-inspiring experience, like the celebration of some religious rite, this was a little sad." The American tourists he observed in Paris might have stepped from the pages of *Dodsworth*: "flat voiced, flat chested women," their men "already suspicious and slightly hostile to Europe," hiding behind the comic section of the Paris *Herald Tribune*.[90]

Years later an observer described Kennan's "line of reasoning in the 30s and 40s" as "one associated with the old established classes of Europe, especially Central and Eastern Europe." Kennan replied, "The observation that I am intellectually a conservative European shows much penetration."[91] The remark obviously referred to Kennan's concern with the Bolshevik menace, but that was not all. His statement about the "momentous, awe-inspiring" transition captured his concern to preserve the cultural integrity and mission of the Old World from the prospect of American, as well as Bolshevik, submersion. By the mid-thirties there is in Kennan a consciousness of the kind of threat Martin Heidegger referred to in 1932:

89. GFK, *Sketches*, 37, 43. This trip is mentioned in *Memoirs*, 1: 75–76, where GFK implies for some reason that it occurred in 1936 rather than 1938.

90. GFK, "Fair Day Adieu!" chap. 2.

91. George Kateb, "George Kennan: The Heart of a Diplomat," *Commentary*, 45, no. 1 (Jan. 1968), 21–26; GFK to Kateb, Dec. 15, 1967, GKP, 67OL, box 31.

This Europe, which in its ruinous blindness is forever on the point of cutting its own throat, lies today in a great pincers, squeezed between Russia on one side and America on the other. From a metaphysical point of view, Russia and America are the same: the same dreary technological frenzy, the same unrestricted organization of the average man.

Thomas Mann feared the "civilizing [in Spengler's sense], rationalizing, utilitarianizing of the West"; Karl Jaspers held views similar to Heidegger's in the early thirties.[92] It was the same preoccupation expressed by Lewis – albeit through a European character – in 1929:

> We are all at heart Pan-Europeans. We feel that the real Continental Europe is the last refuge of individuality, leisure, privacy, quiet happiness. ... America wants to turn us into Good Fellows, all provided with the very best automobiles.... And Russia wants to turn us into machines for the shaving off of all the eccentricities which do not belong to the lowest common denominator.[93]

An older, subtler American rendering of this theme is Henry James's *The American*.[94] It is the story of the quest of Christopher Newman, the finest example of New World manhood, strapping, self-made, sympathetic, to woo – in effect to buy – the most exquisite specimen of Old World aristocratic womanhood, the beautiful Claire de Bellegarde. The suitor's aggressive presumption upsets the Bellegarde family, who, though they need an infusion of cash, refuse to dishonor themselves by accepting the American offer. The prospective bride is driven to break with her family, but rather than disobey her mother and elder brother she opts for a convent, her life, for all practical purposes, destroyed. The American leaves Europe bewildered, shorn of his animal self-confidence, defeated. Even with the best of intentions, the blind energy of America, in colliding with the delicate equilibrium of Europe, has brought unhappy consequences for both. The moral is the necessity of mutual autonomy, respect, and self-restraint – to paraphrase Kennan, the need to preserve the sacred differentness between the Old World and the New.

The fear that the Old World was losing its ballast and vitality, that the center could not hold, was henceforth an essential part of Kennan's

---

92. Heidegger quoted in Thomas Sheehan, "Heidegger and the Nazis," *New York Review of Books*, 35, no. 10, (June 26, 1988), 44. Sheehan makes the point about Jaspers in the same article. Mann quoted in Peter Gay, *Weimar Culture* (New York: Harper & Row, 1968), 15.

93. Lewis, *Dodsworth*, 232–33.

94. Henry James, *The American* (Harmondsworth: Penguin Books, 1986); first serialized in 1876–77.

outlook: "Poor Riviera. It had become only one great brothel ... and in its empty sterility one sensed the breakdown of European society and the approach of a new debacle."[95] It is easy to see how Americans with a similar perspective – Pound for one – saw the salvation of the West in a brand of European extremism or might look, with Heidegger, to a resurgent Germany to restore equilibrium between the center and the flanks. That Kennan's loyalties were divided is suggested by the quotation he chose from Shakespeare to introduce his diary:

> The sun's o'ercast with blood: fair day adieu!
> Which is the side that I must go withal?
> I am with both, each army hath a hand;
> And in their rage, I having hold of both
> They whirl asunder and dismember me.[96]

But the fact that his loyalties remained *divided* distinguishes Kennan from the European and expatriate American "organicist conservatives." There was something basic that did not allow him to relinquish his loyalty. It had to do with his sense of duty; he referred to it as a "matter of self-respect and of a deeper faith in the values of our [American] civilization."[97] Kennan is connected in the end with those native figures whose exile was temporal rather than spatial, who found an intellectual home of sorts in the past, especially in the eighteenth century. As we have seen, the cyclical rediscovery of the eighteenth century is an eternal theme of U.S. political and cultural history. The generation of Theodore Roosevelt, Mahan, and Lodge had wrapped themselves in the mantle of Hamilton just as Franklin Roosevelt had rediscovered Jefferson, the democrat and enemy of plutocracy.[98] Henry Adams, a self-styled "relic of the eighteenth century," had exalted that period over subsequent ones; *The Education* became the "younger generation's primer in history" after it was released in 1918.[99] For the conservative critic Irving Babbitt, the twenties generation of rebels, exiles, and debunkers were the "ill-begotten children of Rousseau."[100] The slightly younger Kennan had partaken of their spirit, one that quickly evaporated after October 1929.

The Adams family hover like muses above Kennan, especially the

---

95. GFK, "Fair Day Adieu!"
96. Ibid., title page, from *King John*, act III – hence the title of the diary.
97. *Memoirs*, 1: 77.
98. See Chapter 1, this volume.
99. Henry Adams, *The Education*, 259; see also Alfred Kazin, *On Native Grounds* (New York: Harcourt, Brace, & World, 1942), 194.
100. Kazin, 198.

Adamses of *The Degradation of the Democratic Dogma*. Henry's murky, prolix musings on the law of entropy are put in context by Brooks's introductory essay. The Adams brothers saw the defeat of their grandfather, John Quincy Adams, by Andrew Jackson as the fatal point of no return in American history. The election of 1828 had signified the end of the promise of enlightened Federalist rule and the rationally controlled development of the interior. With Jackson came the deliberate creation of a mass democracy and "spoils system," the triumph of avarice and competition, both political and economic. "Democracy," wrote Brooks, "was an infinite mass of conflicting minds and of conflicting interests." Though it might be temporarily mastered by demagogues like Jackson, such a system was essentially rudderless and tended toward self-degradation. Its effect, finally, had been

> to turn enormous numbers of women into the ranks of the lower paid classes of labor, but far worse, in substance, to destroy the influence of women in modern civilization.... The woman, as the cement of society, the head of the family, and the centre of cohesion, has, for all intents and purposes, ceased to exist.[101]

Kennan explained his propensity toward the eighteenth century as the natural result of his family's estrangement from the nineteenth and twentieth: "In pioneer families such as ours the eighteenth century lasted a half century longer than the name suggests – down to the 1860s – just as it did in the American South, and in Russia." His father tended "to take refuge in the eighteenth century of his youth."[102] Kennan's interest in the eighteenth century political tradition began around 1930 when he read Charles and Mary Beards's *The Rise of American Civilization*. He wrote his Russian friend Volodia of his surprise that John Adams, Hamilton, and the Federalists had never intended to create a mass democracy. Moreover, "If they disapproved of democracy for a population predominately White, Protestant and British, faced with relatively simple problems, would they not have turned over in their graves" at the thought of democracy extended to masses of poorly educated blacks and Southern European immigrants? In the same letter he contrasted the lives of people trapped in a middle-class routine with the "pride and assurance" of a young "aristocratic couple" whom he met in New York. Of the *New Republic* and the *Nation*, he noted, "I may be wrong...but I seem to detect an unproductive bitterness, a theoreticalness, and a negative dogmatism which

101. Henry Adams, *The Degradation of the Democratic Doctrine* (1919), introduction by Brooks Adams (New York: Peter Smith, 1949), 109, 119.
102. *Memoirs*, 1: 7–8.

might well result from always having kept so completely away from participation in practical politics."[103]

There was more than a trace of romantic egotist – and sophomoric snob – in Kennan at this point; there are also signs of his intellectual trajectory. In his dislike of the leading eastern liberal magazines – and of a posture that a later age would call "radical chic" – there were shades of Amory Blaine, the "spiritually unmarried man" and sensitive middle westerner. Amory had upbraided his Princeton roommate:

> Look at you; you're on *New Democracy*, considered the most brilliant weekly in the country. . . . What's your business? Why, to be so clever and interesting and as brilliantly cynical as possible about every man, every doctrine, book, or policy that is assigned to you to deal with.[104]

Certainly there was something a little fatuous about privileged youths defending the downtrodden – and their international champion, Stalin's Russia – from the sanctuary of their editorial offices. There was also a touch of envy in Amory and Kennan: the liberals had the limelight. Liberal opinion makers, in any event, were nearly always the main target of his periodic outbursts on the subject of the Russians.[105]

Kennan's dislike of American liberalism was a fillip in his discovery of the eighteenth century; he could no more identify with the contemporary alternative – Rotary Club conservatism – than could Lewis or Fitzgerald. The Adams–Hamilton tradition was another window of escape to someone who had by now taken to heart his father's distress about the deteriorating landscape of American life. The decay of the Federalist system, based, inter alia, on limited suffrage and the rule of a meritocratic elite, provided an explanation for the degeneration of U.S. politics and pointed to the solution.

Caesars old and new

Kennan accords a secondary role to ideology in his view of political behavior.[106] Ideology, Marxist or otherwise, is more often than not a

---

103. GFK to Volodia Kozhevnikoff (a member of the Russian family Kennan was close to in Berlin), Oct. 20, 1930. Quoted in C. B. Wright book manuscript, 38–29. CBW KBP, GCML.
104. Fitzgerald, *This Side of Paradise*, 214.
105. The "long telegram" is a classic example. An earlier example is the letter to Walt Farris, Jan. 12, 1931, in which he argued the incompatibility of the U.S. and Soviet systems. When they fell out, the U.S. liberals "who now find the Soviets so pleasant, will be the first ones to be crushed in the clash." CBW KBP, GCML.
106. On this point, see Louis Halle, "The World of George Kennan," *New Republic*, 145 (Aug. 7, 1961), 21–3. For a highly critical treatment of this point see Stephanson.

tool or smoke screen behind which lurk more "permanent character-istics."[107] This tendency is connected to an underlying impatience and dislike of all elaborate intellectual systems laying claim to obedience and scientific truth, as well as to the Protestant conviction that indi-viduals are ultimately responsible for their acts. One senses that the dislike and discounting of ideology were also related to a romantic preoccupation with self-expression and authenticity as opposed to the imitation of accepted, classical standards.[108] What counts in Kennan's intellectual world are such factors as climate, geography, and natural resources, organically shaping character and behavior in ways that are deep and unalterable in the short run – the kind of principles drummed into him by Professor Joseph C. Green at Princeton.[109] Equally import-ant are human passion and fallibility: the love of power, wealth, and glory, avarice, envy, fear, and pride. Here again Kennan's outlook has an eighteenth century cast[110] and suggests the influence of the book that he claimed in the forties had been the most influential of his life, *The Decline and Fall of the Roman Empire* by Edward Gibbon.

Gibbon (1737–94), like other Enlightenment thinkers, was funda-mentally concerned with the problem of civic virtue, "the passion for the public good,"[111] which was thought to have animated the citizen of the classical republic and was rooted in landholding and the qualities of hardiness, frugality, and arms-bearing dexterity that life on the land engendered. Like Hume, Smith, and Hamilton, Gibbon recognized that the modern civilization in which he lived, based increasingly on self-interest, commercial wealth, and mobile as opposed to real property, was inevitably subversive of civic virtue, and that the very success of a republic contained the seeds of its destruction:

> The republic was vulnerable to corruption, to political, moral, or economic changes which destroyed the equality on which it rested, and these changes might occur not accidentally but in consequence of the republic's own virtue. Because it was virtuous, it defeated its enemies; because it defeated its enemies, it acquired empire; but empire brought to some citizens – chiefly military commanders and economic speculators – the opportunity

---

107. On Russia's "permanent characteristics as a world power," see GFK lecture on Russia, May 20, 1938, GKP, box 16.
108. On this point see *Memoirs*, 1: 8, 15, 514.
109. For Kennan's comments on Professor Green's course, see ibid., 14.
110. It has been argued that the Age of Reason might have been called the "Age of Passion" or the "Age of Human Nature" for all the attention paid to these subjects. Gerald Stourzh, *Alexander Hamilton and the Age of Republican Government* (Stan-ford, Calif.: Stanford University Press, 1970), 76.
111. Ibid., 64.

to acquire power incompatible with equality and uncontrollable by law, and so the republic was destroyed by success and excess.[112]

In the great debate between the ancients and the moderns, Gibbon, like Hamilton, sided with the latter; that is, he believed that the rise of a commercial economy and the culture and comfort it had afforded

> had been worth the loss of virtue which it entailed. . . . But the ancient image of virtue was never overthrown or abandoned, and in consequence, it had to be recognized that the virtue of commercial and cultivated man was never complete, his freedom and independence never devoid of the elements of corruption. No theory of human progress could be constructed which did not carry the negative implication that progress was at the same time decay.[113]

This sophisticated ambivalence and historical skepticism toward modern civilization provided an intellectual foundation and congenial framework for Kennan's instinctive doubts. The paradox of progress, the loss of virtue and vitality entailed in the transition from agrarian self-sufficient to complex capitalist forms of social organization, were after all at the center of Kennan's own concerns. Like Chekhov's, Gibbon's fatalism was combined with an equanimity and optimism that appealed to Kennan.

Certainly there was food for thought in Gibbon's treatment of the Roman republic and the vicissitudes of Western history until the fall of Constantinople. Louis Halle claimed that Gibbon explained Stalinism for Kennan better than did Marx.[114] An apt precedent was the paranoid despotism of Constantine, who weakened the army for fear of conspiracy, impoverished agriculture to finance a parasitical bureaucracy, and embraced a new, fanatical religion to cement his rule.[115] In the thirties, Kennan compared the purges to "a grim palace revolution." Stalin's fundamental concern, he later wrote, "was the protection of his

---

112. J. G. A. Pocock, "Gibbon's *Decline and Fall* and the Worldview of the Late Enlightenment," in *Virtue, Commerce and History* (Cambridge: Cambridge University Press, 1985), 145–46.

113. Ibid., 148.

114. See Halle. Halle served under Kennan on the Policy Planning Staff in the late forties and was a personal friend.

115. "The same timid policy of dividing whatever is united, of reducing whatever is eminent, of dreading every active power, and of expecting that the most feeble will prove the most obedient, seems to pervade the institutions of several princes, and particularly those of Constantine." Edward Gibbon, *The Decline and Fall of the Roman Empire* (Chicago: Encyclopedia Britannica Great Books Edition, 1952), 1: 247.

personal position." His "favored strategy," both internally and externally, "was a simple one . . . 'divide and rule.'"[116]

Gibbon had much to say about early Russian history: the repeated attempts by Russian tribes to plunder Constantinople, the moderating effect of Christianity, the belief that "the Russians . . . should become masters of Constantinople." He saw modern Russia as a "civilized empire" but hazarded, "Perhaps the present generation may yet behold the accomplishment of the prediction."[117] Anticipating and – it appears – inspiring Mackinder,[118] Gibbon traced the impact of the marauding horsemen who poured forth from Asia over the millennium 400–1400. It was the Goths, pressed from behind by the Huns, who shattered the defenses of the Empire in the fifth century.[119] In the thirteenth it was the turn of Gengis Khan and Timour. Gibbon recounted the Roman containment of the nations beyond the Rhine and the Danube,[120] as well as the confrontation between land and sea power dear to Mahan and Mackinder, and an episode that gives pause to the modern reader. Timour,

> the lord of so many *tomans*, or myriads of horse was not master of a single galley. The two passages of the Bosphorus and the Hellespont, of Constantinople and Gallipoli, were possessed, the one by the Christians, the other by the Turks. On this great occasion they forgot the difference of religion, to act with union and firmness in the common cause.

Timour had been contained with relative ease; his ambition to conquer the world Gibbon called a "remote and perhaps imaginary danger."[121]

In the meantime, however, the Tartar hordes had spread "to the Black Sea and both Moscow and Kiow . . . were reduced to ashes; a temporary ruin, less fatal than the deep, perhaps indelible, mark which a servitude of two hundred years has imprinted on the character of the Russians."[122] When Kennan himself described Russia's "permanent characteristics," he invoked the vast, defenseless spaces and a political culture marked by dogmatism and servility.[123] Like Gibbon he saw Russia as distinct culturally from Asia but not planted in the West. The

---

116. GFK, "Fair Day Adieu!"; *Russia and the West Under Lenin and Stalin* (New York: Mentor Books, 1960), 239; *Memoirs*, 1: 70.
117. Gibbon, 2: 443–47; on contemporary Russia see also "General Observations on the Fall of the Roman Empire in the West," ibid., 632.
118. On Mackinder see Chapter 1, this volume.
119. Gibbon, 1: 414–18.
120. Ibid., 2: 494.
121. Ibid., 503.
122. Ibid., 484.
123. GFK lecture on Russia, May 20, 1938, GKP, box 16.

promising periods of Russian history occurred when its rulers looked westward, while messianic Slavophilism was a natural countertendency. In 1942, he referred to the revolutionary regime as the "renewed triumph of the Slavophils."[124] Stalin, as Kennan later depicted him, was Asiatic by comparison to European Russians (including Lenin) – he sprang from "the seething, savage underworld of the Transcaucasus" – but distinct from the unfathomable world of China.[125]

A fundamental lesson Kennan absorbed from Gibbon is connected to the theme of virtue–progress–empire–decline, as applied to the United States itself. It was the United States, after all, that was in the throes of transition from republic to empire, whose commercial success undermined its agrarian roots, whose political system felt the effects of immigration by diverse races and cultures. Gibbon traced the decline of Rome to the reign of Caesar Augustus, the first emperor, who had emerged victorious after twenty years of civil war. Augustus's fatal step was the destruction of the independence of the Senate: "The principles of a free constitution are irrevocably lost when the legislative power is nominated by the executive."[126] Gibbon was not defending democracy: "The citizens exercise the power of sovereignty, and those powers will first be abused and afterwards lost, if they are committed to an unwieldy multitude."[127] Rather, Augustus had completed the work of the civil wars that had undermined the constitutional position of the virtuous, arms-bearing and landowning classes represented in the Senate. Their loss of power and responsibility, followed by years of peace, "introduced a slow and secret poison into the vitals of the empire. The minds of men were gradually reduced to the same level, the fire of genius was extinguished, and even the military spirit evaporated."[128] The plebeian classes had been the emperor's accomplice: "Viewing with a secret pleasure, the humiliation of the aristocracy, [they] demanded only bread and public shows."[129]

Kennan's disaffection from the American system arose from his observation of urban politics, to which Gibbon's remark about the "unwieldy multitude" could easily be applied.[130] The force of Gibbon's

124. GFK lecture given at Bad Nauheim in 1942, GKP, box 6.
125. GFK, *Russia and the West*, 231, 259.
126. Gibbon, 1: 25.
127. Ibid., 14.
128. Ibid., 23.
129. Ibid., 24.
130. Kennan quotes this passage from Gibbon in *Democracy and the Student Left* (Boston: Little, Brown, 1968), 206; mentioned by Stephanson, 225. On this point see also Barton Gellman, *Contending with Kennan* (New York: Praeger, 1984), chap. 4.

argument grew stronger as Kennan contended in the thirties with the consequences of popular government. Around the time his first child was born in 1933, Congress reacted to the economic crisis by cutting Foreign Service remuneration by about 60 percent, "abruptly, without warning."[131] A second incident occurred in late 1933. Kennan had recommended that extra care be taken to guarantee the rights of U.S. citizens in the Soviet Union after diplomatic recognition. The president ignored the advice, if he was even aware of it, in his dealings with Foreign Minister Litvinov. This remained in Kennan's mind

> the first of many lessons ... on one of the most consistent and incurable traits of American statesmanship – namely its neurotic self-consciousness and introversion, the tendency to make statements and take actions with regard not to their effect on the international scene ... but to their effect on those echelons of American opinion, Congressional opinion first and foremost, to which the respective statesmen are anxious to appeal.[132]

Kennan added, "Each statesman has to be the judge of the compromises he must make, in the form of a certain amount of showmanship and prestidigitation in order to retain the privilege of conducting foreign policy at all. No one understood this better than FDR."[133]

There is no need to belabor the alienation of Kennan and his colleagues in the Division of Eastern European Affairs (EE) from the Roosevelt administration – the story has been told many times.[134] The crowning indignity was the arrival of Joseph Davies, a liberal businessman, as ambassador and the breakup of the division in 1937. Davies, who landed in the midst of the purge trials, was immediately suspected

> of a readiness to bend both the mission and its function to the purposes of personal publicity at home. What mortified us most of all was the impression we received that the President knew nothing about, or cared nothing about, what we had accomplished in building up the Embassy at Moscow. ... Had the President wished to slap us down and mock us for our efforts in the development of Soviet–American relations, he could not have done better than with this appointment.[135]

Five months after the Davies appointment, "the entire [EE] shop ... was liquidated." Kennan suspected the White House; in fact, FDR had

131. *Memoirs*, 1: 41.
132. Ibid., 53. See also GFK to Charles Taquery, Dec. 22, 1965, GKP, box 31 65OL.
133. *Memoirs*, 1: 54.
134. See, e.g., Yergin, Issacson and Thomas, chap. 5; Stephanson, pt. 1; Mayers, 29–47.
135. *Memoirs*, 1: 82–83.

approved the move, though Welles was directly responsible.[136] Kennan was transferred from Moscow and ended at the Russian desk of the consolidated Department of European Affairs. Kennan, Davies wrote, had been in Russia "too long for his own good."[137] After a year he was taken off Russian affairs altogether until 1944.

By the mid-thirties Kennan profoundly dissented from official policy: "Never – neither then nor at any later date," he wrote in his *Memoirs*, "did I consider the Soviet Union a fit ally or associate, actual or potential, for this country. The idea of trying to enlist Soviet strength in a cause for which we were unwilling to develop and mobilize our own seemed to me particularly dangerous."[138] Kennan has little to say about other aspects of the administration's policy, but he must have been alarmed by its apparent unwillingness to go beyond rhetorical posturing (e.g., the 1937 Chicago speech), its costly, vainglorious crusading at home (e.g., the Supreme Court battle), and its exaltation of Latin America, a part of the world for which Kennan lacked the slightest familiarity, affinity, or regard.[139] Kennan undoubtedly sensed the hostility, cynicism, and moral smugness with regard to Europe pervading the administration. But what he considered truly intolerable about Roosevelt was what seemed his blithe contempt for the virtuous professional diplomats. To add insult to injury, FDR played his handful of court favorites – the Grotonians Welles and Phillips – into whose circles he could scarcely hope to enter. (Kennan would send his only son to Groton.)

In the aftermath of the "purge" of EE, Kennan renewed the "philosophic and political discussions" begun with his colleague Bernard Gufler at Princeton.[140] It was at this point that he produced his now well-known philippic "The Prerequisites: Notes on the Problem of the United States in 1938." It combined two basic features of his outlook, a critique of modern American culture reminiscent of Adams and Lewis and eighteenth century political conservatism. The document is noteworthy for the coherence, if not the practicality, of its recommendations. Kennan "held no brief for the rule of the majority in the U.S." "We do

136. Ibid., 84; see also Chapter 2, this volume.
137. Davies to Robert Kelley, Feb. 10, 1937, Joseph Davies Papers, box 3, Library of Congress.
138. *Memoirs*, 1: 57.
139. When he later visited Latin America, he wrote, "It seems to me unlikely that there could be any other region of the earth in which nature and human behavior could have combined to produce a more unhappy and hopeless background for the conduct of human life." Ibid., 480.
140. Ibid., 85.

not consider the mass of our own population sufficiently enlightened, sufficiently homogeneous in its political thought to be capable of taking responsibility for government." Political power, in any event, was "largely exercised by a conglomerate minority composed of professional politicians and powerfully organized special interests." Kennan proposed a return to eighteenth century principles by limiting the suffrage to white males born in the United States: "A certain number of highly intelligent and right-minded people would not be allowed to vote... by way of compensation, the ground would be taken out from under the feet of a large number of useless and harmful politicians" – of the type, presumably, who had cut the pay of the Foreign Service to curry favor with the voters. Kennan was scathing on the subject of American women, for whom the loss of direct political power might restore a measure of "strength and dignity." Here was his most explicit statement on the postpioneer and – as of 1920 – politically empowered female. It read for all the world like a piece of dialogue from Sinclair Lewis:

> Her club life has become a symbol of futility and inanity. In national politics she has placed her enormous power in the hands of bigots, charlatans and racketeers. Finally she has not even done well by herself. She has ruined in large part some of the greatest aspects of her own sex. She has become in comparison with women of other countries delicate, high strung, unsatisfied, flat chested and flat voiced.[141]

At the center of Kennan's reformed system was not a charismatic leader; on the contrary, his concern was to check the Caesarist tendencies of the existing system. He favored rule by "a minority selected from all sections and classes of the population... on the basis of individual fitness for the exercise of authority."[142] He was speaking, in effect, of the kind of republican senate of public-spirited worthies evoked by Gibbon, a model, in turn, for Federalists like Hamilton. Needless to say, there was little use in pressing such ideas – even if the underlying assumptions were probably more widely shared in the interwar period than is commonly supposed. Nor were they a passing fancy: years later he called for the creation of "a panel or pool of outstanding people, that would comprise perhaps 500–1000 souls.... One could then say to the electorate: 'You can nominate people for election to the

---

141. The author has not had access to the original of this document, which is no longer available in the Kennan papers. The document has, however, been quoted at length by a number of writers. See, e.g., C. B. Wright book manuscript; Issacson and Thomas, 171–72; Stephanson, 216–21; Mayers, 49–54; Walter Hixson, *George F. Kennan: Cold War Iconoclast* (New York: Columbia University Press, 1989), 7–8.
142. GFK, "The Prerequisites."

Senate – but only from this body' . . . I am talking of a 'meritocracy.' "[143]

Franklin Roosevelt represented for Kennan what Jackson had represented for the Adams brothers, and the Emperor Augustus for Gibbon. Certainly – along with Stalin – the president was a central influence in the development of his outlook. In his bitter frustration with the administration, Kennan might have found wry satisfaction in knowing that Adolf Berle began letters to FDR (until the White House secretaries stopped him) not as "Dear Mr. President," but "My Dear Caesar."

Europe, Russia, and America

Kennan later said of Roosevelt as foreign policy leader:

> The truth is – there is no avoiding it – that Franklin Roosevelt, for all his charm and skill as a political leader, was, when it came to foreign policy, a very superficial man, ignorant, dilettantish, with a severely limited intellectual horizon. . . . Roosevelt knew nothing about Russia and very little about Europe. This in itself would not have been so bad. What was worse was that he did not seek or value the advice of those who did know something about these places.[144]

This was a judgment deeply rooted in Kennan's personal feelings and experience in dealing with the problems of Germany and Russia. Those countries constituted part of a single problem: "Since to my mind a sensible policy toward Germany was the first requirement of a sound postwar policy with relation to the Soviet Union itself, the despair, and in some instances, horror . . . with which I viewed our immediate postwar policies towards Germany did more to give me a sense of hopelessness and frustration . . . than did such differences as I had with the administration over the handling of our bilateral relations with Moscow itself."[145]

Needless to say Roosevelt did have at least two close advisers who knew something about Russia and Europe. Adolf Berle and William Bullitt stood somewhere between – in a sense they bridged – two basic tendencies of thought in twentieth century American diplomatic culture: the protocontainment outlook with its emphasis on Anglo-Saxon solidarity, sea versus land power, the need to turn German and Japanese

143. Quoted in Barton Gellman, 201–2. See also GFK, *Around a Cragged Hill*, 236–48, for his proposal for an American council of state.
144. GFK comment during symposium, "Allied Leadership during World War II," published in *Survey*, 21 (Winter–Spring 1975), 30. See also Kennan's introduction to Bullitt, ed., xiv–xv.
145. *Memoirs*, 1: 175.

strength against Russia; and the Europhobic-hemispheric outlook of Sumner Welles, which placed its hopes in the Good Neighbor policy and viewed France and Britain with contempt. As has been seen,[146] FDR did accept the counsel of Berle and Bullitt, but only to a point. FDR shared the view that the United States should not become involved in a war to uphold the Versailles settlement, that revision was necessary, that the victors bore much of the blame, and that the Western Hemisphere was the last bastion of civilization. But he discounted the dire predictions about Russia and the desire to reconsolidate East and Central Europe.

In the political-ideological constellation of the thirties, Kennan found himself remarkably close to Berle and Bullitt. Though there is little evidence that Kennan read the turn-of-the-century geopoliticians, their ideas had been adopted by the older generation of diplomats with whom Kennan was in contact. Kennan had studied Russia from the standpoint of Berlin, and he had absorbed Gibbon, the grandfather of the protocontainment view. He had a natural sympathy for the views of the elder Kennan, the leading American crusader against czarist Russia.[147] Because he had not been involved directly in the events of 1917–19, Kennan had not felt the whole gale of Wilsonian idealism nor the bitter letdown of Versailles. Neverthless, he had felt on graduating from Princeton "the promptings of a vague Wilsonian liberalism [and] a regret that the United States had rejected membership in the League of Nations." He later said, "I think much more highly of Wilson than people might suppose." There was a streak of frustrated Wilsonian idealism in his makeup that occasionally shone through. He had been close enough in age to feel the magnetic pull of Amory Blaine and the "lost generation" of the twenties. There was his initial, guarded hope that things might go differently with the Russians after 1933 and a feeling that the victors shared responsibility for the failure of 1919 – he later spoke of the "vengeful, emotional and unrealistic spirit that dominated French policy." Such sentiments linked him, to a point, with the ex-Wilsonian *jeunesse radicale*.[148]

In the hierarchy of the Roosevelt administration, Kennan stood light-

---

146. See Chapter 2.
147. See GFK, *Soviet–American Relations*, vol. 1: *1917–1920, Russia Leaves the War* (Princeton, N.J.: Princeton University Press, 1956), 12; also vol. 2: *The Decision to Intervene* (Princeton, N.J.: Princeton University Press, 1958), 333, 358. See also Travis, 256–57, 292–93.
148. *Memoirs*, 1: 16, 94. Kennan said of Wilson, "I hold him to be a far greater man than FDR whose historical status I expect to decline as that of Wilson rises." GFK to Augie, Aug. 17, 1956, GKP, box 31.

years from Berle, a New Dealer and member of the inner court. They would have had much to say to each other and did meet briefly in 1942. Kennan's relationship with Bullitt was one of the most important of his life. Bullitt made a vivid impression: "handsome, urbane, full of charm and enthusiasm, a product of Philadelphia society and Yale but with considerable European residence and with a flamboyance of personality that is right out of F. Scott Fitzgerald."[149] Kennan saw him "as a member of that remarkable group... born just before the turn of the century (it included such people as Cole Porter, Ernest Hemingway, John Reed, and Jim Forrestal...) for whom the First World War was the great electrifying experience of life. They were a striking generation, full of talent and exuberance."[150] Bullitt launched Kennan's career by taking him to Moscow in 1933. They did not remain close after an initial period,[151] but each left his mark on the other. Kennan witnessed the ambassador's fruitless wrangling with Litvinov over the Russian war debt and Comintern activities in the United States. Kennan's advice to expect little from the Soviet Union was incorporated into Bullitt's outlook and dispatches by the time the latter left Moscow in 1936.[152] When Bullitt became a precocious advocate of what would eventually be called containment, Kennan could claim the role of stimulator and heir apparent.[153]

At the same time, Kennan's position between September 1938 when he was assigned to Prague and his return from Germany in early 1942 – after several months' internment – was a rather solitary one and, among contemporary U.S. diplomats, unique. No one saw or *felt* the interconnected problem of Europe, Russia, and America from the same set of angles, or with the same intensity, as Kennan. From the viewpoint of a conservative German, the problem of the late thirties was how to prevent European civilization from being crushed, culturally and geopolitically, between the two non-European giants. From the viewpoint of a middle western American, the problem was how to contain the Augustan tendencies in American domestic and foreign policy. Kennan's "isolationism" was always double-edged: it was concerned with pro-

---

149. GFK quoted in Will Brownell and Richard N. Billings, *So Close to Greatness: A Biography of William C. Bullitt* (New York: Macmillan, 1987), 104.

150. GFK, Introduction to Bullitt, ed., xv–xvi. Bullitt was born in 1891.

151. This is according to Loy Henderson. Issacson and Thomas, 163.

152. On this point see C. B. Wright book manuscript, 59.

153. For a discussion of Bullitt's January 1943 memorandum to FDR calling, inter alia, for an Anglo-American line in Eastern Europe to block the Russians see Chapter 3, this volume. Of this memo Kennan later wrote, "It deserves a place among the major historical documents of the time." Introduction to Bullitt, ed., xiv.

tecting the United States from foreign entanglement but in equal measure with protecting Europe from the United States. Finally, from the viewpoint of a Chekhovian Russian, the problem was to create conditions that would allow for the natural evolution of the regime. It was this complex perspective-cum-agenda that explains Kennan the contradictious planner and statesman after 1945.

From each viewpoint, Germany was central. With his Central European sense of cultural vulnerability and geopolitical claustrophobia, his view of Versailles and of Bolshevism, one might expect to find in Kennan's outlook the kind of agnostic, even sympathetic attitude toward Hitler, or rather his revisionist program, that marked the views of Berle, Bullitt, and countless non-Nazi Europeans. There are traces of such an attitude in his 1935 paper "The War Problem of the Soviet Union," in which he gave a limited interpretation to Hitler's aims.[154] At the time of the September 1938 crisis, he wrote:

> It is generally agreed that the break-up of the limited degree of unity which the Hapsburg Empire represented was unfortunate for all concerned. Other forces are now at work which are struggling to create a new form of unity.... To these forces Czechoslovakia has been tragically slow in adjusting herself.... The adjustment – and this is the main thing – has now come.[155]

Such reasoning was identical to Berle's: a natural, necessary process of reconsolidation was at work; Hitler, willy-nilly, was its agent; the result, on balance, was positive for the West.[156]

The occupation of the rest of Czechoslovakia in 1939 was the end of illusions – including Kennan's – but then he had not had many. Nazi behavior can have come as little surprise to someone who had admired George Messersmith in Vienna and who had written two years before Hitler's accession that the Germans' "only conception of the relation between human beings in essence [was] that of slave and master." In a remarkable phrase that summed up his view of the German problem, he wrote, "they are the final hope...they are now the final despair of Western European civilization."[157] Perhaps he had already read Gibbon's description of the savagery of German tribes that, under

---

154. For copy see GKP, box 1; also cited in *Memoirs*, 1: 70–72. Kennan discounted German designs on the Ukraine.

155. GFK, *From Prague after Munich* (Princeton, N.J.: Princeton University Press, 1968), 5. This is a collection of Kennan's reports written at the time. See also *Memoirs*, 1: 95.

156. See Chapter 2, this volume.

157. On Kennan's view of Messersmith, see *Memoirs*, 1: 66. GFK letter to Walt Ferris, Jan. 12, 1931, quoted in C. B. Wright book manuscript, 9, n. 66.

Roman tutelage, added to the backbone of the Empire.[158] Kennan was saying that the Germans alone had the strength to be the anchor and bulwark of an autonomous Europe but left to their own devices were tragically unfit to play the role.

Kennan's most interesting attempt to deal with the German problem before Pearl Harbor was occasioned by the sudden descent of Sumner Welles on Europe in February 1940. Kennan had been attached to the Berlin Embassy as of September 1939 and was sent to Rome to meet the mission. Kennan described his encounter with the most Olympian of FDR's advisers:

> Mr. Welles seemed unaware of my presence and evinced no interest on my views on Russia. So little did I enter into the ken of the party that on leaving Rome for Berlin they forgot me entirely. I learned of their departure only when I happened to see the cavalcade of official cars pass me on the street, late one evening, on its way to the station.[159]

The incident is an apt summary of Kennan's position and attitude with respect to the Roosevelt administration. He nonetheless produced a paper for the mission that sheds light on his views. He tried to dispel the idea of a negotiated peace with Germany and of dealing with much-vaunted moderates who might be waiting in the wings. This was before his contact with several of the leading opponents of Hitler, in particular Count Helmuth von Moltke, whose courage and idealism deeply moved him.[160] He also emphasized that the clock could not be set back: "Germany has simply been unified and thoroughly so. . . . Hitler is now stamping out the last vestiges of particularism and class differences. . . . German unity is a fact."[161] Kennan concluded, paradoxically, that if a "sound political basis for Europe" were to be found, it was in

> a frank recognition of the value of particularism in European life and its essence must be in the reestablishment of the delicate balance thrown out of adjustment by the rise of national states in Germany and Italy and the demise of the Hapsburg Empire. A unified Europe is, for anyone who knows it, an ugly picture. Standardization, an elemment of cohesion at home, bears with it nothing but the seeds of dissolution for Europe.

Germany "must become not only one but many kingdoms and the bonds of dynasty whose strength lies in their apparent absurdity must again be stretched across the continent."[162]

158. Gibbon, 1: 92–95.
159. *Memoirs*, 1: 116.
160. Ibid., 19–24.
161. Ibid., 118, quoting "Article on German Nationalism."
162. "Article on German Nationalism," Feb., 1940, GKP, box 1.

Kennan was obviously thinking of something different from dismemberment à la Roosevelt or Welles: a formula not to weaken Europe or to open it to a flood of American imports, but to restore its internal balance. He was groping for a structure that would render German nationalism harmless and reestablish a sense of the cultural community of Europe, while avoiding the American precedent of homogenization and leveling. He emphasized that the Americans were not "the ones to devise the readjustment . . . it runs counter to our own ideas, our own institutions. It demands far more than we could ever give in historical insight, in perspective. The worlds are so different [*vive la différence!*] that any projection of our own conception onto European problems is almost bound to be invidious."[163] The same spirit moved him to take an extraordinary personal initiative – leading to his first meeting with FDR – as counselor of legation at Lisbon in 1943 in order to prevent what he feared would be the economic debauching of the Azores by gigantic U.S. bases and the upsetting of Portugal's delicate international position.[164]

Immediately after the German invasion of the Soviet Union in June 1941, Kennan wrote Loy Henderson in Washington:

> Throughout the war, the Moscow government has been most vehement in insisting that its own policy was based on sheer self-interest and in expressing its determination to do nothing to aid any warring power. It has thus no claim on Western sympathies. . . . Such a view would not preclude the extension of material aid wherever called for by our own self-interest. It would, however, preclude anything which might identify us politically or ideologically with the Russian war effort.[165]

One can imagine Kennan's reaction to the exile of Henderson to Baghdad and the dispatch of Joseph Davies to court Stalin in 1943.[166] Practically alone among U.S. officials in 1939–41, Kennan visited Nazi-occupied Europe and studied the techniques of German control. What he saw appeared to confirm Gibbon's view that "there is nothing more contrary to nature than the attempt to hold in obedience distant provinces." With no message for Europe but German nationalism, the Nazis would have either to maintain a permanent military occupation or to allow their satellites to "pursue aims by no means identical, and at times even in conflict with" their own.[167] He also observed the adminis-

---

163. Ibid.
164. See *Memoirs*, 1, chap. 6, esp. 151.
165. Ibid., 133–34.
166. See Chapter 2, this volume.
167. *Memoirs*, 1: 129–30. Gibbon is quoted by Kennan. See also GFK, "The Technique of German Imperialism in Europe," Apr. 1941, GKP, box 23; GFK to J. Riddleberger, Nov. 20, 1941, assessing the German position. GKP, box 28.

trative structures the Germans had set up to tie together aspects of the Continental economy – banking, transport, raw material allocation. He recommended that these structures be taken over and run by the Allies to facilitate the postwar transition.[168]

Between mid-1942 and mid-1944, Kennan's position took on certain permanent characteristics. This was connected to his observation of the de facto economic integration of the Continent under Hitler (Chekhov had said, "There is nothing good that has not had evil germs in its beginning"),[169] as well as with the prospect – virtually certain after Roosevelt's declaration of unconditional surrender and the Red Army victories of 1943 – of Soviet encroachment on Germany. Perhaps Kennan's evolution was in some way related to his fleeting contact with Adolf Berle – it was Berle who solicited Kennan's views on Germany in June 1942. Berle was mulling over the problem of European federation at the time.

Between January and May 1944, Kennan was political adviser to John Winant, FDR's ambassador to London and representative to the European Advisory Commission (EAC), the body charged with preparing the German surrender terms and occupation zones. He now came into contact with high-level planning and was appalled by what he saw. Kennan had by this time met von Moltke, whom he envisioned as a leader of a reborn pro-Western Germany. When he read a State Department paper proposing the removal of entire categories of Germans (a total of 3 million people) from the state apparatus, he replied that mass punishment would place an unsustainable burden on the liberal elements while making martyrs of the nationalists. Defeat itself would discredit the extremists, while a new political leadership must be allowed to emerge naturally and organically.[170]

During this period Kennan was involved in an episode that, while minor, is one of the more curious and ironic of the war. The EAC was devoid of decision-making power, as FDR had intended. The British and Russians – who took the EAC more seriously – had reached an agreement on the line between the Soviet and two Western occupation zones in early 1944. On March 8, the U.S. EAC delegation was ordered

---

168. *Memoirs*, 1: 417; GFK memo on Germany, June 18, 1942, CBW KBP, GCML.
169. Anton Chekhov, *Ward No. 6*, in Leo Hamalian and Vera Von Wiren-Garczynski, eds., *Seven Russian Short Novel Masterpieces* (New York: Popular Library, 1967), 393.
170. *Memoirs*, 1: 175–78. See also GFK letter to Robert Murphy, U.S. political adviser for Germany, May 10, 1945, GKP, box 28. On same subject, see GFK to Sir L. Woodward, Mar. 4, 1965, GKP, box 31; GFK to G. Van Roon, Mar. 14, 1962, GKP 31.

by the War Department to present a counterproposal placing the U.S. zone much farther to the east (incorporating 51 percent of the population and 46 percent of the land area of Germany) and cutting "apparently without rhyme or reason across geographic and administrative boundaries."[171] Kennan believed the proposal was absurd. He surmised from a colleague that it was based on a line that FDR himself had penciled on a map in November 1943. The impasse led to a trip to Washington and Kennan's decision to go directly to the White House, where he had been briefly the previous October on the Azores bases matter. This was an extraordinary move for a relatively junior officer. One writer speaks of Kennan's "agonizing quest for personal recognition," and this was certainly the reaction of his colleagues at the time.[172]

Arriving at the Oval Office, Kennan had trouble this time in getting through to Roosevelt why he had come. The president "was already locked into his celebrated conflict with the British over which of us should have the Northern, and which the Southern, of the contemplated two Western zones. This was what was on his mind, and this was what he wanted to talk about."[173] When Kennan explained that it was the east–west, not the Anglo-American, line that he was concerned about, FDR "laughed gaily" and said that the War Department proposal was something he had once drawn "on the back of an envelope." He agreed to the Anglo-Soviet proposal and the necessary orders were sent. Kennan's intercession, in effect, resulted in the east–west division of Germany being drawn farther to the west than might have been the case if FDR had persisted with his notion. Kennan personally favored a line as far east as possible but had strict orders from the State Department not to volunteer his own opinion.[174] In any case, Kennan admitted, he was no match for the Roosevelt technique of "charming you right out of the room before you could say anything."[175] Still, he now understood that Roosevelt was more preoccupied with British wiles and with positioning the United States to leave Europe than with Russia. FDR was also intent on punishing the Germans and saw the war as a simple extension of the first: "All evidence suggests that at no time did he ever become aware of the difference of the social forces from which Wilhelm II and Hitler drew, respectively, their strength. I don't think he ever

171. *Memoirs*, 1: 168.
172. Hixson, 14.
173. *Memoirs*, 1: 171.
174. Ibid., 171. See also GFK to E. Durbrow, Dec. 2, 1963, GKP, box 31.
175. George Urban and George Kennan, "A Conversation with George Kennan," *Encounter*, 47, no. 3 (Sept. 1976), 26.

realized that Hitler's following was predominantly petty bourgeois and that the conservative land owning and military circles, which had played so prominent a part in World War I, viewed Hitler with distaste and distrust."[176]

Kennan had had a firsthand look at what he later called the "entire complex of illusions and calculations and expectations" constituting the "Rooseveltian dream."[177] A policy of punishment, he wrote, would mean "renouncing the aid of the strongest people in Europe in the rebuilding of European society." Kennan had his own misgivings about a united Germany, but now called for partition "within the framework of European federation." A new Germany within a "wider federation" would allow the Anglo-Americans to "enlist" Germany "in the interests of the continent as a whole."[178] He returned to the theme in June 1944:

> I should certainly not recommend any hasty and grandiose schemes for the United States of Europe and I feel any real movement for federation should stop for the time being at the Pyrenees and the Baltic Sea. But some degree of federation for Central and West Europe ... seems to offer the only way out of this labyrinth of conflict which is Europe today.

In this talk, given on the eve of his return to Moscow, Kennan declared his dissent from "the general lines of thinking in our country ... with respect to future policy towards Europe." Except perhaps for Berle and Bullitt – the former was destined for exile to Brazil, while the latter had now joined the entourage of Roosevelt's nemesis, Charles de Gaulle – no American had understood the implications of Roosevelt's Europe earlier than Kennan or would invest more energy in a personal countervision.[179]

176. GFK to Louis Halle, Dec. 15, 1964, GKP, box 31.
177. See GFK lecture in Geneva, "The Shattering of the Rooseveltian Dream," May 1, 1965, GKP, box 21; GKP lecture, "The Roosevelt Error," Oct. 12, 1955, GKP, box 19.
178. See GFK letter (unsent) to John Winant, Mar. 1944, copy in CBW KBP, GCML.
179. GFK, "Remarks to Officers at the Dedication of the Legation at Lisbon," June 1944. After his break with FDR, Bullitt offered his services to General de Gaulle and was made an officer in the French army for the rest of the war.

5

Three worlds instead of two: Kennan and Europe, 1944–1950

A driving force

Controversy has pursued Kennan since the day he made his famous pronouncements in 1947. Kennan, his defenders, and detractors have debated the instruments, scope, and ultimate purpose of containment, the degree of foresight in Kennan's mind when he advanced the concept, and his consistency over time. Kennan later argued that his intention had been "the political containment of a political threat," that the policy was to be applied in a few select areas – Western Europe and Japan – and would lead to an eventual settlement with Moscow.[1] On the basis of Kennan's statements in the forties, his defenders back these claims.[2] Other commentators argue that Kennan's notion was geographically indiscriminate, that it made no distinction between political and military means, and that Kennan was either a self-conscious globalist or else a kind of scorcerer's apprentice.[3] Their critique seems

1. Mr. "X," "The Sources of Soviet Conduct," *Foreign Affairs*, 25, no. 4 (July 1947), 566–82; *Memoirs*, 1: 358, chap. 15; GFK, "Reflections on Containment," in T. L. Deibel and John Lewis Gaddis, eds., *Containing the Soviet Union: A Critique of U.S. Policy* (Washington, D.C.: Pergamon-Brassey's International Defense Publishers, 1987), 17.
2. See, e.g., John Lewis Gaddis, "Containment: A Reassessment, *Foreign Affairs*, 55, no. 4 (July 1977), 873–87. See also his *Strategies of Containment*, chap. 2. Another sympathetic, and exceptionally thorough, account of Kennan's policy-making role and influence as head of the PPS is Wilson Miscamble, *George F. Kennan and the Making of American Foreign Policy, 1947–1950* (Princeton, N.J.: Princeton University Press, 1992).
3. See Eduard Mark, "The Question of Containment: A Reply to John Lewis Gaddis," *Foreign Affairs*, 56, no. 3 (January 1978), 430–1. Mark says that the thrust of Kennan's containment was military and global. See also C. Ben Wright, "Mr 'X' and Containment," *Slavic Review*, 35, no. 1 (March 1976), 1–31, and Stephanson, 92–97. Both Wright and Stephanson say that Kennan did not distinguish between military and political means before 1948 and that he "simply did not see where some of his ideas

inspired by the original broadside delivered at Mr. "X" by Walter Lippmann in September 1947. Lippmann dismissed containment as a "strategic monstrosity," a futile, misdirected policy, and totally unsuited to the American political context. Kennan claimed to agree with much of this criticism while insisting that it did not apply to his version of containment.[4]

Though it is hardly possible to avoid entering into this controversy, the main purpose of this chapter is to trace the working out of Kennan's approach to the European Question between 1944 and 1950. In fact, Kennan's concept of containment did not spring fully developed from his consciousness in 1946 or 1947. We are dealing after all with the interaction between a not yet fully formed outlook and outside stimuli and events. To this could be added Kennan's own caveat that the statements and contributions of a government official "speaking in a governmental context, are not always indicative . . . of his own personal preferences."[5] It would be unreasonable to expect perfect accord among the vast number of speeches, memoranda, and comments generated by Kennan as National War College lecturer and director of the Policy Planning Staff.

It is also true that Kennan did not always weigh his words carefully or gauge their effect. A. J. P. Taylor wrote that Kennan "never appreciated the deeply emotional basis of his own outlook and was thus surprised when he evoked emotion in others."[6] This is partly true. During the period from mid-1944 to mid-1946, Kennan was driven by personal ambition, combined with a strong sense of exclusion and moral indignation. The Milwaukee clergyman who heard Kennan speak in 1946 caught something essential when he said, "Boy, you missed your calling." At some point, however, Kennan did become aware of the emotional wellsprings of his views. In 1949 he warned: "We must

might lead." Wright, 31. For another critical treatment, see Hixson. David Mayers casts Kennan "in a somewhat more negative light" than Gaddis: he "was more uncertain intellectually and more of a Cold Warrior in the late 1940s than he later wanted to admit." At the same time, Mayers emphasizes "the primacy of diplomacy" in Kennan's approach and dismisses Mark's charges. Mayers, 105–6 and chap. 6.

4. See Walter Lippmann, *The Cold War* (New York: Harper Bros., 1947), containing the author's September 1947 columns published in the *New York Herald Tribune*. See also *Memoirs*, 1: 357–61.

5. GFK, "George Kennan Replies [to C. Ben Wright]," *Slavic Review*, 35, no. 1 (March 1976), 36.

6. A. J. P. Taylor, Review of GFK, *Memoirs*, *Observer*, Jan. 28, 1968. On this point see also Kateb.

avoid letting emotion influence our judgements. *Emotion may be the driving force behind an effort to get at the bottom of our problems* and establish the truth, but it must never be allowed to become the method by which that inquiry is conducted."[7] This rings like a lesson learned from his own experience during the previous several years.

What renders Kennan's diplomatic project fundamentally consistent is his deeply emotional commitment to a set of objectives that grew naturally out of his earlier experience: an autonomous Europe, defined to encompass most of the territory west of the Soviet Union's interwar borders, a more liberal regime in Russia, and a self-contained United States. By 1950 he had incorporated his objectives into a coherent vision whose features had been recognizable since at least 1938.

7. *Memoirs*, 1: 299; GFK lecture, "Diplomacy as Intellectual Inquiry," Aug. 30, 1949, GKP, box 17; emphasis added.

The "seeds of a new convulsion"

We have seen how, after mid-1944, Franklin Roosevelt allowed his own postwar conception, based on great-power regional hegemony, to become scrambled in the popular mind with the universalism of Cordell Hull. FDR had come to embody William McNeill's myth. Its ingredients and emotional appeal were essentially Wilsonian. Among other consequences of this development was the counterattack of the anti-Wilsonian skeptics. With the possible exception of Bullitt, no one had taken the failure of the Fourteen Points more personally or denounced Wilson more bitterly than Walter Lippmann.[8] In *U.S. War Aims*, published in mid-1944, Lippmann dismissed the administration's Wilsonianism as a set of "prejudices formed in the Age of Innocence, in the century of American isolation." The United States "had then no need to arm, no need to find alliances, no need to take strategic precautions; Wilson's principles were a demand that the whole world take vows to live forever after on the same terms." Lippmann called for a peace on the basis of existing "historic civilized communities" – an "Eastern [Soviet] regional system" and an "Atlantic Community" with the United States, Britain, Canada, and France at its core. "Organic consultation" among the four was a wise policy regardless of future relations with the Russians – concerning which Lippmann was less optimistic than he had been in 1943. Lippmann called for the incorporation of Germany into the Atlantic Community in order to foster its dependence on Atlantic instead of middle European markets. "There is no other place for a peaceable Germany. For Germany must have a place somewhere."[9]

Such ideas had been in the air for forty years. Henry Adams had mused about an Atlantic combine: "If Germany could be held there, a century of friction would be saved."[10] The importance of splitting German and Russian power was central to the Anglo-Saxon geopoliticians, while the notion of a small, liberal Germany oriented toward overseas markets – as opposed to the big, autarchic, continental Germany of Hitler's conception – had been one of the classic options in German geopolitical discussion. At eighty-two, Halford Mackinder himself called, in effect, for a British–American–French alliance. He warned: "If the Soviet Union emerges from this war as conquerer of Germany, she must rank as the greatest land Power on the globe. . . .

8. See Steel, chap. 13.

9. Walter Lippmann, *U.S. War Aims* (Boston: Little, Brown, 1944), 118–28, 175–80. See also "The Big Four and World Peace: A Debate by Welles, Lippmann," *Newsweek*, Aug. 21, 1944, 96–107.

10. Henry Adams, *The Education*, 438–39.

The Heartland is the greatest natural fortress on earth. For the first time in history it is manned by a garrison sufficient both in numbers and quality."[11]

After mid-1944, Kennan devoted himself to exposing "the Rooseveltian dream."[12] He had probably read Lippmann's 1944 argument; in any event, he was on a similar wavelength at the time. In a February 1945 letter to Charles Bohlen, Kennan called for the recognition of Soviet and Western spheres of influence in Europe and condemned the administration's UN policy for "allowing the Russians to think that we were proposing a cleverly disguised statute for the collaboration of the strong in the browbeating of the weak."[13] On the same occasion, he spoke of an "Atlantic Community," of the need to incorporate as much of Germany as possible into the Western orbit, and of the conflict between Atlantic sea power and "jealous Eurasian landpower."[14] Both Lippmann and Kennan were saying that now that it was installed on the Continent the United States could not simply pack its bags and go home before organizing the West.[15]

Unlike Lippmann, however, Kennan saw German strength as a necessary ballast for Europe and was inclined to think in terms of a "continental option." Unlike Lippmann, he advanced the idea of a federation including Schleswig-Holstein, the Hanseatic cities, Hanover, the Rhineland, Baden-Württemberg, Bavaria, Allied-occupied Austria, along with Denmark, Holland, Belgium, Switzerland, Italy, and France. The Anglo-Saxons would stand behind, but were not part of, such a combination. He did not see this as "a very happy program" – it amounted to "a partition of Europe" – but it was a question of saving what could be saved from Roosevelt's policy of fragmentation and abandonment.[16] Finally, unlike both Lippmann and the Roosevelt administration, Kennan rejected the idea of a permanent "Russian regional system." Already – before Lippmann himself – he was wrestling with the problem of how to bring about the return of Russian power to

---

11. Mackinder, "The Round World and the Winning of the Peace," *Foreign Affairs*, July 1943, reprinted in *Democratic Ideals*, 265–78.
12. GKF lecture, "The Shattering of the Rooseveltian Dream," May 1, 1965, GKP, box 21.
13. See GFK to Charles Bohlen, Feb. 1945, GKP, box 28. See also Bohlen, 175.
14. For Kennan's December 1944 use of the term see *Memoirs*, 1: 214; GFK to Bohlen, cited in note 13.
15. The United States had "no choice but to lead our section of Germany . . . to a form of independence so prosperous, so secure, so superior, that the east cannot threaten it." GFK, "Political Questions – Germany," 1945, GKP, box 25.
16. GFK to Bohlen, cited in note 13.

its "natural borders."[17] For Kennan – following Bullitt – the "natural borders" of Europe and Russia seem to have corresponded to the frontiers established between 1918 and 1923 (the end of the war and the Riga Treaty), with prudent adjustments in favor of the White Russians and Ukranians who had been incorporated into Poland. In his letter to Bohlen, Kennan admitted that Russia's war effort had been "masterful and effective and must, to a certain extent, find its reward at the expense of other peoples in eastern and central Europe." But he failed "to see why we must associate ourselves with this political program."[18]

In his seminal paper, "Russia's International Position at the Close of the War with Germany," written in May 1945, Kennan staked out his long-term position. "It should not be forgotten," he argued, "that the absorption of areas in the west beyond the Great Russian, White Russian, and Ukranian ethnological boundaries [Poland, Finland, and the Baltic states] is something at which Russia has already tried and failed."[19] The western provinces of the czarist empire had become "the hotbed out of which there grew the greater part of the Russian Social Democratic Party which bore Lenin to power." The subsequent loss of those territories had facilitated Stalin's consolidation of power, but now Moscow found itself saddled with them once again. Kennan raised the possibility that

> the seeds of a new convulsion are already being sown, as the seeds of the Russian revolution were planted by the condemned Decembrists. . . . And if this same telescoping of time continues, *another five or ten years*, should find Russia overshadowed by the clouds of civil disintegration which darkened the Russian sky at the outset of this century. Will this process again be hastened and brought to maturity by the germs of social and political ferment from the restless conquered provinces of the West?

Kennan's analysis of the difficulty the Russians would have in digesting their conquests was based on his reading of Gibbon and on his observation of Nazi Europe in 1939–41. The Russians lacked the administrative skill of the Germans, while their ideological message was unlikely to fire the imaginations of the Eastern Europeans. The Russians

17. This, he later said, had always been the "outstanding task of postwar statesmanship for the Western countries." GFK to J. Whelan, July 3, 1959, GKP, box 31.
18. Since the Warsaw uprising of August–September 1944, Kennan had favored a "political showdown" with Moscow. He argued that the movement of Poland's border to the Oder–Neisse line put the postwar Polish state at the mercy of Moscow for protection against German revanchism and that the notion of an independent Poland within such borders was a farce. Bohlen, 175; *Memoirs*, 1: 211–15.
19. GFK, "Russia's International Position," reprinted in *Memoirs*, 1: 532–46.

faced a vast police operation, probably beyond their means, at least in those areas not contiguous with the USSR.[20]

Kennan pursued a related theme, the disaffection of the Russian people. Shortly after returning to Russia, he had written (September 1944), "Through war through peace, through war through suffering... there goes on that vast organic process which can only be described as the spiritual life of the Russian people." Observing the wartime Russians' hunger for religious and cultural sustenance, he had written, "On every hand we see the people of Russia reverting quietly, triumphantly, to that point at which their spiritual and cultural development was interrupted by the violence and conceit of the revolution. We see them taking up the threads again where they once left off."[21] No statement was more revealing of the subjective hopes and feelings that animated Kennan's policy advice. In May 1945, he was more cautious but still argued that there were "no longer many illusions among Russian people as to the moral or spiritual quality of all that the state represents." Kennan concluded that "Russia will not have an easy time in maintaining the power which it has seized over other peoples in Eastern and Central Europe unless it receives both moral and material assistance from the West."[22]

Such assistance, Kennan feared, was exactly what the Kremlin had come to expect from the United States. There was talk of a major postwar loan, while Moscow looked to the United Nations "to enlist automatically the support of the Western democracies against any forces which might undertake the liberation of the [Eastern European] peoples." On the other hand, if the West were able to "muster up the political manliness to deny Russia either the moral or material support for the consolidation of Russian power throughout Eastern and Central Europe, Russia would probably not be able to maintain its hold successfully for any length of time over all the territory over which it has today staked a claim. In this case, the lines would have to be withdrawn somewhat."[23] Moscow would answer by exploiting the full "nuisance value" of the Western European Communists, but if the West were able to "stand firm through such a show of ill-temper... Moscow would have played its last real card."[24] Kennan believed, in other words, that

---

20. Ibid., 534–5, emphasis added.
21. GFK, "Russia, Seven Years Later" (Sept. 1944), reprinted in *Memoirs*, 1: 503–31.
22. GFK, "Russia's International Position," 542–43.
23. Ibid., 545–46. When he wrote his memoirs, Kennan added emphasis to the words "all" and "somewhat."
24. "Further military advances in the West could only increase responsibilities already beyond the Russian capacity to meet." Ibid.

the nationalist challenges to Soviet control emanating from the empire might shake the foundations of the Kremlin's position at home. The most striking feature of Kennan's early postwar outlook, the main premise of his policy recommendations, was not the resiliency, but the fragility – political, economic, moral – of the Stalinist regime. The determination of whether Kennan's view was based on wishful or realistic thinking depended at least partly on whether the kinds of Western policies most likely to exploit the purported weakness of the regime were implemented or not.[25]

The nature of containment

The last two years "have been hard ones ... I am really tired," Kennan wrote on his return from Moscow in the spring of 1946. He considered quitting the Foreign Service before his appointment as "deputy for foreign affairs" at the new National War College in Washington.[26] "I felt keenly," he later said, "the fact that people such as Alger Hiss and Stettinius and Harry Hopkins, who knew nothing about Russia, were at the President's side ... whereas I was side-tracked in Moscow."[27] There were elements of sibling and professional rivalry in his close relationship with Bohlen, someone who had also been at FDR's side. When Kennan visited Yalta many years later, he thought he recognized himself in place of Bohlen in the official portrait of the conference.[28] Bohlen became a close aide to the new secretary of state, James Byrnes, in mid-1945. It was Byrnes's attempt to continue a policy of conciliation at the Moscow conference in December 1945 that caused Kennan to "boil over."[29] Shortly thereafter, he received a request from the Treasury Department for an explanation as to why Moscow did not show more enthusiasm about the World Bank and International Monetary Fund. To Kennan's

25. Eduard Mark is right to stress this feature of Kennan's view in "The Question of Containment." However, his claim that it is nowhere mentioned in Kennan's memoirs is odd in view of the inclusion of the paper "Russia's International Position" in the appendix, as well as of an extensive citation from the lecture of September 17, 1946, in *Memoirs*, 1: 303. Another author who stresses Kennan's hopes for the collapse of the regime is Hixson, at 31, 36, 37, 41–45.
26. See GFK to Bruce Hopper, Apr. 17, 1946; GFK to E. Durbrow, Jan. 2, 1946. GKP, box 28.
27. GFK letter to Wilson Miscamble, July 14, 1978, cited in Miscamble, "George F. Kennan, the Policy Planning Staff, and American Foreign Policy, 1947–1950," Ph.D. diss. (University of Notre Dame, 1980), 23.
28. See GFK, *Sketches*, 255.
29. *Memoirs*, 1: 284–88, 560–65. See also the paper he wrote at the time, "The U.S. and Russia," GKP, box 23.

astonishment his opinion had been asked. "Here was a case where nothing but the whole truth would do."[30] The result was the eight-thousand-word dispatch that brought him to the attention of Secretary of the Navy James Forrestal and other high officials.

The purpose of the "long telegram" was to confront his old bugbear – fashionable but uninformed liberal opinion – with arguments so stunning and unanswerable that the field would be cleared for a new approach to Russia. It was an utter waste of breath, Kennan said, to talk of friendship with the Soviets. The regime had a vested interest in a hostile outside world and was impervious to reason. "In summary we have here a political force committed fanatically to the belief that with the U.S. there can be no permanent *modus vivendi*, that it is desirable and necessary that the internal harmony of our society be disrupted, our traditional way of life be destroyed, the international authority of our state be broken, if Soviet power is to be secure." Here was the verdict of someone who had invested considerable psychic energy in trying to break through the reserve and evasiveness of Soviet society – to no avail. As one whose *personal* efforts had met with frustration, he found Henry Wallace's charge that the United States had not done enough to communicate with and reassure Russia "preposterous and fantastic."[31]

Once the "Rooseveltian dream" had been disposed of, the United States could exploit its great advantages. The Soviet regime was "highly sensitive to [the] logic of force. For this reason it can easily withdraw – and usually does – when strong resistance is encountered at any point. Thus, if the adversary has sufficient force and makes clear his readiness to use it, he rarely has to do so. . . . Gauged against [the] Western World as a whole, [the] Soviets are still by far the weaker force." Sooner or later, the regime would face the "supreme test" of transition following Stalin's death. "By virtue of recent territorial expansion" it faced the strains that had "once proved a severe tax on Tsardom." Therefore, "we may approach calmly and with good heart the problem of how to deal with Russia." The United States could not turn its back on the consequences of its position, especially with regard to the Western Europeans: "They are seeking guidance rather than responsibilities. We should be better able than the Russians to give them this. And unless we do the Russians certainly will." "Much depends," he concluded, "on the health and vigor of our own society. . . . Every courageous and incisive measure to solve the internal problems of our own society . . .

30. Nowhere in Washington, he wrote, had hopes for "postwar collaboration with Russia been more elaborate, more naive, or more tenaciously (one might almost say ferociously) pursued than in the Treasury Department." *Memoirs*, 1: 292–93, 298.
31. See GFK to Secretary of State, Feb. 22, 1946, *FRUS*, 1946, 6: 696–709.

is a diplomatic victory over Moscow worth a thousand diplomatic notes."[32]

There were moments when the spectacle of a prostrate and disoriented world seemed to ignite the embers of Wilsonian idealism in Kennan's makeup, but the impulse was dampened by the admonition "Physician, heal thyself."[33] In September 1946, he asked whether the United States had a "positive philosophy applicable to other people." His own answer was, "I just don't know.... Perhaps I can see both sides.... I am still trying to think it out." In any event it was best to say, " 'You will have to solve your own problems' " and that " 'We are trying to put you in a position to help yourself.' "[34]

Kennan was grappling with the questions of the means of American power and its geographical scope. Perhaps the controversy about his intentions might have been avoided if historians, including Kennan, had simply reread the passage in his *Memoirs, 1925–1950* where (commenting on the lecture he had delivered on September 17, 1946), he said, "The tough side [of the Russian political personality] could only be confronted by superior military and political force." The United States would be able, "if our policies are wise and non-provocative, to contain them both militarily and politically for a long time to come."[35] Military power was an indispensable component of diplomatic strength, one whose very existence was the best guarantee that shots would not be fired.[36] But he clearly distinguished between the essentially *passive* military component of containment, on one hand, and *active* political and economic measures, on the other. In fact, Kennan's notion of containment was deeply conditioned by his desire to bring military power under political control. This arose from his at times humiliating dealings with the U.S. military over the Azores and the German occupation zones.[37] After his clashes with the War Department, he was

---

32. Ibid.
33. After the Byrnes visit to Moscow, he had spoken of the danger of "losing – for the second time in 3 decades – the moral leadership of Europe which was ours for the taking." His concern at this point was that, Roosevelt's hopes having proven an illusion, the United States would simply decide to abandon Europe in a fit of pique or panic. See GFK, "The U.S. and Russia."
34. GFK lecture, "Measures Short of War," Sept. 16, 1946, GKP, box 16.
35. *Memoirs*, 1: 302, 304.
36. On this point, see the "long telegram," cited in note 31. See also Mayers, 123. Kennan developed this point on a number of occasions. See, e.g., the lecture "Russia," Oct. 1, 1946, GKP, box 23; "Current Problems of Soviet–American Relations," May 9, 1947, GKP, box 23; PPS 23, Feb. 24, 1948, *FRUS*, 1948, 1: 519.
37. See Chapter 4, this volume. On the Azores see also GFK lecture, "Problems of Diplomatic–Military Collaboration," Mar. 7, 1947, GKP, box 23.

ordered to stay out of the business of the military supply mission at the Moscow Embassy. When he presumed to question a Soviet order for U.S. movie film, he received the most severe reprimand of his career.[38] Under Roosevelt, what Kennan called "military pro-Sovietism" had flourished.[39] Observing the postwar occupation of Germany, Kennan felt that the U.S. "military authorities were still deeply affected by . . . the disgraceful anti-British and pro-Soviet prejudices that certain of our military leaders had entertained during the war."[40] Kennan feared the use of force because once that Pandora's box was opened the soldiers would acquire the leverage that would allow them to dictate to the diplomats. In 1947, he wrote, "Many of the disasters that befell the Foreign Service and also American foreign policy resulted from the fact that there were simply no men high up in the Service who had both the prestige and the guts to talk up successfully to the military leaders."[41] Kennan was probably suggesting that he had possessed the latter quality, but not the former.

Any power in the position of the United States after 1945 was bound to receive requests for aid and intervention from diverse quarters and to find its credibility at stake depending on its response. Areas of little or no traditional or intrinsic interest acquired symbolic importance, and opportunities to overextend oneself abounded. Vital and nonvital interests might be distinguished from each other as an intellectual exercise, but such calculations could well prove worthless in real life. This was the set of dilemmas that Lippmann analyzed in his famous September 1947 columns. Kennan had been trying to come to grips with them well before that date. Sometimes he spoke like a global interventionist: In January 1947, he said that U.S. forces should be "in a position to be moved anywhere on short notice and to undertake the defense of the interests of this country or of the world community."[42] His hope was that the capacity to move them would make movement unnecessary – their "mere existence does the trick." Kennan was also frankly recognizing the implications of a state of affairs in which the United States alone would be able to act if certain traditional Western interests were challenged. His concern, however, was to change that

---

38. See GFK to T. A. Julian, Mar. 31, 1965, GKP, box 31. Kennan was reprimanded by General John Deane.
39. See lecture of May 1, 1965, "The Shattering of the Rooseveltian Dream," GKP, box 21. See also *Memoirs*, 1: 308–10.
40. *Memoirs*, 1: 257.
41. See GFK to W. Gallman, Mar. 14, 1947, GKP, box 28.
42. GFK lecture, "Requirements of National Security," Jan. 23, 1947, GKP, box 16. See also "The World Position and Problems of the U.S.," Aug. 30, 1949, GKP, box 17.

situation as rapidly as possible by restoring the *natural* barriers to Russian power, the British Empire, Germany, and Japan. Like the old Imperial Defence, Kennan's "global interventionism" contained an element of bluff; unlike British strategy, it was a transitional expedient until the United States could remove itself from the breach.[43]

American policy in 1946 was to exert diplomatic pressure against the Russians along the British imperial perimeter (in Iran in February–March, in Turkey and the Straits in August), culminating in the assumption of responsibility for the eastern Mediterranean in February–March 1947. It was during this relatively brief period that Washington followed something like the famous formula set forth in "The Sources of Soviet Conduct": "the adroit and vigilant application of counterforce at a series of constantly shifting geographical and political points, corresponding to the shifts and manoeuvres of Soviet policy, but which cannot be charmed or talked out of existence." The latter phrase, along with Kennan's insistence on the Kremlin's interest in a hostile foreign environment, indicated his abiding fixation on the "Rooseveltian dream." Characteristically, the target of this article was the "puerile defeatism" of the liberal intellectuals who argued that a firm policy toward Russia would lead to war. On the contrary, Kennan said, a firm policy was necessary to prevent "a deterioration . . . which would eventually be bound to engage our military interests."[44]

"The Sources," written in December 1946, is the clearest possible evidence of the compensatory and transitory nature of containment as Kennan saw it and of its basic purpose: to change the Soviet Union. Virtually half of the article dealt with the crisis of the regime. Even so, he had not gone "nearly as far" as he might have with his argument because he did not want "to give the Russians the opportunity to say that anyone here was advocating the overthrow of the Soviet Govern-

---

43. To say, as Eduard Mark does, that he grew less, rather than more, discriminating about U.S. interests over time seems to me to be missing the basic point. On military force "doing the trick," see "Russia's National Objectives," Apr. 10, 1947, GKP, box 17. Needless to say, an effective policy of intervention required a degree of executive flexibility and independence from public and congressional interference that was foreign to American experience. Few people were more conscious of this than Kennan. Among countless statements concerning the institutional inadequacy of U.S. foreign policy, see GFK, "Planning Foreign Policy," June 18, 1947, GFK, box 17.

44. Mr. "X," "The Sources of Soviet Conduct." On the circumstances surrounding the writing of this article see *Memoirs*, 1: 354–56; also GFK, "Reflections on Containment." On U.S. intellectuals see unsent letter to Lippmann, Apr. 6, 1948, GKP, box 17. On this point see also GKP lecture "Russia and the Russians," Jan. 21, 1950, GKP, box 18.

ment."[45] "The outstanding circumstance surrounding the Soviet regime," he argued, was that the process of consolidation had never been completed. It now faced the physical exhaustion and disillusion of the populace, the economic consequences of the war, and the impending transfer of leadership that might "shake Soviet power to its foundations." He noted the possibility of a serious generational conflict in the party:

> If disunity were ever to seize and paralyze [it], the chaos and weakness of Soviet society would be revealed in forms beyond description. For we have seen that Soviet power is only a crust concealing an amorphous mass of human beings. . . . The possibility remains (and in the opinion of this writer it is a strong one) that Soviet power, like the capitalist world of its conception, bears within it the seeds of its own decay, and that the sprouting of these seeds is well advanced.

"The possibilities for American policy [were] by no means limited to holding the line and hoping for the best." On the contrary, the United States had

> it in its power to increase enormously the strains under which Soviet policy must operate, to force upon the Kremlin a far greater degree of moderation and circumspection . . . and in this way to promote tendencies which must eventually find their outlet in either the break-up or gradual mellowing of Soviet power.

Here was the true objective and promise of containment. Kennan indicated a time frame of from ten to fifteen years.[46]

Kennan's statement was extraordinary, given the need for caution on the subject.[47] He assumed the existence of moderates and potential interlocutors within the Soviet regime,[48] but his deeper faith in contain-

---

45. GFK unsent letter to Lippmann, cited in note 44.
46. GFK, "The Sources of Soviet Conduct," 569, 577–82.
47. He was increasingly concerned not only about the Russian reaction, but about hotheads in the United States: "No one," he said in 1949, "wishes more fervently than I, nor on the basis of more bitter personal experience, for the end of Communist power in Moscow," but it was preferable and possible to encourage that development diplomatically rather than risk a preventative war. GFK lecture, Aug. 30, 1949, GKP, box 17.
48. See "The U.S. and Russia," *Memoirs*, 1: 560–61. Here he spoke of "helping our friends in Russia to prove that aggression does not pay." See GKP, box 23. On Dec. 29, 1946, he said that the United States must leave the door open to strengthen the moderate forces that exist within the USSR. See discussion following the lecture "Russia's Split Political Personality," GKP, box 16. He expressed the same view in PPS 23, Feb. 24, 1948, *FRUS, 1948*, 1: 523. See also an earlier unsent letter to H. Freeman Matthews (1945, undated), GKP, box 17, in which Kennan wrote, "I

ment arose from a belief in the organic nature of political life and in the natural rhythm of Russian history. In September 1944, he had spoken of the "vast organic process" constituting the "spiritual life of the Russian people." In May 1947, he said that totalitarianism was "essentially a device of despair coming from specific and particularly painful problems of adjustment at given stages in the development of individual peoples; and that it is therefore by nature a temporary phenomenon." He later referred to the "renewed evolution of the Russian state in the direction of greater liberalism which I believe to be entirely possible... but which must be a spontaneous Russian process." In January 1949, he spoke of allowing "the natural fluctuations of Russian state behavior to do their work."[49] There was something going on – a natural process – which no one could dictate but which the West, like Spengler's gardener, was in a position to affect. His most explicit statement of the "Spenglerian" nature of containment, as he saw it, was the following (August 1948):

> Such alterations [in the psychology and outlook of peoples] can flow only from the organic political experience of the people in question. The best that can be done by one country to bring about this sort of alteration in another is to change the environmental influences to which the people in question are subjected, leaving it to them to react to those influences in their own way.[50]

On another occasion he said, "The great problems of foreign affairs are part of the problems of nature. Like many natural things they yield only to correct treatment applied steadily and consistently over a long period of time."[51]

Kennan was no doubt aware that Spengler himself had seen Russia's historical relation to Europe as a case of what he called "pseudomorphosis," in which "an older alien Culture [the West] lies so massively over the land that a young Culture [Russia] cannot get its breath.... The suppressed Culture can only hate the distant power with a hate that grows to be monstrous." Spengler saw Bolshevism, like "Petrinism"

believe that the efforts of those Russians who sincerely desire collaboration with the West are being constantly and successfully sabotaged by bigoted and chauvinistic internal authorities whom not even Stalin can really call to account without producing a major internal crisis."

49. See *Memoirs*, 1: 510; see also lectures of May 2, 1947, and May 31, 1948, box 17, GKP; notes for seminar at Princeton University, Jan. 23–26, 1949, box 17, GKP.
50. PPS 38, Aug. 18, 1948, RG 59, Records of the Policy Planning Staff (PPS), box 731, NA.
51. GFK lecture, Jan. 16, 1953, GKP, box 13.

(the Westernizing tradition of Peter the Great), as a new form of this tragic pseudomorphosis, but one that would eventually be thrown off by a Russian people whose spiritual vitality, represented by Dostoyevsky, stood in opposition to the decadent West. "To Dostoyevsky's Christianity," said Spengler, "will the next thousand years belong."[52] Kennan also saw Russia as culturally distinct from Europe; he was attracted by the spiritual depth of its people and foresaw a similar fate for the regime. But he rejected the idea of ultimately unbridgeable divisions and counterpoised cultural destinies. He suggested that "the vast creative abilities of Russia" might contribute to the rescue of Western civilization.[53] He wished, in the final analysis, to lower the barriers, to promote a kind of cross-fertilization, to allow Russia – it was the liberal Chekhov, not the religious Slavophil Dostoyevsky, with whom he identified – to overcome its inferiority complex, while preserving its cultural uniqueness.

A double message

The events of spring 1947 – the Greek–Turkish crisis, the proclamation of the Truman Doctrine, the failure of the Moscow Conference of Foreign Ministers to agree on Germany – propelled Kennan to center stage. He favored aid to Greece, not only to avoid the psychological repercussions in Western Europe of a successful Communist insurrection, but because a Communist defeat might set in motion the kind of reverse domino effect that he hoped for at the time.[54] Kennan, however, was not happy about the sweeping implications of Truman's March 12, 1947, speech and had tried unsuccessfully to change it.[55] Henceforth, his dilemma was how to maintain sufficient pressure on the Soviet Union to encourage internal change while avoiding a dispersion of American resources.

Kennan became head of the Policy Planning Staff (PPS) on May 6, 1947. In its first major paper, the PPS urged the removal of "damaging impressions" left by Truman's pronouncement.[56] In the same memo

---

52. Spengler, 268–74.
53. In "Russia Seven Years Later," *Memoirs*, 1: 528.
54. If Western European Communists were "to start on the backward slide," it was possible to imagine "a general crumbling of Russian influence and prestige which would carry beyond those countries, and into the heart of the Soviet Union itself." GFK lecture, "Russia's National Objectives," Apr. 10, 1947, GKP, box 17.
55. *Memoirs*, 1: 315, 321.
56. These impressions were: "a. That the United States reaction to world problems is a defensive reaction to Communist pressures and that the effort to restore sound

Kennan set out the essential features of the subsequent Marshall Plan. It was the Marshall Plan, Kennan later wrote, that "finally broke through the confusion of wartime pro-Sovietism, wishful thinking, anglo-phobia and self-righteous punitivism in which our occupational policies in Germany had thus far been enveloped." Its launching represented Kennan's vindication, the culmination of his crusade against Roosevelt's vision of Europe. With the State Department firmly in control of the policy-making process – or so it seemed – the plan initiative also marked the victory of virtuous professionalism over the dilletantism of the past. As head of the PPS, Kennan suddenly found himself a public figure and courted by the press.[57]

The moment of triumph was brief. Kennan's new problems began with the publication of "The Sources of Soviet Conduct" in June 1947. Secretary of State Marshall, for one, was shocked by the publicity the article garnered its author,[58] and Kennan's credibility may have suffered as a result. Neither the controversy surrounding the article nor Lippmann's attack in September caused him to question his basic agenda at the time. By his own admission, however, his vanity, and the attention his words seemed to attract, led him to deceive himself as to the real influence he exerted.[59]

A more basic problem arose from the nature of Kennan's analysis of Soviet reality. "Sources," like all of his important pronouncements, contained a double message. The first part, aimed at liberal intellectuals and residual Rooseveltians, was that it was impossible to make common cause with a regime whose leaders depended on a hostile outside world in order to maintain their internal position and would not sleep soundly in their beds until they had witnessed the destruction of the West. This

economic conditions in other countries is only a by-product of this reaction and we would not be interested in doing it if there were no Communist menace; b. That the Truman Doctrine is a blank check to give economic and military aid to any area of the world where the Communists show signs of being successful." PPS memo, May 23, 1947, *FRUS*, 1947, 3: 229. On the circumstances surrounding Kennan's appointment to the PPS, see Miscamble, *George F. Kennan*, 10–11.

57. See the Alsop brothers, "The Kennan Dispatch," *New York Herald Tribune*, May 23, 1947; James Reston, "A New Role for the State Department," *New York Times*, May 25, 1947; Neal Stanford, "Planning Staff for Foreign Policy," *Christian Science Monitor*, May 26, 1947; Oliver Pilat, "Close-Up: Diplomatic Chief of Staff," *New York Post*, June 4, 1947; Brooks Atkinson, "America's Global Planner," *New York Times Magazine*, July 13, 1947; Richard Stokes, "Modern Version of 'The Thinker,'" *Washington Sun Star*, Aug. 24, 1947; Philip Harkins, "Mysterious Mr. 'X,'" *New York Herald Tribune*, Jan. 4, 1948.

58. See Kennan's own extensive discussion of the article and its effect, *Memoirs*, 1: chap. 15.

59. Ibid., 314.

part of the message had now hit home. Increasingly it corresponded to the popular perception of the Soviet Union in 1946 and became all too credible thanks to the Truman administration's clamorous public campaign to sell aid to Greece and Turkey in 1947. The second, essential part of Kennan's message was that the Soviet regime was not a mortal threat to the West – the Russians were not "ten feet tall." On the contrary, the regime was in the throes of a serious crisis and already overextended in Europe. What Kennan did not immediately realize was that, while the first part of his message was plausible to a lay audience, the second part was much less so and seemed logically inconsistent with the first. Thus the second part and the policy recommendations that followed from it tended to be discounted or ignored. In fact, Kennan's conviction that the regime was overextended and tottering was based on a rather unique feel for Soviet reality and highly refined intuition. The notion that the Soviet Union was implacably hostile but also liable to collapse and therefore not seriously threatening was simply not credible to a public (and elite) audience whose image was based not on firsthand knowledge of the system's backwardness and vulnerability but on the performance of the Red Army and Soviet ruthlessness after the war in Eastern Europe. Kennan had been behind what he thought was the Potemkin village of Soviet power. His audience had not. Once again, it was Kennan's special knowledge, his professional "virtue," that cut him off from the American scene.

This basic difference of perspective became evident during the launching of the Marshall Plan. The purpose of the plan, as Kennan saw it, was not to divide Europe but to hasten its reunification, not to entangle the United States in Europe, but to allow it to go home. Kennan had little enthusiasm for the New Deal and Keynesian-inspired technocrats who flocked to the Economic Cooperation Administration (ECA), the Marshall Plan bureaucracy. Their aim was to export an American model of material prosperity and social peace based on perpetual economic growth and higher productivity. For Kennan the Marshall Plan was the preeminently political and psychological offensive, with hoped-for repercussions at the heart of the Soviet system, that he had called for in April 1947.[60]

He insisted that the offer of participation be extended to the Eastern Europeans and the Soviet Union itself. In so doing, he thought, the United States was implementing a policy designed to prevent the consolidation of Soviet power in Eastern Europe.[61] He had never seen the

60. See GFK, "Russia's National Objectives."
61. See Mayers, 140–41.

partition of Europe along the Stettin–Trieste line as anything but temporary and defensive. As he explained it in 1948:

> By forcing the Russians to permit the satellite countries to enter into a relationship of economic collaboration with the west of Europe which would inevitably have strengthened east–west bonds and weakened the exclusive orientation of these countries toward Russia or to force them to remain outside this structure of collaboration at heavy economic sacrifice to themselves, we placed a severe strain on the relations between Moscow and the satellite countries.[62]

Unfortunately for Kennan, most of his fellow policy makers – Bohlen, Under Secretary of State for Economic Affairs William Clayton, Under Secretary of State Dean Acheson – while they no longer believed in a general political settlement with the Russians, were still sufficiently Rooseveltian in their basic assumptions that they did not seriously question the inevitability of a Soviet sphere of influence in the East. Kennan thought he had buried the "Rooseveltian dream," but its legacy lived on. His colleagues went along with Kennan on the invitation to the Eastern countries because they saw it as a device to place the onus of dividing Europe on Moscow – not because they were preoccupied at the time with overcoming the division itself. For the most part, moreover, they were now committed to the liberal economic and social vision coalescing around the plan. Kennan seems to have been oblivious to this basic difference of perspectives in May 1947 and was surprised when it emerged.[63]

62. PPS 38, 86, cited in note 50.
63. The difference has not been sufficiently appreciated by historians. For example, Michael Hogan suggests, in his generally excellent account, that Kennan saw the invitation to the USSR and Eastern Europe as a way to consolidate a Western bloc. In this way he was opposed to younger Wilsonian officials who still believed in "One World." Hogan, *The Marshall Plan: America, Britain and the Reconstruction of Western Europe, 1947–1952* (Cambridge: Cambridge University Press, 1987), 44–45, 442. Hogan draws on John Lewis Gaddis, "The United States and the Question of a Sphere of Influence in Western Europe, 1945–1949," in Olav Riste, ed., *Western Security: The Formative Years – European and Atlantic Defense* (Oslo: Norwegian University Press, 1985). Gaddis suggests that Kennan's position changed one hundred and eighty degrees on the question of east–west partition of Europe between 1945 and 1949. He favored it until 1948–49, but then changed his mind (see 67, 82). This somewhat overlooks the fact that Kennan wished to draw a line in Central Europe in 1945 in order to stop the Russians from taking *everything*. He always emphasized the weakness of the Soviet position and saw the Marshall Plan as a way of hastening, not postponing or renouncing, the withdrawal of the Russians from Eastern Europe. Gaddis suggests this at one point (73–74) in his article. Kennan later acknowledged the probable existence of differing objectives and assumptions underlying the offer of aid to the East among his colleagues, while insisting on the sincerity of his own hope

The other virtue of the Marshall Plan, as Kennan saw it, was that it would oblige the Western Europeans to accept the revival of German strength, paving the way for American withdrawal. Two weeks after Marshall's Harvard address, Kennan defined the crisis in Europe as "largely psychological"; the shadow of the Kremlin fell across many countries that would otherwise be of little concern to the United States. "In these circumstances," he went on, "it may well be that we are overextended . . . it may be that we have undertaken too much: That there is a serious gap in peacetime policy between the things we have set out to do and our own capabilities for doing them."[64] In other words, let us restore responsibility for Europe to the Europeans.

But a new question was emerging, one that had hardly occurred to Kennan: did the Europeans want to reassume responsibility for their fate? In August Kennan visited Paris, where the Western Europeans – Molotov having come and left – were trying to prepare a joint proposal in response to Marshall's offer. Kennan found weak leaders presiding over feeble governments; some, particularly the Scandinavians, were "pathologically timorous about the Russians." Britain was "seriously sick." He reluctantly concluded that the United States could not ask the Europeans what kind of plan they wanted; it would be necessary "just [to] *tell* them what they would get." The fact that they wanted to have the law laid down to them was a measure of "Europe's pathetic weakness, and Europe's consciousness of that weakness."[65]

Late 1947 to early 1948 was a vexatious time for Kennan. As a consequence of its reverses in Western Europe – the French and Italian Communist parties had been forced into opposition in May – Moscow was clamping down in the East. Kennan still expected that Soviet power there would crumble, but now feared that in such circumstances the Kremlin might "resort to desperate measures."[66] This was an argument not for writing off Eastern Europe, but rather for trying out new methods to promote Soviet withdrawal. In the United States, meanwhile, Congress gave control of the Marshall Plan to its bureaucratic creature, the ECA, thus ending the State Department's brief hegemony

to include the Eastern satellites in the plan. See GFK lecture, "The Marshall Plan and the Future of Europe," Berlin, June 25, 1987. See also Kennan interview given in February 1953 as part of the oral history of the Marshall Plan prepared by Harry B. Price, HSTL; Miscamble, *George F. Kennan*, 52.

64. GFK, "Planning Foreign Policy," June 18, 1947, GKP, box 17, excerpts in *Memoirs*, 1: 348–52.
65. Kennan report, Sept. 4, 1947, *FRUS*, 1947, 3: 397–405.
66. GFK, "Resumé of the World Situation," Nov. 6, 1947, *FRUS*, 1947, 1: 774.

over European policy. Finally, there was the continuing paralysis of Western Europe – connected, Kennan believed, to the largely irrational fear of Soviet attack and of the local Communists. Upon his return from Moscow in early 1946, Kennan wrote, he had been impressed by the "weakness of Russia's position," by "the ease with which they could be held and pushed back." "Today I think I was wrong – not in my analysis of the Soviet position, but in my assumption that this Government had the ability to 'operate' politically at all in the foreign field." The ECA's handling of Marshall aid would be "cumbersome, inflexible, and unpolitical."[67] The social-economic vision of the economists and businessmen would prevail.

Nothing bothered Kennan more than Western European Communism – an essentially Latin phenomenon. Behind his attitude was a not so latent antipathy toward Latin society and belief in the moral-intellectual rigor of the North.[68] At one point he said that Communist control over France or Brazil would serve, while it lasted, to discredit the Left: in neither case would rescue be forthcomimg from Moscow.[69] He almost seemed to be saying, "Let those countries have a taste of Communism. That will teach them." Italy was different, since an insurrection might be supported by the Yugoslavs or Russians. Kennan's deep irritation with the apparent unwillingness of the local elites to take responsibility for their own affairs and their attempt to play upon their vulnerability to extract aid from the United States may help to explain his suggestion that the Italian Communist Party be outlawed before the April 1948 elections. Kennan was badly out of touch with conditions in Italy – he was in the Far East at the time.[70] The recommendation also indicates that Kennan was affected by the fear that swept the West following the

---

67. GFK, "Notes on the Marshall Plan," Dec. 15, 1947, GKP, box 23. On the ECA see also PPS 23, *FRUS*, 1948, 1: 512–13.

68. Maybe he saw the Grand Inquisitor's words as applying with particular force to the French and Italian masses: "I tell thee that man is tormented by no greater anxiety than to find someone quickly to whom he can hand over that gift of freedom with which the ill-fated creature is born. But only one who can appease their consciences can take over their freedom.... Oh, we shall allow them to sin, they are weak and helpless and they will love us like children because we allow them to sin.... And they will have no secrets from us ... and they will submit to us gladly and cheerfully." From the Grand Inquisitor to Christ in Dostoyevsky's *The Brothers Karamazov*, quoted by GFK in *Presbyterian Life*, March 1954.

69. See GFK, "The Problems of U.S. Foreign Policy after Moscow," May 6, 1947, GKP, box 17; see also "Relations with Russia," Dec. 3, 1947, GKP, box 17.

70. GFK to Secretary, Mar. 15, 1948, *FRUS*, 1948, 3: 849. The Popular Front had little chance of winning the elections (one may even question whether its leaders desired victory).

Czech coup in late February 1948 and General Lucius Clay's message from Berlin that war might come "with dramatic suddenness."[71] It was only on his return (followed by hospitalization for an ulcer attack) that he grasped the dimensions of the "war scare" and sensed the new mood in which the concern about *military* security overshadowed all others.

Kennan set out his own concerns on the eve of his departure for Japan in February 1948. "In the long run," he observed, "there can only be three possibilities for the future of Western and Central Europe. One is German domination. Another is Russian domination. The third is a federated Germany, into which the parts of Germany are absorbed but in which the influence of the other countries is sufficient to hold Germany in her place." Without the Germans, there could be no real European federation. Germany's economic integration with Europe had to be accelerated in order to transcend the Germans' "defiant nationa-lism" and "collective egocentrism." The United States must accept the bankruptcy of its own moral influence and "force the Germans to accept responsibility" for their affairs.[72] In the Mediterranean, Kennan believed, the United States did "not possess the weapons which would be needed to enable it to meet head-on the threat to national indepen-dence presented by the Communists elements." In the Middle East, U.S. policy should support the British position. In the Far East, the United States was "greatly over-extended in our whole thinking about what we can accomplish, and should try to accomplish in that area."[73] (He later referred to "the ridiculous attempt by FDR to build up China into our closest and greatest ally, even at the expense of our relationship with Britain.")[74] The kinsman of the elder George Kennan would shortly help to change U.S. occupation policy in Japan with the aim of trans-forming it into an independent power center on the Soviet periphery.[75]

Kennan's most important suggestion at this point had to do with the Soviet Union itself. Thanks to the psychological success of the Marshall

---

71. See *Memoirs*, 1: 400. In his March 15 cable sent from the Far East, Kennan said that "the savage abruptness and cynical unconcern for appearances of recent action in Czechoslovakia leads me to feel that Kremlin leaders must be driven by a sense of extreme urgency. They are probably realizing that they are basically over-extended in eastern Europe and that unless they can break the unity of western Europe and disturb the ERP pattern, it will be difficult for them to hold on in eastern and central Europe. . . . If this analysis is correct then there is indeed a real and new element of danger in the present situation, and we must be prepared for all eventualities." *FRUS*, 1948, 3: 848–49.

72. PPS 23, Feb. 24, 1948, *FRUS*, 1948, 1: 510–29.

73. Ibid., 523–24.

74. GFK to Harold Hochschild, Oct. 6, 1964, GKP, box 31.

75. *Memoirs*, 1: 368–96, for Kennan's own account.

initiative, the Russians might be in a frame of mind "to do business seriously with us about Germany and about Europe in general." Talking to Moscow did not represent a "true change of heart" on his part; it arose from Kennan's long-standing belief that Russian domination of Eastern Europe was unnecessary and untenable.[76] "What the Russians will want to do," Kennan thought, "will be to conclude . . . a sphere-of-influence agreement similar to the one they concluded with the Germans in 1939." But the United States should convince them that it would be worth their while "to reduce Communist pressures . . . to a point where we can afford to withdraw all our armed forces from the continent and the Mediterranean."[77] Kennan's confidence in his own ability and influence was very much intact: he called for secret preliminary talks with Stalin conducted by someone with qualifications that practically he alone possessed.[78] In Japan, he acted out a script that might have been written by the elder Kennan, helping to nail shut the coffin of Roosevelt's Pacific dream.[79] Unfortunately for Kennan, this episode of personal destiny fulfillment caused him to be absent from Washington at a crucial turning point in U.S. relations with Europe.

"The fateful confusion"

Kennan's moment of glory as a policy maker had coincided with a general reaction against the Rooseveltian vision of a Europe retired and reduced. It was a reaction that he had both anticipated and brilliantly expressed. Once Roosevelt's Soviet policy had been discredited – once the Western Europeans themselves had regained a degree of diplomatic initiative – Kennan found himself fighting a defensive battle on behalf of objectives that he had mistakenly assumed were widely shared: a strictly contained American policy, the transformation of the Soviet system, the restoration and unity of Europe as he defined it: from Brest to Brest-Litovsk. In an April 1948 letter to Lippmann (unsent), Kennan referred to what he had been fighting since 1944 as "the fateful confusion between the 'one world' and the 'two world' concepts." "One world" represented FDR's policy of collaboration with the Soviet

---

76. On Lippmann's possible influence, see ibid., 360, 365; on alleged "change of heart," see Issacson and Thomas, 436.
77. *FRUS*, 1948, 1: 522.
78. That is, an objective, expert, discreet, and Russian-speaking negotiator. See ibid., 522.
79. Kennan considered his part in reversing U.S. occupation policy in Japan "after the Marshall Plan, the most significant, constructive contribution I was ever able to make in government." *Memoirs*, 1: 393.

Union; "two worlds," the false alternative of perpetual confrontation.[80] Kennan's personal conception had always been tripolar.

Like Bohlen, the other leading student of the Soviet Union, Kennan greeted the idea of a formal alliance between the United States and Western Europe with a certain disbelief. During the Berlin blockade (June 1948 to May 1949), he did not rule out the possibility of war, but he did not believe the Russians had any interest in trying to conquer Western Europe. An alliance served only to focus their attention on military competition while turning peripheral, indefensible areas like Italy, Greece, and Turkey into liabilities and diverting energy from the main task, economic rehabilitation.[81] Finally, an alliance implied a permanent U.S. military establishment in Europe – the kind of self-perpetuating satrapy accountable only to itself and its congressional sponsors that Kennan had set out to get rid of in Japan.

It was preposterous to Kennan that the New World should become permanent tutor to the Old. Among other things, what henceforth set Kennan apart was that his notion of the balance of power,[82] unlike the conventional idea, had a cultural and aesthetic component. The rationale of the balance, as he had seen it since the thirties, was to preserve the cultural, as well as the territorial, integrity of continental Europe from the modernizing, homogenizing, debauching forces inherent, albeit in different ways, in both Soviet and American life. For someone who had cringed at the sight of the U.S. Olympic team arriving in Germany in 1936, the spectacle of American soldiers covering Europe with chewing gum and comic books represented the fulfillment of Lewis's 1920 prediction that Main Street civilization would prove difficult to contain. Kennan was profoundly out of sympathy with the idea, now bound up with the Marshall Plan, that Europe's salvation lay in the wholesale adoption of American techniques, products, values, and institutions, that the purpose of American aid was to market the notion that "you too can be like us."

Kennan was prepared to indulge Europe's phobias by offering a unilateral U.S. guarantee of the emerging "Western Union."[83] But the

---

80. GFK to Lippmann (unsent), Apr. 6, 1948, GKP, box 17.
81. *Memoirs*, 1: 408–15. On the possibility of war, see PPS 33, June 23, 1948, *FRUS*, 1948, 1: 619, 621. See also PPS 38, Aug. 18, 1948, 395. RG 59, PPS Records, box 731, NA.
82. For one of his many statements on this subject, see memo to Secretary of State, Jan. 20, 1948, *FRUS*, 1948, 3: 7.
83. See GFK memo to Under Secretary of State Robert Lovett, Apr. 29, 1948, ibid., 109; *Memoirs*, 1: 406–7. The Western Union grew out of the security pact launched by British Foreign Secretary Ernest Bevin, including Britain, France, and the Benelux.

prospect that U.S. policy might be working toward something other than the restoration of an independent power center left him incredulous and perplexed. Awareness of the leverage the Europeans had achieved over U.S. policy by stressing the Soviet danger inclined him to resist. After the effort to rescue Europe from Stalin and Roosevelt, the possibility that the Europeans were prepared to accept the division of the Continent with equanimity, that they were shunning their responsibility to reincorporate Germany, that they preferred U.S. protection to autonomy filled Kennan with disgust.[84] Meanwhile, the division of Europe was powerfully reinforced by the so-called London program negotiated by the Western powers in 1948 for an independent western German state. From Kennan's perspective, this program, together with the nascent Atlantic pact, provided the very external threat that the Kremlin required to shore up its position in Eastern Europe and at home. The Soviet blockade of Berlin, provoked by the London program, in turn galvanized popular support for the North Atlantic Treaty and a western German state.

These developments were all the more untimely, even tragic, he believed, because they came precisely at the moment when the initial stage of containment was starting to bear fruit. Kennan seized upon the break between Tito and Stalin in June 1948. He wrote on June 30, "A new factor of fundamental and profound significance [had] been introduced into the world Communist movement."[85] In mid-August he wrote:

> The disaffection of Tito, to which the strain caused by the ERP problem undoubtedly contributed in some measure, has clearly demonstrated that it *is* possible for stresses in the Soviet–satellite relations to lead to a real weakening and disruption of the Russian domination. It should therefore be our aim to continue to do all in our power to increase these stresses and at the same time to make it possible for the satellite governments gradually to extricate themselves from Russian control.[86]

But whether Tito's challenge foreshadowed the general withdrawal, or even crumbling, of Soviet power that Kennan had predicted depended in part on U.S. policy.

In Tito's break is to be found the immediate origin of Kennan's "Program A" for a united Germany. It was not so much a "major

---

84. On the Western Europeans and the German problem, Kennan said, "They also shun what I think is their real responsibility." GFK lecture, "Contemporary Problems of Foreign Policy," Sept. 17, 1948, GKP, box 17.
85. PPS 35, June 30, 1948, *FRUS*, 1948, 4: 1080.
86. PPS 38, Aug. 18, 1948, RG 59, PPS Records, box 731, NA, 386–87; emphasis in original.

change of outlook"[87] as a way of pursuing classic objectives, the roll-back of Soviet power and the conversion of German strength into the anchor of an autonomous Europe, under the conditions of 1948. Kennan had never believed in partition. In 1940, he had said that regardless of what happened to Hitler German unity was "a fact."[88] The idea that Germany could or should be cut off permanently from its natural commercial and cultural habitat in Eastern and Central Europe would have struck him as absurd. His February 1945 call for an east–west division running through Germany was contingent on immediate circumstances, including his personal anger over Yalta.[89] Dividing Germany was not an end in itself; it was the only way to prevent the Russians from controlling all of Germany at the time. To be sure, Kennan wondered whether Allied acceptance of the Oder–(western) Neisse line at Potsdam, leaving Germany without its bread-basket, had not compromised chances for a united Germany independent of Moscow. If so, the United States had little choice for the time being but to "rescue the Western zones of Germany by walling them off against eastern penetration."[90] In May 1946, Kennan was still trying to discredit policies of collaboration with Moscow that might actually facilitate the otherwise problematical Russian task of absorbing Eastern Europe. In that spirit he proposed (May 1946) "the economic unification of Germany *not only* within the Oder–Neisse boundary but also generally within the old boundaries, excluding East Prussia."[91] A year later, he was still worried about Soviet control of all of Germany. To that prospect partition, though "undesirable," was still to be preferred.[92]

In mid-1948, Kennan saw a way to replace this essentially tactical policy. He argued for a broad settlement of the German problem, including the withdrawal of foreign troops to seaside garrison areas; free, all-German elections; and the creation of a central government. "First, it is basically a question of timing. Some day our forces must leave Central Europe. Some day Soviet forces must leave. Some day Germany must again become a sovereign and independent entity." He

---

87. This is Stephanson's view (114–15, 144). Stephanson is right to stress the connection between Tito's break and Kennan's reexamination of the German problem (145).
88. See his February 1940 paper written for the Sumner Welles mission cited in Chapter 4, this volume.
89. There was clearly an element of pique in his call for the partition of Europe around the time of Yalta.
90. See GFK to Secretary, Mar. 6, 1946, *FRUS*, 1946, 5: 519.
91. GFK to Carmel Offie, May 10, 1946, ibid., 556; emphasis in original.
92. His reluctant acceptance of division was also connected to the Russian razing of East Prussia (an area, he noted, of the same size and richness as Wisconsin), whose gruesome results he had witnessed from the air. GFK, "Russia's National Objectives."

acknowledged the counterarguments, in particular "the absence of some real [European] union" in which to fit Germany and "the risk which surrounds the behavior of such a [larger] Germany in the future as a powerful member of the European Community."[93] But the lack of progress toward a federation was due to the "weariness and timidity and lack of leadership" of the other Europeans. Between the lines he was presumably saying that reunifying Germany was a way of forcing the other Europeans to create the kind of deep federation that could safely house the Germans.[94]

In August and September 1948, Kennan laid out his famous notion of the five areas of military-industrial power – the United States, Britain, the Ruhr, Japan, and the Soviet Union.[95] He did so in the context of Program A and of his disagreement with the Office of European Affairs (EUR) over the scope of the Atlantic pact. If there had to be an alliance, Kennan preferred a two-anchor structure with limited membership, while EUR favored a single, broader grouping.[96] Since four of the five areas were already in Western hands, the five-center notion was essentially a way of reiterating the old problem of dividing German and Russian power. In the same lecture Kennan spoke of "the maneuvering of Russian power back into the Russian border." Since the Russians were now facing the disintegration of their sphere, they would try to hold on even more tightly to what they had. Still, "we must get them out. We cannot settle for them remaining there indefinitely."[97] The way was Program A: it would give the Russians a relatively graceful exit. Since U.S. troops would also withdraw, it would weaken the one effective argument the Russians had to justify their presence to the Eastern Europeans: protection of the area against a resurgent Germany allied to the United States.

Kennan and the PPS proposed Program A (November 1949) as the position to be taken by the United States in the case of a future Council of Foreign Ministers (CFM) meeting on the German problem.[98] But unification ran directly counter to the efforts of EUR and of the military authorities who were engaged in a complicated argument with the French over the powers to be granted to the new western German government. Kennan had already anticipated another basic problem:

93. PPS 37, *FRUS*, 1948, 2: 1287–97.
94. Ibid., 1295–96.
95. See GFK lecture, "Contemporary Problems of Foreign Policy," Sept. 17, 1948, GKP, box 17; see also Gaddis, *Strategies of Containment*, chap. 2.
96. On this disagreement see GFK to Lovett, Aug. 31, 1948, *FRUS*, 1948, 3: 225.
97. GFK, "Contemporary Problems of Foreign Policy."
98. *FRUS*, 1948, 2: 1321–38. See also *Memoirs*, 1: chap. 18.

At every turn we find this terrible dilemma that what appears to be the sensible thing to do about Germany is the thing that our own allies are most reluctant to do. We then are before the choice of whether we should do things which we think in the long run will undermine the power of Western Europe or things which would cause us to depart from the company of our allies.[99]

Clay told a U.S. official: "Our French friends, if they saw it [Kennan's proposal,] would immediately reclassify you and me as 'les meilleurs amis.' "[100]

Kennan was worried about a split between the United States and its allies, but he was inclined to pursue what he saw as the higher interests of Europe and let the chips fall where they may. He did not want U.S. policy toward Europe determined on the basis of calculations of what the Europeans wanted in the immediate future or were likely to accept. Such a course was no more sensible or honorable, he thought, than allowing policy to be dictated by what American politicians would be likely to support.[101]

Kennan, Acheson, and the vision of three worlds

That Kennan had achieved prominence under General Marshall was not without its ironic aspects. Kennan's disagreements with the secretary were of a rather basic order.[102] During the war, at least, Marshall had personified the "military pro-Sovietism" that Kennan had deplored. As secretary, Marshall did not fight to keep control of the European Recovery Program (ERP) in the hands of the State Department and lent his prestige to the projects Kennan opposed, the London program and the North Atlantic Treaty. Whatever Marshall's failings, however, Kennan believed that the austere Virginian came closer than anyone to embodying the eighteenth century virtues of disinterested public service and moral strength. For his part, Marshall had given the PPS – his own creation – an exalted place in the department. He had appreciated Kennan's abilities during the launching of the ERP and allowed him to play the role of thinker-in-residence and, for a brief time, *éminence grise*, to which the younger man aspired.

With the advent of Dean Acheson, Kennan recalled, there was

---

99. GFK, "Contemporary Problems of Foreign Policy."
100. *FRUS*, 1948, 2: 1320, n. 1.
101. On this point see *Memoirs*, 1: 413–14.
102. Kennan himself hints at this. See ibid., 345–46.

a perceptible change in the position and possibilities of the Planning Staff. He [Acheson] was a man who dealt, in his inner world, not with institutions but with personalities; and he was not always, I thought, a good judge of the latter. My Foreign Service experience was not only strange to him but was in his eyes, I suspect, of dubious value as a preparation for statesmanship or anything else.... There were times when I felt like a court jester, expected to enliven discussion, privileged to say the shocking things, valued as an intellectual gadfly on the hides of slower colleagues but not to be taken fully seriously when it came to the final, responsible decision of policy.[103]

There was, in other words, a new chemistry at work. The difference in age – Kennan was eleven years younger – was perhaps too slight to allow the kind of filial deference on Kennan's part that might have smoothed relations; nor, though he was from the same generation, did Acheson possess the romantic allure of Forrestal or Bullitt. Kennan liked and esteemed Acheson but felt a certain intellectual superiority; for all his savoir faire, Acheson was without European experience, without languages, without a historical education. From Kennan's standpoint, Acheson had enjoyed the advantages but suffered from the provincialism and cultural limitations of the Northeastern WASP elite. By origin he was a domestic political animal whose patrons, along with Felix Frankfurter, had been Hull and FDR. But Acheson was also the kind of figure apt to trigger Kennan's old middle western diffidence and undergraduate insecurities: he felt engaged in a social, as well as an intellectual – the two realms now overlapped – competition for influence. Thus he came to miss his hierarchical, quasi-military relationship with Marshall. While ostensibly impersonal, their connection had seemed to guarantee an automatic and respectful hearing for Kennan's views.

In fact, Kennan probably exerted more influence on Acheson in 1949 than his recollections imply. The real problem was that Kennan's ideas were now seriously diverging from those of his other colleagues. He continued to back Program A and possible negotiation with the Russians.[104] As chairman of the National Security Council "Steering Committee" on Germany, he was charged with finding agreement with the Pentagon and the ECA. By early March he had decided to go to Germany himself.

Kennan's March 1949 visit rekindled old feelings of empathy and solicitude, mixed with what he called "an almost neurotic distaste" for Germany's occupiers and tutors. He was especially moved by the destruction of Hamburg – not like Berlin a symbol of Nazi hubris,

103. Ibid., 426.
104. See GFK paper on German policy, Mar. 8, 1949, *FRUS*, 1949, 3: 96–102.

but a "comfortable, good-humored seaport community, dedicated like so many of our own cities [read Milwaukee] to the common-sense humdrum of commerce and industry."[105] "The tragedy of the decent Germany was in just sufficient degree my own tragedy that I could not close my eyes to it." Later he realized that he may have reacted with greater anguish than the Germans themselves to the indignities of the occupation.[106] His German contacts echoed his view that the new political class needed "responsibility thrust upon them."[107] Kennan discussed the idea of a simplified "occupation statute" with the French foreign minister Robert Schuman.[108] A colleague later gave Kennan main credit for conceiving the Allied High Commission that replaced the military governorship after agreement among the U.S., French, and British foreign ministers at Washington in April 1949.[109] As for Program A, however, the visit provided no encouragement. The mayor of Berlin was more concerned with creating a western German government than a settlement with the Russians. A German-American friend advised that the West "cling to the split Germany as the only hope for the consolidation of Western Europe. A united Germany would probably be indigestible."[110]

Among the factors eventually dividing him from Acheson, Kennan stressed their different cultural backgrounds:

> He, having never lived in Eastern Europe or Russia (and perhaps sharing Sigmund Freud's view that the people east of the Elbe were baptized late and very badly), considered the possibility of agreement for the withdrawal of the Russian forces from the Eastern zone of Germany to be of relatively small importance and thus expendable, whereas our occupational establishment in Western Germany, and the Western unity it symbolized, were definitely not. I, on the other hand, haunted by memories of long residence in both Germany and Russia, considered our occupational establishment in Western Germany decidedly expendable, but clung desperately to the hope of getting the Russians to retire someday from the heart of the continent.[111]

105. *Memoirs*, 1: 435–37.
106. Ibid., 428–29, 447.
107. Ibid., 432. Kennan is referring to a conversation with the mayor of Berlin, Ernst Reuter.
108. *FRUS*, 1949, 2: 113–14.
109. Richard Bissell Oral History Interview, HSTL. On this point see also GFK to Under Secretary of State James Webb, Feb. 25, 1949, PPS Records, box 20042, RG 59, NA; GFK letter to Acheson (unsent), Mar. 29, 1949, GKP, box 23.
110. *Memoirs*, 1: 423–33. Kennan does not identify the German-American, but it may have been Felix Gilbert, who served in the occupation and was later a Princeton colleague.
111. Ibid., 445.

Kennan's Milwaukee–Berlin formation divided him not only from Acheson but from his West German interlocutors as well. Kennan must have realized that Konrad Adenauer and the leadership of the Christian Democratic Union (CDU), while basically committed to reunification, were prepared to live indefinitely with a solution that isolated the Socialist strongholds of Saxony and Berlin. For the Rhinelander Adenauer, the Elbe was a natural dividing line between the civilized European and non-European worlds. Kennan found himself isolated by his idealistically broad conception of the West.

Rumors of the existence of Program A prompted semipanic in Paris and soothing denials from Washington.[112] The program had already received a mortal blow during a meeting on March 31. In a discussion of the possibility of negotiations with the Russians, Foreign Secretary Ernest Bevin told Acheson, "If the Soviets withdraw from Europe they will want us to do so also, but this would frighten the European population." When Acheson mentioned a "sort of peripheral withdrawal" (Program A), Bevin said that he had "never seriously considered that possibility."[113] On May 10, Bevin warned Acheson that German leaders were adamantly opposed to any kind of reunification other than the annexation of the eastern zone under the provisions of the West German Basic Law.[114] Acheson's May 11 memorandum outlining the U.S. position at the CFM included a cautious reference to regrouping troops, but this brought Bevin's warning that mere mention of the possibility might have an "unsettling effect on public opinion in Europe."[115] Kennan commented bitterly, "Piece by piece, in our own deliberations here and in the concessions we have made to French and British feeling in Paris, the essentials of this program [A] have been discarded."[116]

In mid-1949, Kennan made a final attempt to regain the initiative. In April, he had solicited an invitation to go to England to discuss Anglo-American relations and the connection of both countries to the Con-

---

112. On the demise of Program A see ibid., 444: Bohlen, 284–85; Miscamble, *George F. Kennan*, 158–69; Lucius Clay, *Decision in Germany* (Garden City, N.Y.: Doubleday, 1950), 438–39. The military was particularly upset by the implications of the plan.
113. *FRUS*, 1949, 3: 157.
114. Ibid., 870–72.
115. Ibid., 873, 875. Miscamble's is probably the most thorough account of the Program A episode, but his suggestion that Acheson was still open to German reunification in May 1949 on anything other than terms acceptable to Adenauer seems misleading to me. See *George F. Kennan*, 167.
116. Kennan memo to Acheson, May 20, 1949, in Miscamble, *George F. Kennan*, 89.

tinent. Using the Foreign Office's invitation,[117] Kennan launched a basic review of U.S. policy toward Europe, leading to his July paper, PPS 55. Kennan's vision of Europe crystallized against the background of an increasingly assertive West German government and the emerging crisis of the Marshall Plan. By early 1949, ECA officials had become alarmed by the prospect of a European balance-of-payments deficit of up to $3 billion per annum after the end of the plan in 1952. Intra-European trade, national production, and capital investment continued to improve, but there had been little progress toward the kind of European-wide integration that ECA officials believed would rationalize industry, lower costs, and render Europe independent of outside help. With an American recession in 1949, European dollar earnings declined, threatening a proliferation of trade and currency controls and the collapse of U.S. plans for an economic regime based on nondiscrimination and stable noncommunist governments.[118]

British policy was a critical factor in 1949. A year earlier Bevin had launched the idea of a British-led Anglo-Continental economic union. Its unspoken purpose was to prevent Europe and the Commonwealth from being crushed between the Soviet Union and the United States.[119] Such ideas had wide currency in the Foreign Office and had been advanced during the war by Eden and Smuts.[120] But a coalition of pro-Empire, Treasury, and left-wing Labour Party spokesmen had soon forced Bevin to water down plans for a supranational entity. In mid-1949, faced with a run on sterling at least as serious as the crisis of August 1947, the British government seemed prepared to oppose even modest amounts of European integration and fall back on autarchy within the sterling bloc.[121] Such a step, in turn, would provoke a severe reaction on the part of U.S. officials like Treasury Secretary John Snyder, who blamed Britain's problems on socialism, and Averell Harriman, who believed the British had broken their promises on European integration.[122]

Kennan, the PPS, and a group of outside consultants[123] took up the issue of European unity in May–June 1949. Their question was: "In what geographic area and in what framework of membership did we

117. See Jebb to GFK, Apr. 7, 1949, *FRUS*, 1949, 4: 289–91.
118. See Hogan, *The Marshall Plan*, 208, 238.
119. Ibid., 112–14.
120. See Chapter 3, this volume.
121. Hogan, *The Marshall Plan*, chap. 6.
122. Harriman was now special representative in Europe for the ECA.
123. These included Arnold Wolfers, Reinhold Niebuhr, Hans Morgenthau, and Robert Oppenheimer. On this subject see Miscamble, *George F. Kennan*, chap. 9.

wish to see the movement toward European unification proceed, over the long term, and how far did we really wish it to go?" Another way of posing the question, Kennan said, was "whether there are to be two worlds or three."[124] For Kennan the situation contained an unassailable logic. He envisioned two natural federal groupings: the United States, Britain, and Canada, on one hand; France, Germany, and the smaller European countries, on the other. The first was essentially Anglo-Saxon (though it might include Norway and Britain's traditional ally, Portugal), maritime, and extra-European in interests and mentality; the second, relatively land-bound and Continental.

Kennan reasoned on the basis of the recent Marshall Plan as well as longer-term historical experience. It was obvious from the attitude of the British toward the fledgling Organization of European Economic Cooperation (OEEC) that they constituted a basic obstacle, or "ceiling," to progress toward European federation.[125] Kennan did not blame Britain. After all, its interest and instinct had always been to try to break up any Continental combination it could not control. In order to safeguard the process of European integration, and to prevent new burdens from falling on America's shoulders, Britain's political talents and limited resources were better employed in the defense of vital Western interests *outside* of continental Europe. With time the venerable mother country would probably come more and more under the wings of its robust New World children. The United States would have to underwrite and gradually liquidate the sterling system, a price well worth paying if it meant "the continental countries would be free of the greatest barrier to rapprochement among themselves."[126] In any case, the United States would have to restrain Britain's natural but now misguided impulse to prevent the true unity of Europe. By 1949 – and probably well before – Kennan saw Britain as a fundamentally decadent power, but still strong enough to undermine an emerging European structure. He acknowledged that if the United States and Canada were to join a European federation, the British would abandon their objections. But such a federation could not extend to Eastern Europe. The Russians would never allow their satellites to be part of an entity organized and dominated by the Americans, while the notion of a federation "extending from San Francisco to the eastern Carpathians and the Pripet Marshes" – the natural borders of Europe – did not

124. *Memoirs*, 1: 451. See also Minutes of PPS meeting May 18, 1949, PPS Reords, box 32, RG 59, NA.
125. *Memoirs*, 1: 453–54; see also PPS 55, PPS Records, RG 59, NA.
126. Minutes of PPS meeting, May 25, 1949, PPS Records, box 32, RG 59, NA.

make any sense.[127] The gap in historical experience, economic development, and political tradition between Eastern Europe and the Anglo-Saxon maritime states was too vast to allow federation in anything but name.

The beauty of the separate Continental grouping was that it would deal simultaneously with the problems of American overextension, providing a place in Europe for the Eastern satellites, counterbalancing Russian power, and what to do with Germany. Beneath this notion lay Kennan's old conviction that Europe's only salvation lay in harnessing Germany's strength and talent, something possible only within the kind of real federation that without British obstructionism might actually be built. In the absence of unification, he believed, the Germans might eventually take the issue into their own hands in the spirit of "a plague on both your houses."[128] During the 1949 election campaign, both CDU and Social Democratic candidates denounced Allied restrictions on German sovereignty and the dismantling of German industry. Kennan's analysis also drew on his personal experience of the Weimar period and the mood of pessimism, vulnerability, and geopolitical claustrophobia that had characterized the Central European cultural climate. The Germans, he believed, needed physical and psychic space in which to express themselves and vent their extraordinary energies. Damming them up within another "over-crowded, occupied and frustrated semi-state" would produce another tragic explosion – thus Kennan's insistence on outlets for German immigration, to Africa, for example, and on using the idea of Europe "to create something larger... to which German loyalties and attention would be attracted."[129] The idea of a rump West Germany, economically dependent on overseas markets, the old "small German" and 1944 Lippmann model, was obviously familiar to Kennan but he considered it unfeasible. Needless to say, neither he nor anyone else foresaw the dimensions of the subsequent "economic miracle," while the prospect that the Germans would react to their second defeat by adopting America and its consumer civilization as a kind of *Ersatzfaterland* was, for someone like Kennan, virtually inconceivable.

In short, Kennan's 1949 vision of a Continental bloc sprang naturally

127. *Memoirs*, 1: 454.
128. GFK to Acheson, May 20, 1949, *FRUS*, 1949, 3: 889.
129. GFK letter to Bohlen, Nov. 7, 1949, GKP, box 28; see also Minutes of PPS meetings, June 13 and 14, 1949, PPS Records, box 32, RG 59, NA. On possible German immigration and technical assistance to Africa, see Minutes of PPS meeting, June 3, 1949, PPS Records, box 32, RG 59, NA. This was all the more urgent because of the influx of millions of refugees from the East.

from his interwar Berlin perspective. He saw no point in denying that Germany was the political and economic magnet around which the smaller Central and Eastern European raw-material-producing countries would cluster. This had been true before 1914, when Germany and Austria had exercised a relatively benign hegemony. Kennan told Acheson in October 1949 that the Germans knew much more about how to organize the area, including Poland, Czechoslovakia, and Yugoslavia, than did the United States or Britain: "It often seemed to me during the war living over there that what was wrong with Hitler's new order was that it was Hitler's." Along with Bullitt and Berle, moreover, Kennan presumably believed that not everything Hitler had tried to do ran counter to the interests of the West,[130] nor had his geopolitical analysis been entirely wrong. Shortly before the end, Hitler had observed:

> If fate had granted to an aging and enfeebled Britain a new Pitt instead of this Jew-ridden, half-American drunkard, the new Pitt would at once have recognized that Britain's traditional policy of balance of power would have to be applied on a different scale, and this time on a worldwide scale. Instead of maintaining, creating and adding fuel to Europe's rivalries, Britain ought to do her utmost to encourage and bring about a reunification of Europe. . . . The crucial new factor [since Pitt's day] is the existence of those two giants, the United States and Russia.[131]

Here in a sense – minus the Nazi ideology and vulgarity – was Kennan's own message in 1949: German hegemony in Eastern and Central Europe – a version of the so-called big German or Continental option – had a certain historical and economic inevitability, and Germany alone could provide the margin of material resources necessary for an *inherent* European balance vis-à-vis the superpowers. The alternative was prolonged American hegemony over Western Europe in tandem with Soviet domination of the East. Creating a Continental receptacle in which the Eastern satellites might be collected was also an urgent matter for Kennan. In August 1949, he again stressed the weaknesses of the Soviet position in the East and the need to encourage, as an interim step, heretical Communist regimes.[132] The prospects for such a development would be greatly enhanced by the withdrawal of Soviet troops from

---

130. On this point see Chapter 2, this volume.
131. Minutes of PPS meeting, Oct. 18, 1949, PPS Records, box 32, RG 59, NA. Hitler quoted in David P. Calleo, *The German Problem Reconsidered* (New York: Cambridge University Press, 1978), 109.
132. PPS 59, Aug. 25, 1949, *FRUS*, 1949, 5: 21–26. See also NSC 58/2, Dec. 8, 1949, ibid., 42–55.

Eastern Europe, something, in turn, that was unlikely to happen as long as U.S. troops remained in Germany.

It is fitting that Kennan's last important contribution – and also his demise – as director of the PPS was connected to his vision of two federal groupings, allied through the Atlantic pact but politically and economically distinct. No official action had been taken on Kennan's proposal by the time of the U.S.–British–Canadian talks in September 1949, but the U.S. position, and the sheer fact that secret, exclusive tripartite talks were conducted, reflected Kennan's view. It was Kennan who prepared Acheson's briefing paper for the negotiations and who arranged for conciliatory language to be inserted into a speech given by President Truman just before Bevin and Chancellor of the Exchequer Stafford Cripps arrived.[133] The talks led to the devaluation of sterling in return for U.S. aid and concessions. The United States conceded the need for further sterling bloc discrimination against the dollar and agreed – at least in Kennan's interpretation – that Britain's non-European commitments should take precedence over its European role. Discussions also took place with a view to restoring Anglo-American atomic energy collaboration, which had been brusquely cut off by the Atomic Energy Act of 1946. In a meeting on September 13 of the Combined [U.S.–British–Canadian] Policy Committee on Atomic Energy, Kennan expained why, in his words, "the conclusion had been reached in the [State] Department that an attempt should be made to link the United Kingdom more closely to the United States and Canada and to get the United Kingdom to disengage itself as much as possible from Continental European problems."[134]

Three days later, on orders from Under Secretary of State James Webb, the procedure governing PPS papers was abruptly changed. The papers were no longer to go directly from Kennan to the secretary, but would be reviewed, and if necessary changed, to reflect the opinions of other high officials. As Kennan immediately understood, "a question of confidence" had been raised. On September 29, 1949, he asked to be relieved as head of the PPS. Kennan indicates in his memoirs that the paper at issue concerned Yugoslavia,[135] but it seems almost certain that

---

133. *Memoirs*, 1: 454–61. The briefing paper Kennan refers to in his memoirs is presumably PPS 62, Sept. 3, 1949, printed in *FRUS*, 1949, 4: 822–30.

134. On the September 1949 talks see Hogan, *The Marshall Plan*, 261–65; Alan Milward, *The Reconstruction of Western Europe* (Berkeley: University of California Press, 1984), 335–61. For Kennan's presentation see *FRUS*, 1949, 1: 521. Britain's sterling debt, according to the PPS, amounted to the equivalent of $13.5 billion. Ibid., 824. The talks created a tripartite organization, separate from the OEEC, to deal with Britain's enormous sterling debts.

135. *Memoirs*, 1: 465–68.

Webb's move was connected to PPS 55, setting out Kennan's European vision, and to the outcome of the tripartite talks, reflecting Kennan's line. The general department view of the talks was anything but enthusiastic. This, in turn, reflected the reaction of the continental Europeans.[136]

In all probability the "vote of no confidence" reflected the belief that Kennan's personal preferences had determined high policy – before PPS 55 had been officially accepted by the secretary of state. The desire to cut Kennan down to size must have been building in certain quarters since the disagreements over NATO and Program A; perhaps it was fueled by the fact that a prominent newspaper column had effusively praised Kennan's British policy just before the tripartite talks.[137] There were still plenty of people who recalled Kennan's wartime "bureaucratic end-runs" and personal protagonism. There is some irony in the fact that Kennan's downfall in September 1949 was not connected to a disagreement with Acheson himself. If anything, it had to do with what others saw as his excessive influence over the secretary and to the fundamental *agreement* between them on the necessity of a "special relationship" with Britain.

The specific reason for the negative reaction to the tripartite talks was the "abandonment" of France. In his *Memoirs* Kennan observes:

> Not specifically expressed in the paper [PPS 55] but an integral part of the thinking that lay behind it and freely expressed to all with whom I discussed it, were two additional assumptions. One was that Germany, while perhaps contributing in certain suitable ways to arrangements for the defense of Western Europe, would themselves remain outside of the NATO pact and without armed forces of their own. The other assumption was that the driving force behind any movement toward political unification on the continent, and the dominant influence within any federal union that came into being, would be, naturally and unquestionably, France.[138]

The record suggests that this statement may well reflect what he hoped for and preferred, but does not fully capture what he was saying in 1949. On May 20, Kennan told his staff, "I am afraid that while we cannot say so, what we have to do is to persuade the Europeans to find

---

136. Kennan said that the French "lost no time in staging tantrums of anxiety and discontent." Ibid., 462. This was partly due to the fact that the British devaluation of 30%, announced on September 18, took France and the Benelux countries by surprise and created havoc for their policy calculations.

137. For the article praising the idea and attributing Truman's recent speech to Kennan, see the Alsop brothers, "Boldness at Last," *New York Herald Tribune*, Sept. 2, 1949.

138. *Memoirs*, 1: 455.

a way to permit Germany's leadership to become manifest without involving military and political controls of a nationalist Germany over the other countries of Europe."[139] On June 13, he observed, "The Germans are natural leaders and the only potential unifiers in Europe. I am afraid our solutions are ignoring these basic facts."[140] On June 14, when Arnold Wolfers stressed the need to reassure France, Kennan replied:

> We have spent four years since the war ended trying in utter sincerity to do exactly what you have been talking about.... I don't know what more we could have done. The French meanwhile have given us no hope that they would seize and exercise leadership if the gap left by Germany is going to be filled. Is our position towards France to be utterly independent from what they do?[141]

Kennan probably realized that there was no better way to oblige the French to take the lead in creating a European federation than to confront them with the prospect of a revived and independent Germany.

By the time Kennan met with Acheson in October 1949 to prepare a policy statement for discussion by U.S. officials in Paris, he had felt the wrath of American Francophile opinion. Walter Lippmann, whose Atlantic Community included France, derided Kennan's view.[142] Charles Bohlen, now counselor at the Paris Embassy, lectured him: "We must again permit no ground for the Continental Europeans' believing that we have any special understanding with Great Britain and Canada."[143] Other branches of the State Department attacked PPS 55 on similar grounds.[144] For his part, Kennan doubted the wisdom of pandering to "what is in reality the lack of confidence of the French in themselves," but accepted the need to stress the Anglo-American military guarantee.[145] The secretary's carefully worded statement to U.S. ambassadors in Europe stated that "the key to progress towards integration is in French hands.... France and France alone can take the decisive leadership in integrating Western Germany into Western Europe." But if it failed to rise to the occasion, the United States would have to give the German horse its head. "I believe," said Acheson, "that this may be the last chance for France to take the lead." In effect, he struck a

---

139. Note on PPS discussion of May 20, 1949, PPS Records, box 32, RG 59, NA.
140. Minutes of PPS meeting, June 13, 1949, PPS Records, box 32, RG 59, NA.
141. Minutes of PPS meeting, June 14, 1949, PPS Records, box 32, RG 59, NA.
142. Walter Lippmann, "Whither Britain?" *New York Herald Tribune*, Sept. 26, 1949.
143. Bohlen to GFK, Oct. 6, 1949, GKP, box 28.
144. Hogan, *The Marshall Plan*, 269.
145. GFK to Bohlen, Oct. 12, 1949, GKP, box 28.

compromise between Kennan's and the diametrically opposite line that Britain be given a crack of the whip on its hindquarters and a firm shove into Europe: "We will encourage the U.K. to move as far and as fast as it can in strengthening its ties to the continent, though we recognize there are good reasons why the U.K. feels that it would have to stop short of steps involving merger of sovereignty at this time."[146]

Kennan's view, still implicit in the secretary's message, received a thrashing at the hands of Bohlen, Harriman, Ambassadors Lewis Douglas (Britain), David Bruce (France), and James Dunn (Italy), and the U.S. high commissioner for Germany, John McCloy. Harriman was the leading exponent of the whip-cracking approach; Britain, the main beneficiary of the Marshall Plan, was simply not cooperating and should be told so "bluntly and immediately." For Bruce, the British economy was "so intertwined with the European economy that no integration of Western Europe [was] conceivable without the full participation of the U.K." Like Douglas, he stressed the weakness of the British world position, leaving them no real option but Europe. All rejected any suggestion of German rather than French leadership, while adding that the latter could emerge only under the "umbrella" (Harriman's expression) of the North Atlantic Treaty.[147] Acheson's representative at the meeting reported "complete unanimity of opinion" that the British were needed in Europe to prevent the possibility of German domination and to reassure the French.[148] They turned Kennan's thesis on its head.

The old differences of background and perspective between Kennan and the others had now come home to roost. Harriman, Bruce, and Bohlen were deeply preoccupied with the need to avoid French fears of isolation on the Continent by providing them with iron-clad guarantees. According to their conventional wisdom, the failure of the British and the Americans to provide such guarantees had been the basic cause of the French failure to take the initiative against Germany in the thirties, of appeasement, and of the eventual debacle. Bohlen, Bruce, and Harriman looked at the situation squarely from the standpoint of Paris, where, it so happened, they all resided at the time. Having lost the classic option of alliance with Russia or a system of smaller Eastern

---

146. Acheson to U.S. Embassy at Paris, Oct. 19, 1949, *FRUS*, 1949, 4: 469–72. See also Kennan's comments on France during the department meeting attended by Acheson to prepare the message. Minutes of meeting, Oct. 18, 1949, PPS Records, box 32, RG 59, NA.

147. *FRUS*, 1949, 4: 472–96.

148. Assistant Secretary of State for European Affairs George Perkins to Acheson, Oct. 22, 1949, ibid., 342–44.

European states, the French had even less choice than in the thirties as far as reliance on the Anglo-Saxons was concerned. De Gaulle, to be sure, favored a more independent policy, but Bohlen and Harriman had acquired a Rooseveltian hostility toward the general. As for what to do with Britain, their conventional view also reflected the lingering influence of FDR. Roosevelt had always tried to push the British into taking responsibility for Western Europe, combined with a scaling-down of Britain's overseas commitments.

The disagreement between Kennan and his old companion Bohlen had a poignant aspect. Kennan's insistence on the essential *weakness* of the Soviet position no doubt struck a responsive chord in Bohlen. From Bohlen he could also expect sympathy for the idea that Europe did not end at the Elbe but stretched to the Carpathians and Pripet Marshes. But their common Russian experience counted for less in the end than the contrasts between a Cambridge Avenue, Milwaukee–Berlin formation, on one hand, and a Cambridge, Massachusetts–Paris education, on the other. Bohlen, who had learned his Russian in Paris in the late twenties, had absorbed the French geopolitical anxieties of the period; he had a sympathy for France and sense of its centrality that Kennan lacked, along with a Rooseveltian view of Britain.[149] For Kennan's part, there is no evidence that he felt any pangs of conscience about the Anglo-American failure to back France against Germany in the thirties. He was more inclined to the Berle view that France's troubles arose from the misbegotten peace of 1919 and that the French had themselves to blame. From his Central European perspective, Germany had to be the guts and brawn, even if not the guiding brain, of a European federation. The alternative was a continent subordinated to the non-European powers, a prospect that did not appear to trouble the Rooseveltian Bohlen.

After a heated exchange of letters with Bohlen, Kennan admitted that his estimate of his own usefulness in Washington had been shaken.[150] Once more, however, Kennan probably underestimated the practical impact of his views. After September 1949, U.S. policy makers generally accepted the notion of British distinctness, or "exceptionalism," with respect to European integration – even if the "no Europe without

---

149. For Bohlen's position on the United States, Britain, and the Empire, see Minutes of PPS meeting, Jan. 24, 1950, which is also an excellent summary of the Kennan–Bohlen argument. *FRUS*, 1950, 3: 617–22. See also T. Michael Ruddy, *Cautious Diplomat: Charles E. Bohlen and the Soviet Union* (Kent, Ohio: Kent State University Press, 1986), 94–95.

150. GFK to Bohlen, Nov. 17, 1949, GKP, box 28. See also letters cited in notes 143 and 145.

Britain" school survived. It also appears that at least one influential Frenchman got the message that Kennan presumably wished to send. When Jean Monnet launched the "Schuman Plan" for a European coal and steel community in the spring of 1950, his argument was that France, having failed to dismember Germany, must shake off its pessimism and self-absorption and take the initiative in building a federal Europe in partnership with Germany. The alternative, he warned, was American sponsorship of an autonomous, resurgent Germany that would once again overshadow France.[151]

"The whole ominous significance"

Kennan's final parting of the ways with the Truman administration had to do with the reaction of the United States to the Soviet atomic test in September and the defeat of the Chinese Nationalists in October 1949. These events served to accelerate trends that were fundamentally at odds with Kennan's three-world vision. They increased the likelihood of a long-term U.S. protectorate over Western Europe and a permanently divided continent. Early 1950 saw the decision to develop the hydrogen bomb, while the formulation of NSC 68 presaged the kind of geographically limitless anti-Soviet alliance and generalized imperial responsibilities that Kennan had deplored.[152]

Kennan looked with a certain disbelief on the prospect that his objectives were to be supplanted by the ones he had opposed.[153] His increasing preoccupation with the loss of a sense of proportion in U.S. policy also arose from the awareness of his personal fall from grace. He concluded that the role of professional planner-cum-*éminence-grise* that he had coveted, outside the regular chain of command, had been a failure.[154] In fact, his assumption that he could shape minds through the power and artistry of the written word had been, to a degree, the product of personal presumption; his faith in his own ideas and intuition had at times rendered him oblivious to the real views of his

151. Jean Monnet, *Memoirs* (Garden City, N.Y.: Doubleday, 1978), chap. 12.

152. *Memoirs*, 1: 474–75. On NSC 68 see Paul Hammond, "Prologue to Rearmament," in Warner R. Schilling et al., *Strategy, Politics, and Defense Budgets* (New York: Columbia University Press, 1962), 267–387.

153. Paul Nitze replaced Kennan as director of the PPS on January 1, 1950. In February, in his new role of counselor, Kennan urged Acheson to consider systematic indoctrination of department officials in order to correct misconceptions about U.S. objectives. See GFK memo to Acheson, Feb. 17, 1950, *FRUS, 1950*, 1: 65–66. See also excerpt from GFK diary, quoted in *Memoirs*, 1: 468.

154. *Memoirs*, 1: 467.

colleagues. It is this intense reflectiveness connected with what he saw as his personal failings that lends force and pathos to Kennan's end-of-career injunction against pride and self-delusion in U.S. foreign policy.

The Kennan of late 1949 was the Chekhovian critic of humanity's thralldom to technology, once again looking back to the preindustrial era as a time of relative equilibrium and contentment. His experience as a policy maker had served to confirm his distaste for the nineteenth century – an epoch whose unbounded faith in science had ultimately produced atomic energy and the bomb. The vulnerability of modern society to totalitarianism was linked, he wrote, to "the disintegration of basic social groups in which the individual found the illusion of security through the sense of belonging – namely, the family, the local community, the neighborhood. . . . what is causing these groups to disintegrate is the urbanization of life – that is, the revolution in living wrought by modern technology."[155] How, he asked, could the United States presume to solve the rest of the world's problems by exporting such a way of life?

Speaking of the vast changes in store after 1900, he observed that only a few people – for example, the Adams brothers – "seem really to have caught the whole ominous significance of what [was] in the making." Brooks had foreseen the decline of Britain, and a day "'when two great systems [would] be left pitted against each other.'" Henry had looked "with fascinated horror at the dizzy acceleration of progress in science."[156] Kennan might have added that his own father had glimpsed the shape of things to come. Kennan turned increasingly, at this point, to the Federalist tradition. He quoted John Quincy Adams's dictum that the United States "does not go abroad in search of monsters to destroy." Nor should it aspire to "infuse into others a foreign will to the exclusion of their own."[157] From the Adams brothers' critique of industrial modernity it was but a short step to their grandfather's diplomatic precepts – and thence to an even more straitened, seventeenth century New England notion of national interest and mission with its emphasis on self-perfection and self-control.

Within the State Department there was still one colleague who might

---

155. GFK memo, Oct. 17, 1949, *FRUS*, 1949, 1: 404–5. See also Jerald A. Combs, "The Compromise That Never Was: George Kennan, Paul Nitze, and the Issue of Conventional Deterrence in Europe, 1949–1952," *Diplomatic History*, 15, no. 3 (Summer 1991), 361–86.

156. GFK lecture, "Where Do We Stand?" Dec. 21, 1949, Dean Acheson Papers, box 62, HSTL.

157. GFK lecture, "Foreign Aid and the Formulation of National Policy," Nov. 10, 1949, GKP, box 17.

have been expected to sympathize with Kennan's views, someone who had listened attentively to Kennan on Russia and other subjects. Kennan had tried to appoint him deputy head of the PPS in 1947, an idea that Acheson had adopted in mid-1949. He was a middle westerner who had been drawn to Wilson in 1919, who sympathized with German revisionism, and who had steeped himself in Spengler. His foreign policy views in the thirties closely paralleled those of the older *jeunesse radicale* isolationists like his fellow German-American, Berle; Bullitt, whom he knew personally; and Forrestal, his boss and patron. His personal affection for Kennan ran deep.[158] Nonetheless, Paul Nitze represented a classic case of someone (Acheson eventually was another) who had taken to heart the first part of Kennan's message – that the Soviet regime was by its nature profoundly hostile to the West – while ignoring or discounting the second – that the Soviets were already overextended and had no intention to attack.

Kennan's disagreement with Nitze came to a head in early 1950. Nitze was deeply impressed by the potential of nuclear weapons. It appears that he had been marked for life by the surprise attack at Pearl Harbor. Though he did not see nuclear weapons as a panacea or substitute for conventional military power, he was naturally attracted by an instrument that might serve as a surrogate for the will and resolve of the American people in the international arena, something in which, as a former isolationist, he had little faith. He was intent on demystifying atomic weapons in the minds of people who believed that they could not be considered "normal" weapons. Kennan, in contrast, insisted on a philosophical distinction between weapons of mass destruction and conventional weapons. The former, he argued, could not be used to pursue the traditional ends of warfare: "They reach backward beyond the frontiers of Western civilization to the concepts of war which were once familiar to the Asiatic hordes. They cannot really be reconciled with a political purpose directed to shaping rather than destroying, the lives of the adversary." Kennan conceded that a supply of bombs should be kept on hand for purposes of deterrence and retaliation, but he rejected a strategy based on their first use. Even so, he feared that the possession of even a small number would "impart a certain eccentricity" to military planning and preferred, in the end, "an imperfect system of

158. On Nitze's background see Strobe Talbott, *The Master of the Game* (New York: Knopf, 1988), 23–46. See also David Callaghan, *Dangerous Capabilities: Paul Nitze and the Cold War* (New York: Harper & Row, 1990), 11–61. For some details, including Nitze's attraction to Wilson, I rely on my conversation with Nitze, Apr. 29, 1990, Bologna, Italy.

international control" to possession of the weapon.[159] Probably he foresaw that the United States would come to rely on the relatively cheap expedient of nuclear weapons to maintain its protectorate over Europe. This prospect served only to reinforce his attachment to his basic vision. To Nitze, who had sifted the rubble at Tokyo and Hiroshima, concluding that the difference between conventional and atomic attack was only a matter of degree, Kennan answered:

> Take but degree away – untune that string
> And hark what discord follows ...
> Then everything includes in power –
> Power into will, will into appetite,
> And appetite, a universal wolf,
> So doubly seconded with will and power,
> Must make perforce a universal prey
> And last eat up himself.[160]

Kennan was pleading for a sense of proportion lest the bomb, like Henry Adams's Dynamo, become an object of worship, lest an inanimate object replace the human qualities of bearing and persuasion.

Logically, the alternative to reliance on nuclear weapons was the conventional rearmament of the United States and Western Europe. By late 1949, the question of German rearmament was in the air.[161] Kennan himself had called all along for the rebuilding of the natural barriers to Russia. What could that mean if not the revival of armed strength, especially at a time when both Germany and France had ceased to exist as military powers? Kennan was rather at a loss to give a clear and consistent answer to this question. In the end he could only repeat his earlier argument that steps to militarize the confrontation with the Soviet Union would only provoke the kind of reaction that one presumably wanted to avoid.[162] To build up the economic strength and self-confidence of Japan and Germany was one thing; to turn them into armed clients and military outposts was another.[163] For Kennan, the alternative to militarization of the cold war remained the disengagement of U.S. and Soviet forces. In theory, the issue remained open until June

159. GFK (private) memo to Acheson, Jan. 20, 1950, *FRUS*, 1950, 1: 37–39.
160. Ibid., 36. Kennan is quoting from Shakespeare, *Troilus and Cressida*.
161. See, e.g., Dorothy Thompson, "Crisis in Germany on Rearming Issue Seen in Next Year," *Washington Star*, Dec. 24, 1949.
162. See Minutes of PPS meeting, Oct. 11, 1949, *FRUS*, 1949, 1: 415; GFK to Acheson, Feb. 17, 1950, *FRUS*, 1950, 1: 160–67.
163. The problem, he thought, was still essentially one of internal security, and he called for efficient police and paramilitary forces. See GFK to Lewis, Apr. 24, 1950, *FRUS*, 1950, 4: 681–82.

24, 1950. With the invasion of South Korea, widely interpreted as the first move in a general Soviet offensive, the arguments against U.S. and German rearmament were swept aside. But even before Korea, the argument Kennan deplored, that the United States must accommodate itself to European fears and anxieties, had won the day.

A moral-historical edifice

On the final page of the first volume of his memoirs, Kennan described his departure from Washington during the crisis and confusion of September 1950.[164] Thus began his inquiry – interrupted by spells of government service, including his brief ambassadorship in Moscow[165] – into the deeper causes of the transformation of America's world position. His basic purpose was didactic: he wrote history in order to demonstrate certain deeply held convictions about the modern world.

Kennan built his moral-historical edifice on the belief, always inherent in his outlook, that the great watershed in modern life was August 1914.[166] A series of fateful consequences flowed from the outbreak of the war: the shattering of the Austro-Hungarian Empire, the interruption by the Bolshevik Revolution of the precarious but promising evolution of the Russian state toward liberalism, the weakening of French and British power, the upsetting of the traditional American relationship to the Old World, including the intervention in Russia, an event full of unfortunate repercussions for relations between the two countries. Finally, the war broke what in Kennan's view was the inevitable and, all things considered, desirable trend of the late nineteenth century toward a relatively benign German hegemony over continental Europe and toward an entity that would have been able to balance Russian power on its own. Pre-1914 European statesmen had failed "to recognize that in the face of the growing power of the outside world, especially Russia, Old Europe could particularly ill-afford any division that tended... to weaken her power as a whole." In those

---

164. *Memoirs*, 1: 500.
165. Also as an adviser and negotiator during the Korean War and as ambassador to Yugoslavia.
166. The First World War was "*the* great seminal catastrophe of the century – the event which, more than any other, excepting only, perhaps the discovery of nuclear weaponry and the development of the population-environmental crisis, lay at the heart of the failure and decline of this Western Civilization." GFK, *The Decline of Bismarck's European Order: Franco-Russian Relations, 1875–1890* (Princeton, N.J.: Princeton University Press, 1979), 3–4. On Kennan as historian see also Michael Polley, *A Biography of George Kennan: The Education of a Realist* (Lewiston, N.Y.: Edwin Mellen Press, 1990), chap. 6.

circumstances, "the effort to prevent the gradual and natural development of Germany's importance to Europe – a development indicated by all the factors of the new age: geographic, demographic, political and economic – simply could not be worth the candle."[167] With all of its faults, Wilhelmine Germany was a country "run by conservative but relatively moderate people, no Nazis and no Communists, a vigorous Germany, united and unoccupied, full of energy and confidence."[168] Though Western statesmen might have taken positive steps after 1918 – including a far more sympathetic attitude toward Weimar[169] – the Second World War followed almost ineluctably from the first. Who in his right mind would not trade the Germany of 1933 or 1953 for the Germany of 1913? In a sense, Kennan's whole opus as a diplomat had consisted of the effort to put the train of history back on the track from which it had been tragically derailed in 1914.

Kennan's inquiry into the failure of pre-1914 statesmanship led him, over the years, to focus on the new relationship, "the fateful alliance," consummated between France and Russia in the early 1890s. Despite the bombast and unbalanced quality of its diplomacy, Kennan saw the Germany of his boyhood as an essentially satisfied power; it was France and Russia that, in their territorial revisionism, anti-German nationalism, and blindness to the consequences of modern warfare, had conspired to overthrow the status quo.[170] Not surprisingly, Kennan traced this colossal failure of vision to the passing of an older generation of statesmen. Bismarck, Palmerston, the emperor Wilhelm I were, for Kennan, "primarily eighteenth century personalities."[171] In this category Kennan no doubt meant to include the Russian foreign minister Nikolai Giers, who had seen the dangers in the Franco-Russian pact but had been unable to prevent it, and his *éminence grise*, the Baltic German Count Vladimir Lamsdorf – with whom Kennan identified himself. Lamsdorf's grasp of international affairs was practically unrivaled, "but his effectiveness was restricted by his neurotic shyness, his unsociability,

---

167. GFK lecture, "Western European Integration," Dec. 3, 1954, GKP, box 18. See also his lecture, "The West in the Twentieth Century: A Personal View," GKP, box 20.
168. GFK, "World War I," in *American Diplomacy, 1900–1950* (New York: Mentor Books, 1951), 51.
169. On this point see GFK, "World War II," in ibid., 71.
170. Both countries permitted their military leaders to plan a war that, once it had begun, would automatically engulf all of the great powers. Kennan made these points in a lecture, "The Franco-Russian Pact," Feb. 19, 1964, GKP, box 21. It is the theme of *The Decline of Bismarck's European Order* and of *The Fateful Alliance: France, Russia, and the Coming of the First World War* (Manchester: Manchester University Press, 1984).
171. GFK, *The Decline of Bismarck's European Order*, xv.

his cultivation of a fastidious privacy and his utter lack of talent [taste?] for that peculiar sort of bureaucratic infighting without which no great foreign office, it would seem, can exist and in the operation of which so many unworthy careers have been established and so many worthy ones broken."[172] Most of the subsequent generation were

> in some respects Victorians, in the sense that they were less secure in their values, more self-conscious, more imitative, more given to enacting a role, than their predecessors. . . . Whereas members of the older generation had been governed in their social and official conduct by the manners of the eighteenth century – clear, schooled, unapologetic, a law unto themselves – the conduct of these late nineteenth century people seemed by comparison, uncertain, histrionic, overacted – always with an anxious eye to spectators.[173]

Kennan would have agreed that the First World War was indeed "the Victorian war," as Amory Blaine had put it.[174]

Kennan saw forces that the Victorian generation of statesmen could neither understand nor control, in particular rabid nationalism. Nationalism, in turn, he saw as "the expression of a crisis of identity on the part of great masses of people displaced by the over-rapid social and economic changes of the nineteenth century." The world of the late nineteenth century

> held millions of people for whom, sometimes because of upward social movement, sometimes because of downward, sometimes because of educational experience, sometimes because of the change from country to city, their familiar and reassuring points of orientation had been lost. . . . In the cultivation of the myth of collective glory – the glory of the national society to which one belonged – one could lend to the individual's experience a meaning, or an appearance of meaning.[175]

These words were written about Russia, but they applied to the America of Thomas Lathrop and Kossuth Kent Kennan, to the jingoism of 1898, and to the anti-German chauvinism of 1917.

On reflection, Kennan found the arguments for America's turn-of-the-century departure unconvincing. By 1950, he was closer to Carl Schurz, the great middle western German-American leader, domestic

---

172. Ibid., 240.
173. Ibid., xv–xvi. Of Wilhelm II, Kennan said, "He was very much a product of the late nineteenth century, with all its inner uncertainties and extravagant pretentions." Ibid., 368.
174. See Chapter 4, this volume.
175. GFK, *The Decline of Bismarck's European Order*, 418–19.

reformer, and advocate of Continental autonomy[176] than to the turn-of-the-century geopoliticians. During the First World War, Kennan argued, instead of using its power to preserve the balance of power, the United States allowed itself to be drawn into an all-out struggle against Germany, while advancing a quixotic program for the abolition of the European state system.[177] Kennan sought the sources of American conduct in the intellectual climate of the Victorian period in which "a legalistic moralistic approach to international problems" had emerged.[178]

Kennan's tirade against "morality" as a guiding force in foreign policy was in reality an attack on what he considered the moral pretentiousness, fatuous optimism, and naive belief in universal progress typical of the nineteenth century middle classes. Into his critique he incorporated Lippmann's view that the long peace of the nineteenth century, the Booth Tarkington "Age of Innocence," had given a fairytale quality to American thinking about international questions. He also adopted Reinhold Niebuhr's view that during the same period middle-class liberals had lost a notion of original sin – a sense of innate human imperfectability – leading to their foolish and dangerous inability to recognize the corrupting power of "self-will" and self-interest in themselves as well as their ideological opponents.[179] Here, for Kennan, was the source of the self-deception, the hubris, what de Gaulle called the "will to power cloaked in idealism," that had characterized American foreign policy since 1898 and whose ultimate expression was FDR.[180] Finally, Kennan's mature outlook drew upon the old melancholia and sense of moral responsibility of someone who had escaped the First World War but who, like Amory Blaine in 1920, was keenly preoccupied by "the spirit of the past brooding over a new generation, the chosen youth from the muddled, unchastened world, still fed romantically

---

176. On Schurz see Hans Trefousse, *Carl Schurz: A Biography* (Knoxville: University of Tennessee Press, 1982), chap. 18.
177. See GFK, "World War I," in *American Diplomacy*. See also lecture, "Where We Stand, Where We Are Going," Aug. 29, 1950, GKP, box 18.
178. See GFK, *American Diplomacy*, 82; "Notes for Essays, Spring 1952, Consisting of 8 Sections" (U.S. External Relations Project), GKP, box 26.
179. See Reinhold Niebuhr, *The Children of Light and the Children of Darkness* (New York: Scribners, 1944), chap. 1.
180. Perhaps Niebuhr's defense of democracy on the basis of human fallibility – "man's capacity for justice makes democracy possible, but man's inclination to injustice makes democracy necessary" – helped to reconcile Kennan to the idea. See Niebuhr, xiii. See also GFK sermon given at the Belgrade Embassy, Mar. 17, 1963, GKP, box 20.

on the mistaken and half-forgotten dreams of dead [Victorian] statesmen."[181]

Kennan's so-called realism was the ultimate expression of his lifelong
anti-Victorian revolt. It was an appeal for a chastened, in essence
Christian, appreciation of human nature, as well as for a higher idealism
based on the principles of minding one's own business and putting one's
own house in order first. Kennan's thinking on foreign affairs in the
end came full circle to rest on the foundation of seventeenth century
New England culture, whence his ancestors had sprung.[182] America's
energies, he believed, should be channeled into building an American
commonwealth: "We do not live just in order to conduct foreign policy.
It would be more correct to say that we conduct foreign policy in order
to live. . . . The greatest thing America can do for the rest of the world is
to make a success of what it is doing here on this continent and to bring
itself to a point where its own internal life is one of harmony and
stability and self-assurance." The basic interest guiding relations with
the rest of the world was to allow a continuation of "this Pilgrim's
Progress towards a better America under the most favorable conditions,
with a minimum of foreign interference, and also a minimum of in-
convenience or provocation to the interests of other nations."[183]

IN EARLY 1950, as Kennan prepared to leave the State Department,
Sinclair Lewis completed what was to be his last novel, *World So Wide*,
in Florence. The theme of the novel, in the words of Lewis's biographer,
was that of Americans searching "for a richer tradition and a longer
continuity than are their own but . . . unable to connect meaningfully
again with that Europe from which historically, they had severed themselves, and which, in fact and in itself no longer exists." In his last
public lecture, given in April 1950, Lewis voiced his fear of "Chicago-
ism," the uncontrolled urbanization and cultural homogenization that

---

181. Fitzgerald, *This Side of Paradise*, 282.
182. Mayers (318) makes a similar point about GFK's New England roots. On this gen-
     eral point see also Joel Rosenthal, *Righteous Realists: Political Realism, Responsible
     Power, and American Culture in the Nuclear Age* (Baton Rouge: Louisiana State
     University Press, 1991), 27, 169–70. It is interesting, and revealing, that Kennan's
     mature conception of God involved a departure from the "all-powerful Deity of
     established Christian doctrine" and of his Victorian forebears. See GFK, *Around the
     Cragged Hill*, 45–47.
183. GFK speech, "The National Interest of the United States," Jan. 30, 1951, reprinted
     in the *Illinois Law Review*, no. 6 (Jan.–Feb. 1951). See also U.S. External Relations
     Project, Part I, "Reflections on the Element of Purpose in the Conduct of External
     Relations," GKP, box 26.

he believed had infected Europe.[184] Nearing the end of his life, Lewis feared the death of what had tied him to the Old World: its nourishing, restorative, and feminine qualities, its harmony with nature, its "good vulgarity of earth."

Unlike his spiritual kinsman, who died in Rome in 1951, but like Lewis's character Sam Dodsworth, Kennan cast his lot with his own country in the end. He remained attached to the Middle West, "with its essential decency, its moral earnestness, its latent emotional freshness," but he sought his Yasnaya Polyana and refuge in the large working farm in Adams County, Pennsylvania, which he had bought on his return from Germany in 1942. The farm was situated on the edge of the Pennsylvania Dutch (Deutsch) country, home to a people for whom Kennan felt considerable affinity and regard.[185] Kennan's rejection of expatriation had to do, aside from practical considerations, with the death of the Europe that had drawn him in the twenties. In Hamburg in 1959, he

> watched the people move along the sidewalk and the stream of traffic coming and going before the station, and pondering the nature of this new Europe.... Never had I realized more keenly the extent to which the Europe of my youth, and the Europe about which I had cared, had left me and receded into the past, just like the America of the same description.[186]

The following year he realized that he had "nothing interesting to say about this sturdy Hamburg... with its startling material success, its heavy motor traffic, its relatively egalitarian style of life, its lack of slums and great houses, its better-dressed, semi-Americanized girls, its relative placidity, its absence of social tensions, of ideology."[187]

Kennan's mature sensibility with respect to Europe combined affection, nostalgia, disillusion, and regret. Already in 1947, he had felt a loss of the resolve, of the will to determine one's own future, that had animated the revolt of de Gaulle and Churchill against Roosevelt in 1944–45 and which he himself had felt to be so intense and desperate in the Europe of the thirties. Looking back many years later, he remarked that "Europe has not only cut itself off from its own past but has lost control of its own destiny." Europe, in short, was no longer really Europe. On another occasion he asked, "Could there have been for the

184. On this point see Mark Schorer, Afterword to Lewis, *Dodsworth*, 360–61.
185. See *Memoirs*, 2: 62–63, 75. On the Pennsylvania Dutch see also GFK letter to Frank, Mar. 23, 1964, GKP, box 31.
186. GFK, *Sketches*, 182.
187. Ibid., 197.

Europeans any other way to go?" Kennan believed that the answer was yes:

> It would have had to take its departure from the deliberate abandonment of the materialism, greed, and decadence of modern society, and to have proceeded to the enthronement in its place of true spiritual leadership and environmental preservation as the primary aims of civilization – to the acceptance of concern, in short, for the quality of man himself, primarily in his moral and spiritual, only secondarily in his material, incorporation, and for the intactness and the wholesomeness of his natural surrounding.[188]

This was the best summing up of what Kennan the man had always searched for in Europe and what Kennan the statesman had envisioned.

188. Ibid., 354–55. These words were written in June 1988.

PART THREE

PART THREE

6

Dean Acheson, 1893–1947: a Victorian for all seasons

Introduction

According to a famous nineteenth century student of transatlantic differences:

> The American, though he dresses like an Englishman and eats roast beef with a silver fork – or sometimes with a steel knife – as does an Englishman, is not like an Englishman in his mind, in his aspirations, in his tastes, or in his politics. In his mind, he is quicker, more universally intelligent, more ambitious of general knowledge, less indulgent of stupidity and ignorance in others, harder, sharper, brighter with the surface brightness of steel, than is an Englishman; but he is more brittle, less enduring, less malleable, and I think less capable of impressions. The mind of the Englishman has more imagination, but that of the American more incision.[1]

Anthony Trollope did not explain these differences, but perhaps they had to do with the fact that the tasks of pioneering and economic development called for cutting power rather than imagination, and with the prevalence in America of minds, to paraphrase Burke, sharpened but narrowed by study of the law.

Dean Gooderham Acheson's cultural makeup was a subject of considerable interest to his British contemporaries. To a British journalist, Acheson "was brought up to be an English gentleman. He thinks like an English gentleman. He behaves like an English gentleman. He even writes like an English gentleman."[2] An English academic recalled that Acheson had often been accused by his enemies of being an "imitation Englishman" but

> nothing could be further from the truth. . . . His dress and deportment are of a ramrod stiffness which makes him resemble a figure out of the

1. Anthony Trollope, *North America* (1862) (New York: Knopf, 1951), p. 203.
2. Philip Goodheart, Review of Acheson's *Morning and Noon*, *Sunday Telegraph*, Mar. 19, 1967.

diplomacy of the Austro-Hungarian Empire rather than any product of Eton and Trinity. He has a mind of unusual clarity, very powerful short range vision.[3]

For Acheson's friend Oliver Franks:

> He is not at all an English or British type. He is a pure American type of a rather rare species. He is imbued by a love of cabinet making and gardening, never forgetting and ever going back to the roots from which it all sprang.... He [is] profoundly American in this regard.

Acheson, said Franks, was "a blade of steel."[4]

Trollope himself would probably have seen the young Acheson as a preeminently American rather than an English type. Acheson ate and dressed like an urbane Englishman. But there was an earnestness and sharpness, combined with a kind of temperamental rigidity that perceptive Englishmen recognized as something other than their own. Yet Trollope – who admired British political leadership over American – might have seen traits in Acheson that set him apart from the typical ambitious American who "never soar[ed] so high as the ambitious Englishman... and [was] always fearful of a fall."[5] Trollope might also have seen a combination of qualities – enterprise, determination, self-abnegation – that could not have been more English except that they were more typical of the rising Englishmen of the 1830s and 1840s than of the 1870s and 1880s, and of Dickens's characters than Trollope's own. They were qualities that to late-Victorian eyes were already a little quaint. Acheson's character, Trollope might have surmised, was not so much a "pure American type of a rather rare species" as an English type of an earlier day. Acheson's political outlook, however, would not have seemed exotic to the mid- or late-Victorian observer. As Acheson himself said, "We are nineteenth century people.... We aren't twentieth century people. Our ideas are inherited ideas."[6]

A Victorian ideal

Acheson knew the essential facts of his family background – though not as much "as I could have if I had gotten my father to talk about the

3. Alastair Buchan, "High Postured Leader," *Listener*, April 23, 1970, 11.
4. Sir Oliver Franks, interviewed by David McClellan, June 27, 1964, Oral History Collection, HSTL. "Blade of steel" quoted in David McCullough, *Truman* (New York: Simon & Schuster, 1992), 756.
5. Trollope, 203.
6. Dean Acheson, "Real and Imagined Handicaps of Our Democracy in the Conduct of Foreign Affairs," Speech given at the HSTL, Mar. 31, 1962.

history."[7] He described his father as a powerful moral influence, as well as an "Olympian," detached and slightly mysterious figure. Edward C. Acheson was born at Woolwich in South London in 1858, the son of Alexander Acheson, an Ulsterman of Scottish origin, and Mary Campion, of Cork. Woolwich was the site of the arsenal where the elder Acheson, a veteran of the Crimean War, was stationed at the time. The life of Edward, though details are scanty, reads like the legend of the Victorian self-made man.

The son of a common soldier, he lost his mother at age twelve and went to live with relatives in Cork to escape a hostile stepmother. At fourteen, a penurious orphan, he fled to Toronto, where he worked and slept in a millinery warehouse. Of his secondary education nothing is known, but he attended the University of Toronto, whose "manly, noble" structure had attracted Trollope, and the Wycliffe Theological Seminary. In 1885, he fought under a British general against Louis Riel, the half-breed chief who with his Métis followers had challenged Ottawa from their Saskatchewan stronghold. The Riel rebellion shook the new dominion – it was feared U.S. interests were behind Riel – and its rapid defeat was greeted with joy in English Canada. Edward Acheson became a national celebrity when he was cited in dispatches for trying to rescue a wounded soldier.[8] The handsome mustachioed war hero won the hand of Eleanor Gooderham, daughter of one of Canada's great families. The Gooderhams had come from Diss, in Norfolk, in 1832. They made a fortune in milling, real estate, and whiskey and were powerful backers of the Conservative Party. Dean Acheson recalled that his mother's "enthusiasm for the Empire and the Monarch was not diluted by any corrupting contact with Canadian nationalism."[9]

Edward Acheson ended his career – there is hardly a better term – as a pillar of the establishment: registered Republican, Episcopal bishop of

7. Acheson to M. A. Harper, Feb. 5, 1963, Dean Acheson Papers, Sterling Library, Yale University (hereafter, DAP-SL).
8. On Edward Acheson, see Dean Acheson, *Morning and Noon* (Boston: Houghton Mifflin, 1965), chap. 1; David McClellan, *Dean Acheson: The State Department Years* (New York: Dodd, Mead, 1976), chap. 1; Gaddis Smith, *Dean Acheson* (New York: Cooper Square, 1972), chap. 1; Dean Acheson, notes written for Peale Museum in connection with lectures, Feb. 15, 1962, Dean Acheson Papers, HSTL (hereafter, DAP-HSTL), box 140; letter to Mrs. Harper, cited in note 7. On the University of Toronto, see Trollope, 79. On the Riel rebellion, see J. M. S. Careless and R. Craig Brown, eds., *The Canadians, 1867–1967* (Toronto: Macmillan Co. of Canada, 1967), 95–96.
9. One of Eleanor Gooderham's brothers was mayor of Toronto; another was knighted by King George V. On the Gooderhams see Acheson, *Morning and Noon*, chaps. 9, 10; Careless and Brown, eds., 135; Acheson to Mr. E. Gooderham, undated, DAP-SL.

Connecticut, and chaplain of the state's masonic lodge. Dean Acheson wrote:

> As a prelate he was a baffling man, widely read in theology and Christian doctrine, yet rarely speaking of either, privately or in his sermons, which so far as I can remember dealt more with ethics and conduct. But no conviction could have been deeper than his code of conduct based on perceptions of what was decent and civilized for man inextricably caught up in social relationships. If his goal was the salvation of the soul, it was a salvation by works performed with charity and humor as well as zeal. Through this mixture ran a strong strain of stoicism. Much in life could not be affected or mitigated, and hence, must be borne. Borne without complaint, because complaints were a bore and a nuisance to others and undermined the serenity essential to endurance.

This recalls Samuel Smiles's classic code of conduct for the striving Victorian: hard work, thrift, loyalty, charity, the superiority of wisdom gained from life lived over mere learning gained from books.[10] Acheson's grandfather and father were probably familar with *Self Help*, published in 1859. Edward was living proof of its message about the possibility of progress – progress defined as "the reward of virtue; of diligence and self-education; of providence and self-control."[11]

The origins of this creed, G. M. Young suggests, lie in the Evangelical Christianity that swept through Britain in the early nineteenth century. In its stark belief in the evil of this world, in duty, in the need to purify personal behavior, Evangelicalism was "at war with habit and indifference, with slavery, dueling and bull baiting." As it waned as a religious movement in the early Victorian age, Evangelicism crystallized into a set of social standards. "Evangelicalism had imposed on society its code of Sabbath observance, responsibility, and philanthropy; of discipline in the home, regularity in affairs.... The Evangelical discipline, secularized as respectability, was the strongest binding force in a nation which without it might have broken up."[12] The spirit of Evangelicalism infused politics in the 1830s and 1840s. The 1840s were the decade of Robert Peel, who abolished the Corn Laws, of Disraeli's *Sybil*, and the radical Toryism of Anthony Ashley Cooper, seventh Earl of Shaftesbury.

---

10. Acheson, *Morning and Noon*, 18; Samuel Smiles, *Self Help* (1859) (New York: Lovell, 1884 ed.). On Smiles see Eric Hobsbawn, *The Age of Capital, 1848–1875* (London: Weidenfeld & Nicholson, 1975), 277.
11. The description of the belief in progress is G. M. Young's, *Victorian England: Portrait of an Age* (1936) (London: Oxford University Press, 1959), 10.
12. Ibid., 4, 5.

Shaftesbury, an Evangelical Christian and free trader, led the struggle to adopt the Factory Acts of 1833 and 1847 against the bitter resistance of the Manchester factory owners. "The middle classes know [or ought to know]," said Shaftesbury, "that the safety of their lives and property depends upon their having round them a peaceful, happy and moral population." If there was a strain of thought that inspired the philanthropic conservatism of Edward Acheson, it was 1840s Evangelical Toryism, several of whose leaders (Michael Sadler and Richard Oustler) were Methodists who embraced the Church of England. Dean Acheson compared modern American reformism to the "Tory liberalism" of Shaftesbury, and Herbert Hoover and Robert Taft to the mid-nineteenth century Manchesterians.[13]

Along with its code of conduct, social conscience, and meliorism, Evangelicalism gave believers "that sense of being an Elect People which...became a principal element in late-Victorian Imperialism."[14] Edward Acheson's late-Victorian sanctimony was leavened by a Smilesian humility and Irish sense of the absurd. Eleanor Gooderham was a more class-conscious, spirited, and affable character from whom Dean Acheson acquired a sense of style and erect physical carriage – what Americans considered his "English" traits – as well as, one suspects, his basic worldliness and self-assurance.[15] Not that Edward Acheson raised the Union Jack above his Middletown, Connecticut, rectory and toasted the sovereign's birthday out of deference to his wife.[16] He was patriotic and probably grateful at the thought of belonging to a great extended family stretching from Toronto to Tasmania, united by a common language, tradition, and religion and connected by the worldwide commercial network that had London at its hub. If for Kennan the nineteenth century was a time of false standards and alienating technology, for Dean Acheson looking back it was a period "of greater economic progress than in the entire history of man from the discovery of the wheel until 1900."[17]

The history of the Acheson and Gooderham families was part and parcel of the epic of the British Empire: the vast migration from the mother country – between 1851 and 1880, 5.5 million people left the

13. On Shaftesbury and Evangelical Toryism see ibid., 25, 44–48; R. A. B. Butler, ed., *The Conservatives: A History from Their Origin to 1965* (London: Allen & Unwin, 1977), 117. See also Acheson, *Morning and Noon*, 109; Dean Acheson, *A Democrat Looks at His Party* (New York: Harper Bros., 1955), 41, 46, 47.
14. G. M. Young, 4.
15. On this point see McClellan, 4–5.
16. See Acheson, *Morning and Noon*, 12.
17. On world trade see Hobsbawn, 34; Acheson, "Real and Imagined Handicaps."

British Isles, including a half million for Canada – the outpouring of manufactures, the worldwide spread of capital, the exploration of new continents, the construction of mines, roads, telegraph lines, harbors, and bridges, ultimately the linking of a quarter of the world's population under a single crown.[18] Above all, perhaps, it was the age of the railroad:

> It is impossible not to share the mood of excitement, of self confidence, of pride, which seized those who lived through this heroic age of the engineers, as the railway first linked Channel and Mediterranean, as it became possible to travel by rail to Seville, to Moscow, to Brindisi, as the iron tracks pushed westwards across the North American prairies and mountains and across the Indian sub-continent.[19]

British money and know-how built many of the railroads. It was the newly completed Canadian Pacific that sped Edward Acheson and the Queen's Own Rifles westward in 1885 and guaranteed the swift end of the Riel rebellion.[20] It was the construction of the Grand Trunk Pacific – the brother of his Canadian governess was an engineer on the project – that gave Dean Acheson his own taste of empire building in 1911. The camaraderie and physical exhilaration experienced in helping to cut a railway across northwest Canada made that summer, he recalled, among "the most important few months of my life." After six years of school he regained "a priceless possession, joy in life."[21]

The transition from the mid- to the late-Victorian period was marked by the death of Palmerston, symbol of Britain's unchallenged prestige and power, in 1865 and by the economic downturn after 1873. The last decades of the century were characterized by formal imperialism, protectionism, and the fear of general war, as well as by a more pessimistic cultural climate reflecting the influence of Marx and Darwin. Dean Acheson suggests (asking "*if* his [father's] goal was the salvation of his soul")[22] that Edward Acheson was affected by the skepticism and agnosticism typical of the late nineteenth century. At the same time, as someone who had left Britain as a boy in 1872, he remained essentially early Victorian or mid-Victorian in his aspirations and values. The life Edward Acheson tried to create for his family during the twenty years after the birth of his son in 1893 reflected a sort of Victorian ideal or

---

18. Hobsbawn, 195.
19. Ibid., 55. See also Herbert Feis, *Europe: The World's Banker*, 1870–1914 (New York: A. M. Kelley, 1964).
20. On this point see Careless and Brown, eds., 89.
21. Acheson, *Morning and Noon*, 37.
22. Ibid., 18; emphasis added.

equilibrium between the self-sacrifice, charity, and personal modesty that were responsible for present well-being and the complacent acceptance and enjoyment of material comforts that were the visible rewards of virtue. Of mid-Victorian life, its leading apologist wrote in 1936:

> It was the flower of a brief moment of equipoise, Protestant northern, respectable. It omitted much that a Greek or Italian would have thought necessary to completeness ... yet in the far distance I can well conceive the world turning wistfully in imagination, as to the culminating achievement of European culture, to the life of the university-bred classes in England of the mid-nineteenth century, set against the English landscape as it was, as it can be no more, but of which nevertheless, some memorials remain with us to-day, in the garden at Kelmscott, in the hidden valleys of the Cotswolds, in that walled close where all the pride and piety, the peace and beauty of a vanished world seem to have made their last home under the spires of St. Mary of Salisbury.[23]

The best of all possible worlds

Chance – the opening of a position – brought Edward Acheson to Middletown, Middlesex County, in the Connecticut River Valley, but there may have been few places in North America more suitable for cultivating the mid-Victorian ideal. The town was past its prime as a river port by the turn of the century, but the fortune of an earlier epoch had built the brownstone banks and stately houses that lined its elm-shrouded streets. Here was real "Booth Tarkington provincial innocence" – and unthreatened by encroaching trauma. Certainly it was not the sort of place that bred catastrophism or left a chip on one's shoulder about the modern world. Middletown in 1900 was a tranquil market town with a handful of factories. Residential neighborhoods merged seamlessly with the countryside of which Henry Adams had asked: "What had the United States ... to show in scenery and landscape more beautiful or more willing than that country of meadow and mountain?" Joseph Alsop, who grew up in nearby Farmington, an even more composed and secluded town, wrote, "Somehow that portion of Connecticut, as it used to be, with its fertile farms and little towns, still seems to me a golden place." For Dean Acheson, the last years of the nineteenth century and the early years of the twentieth were "the golden age of childhood." The Connecticut Valley was its Athens.[24]

23. G. M. Young, 99.
24. Henry Adams, *A History of the United States*, 24; Joseph Alsop, with Adam Platt, "The Wasp Ascendency," *New York Review of Books*, 36, no. 17 (Nov. 9, 1989),

Of his parents' adaptation, Acheson wrote that "so strong was the yeast of Connecticut life that it leavened the whole and in almost no time at all the newcomers were New Englanders to the core."[25] It is also true that New England was the most English part of the United States, Connecticut the most English part of New England, and the Farmington–Middletown region the most English part of Connecticut. Connecticut soil nurtured the assiduously Anglophile Alsop and the exquisitely Anglicized Wilmarth Lewis.[26] The original J. P. Morgan hailed from Hartford. Trollope touched something essential about Connecticut when he wrote:

> It is gratifying to see how this new people, when they had it in their power to change all the laws, to throw themselves upon any utopian theory that the folly of a wild philanthropy could devise, to discard as abominable every vestige of English rule and English power – it is gratifying to see that when they could have done all this, they did not do so, but preferred to cling to things English.... The old laws were to remain in force. The precedents of the English courts were to be held as legal precedents in the country of the new nation.... It was still to be England – but England without a King making his last struggle for political power.[27]

Acheson believed that the American Revolution had been the attempt to secure the traditional rights of Englishmen and thus "a political act not a social revolution or a nationalist uprising." Denigration was reserved in the Declaration of Independence not for England but "solely for the villain of the piece, King George III."[28] This was a far cry from the Roosevelt family version.

Connecticut Federalism and individualism blended naturally with Edward Acheson's Evangelical–Victorian ethic. His household knew no clear cultural boundaries between the New World and the Old. Acheson and his sister were U.S. citizens, while his parents and their governess, maid and cook, were British subjects, but "nationality was not a divisive notion." He visited England with his mother at age seven or eight

59; Acheson, *Morning and Noon*, 1. For the reference to Tarkington see Chapter 4, this volume.

25. Dean Acheson, Speech on the 200th anniversary of Holy Trinity Parish, Apr. 17, 1950. Copy in DAP-HSTL.
26. Lewis, three years behind Acheson at Yale, was a Californian who settled at Farmington, where he set up his unique library and collection of Horace Walpole memorabilia. See W. L. Lewis, *One Man's Education* (New York: Knopf, 1967), chap. 12.
27. Trollope, 220. Trollope is referring specifically to Connecticut in this passage.
28. Dean Acheson, "The Prelude to Independence," *Yale Review*, 48, no. 4 (June 1959), 481–90.

and again with his father at fourteen, in 1907. (He made a third trip, to the Henley regatta and Oxford University as a member of the Yale crew, in the summer of 1913.) Among the topics on which he heard his father's strongly held and expressed opinions were the Irish question and Queen Victoria's Diamond Jubilee. Another topic was the Boer conflict. Acheson – in contrast to eighteen-year-old Franklin Roosevelt and most of Middletown – sympathized with the British side.[29]

Perhaps incidents such as this brought home to Acheson that he *was* a cultural anomaly; this must have become even more evident after he entered prep school at age ten. Accounts of his time in "that semi-eternity which begins with homesickness and hazing and snowballs and ends, such seeming ages afterwards, with the white flannels and blue coats of commencement in the full glory of a New England spring," suggest that it was one of tedium and self-doubt.[30] Acheson was neither a misfit-rebel like Louis Auchincloss's Billy Prentiss, who leaves school in disgrace after a puerile gesture of defiance, nor a conformist-diplomat like Franklin Roosevelt, whose emollient shrewdness and calculated deference allowed him to survive unscathed. He was somewhere in between: too proud and flippant to escape the ritual punishment of "pumping," but too stoic and trusting of adult wisdom to attempt futile resistance to authority. His father's complaint against complaining was never to prevent Acheson from doing so; still, if he had been sent to such a harsh place, there must have been a reason. David Copperfield had survived Salem House and was the wiser for it.

There was another contrast between the schoolboys FDR and Acheson. Hazing helped to strip Roosevelt of his English – in any event exotic, foreign – patina. The same early adolescent trauma seems to have hardened Acheson's "English" varnish. It came to constitute a kind of badge of identity against the slings and arrows of his peers. One can imagine that his parents did not discourage Acheson's sense that he was different. Eleanor Acheson clashed with Headmaster Peabody over her son's unwillingness to fit the mold.[31] At Groton Acheson also became aware of his inherited political ideas. Like his father, Acheson sympathized with Theodore Roosevelt's challenge to the Republican

29. Evidence of the early trip is provided by the photograph facing page 146 in McClellan, though there is no mention of it in the text. See also Acheson, *Morning and Noon*, 11, 12.

30. The description is from Louis Auchincloss, "Billy and the Gargoyles," reprinted in *The Romantic Egoists* (Boston: Houghton Mifflin, 1954), 23. For accounts of Acheson at Groton see Acheson, *Morning and Noon*, 24–26; McClellan, 8–9; Issacson and Thomas, 54–57.

31. On this point see Issacson and Thomas, 55.

Party in 1912, while the average Grotty was a stand-pat conservative.[32] Acheson felt closer to his Middletown playmates, the sons of workers and tradesmen, than to the sons of parvenus. His essay "The Snob in America" (written in his last year at school) reflected the early-Victorian values of his father. Snobbery, wrote Acheson, was not to be confused with "that greatest of all necessities," self-respect. ("Self-respect," wrote Samuel Smiles, "is the noblest garment with which a man may clothe himself – the most elevating feeling with which the mind can be inspired.") In contrast to a justifiable feeling of superiority based on real achievement, snobbery was a class feeling, "the abasement of others," and thus deserving of contempt. From what was at heart an earnest piece of social commentary the author shifted into a Twain-esque vein, arguing that the "snob of fashion" is a pardonable and human type compared with the athletic or literary snob. In fact, the essay suggested a certain ambivalence toward the institution of snobbery. After all, might not someone who had been taught not to pretend to be better than he was consider himself a little better than those – the typical Grotties – who never had?[33]

When given the chance to be a snob at Yale, Acheson seems, in late-adolescent fashion, to have risen readily to the occasion. Yale was a period for sowing wild oats, leading to a clash with his father, with whom he was not on speaking terms for at least a year. Success was measured in terms of membership in a senior society; Acheson was tapped for the second most venerable, Scroll and Key. The atmosphere was insouciant rather than conducive to scholarly achievement. Edmund Wilson's remark that the most vigorous minds at Yale were likely "to have their intellectual teeth drawn as the price of their local success" was apt in Acheson's case.[34]

Notwithstanding, a kind of literary culture flourished during the first decades of the century. It did not produce – aside from Sinclair Lewis – novelists of the first rank, but there were distinguished figures in drama, music, poetry, and belles lettres: Clarence Day, Cole Porter, Philip Barry, Archibald MacLeish, Stephen Vincent Benét, Thornton Wilder, and the already mentioned Wilmarth Lewis. These men were not alienated modernists or iconoclasts – Sinclair Lewis does not belong on

---

32. On this point see McClellan, 9.
33. From *The Grotonian*, 1911, copy in DAP-SL. See Smiles, 362. On Acheson's having learned from his parents not to pretend to be better than he was see McClellan, 19; McCullough, 755.
34. Wilson quoted in G. W. Pierson, *Yale College: An Educational History, 1871–1921* (New Haven, Conn.: Yale University Press, 1952), 20. On Yale's atmosphere see also W. L. Lewis, chaps. 7, 8.

such a list – with middle western complexes or radical ideas. Nor were they – in contrast to their Cambridge University–Bloomsbury counterparts – at loggerheads with the notion of original sin. They might have been dandies compared with their parents' generation, but they did not question the older generation's values. They were essentially high spirited young gentlemen whose preoccupations were personal distinction, style, elegance, polish, manners, and conviviality: the ethos of Scroll and Key.

What Acheson, who absorbed something of this atmosphere, found at Yale was fellowship. Wilmarth Lewis and MacLeish became his closest friends. In effect, they were the last of the Victorians, a generation who had lived too long and too well under the pre-1914 pax universalis and were too well indoctrinated in its moral and aesthetic standards to imagine a better time or place. Though they could convince themselves intellectually of the passing of the nineteenth century – of which their undergraduate life had been a kind of Indian summer – they were never able to accept its demise emotionally, and it remained fixed in their imaginations as the best of all possible worlds.

A "sophisticating pursuit"

Acheson was fond of Alexis de Tocqueville's remark that the study and practice of law produced "certain habits of order, a taste for formalities, and a kind of instinctive regard for the regular connection of ideas."[35] He also liked Jean Monnet's observation about the "practical statesmanship" of a certain type of American lawyer who was "peculiarly able at once to understand the uniqueness of unprecedented situations."[36] De Tocqueville also observed that in a society where there were "no nobles or literary men, and the people are apt to mistrust the wealthy ... lawyers consequently form[ed] the highest political class and the most cultivated portion of society." Because of their special knowledge, role, habits, tastes, and "instinctive love of order," they constituted the aristocratic element of the democratic order. De Tocqueville saw Anglo-Saxon lawyers as a single type for whom the law of precedent resulted in a certain "abnegation of his own opinion ... [an] implicit deference to the opinions of his forefathers."[37] In effect, Monnet emphasized the innovative capacity of the American lawyer, de Tocqueville his reverence for the past.

35. Acheson, *Morning and Noon*, 145; Alexis de Tocqueville, *Democracy in America* (1836) (New York: Vintage Books, 1961), 1: 283.
36. Acheson, *Morning and Noon*, 146. This is Acheson's rendering of Monnet's point.
37. De Toqueville, 284–87.

Both insights are required to understand the effects of the law on Acheson's public life. The kind of lawyer Monnet knew possessed a flexibility that would have surprised de Tocqueville, along with a devotion to tradition that would have confirmed his basic view. Felix Frankfurter was the prototype of the socially active, creative lawyer who would have surprised de Tocqueville and the patron of a generation of lawyers whose métier was reform. Frankfurter was also the link between Acheson's generation and the founts of innovative jurisprudence in the late nineteenth and early twentieth centuries, Louis Brandeis and Oliver Wendell Holmes, Jr. Their response to the new conditions created by industrialization paved the way for the "new" lawyers of the period from 1900 to 1940. Frankfurter ignited Acheson's interest in the law and became his lifelong ally, but his real mentors were Brandeis and Holmes.

Brandeis, the "People's Lawyer" and scourge of bigness in American economic life, was already a legend when Acheson, recommended by Frankfurter, became his secretary in 1919. The son of Edward Acheson was naturally impressed by a man whose personal code called for "low heat in his law office to save expense . . . [and] the zealous molding of the lives of the underprivileged so that paupers might achieve moral growth."[38] Acheson was also struck by the severity of his working methods and his passion for "the facts." For Brandeis, "most doubtful points would not be doubtful if all the facts were thoroughly known, not only the facts in regard to the situation, also in regard to the law and its making."[39] Early in his clerkship, Acheson wrote that Brandeis was a moralist and educator who spent much of life "telling stupid people what any idiot ought to have been able to see at a glance." He later realized that Brandeis was also apt to wrap "the mantle of Isaiah around himself" and defend the existence of absolute truth as revealed to the prophets and the poets.[40]

Brandeis's famous dissents were exercises in "judicial self-restraint" in cases where a majority of the Supreme Court voted to overrule attempts by state legislatures to expand workers' rights or to protect civil liberties. Brandeis insisted that the formulas "liberty of contract"

38. G. Edward White, quoted in Bruce Allen Murphy, *The Brandeis–Frankfurter Connection: The Secret Political Activities of Two Supreme Court Justices* (New York: Oxford University Press, 1982), 20.

39. Acheson to Felix Frankfurter, Mar. 15, 1920, in David Acheson and David McClellan, eds., *Among Friends: Personal Letters of Dean Acheson* (hereafter, *Among Friends*) (New York: Dodd, Mead, 1980), 8.

40. Acheson to Felix Frankfurter, Nov. 16, 1920, quoted in Acheson, *Morning and Noon*, 51–53, 95–96.

and "due process" be interpreted in the context of modern social and economic conditions and not be used as weapons to defend capital against labor. As Acheson later put it, "The judicial weighing of the interests involved [in a particular case]" had to be made "*in the light of facts, sociologically determined and more contemporary*" than those that underlay the prevailing conservative judicial approach to labor issues. This, in a nutshell, was the theme of Acheson's own inquiry into the history of laws governing combination from Tudor times until the early nineteenth century.[41]

Acheson's desire to practice labor law waned when he discovered that labor lawyers spent most of their time "straightening out intra-union rows." Thus when Judge J. Harry Covington of the Washington firm Covington and Burling hesitated to hire him in 1921 because of his labor interests, Acheson was able to say that he was "sick of that sort of thing."[42] The justice's practical idealism, meliorism, and moral earnestness nonetheless remained a powerful example. Acheson later wrote: "Suppose he had his vanities and was not proof against the constant drip of adulation. . . . All that is so minor and unimportant, so irrelevant to what he did, to what he stood for. . . . There is nothing here to expose. There is no sham, or pretense, or hypocrisy lurking in the background. There is no need for a Lytton Strachey."[43]

Of Brandeis's brother dissenter, Justice Holmes, Acheson said: "One of the slipperiest words I know is 'great.' But I think the 'greatest' man I have ever known, that is, the essence of man living, man thinking, man baring himself to the lonely universe, was Holmes."[44] Holmes (born 1841) was the most eminent American Victorian: a tall, striking, thrice-wounded Civil War officer, spellbinding talker, as his friend William James described him, "a powerful battery, formed like a planing machine to gouge a deep self-beneficial groove through life."[45] The elderly man whom Acheson knew still cut an elegant Edwardian figure – not for him the Brandeisian cult of austerity – but what struck the younger man more was the philosophy Holmes dispensed in pungent aphorisms and

41. Ibid., 82; emphasis added. Acheson argued that "the laws of property had by the industrial revolution become bad laws . . . in that by law they vested in one class, the power of control over another. The remedy is not to abolish laws of property . . . but to delimit property interests by balancing against them interests of personality, and then introduce into the legal order principles which would secure both interests, thus delimited." Typed manuscript (140 pages), 29, 109, DAP-SL.
42. Acheson to Felix Frankfurter, Apr. 21, 1921, in *Among Friends*, 12.
43. Acheson to Charles Wyzanski, Feb. 27, 1956, in ibid., 113.
44. Acheson to Michael Janeway, May 24, 1960, in ibid., 182.
45. Quoted in Catherine Drinker Bowen, *Yankee from Olympus: Justice Holmes and His Family* (Boston: Little, Brown, 1943), 271.

the caustic property of his mind. Holmes bore the imprint of the Darwinian climate in which old dogmas had been shredded and the notion of humanity engaged in a never-ending contest had become an *idée fixe*.[46] Holmes carried his scorn for dogma and the human appetite for certainty to the point of cynicism; he also believed that human beings could find redemption through duty and action, the essence of their being. Such sentiments appealed to Acheson, son and grandson of soldiers and inheritor of a secularized Evangelicalism.[47] Acheson, like Holmes, was apt to see people simply as not-so-distant relatives of the ape. Both delighted in Clarence Day's essay "This Simian World." When Acheson referred to his enemies of the McCarthy period as the "primitives," Holmes would have understood.

As a scholar and jurist, Holmes applied an evolutionist razor to the popular notion that laws embodied either moral absolutes or some sort of truth independent of historical experience. Holmes wrote:

> A very common phenomenon, and one very familiar to the student of history, is this. The customs, beliefs, or needs of a primitive time establish a rule or a formula. In the course of centuries the custom, belief or necessity disappears, but the rule remains. The reason which gave rise to the rule has been forgotten, and ingenious minds set themselves to inquire how this is to be accounted for. Some ground or policy is thought of, which seems to explain it and to reconcile it with the present state of things; and then the rule adapts itself to the new reasons which have been found for it and enters on a new career. The old form receives a new content, and in time even the form modifies itself to fit the meaning which it has received.[48]

Holmes rejected Brandeis's social reformism, but he relished exposing how "new reasons" and "new content" in the nature of self-serving, pro-property ideologies had attached themselves to legal notions like due process and liberty of contract. The most famous instance was his

46. "For my own part," Holmes said, "I believe that the struggle for life is the order of the world, at which it is vain to repine." "The Soldier's Faith" (1896), in Kenneth Lynn, ed., *The American Society* (New York: G. Braziller, 1963), 164.

47. One of Acheson's favorite citations from Holmes was "Man is born to act. To act is to affirm the worth of an end; and to affirm the worth of an end is to create an ideal." Another was "In nature, the penalty for error is death." See Acheson to Charles Gary, Dec. 11, 1956, DAP-SL; Acheson to Philip Haring, Aug. 9, 1960, in *Among Friends*, 189–90; Dean Acheson to Elizabeth Wenger, May 21, 1970, DAP-SL.

48. Oliver Wendell Holmes, Jr., quoted in Frederic Roger Kellogg, *The Formative Essays of Justice Holmes: The Making of an American Legal Philosophy* (Westport, Conn.: Greenwood Press, 1987), 7.

dissent in the *Lochner* case, when he admonished his fellow judges that "the Fourteenth Amendment [did] not enact Herbert Spencer's *Social Statics.*"[49] From Holmes Acheson acquired a skepticism about doctrine and an eye for the unprecedented situation in which the old rules were obsolete. These were the habits of mind that de Tocqueville, writing before evolutionism and the twentieth century Progressive movement, had not seen in American lawyers but that struck Monnet.

There was an aspect of Acheson's legal education that de Tocqueville would have had no trouble understanding: an attachment to English common law and sense of belonging to a seamless civilization. No discipline produced a stronger grasp of the organic connection of the two sides of the Atlantic. Brandeis's Anglophilia, like Frankfurter's, was an almost childlike feeling of devotion. Holmes's was seasoned by years of travel to England and correspondence with intellectuals like Sir Leslie Stephen, Sir Frederick Pollock, and, in later years, Harold Laski.[50] During the Spanish-American War, Holmes wrote Pollock – without his customary gruffness and "language of cynicism" – "England has behaved nobly to us . . . and I hope we may draw closer together." Early in the Boer War he wrote, "I anxiously wish you speedy success."[51]

When Laski talked about Holmes's disciples – Brandeis, Frankfurter, himself (he might have included Acheson) – he meant people who believed in Anglo-American solidarity and the superiority of the Anglo-Saxon political tradition.[52] Their veneration arose from the belief that nineteenth century English political leaders had demonstrated a talent for timely adaptation unmatched in the United States. For Holmes, there were "more civilized men to the square mile [in England], more

49. Quoted in ibid., 66. In this case a New York state law limiting working hours for health reasons was held unconstitutional by a majority of the Supreme Court on the grounds that the Fourteenth Amendment protection against the deprivation of liberty without due process of law included freedom of contract, and that the right to buy and sell labor was thus protected from regulation by the state.

50. Holmes told Harold Laski, who had written from London about a visit by Frankfurter and Brandeis, "I am glad that Brandeis should see more of England which when we last talked he admired beyond every thing else" (July 30, 1920), in Howe, ed., *Holmes–Laski Letters*, 272. On Holmes in London see Oliver Wendell Holmes, Jr., to Laski, Mar. 1, 1928, in ibid., 1031.

51. See Oliver Wendell Holmes, Jr., to Pollock, May 13, 1898, and Dec. 1, 1899. Mark de Wolfe Howe, ed., *Holmes–Pollock Letters: The Correspondence of Mr. Justice Holmes and Sir Frederick Pollock, 1874–1932* (Cambridge, Mass.: Harvard University Press, 1961), 1: 86, 98. The expression "language of cynicism" is Holmes's own to describe many of his pronouncements. See Samuel Konefesky, *The Legacy of Holmes and Brandeis* (New York: Dacapo Press, 1974), 5.

52. See Laski to Holmes, Aug. 18, 1928, in Howe, ed., *Holmes–Laski Letters*, 1086.

past in every environment."[53] A belief in the ideals of English life helped fill the void created by a compulsively cutting intellect: in a Godless, ever-shifting cosmos, English civilization remained a fixed point.

Acheson later wrote of the late nineteenth century: "Public life in England reached its most luxuriant and brilliant flowering, while in America it sank to depths not plumbed before or since."[54] He was drawn to American leaders with the intelligence to recognize the unprecedented situation created by modern capitalism and the skill to devise practical solutions. Had the Republican Party embraced what Acheson called "positive Tory liberalism,"[55] he would have joined it. But that tradition passed by default to the Democratic Party after Theodore Roosevelt's defeat in 1912. Louis Brandeis cast his lot with the Democrats and became a leading intellectual force behind Wilson's program to regulate American capitalism. In 1920, Acheson followed suit.[56]

Acheson's law firm, Covington and Burling, was created to press claims arising from the World War; it owed its later fortune to the New Deal, which resulted in vast amounts of litigation against the federal government.[57] Such a practice, de Tocqueville had suggested, was not apt to spark sympathy for the masses, but it was a "sophisticating pursuit."[58] Acheson's most challenging work came early in his career, which is one of the reasons he became bored with the law. His clients included the Norwegian and Swedish governments in cases that took him for extended periods to Oslo, The Hague, and Stockholm. His defense of Arizona in the (unsuccessful) attempt to block the Boulder Dam led to his friendship with Lewis Douglas, a young Arizona congressman, who marveled at Acheson's "queer ability to help untie mental knots and snarls."[59] He defended textile manufacturers seeking to raise rates at the time of the Smoot–Hawley Tariff in 1930.[60] His

53. Holmes to Laski, Jan. 14, 1920, in ibid., 232.
54. Acheson letter to *New York Times* on U.S. education, Feb. 2, 1958.
55. Acheson to A. B. Dick, Jr., Nov. 14, 1932, in *Among Friends*, 18–19.
56. Acheson (he was too young to vote in 1912) preferred Charles Evans Hughes to Wilson in 1916, perhaps because the Republican seemed the more Disraelian or more forthright on preparedness for war. On this point see Acheson to Grenville Clark, Oct. 31, 1936, DAP-SL.
57. As Edmund Burling put it, "Businesses all over the country began squealing about what was happening and had to hire lawyers." Burling's obituary, *Washington Post*, Oct. 4, 1966.
58. Dean Acheson, "Lawyers in the Republic," *Esquire*, 56 (July 1961), 100–3. See also de Tocqueville, 283.
59. Lewis Douglas to Acheson, Sept. 21, 1932, DAP-SL.
60. See Acheson's statement to the Joint Economic Committee of Congress, Dec. 5, 1961, 12, DAP-HSTL.

partners Harry Covington, Edward Burling, and George Rublee were veterans of the Progressive Era, but the firm was by the nature of its business an adversary of the Roosevelt administration.

Sir Oliver Franks later observed that two qualities were at war in Acheson as secretary of state: "The historical sense . . . and the lawyer's skill at creating the case which he must argue." By this he seems to have meant that the lawyer's incisiveness exercised on a narrow front on behalf of his client occasionally led him to lose sight of the historical forest for the trees. Acheson himself later said that the "mental discipline of logic" was one of the main assets of the lawyer-turned-foreign-policy-maker. A serious disadvantage, however, was "that in a lawyer's experience his thinking starts from a point of view rather narrowly given him by his client's interests . . . his purpose and scope is delimited for him, even though he has scope within the limits."[61] It is revealing that he looked back on this after 1952 as having been a disadvantage. The hallmark of his approach as secretary of state was the tendency to allow his scope of action and objectives to be delimited by his European interlocutors.

Acheson's "brief encounter" with the Roosevelt administration in 1933 was a fundamental experience.[62] It occurred during the confused, improvisational period of the early New Deal. Acheson shared the view of the internationalist Democrats, Hull, Lewis Douglas (FDR's budget director), and James Warburg, that the way to prosperity included a balanced budget, lower tariffs, and currency stabilization through a return to the gold standard. Roosevelt had endorsed such principles in early 1933.[63] When the president's nationalist and experimentalist instincts prevailed (in his torpedoing of the London Economic Conference in July 1933, followed by the attempt to raise domestic prices by depreciating the dollar), he clashed with his conservative supporters. Acheson was fired as under secretary of the Treasury (a position obtained on the recommendation of Frankfurter) when he declined to support FDR's gold purchase program in late 1933.

61. See interview with Franks, cited in note 4. On his law career in general see Acheson, *Morning and Noon*, chaps. 8 and 10. For Acheson's view see Acheson to Hans Morgenthau, Jan. 3, 1957, DAP-SL.

62. See Acheson, *Morning and Noon*, chap. 9, entitled "Brief Encounter with FDR." See also Schlesinger, *The Coming of the New Deal*, chap. 14; Herbert Feis, *1933, Characters in Crisis* (Boston: Little, Brown, 1966), chap. 22. See also Acheson to Robert Atwood, Sept. 30, 1965, DAP-SL.

63. For example, during his campaign speech at Pittsburgh and his second "fireside chat" on May 7, 1933.

It is difficult to rank Acheson's reasons for opposing Roosevelt. High among them must have been the conviction that the plan to buy gold at a price above the one fixed by statute was illegal and that he might find himself liable should Congress investigate a policy that was not likely to succeed. Acheson saw not only that the underlying theory (raising the price of gold would raise the general price level) was dubious, but also that depreciation amounted to a fraud perpetrated on holders of Treasury securities. FDR had rejected the advice of the so-called New York group, including Acheson, Douglas, and Warburg. In an August 29, 1933, memo, the group had recommended "a revised and more flexible gold standard." As an interim step, they urged a gradual fixing of sterling and the dollar and a rapid (and generous) settlement of the British war debt.⁶⁴ In October 1933, just before adoption of the gold purchase plan, Acheson had taken part in negotiations with the British ambassador Ronald Lindsay and Sir Frederick Leith-Ross, financial adviser to the cabinet. After Acheson spoke to the press, the London *Times* wrote that "the thing was done with such grace and feeling for justice as to make an extremely happy impression everywhere."⁶⁵ Not, however, at the White House, where Acheson's attempt to persuade Roosevelt to liquidate the debt controversy had been rejected. Related to these legal and political considerations in Acheson's mind was an "institutional" factor. The Treasury Department over which he presided "was an extraordinarily able organization. It was much like the British Treasury."⁶⁶ He declined to challenge the able career men who were convinced that the president and his ally Henry Morgenthau of the Farm Credit Bureau were simply wrong.

Acheson's account of the affair also indicates a more emotive reaction; he was offended by FDR's regal, patronizing manner, including the attempt to conduct business from the royal bedchamber. "The impression given me by President Roosevelt carried much of [the] attitude of European – not British – royalty." (The latter was "comfortably respectable, dignified and bourgeois.") "Many reveled in apparent admission to an inner circle. I did not."⁶⁷ Roosevelt triggered an adolescent defiance in Acheson, a refusal to be browbeaten or cajoled by an authority figure whom he did not respect. Acheson's behavior also recalled that of the newly appointed Justice Holmes, who voted

---

64. For a copy of the memo see Acheson, *Morning and Noon*, 243–54.
65. Quoted in ibid., 184.
66. Princeton Seminar transcript, 108, DAP-HSTL. During much of his term, Acheson was acting secretary due to the illness of William Woodin.
67. Acheson, *Morning and Noon*, 185, 191. See also Acheson to F. Frankfurter, Dec. 19, 1958, DAP-SL.

against the wishes of his would-be master Theodore Roosevelt in the Northern Securities case.[68]

The failure of FDR's gold-buying scheme vindicated Acheson. When *Fortune* magazine criticized Douglas for "insensitivity to new intellectual currents," Acheson replied:

> Lew is one of the only living conservatives of the time. When most of the young are willing to scrap the whole political, industrial and financial structure ... Lew believes that the foundations of capitalism, individualism and democracy can be preserved, and at the same time the evils which have produced the damage can be eliminated. It is always unusual to find a man holding firmly to his convictions when an articulate minority are filling the public mind with different ideas, but I don't think that is curious – certainly it would not be curious in England where such creatures are produced in each generation.[69]

Acheson was describing not only Douglas, grandson of a self-made English emigrant, but himself. The "new intellectual currents" referred to "Keynesianism" and to the influence of a man whose assault on Victorian orthodoxy was having reverberations in Washington. Keynes's open letter to Roosevelt in the *New York Times* (December 31, 1933) reflected the nationalistic views of "National Self-Sufficiency" (December 1933). He criticized the gold-buying experiment as theoretically flawed but praised its attempt to subordinate the exchange rate to the goal of domestic recovery. Keynes's advice was that to promote growth of output "public authority must be called in aid to create additional current incomes through the expenditures of borrowed or printed money."[70] In early 1934, Keynes visited the United States and talked to FDR. Whether Keynes actually persuaded the president of his theories is doubtful, but 1934 nonetheless marked the transition of the New Deal to a stage characterized by deficit spending, public works, and regulation of private business.[71] By mid-1934, Douglas had lost his battle against "paper inflation" and was forced out. With Warburg, he organized the "Democrats for Landon" movement in 1936.

68. On Holmes's motivation see Konefsky, 57.
69. Acheson to Archibald MacLeish, his personal friend and *Fortune* editor, Apr. 6, 1934, in *Among Friends*, 21.
70. Printed in Freedman, ed., 178–83. This letter was printed in the *New York Times* but an advance copy was forwarded to FDR by Frankfurter. See ibid., 177.
71. Despite the objection that it is too schematic (see, e.g., Felix Frankfurter's letter to A. Schlesinger in Freedman, ed., Introduction; see also Murphy, 108), the distinction between a first and second New Deal initially noted by Tugwell (326) and developed fully in Schlesinger's *The Coming of the New Deal* remains sound and useful. On

After Keynes's visit to the White House, Acheson wrote a friend: "This has produced discouragement in circles with which you are familiar."[72] The idea of going into debt to abet consumption went against the grain of his outlook. He believed (with Holmes) that there were certain economic – in reality ethical – principles whose violation would exact a price. De Tocqueville wrote that political questions in the United States tended to resolve into judicial questions. The dollar depreciation and deficit-spending controversies indicated that, for Acheson, political questions tended to resolve into questions of personal conscience. The Evangelical legacy did not always sit easily with the lawyer's pragmatism.[73] He had been bred to grasp the nettle rather than shun difficult choices. The conviction of personal superiority he radiated was justified in the sense that few lived by the same code, but the negative side of his shining moral courage was an inflexibility and streak of dogmatism that might not have surprised Trollope.

Acheson, nonetheless, eventually became one of Roosevelt's most articulate supporters. One reason is that he did not relish corporate law and wished to keep open the possibility of another political appointment. Another is that the Republicans failed to adopt the "positive Tory liberalism" that he had prescribed for them, even as the New Deal shifted in 1934. Douglas was out, but so was the National Recovery Administration, centerpiece of the "First New Deal"; the dollar was stabilized in January 1934 against the pound. Beginning in 1934, the New Deal increasingly reflected the influence of Brandeis, Frankfurter, and their protégés, who accepted – in Frankfurter's case actively promoted – Keynesian ideas.[74] Acheson still did not: in 1935 one finds him praising Friedrich von Hayek's anti-Keynesian *Prices and Production* and arguing lawsuits against Ickes's Public Works Administration. Keynes himself called von Hayek's book "one of the most frightful muddles I have ever read."[75]

On the eve of the election Acheson wrote that his ideas were "very

Keynes and FDR see also Herbert Stein, *The Fiscal Revolution in America* (Chicago: University of Chicago Press, 1969), 148–51.

72. Acheson to James Grafton Rogers, July 5, 1934, in *Among Friends*, 23–24. Acheson expressed similar sentiments in letters to Warburg, Jan. 7, 1934 (ibid., 20), and Prentiss Gilbert, Feb. 13, 1934, DAP-SL.

73. On Holmes's economic outlook see Konefsky, 45–46, 59–61; cf. de Tocqueville, 1: 290; Smiles, 328–29.

74. On Acheson's aspiration for the GOP see letter to A. B. Dick, Nov. 14, 1932, in *Among Friends*, 19. For Brandeis's influence on FDR at this point see Tugwell, 326. On Brandeis, Frankfurter, and Keynes see Murphy, 126–28.

75. See Acheson to Warburg, Apr. 3, 1935, DAP-SL; Acheson to Warburg, Oct. 8, 1935, DAP-SL. For Keynes's comment on von Hayek, see Harrod, 435.

confused."[76] Personal experience had taught him, as it had Kennan, to distrust FDR's Caesarist tendencies, but unlike Kennan Acheson also reasoned that the president had fulfilled the statesman's function of attempting "those things which large groups demand as a condition [of] their emotional allegiance to the system." This was a tacit admission that FDR had been obliged to do *something* to respond to public despair about the price level (in 1933 it stood at 60 percent of 1926 levels), even buying gold.[77] If he believed, with de Tocqueville, that his profession was America's natural aristocracy, he had no reason to complain – in contrast to Kennan the diplomat – that lawyers did not have enough influence at the top. The Supreme Court's abandonment of judicial self-restraint in striking down New Deal legislation also drew Acheson closer to the Roosevelt camp. In 1937, he admonished the legal profession with the arguments of Brandeis and Holmes: "If we see in every social question only the seeds of Götterdämmerung, if all our boasted inventiveness turns to the dust of constitutional platitudes and the formulae of dead economists, then we shall be a menace to the very social order we effect to defend and become the instrument of social catastrophe."[78]

There was a final factor in Acheson's decision to back Roosevelt: Hull's Reciprocal Trade Act of 1934. When he endorsed Roosevelt in 1936, Acheson did so in language nearly identical to that of William Clayton, the Texas cotton magnate – and his future State Department colleague. Neither mentioned FDR but expressed hope, in Acheson's words, "that Mr. Hull's liberalism, sanity and patience may increasingly shape the policies of the government."[79]

"The ablest lawyer in Washington"

Acheson's place in the foreign policy constellation of the late thirties was halfway between the orthodox Wilsonianism of Hull and the

76. Acheson to L. Douglas, Sept. 5, 1936, DAP-SL.
77. Acheson to Grenville Clark, Oct. 31, 1936, DAP-SL. On the price level see Schlesinger, *The Coming of the New Deal*, 195. The figures are for wholesale commodity price levels.
78. Acheson's address, "Some Social Factors in Legal Change," Jan. 22, 1937, Chicago Law Club. On the Supreme Court, see Acheson to R. MacDonald, Mar. 11, 1937, in *Among Friends*, 28–29; Acheson to Warburg, Mar. 12, 1937, in ibid., 29–31; Acheson to R. MacDonald, Sept. 29, 1937, in ibid., 33; Acheson to Raymond Lee, July 12, 1938, DAP-SL.
79. In Acheson, *Morning and Noon*, 201. For Clayton's statement see John L. Harper, *America and the Reconstruction of Italy, 1945–1948* (Cambridge: Cambridge University Press, 1986), 7.

progressive Republican activism of Stimson and Ickes. He had little in common with the anti-Sovietism of the protocontainment group in the State Department and even less with the Europhobic-hemispheric tendency of Berle and Welles. He was inclined to believe – here was the link to the Theodore Rooseveltians – that the long peace of the preceding century had rested on naval and military power and that the United States should consolidate the alliance with Britain that had begun to emerge in 1898. The nineteenth century system would have to be put back on track and strengthened on the basis on which it had actually existed, not according to a fanciful blueprint inspired by the reading of Tennyson's "Lockesley Hall." Perhaps Acheson's view of universalistic schemes and of the relationship between the Anglo-American world and its adversaries had been influenced by Holmes, who believed that

> force, mitigated so far as may be by good manners, is the *ultima ratio*, and between two groups that want to make inconsistent kinds of worlds I see no remedy except force.... However I dare say that all this is in the air and that you may say that on these [the League of Nation's] or any other principles it is a good thing if we can unite forces to put down avoidable displays of force.[80]

Acheson's *Morning and Noon* is suspiciously vague about the author's personal feelings for Wilson and his program in 1919; they were probably more positive than he later let on. His attitude toward Hull, Wilson's chief disciple, was one of sympathy and respect. While filtering out the utopian and Anglophobic elements of Hull's message, Acheson was powerfully attracted to the economic goals and the idea of international cooperation. Acheson later blamed the impracticality of the United Nations on the man he called "that little rat," Leo Pasvolsky: "How he possessed poor old Cordell's mind." Brandeis's own meliorism had extended into the realm of foreign affairs. Thus there was a Brandesian liberal as well as a Holmesian realist side to Acheson's international outlook.[81] At this point, Acheson had no developed vision of Europe per se. But from either perspective, Europe was bound to be central: as an indispensable component of the world economy and as a

80. Holmes to Pollock, Feb. 1, 1920, in Howe, ed., *Holmes–Pollock Letters*, 2: 36. Acheson undoubtedly heard such views firsthand at the time. See also Acheson, *Morning and Noon*, 121; McClellan, chap. 4.
81. On Acheson's fondness for Hull, see Dean Acheson, *Present at the Creation: My Years at the State Department* (New York: Norton, 1969), 87–88. On Pasvolsky see Acheson to C. B. Marshall, Oct. 30, 1967, DAP-SL. Brandeis's biographer notes, for example, "Mrs. Brandeis was an avowed pacifist.... The Justice himself undoubtedly sympathized with her views." A. T. Mason, *Brandeis: A Free Man's Life* (New York: Village Press, 1956), 519.

geopolitical entity whose fate was vital to the United States. There was nothing in Acheson's cultural makeup or outlook to cause him to abhor contact with Europe or to view the Atlantic as a historic barrier; his nightmare was the opposite: that the United States would find itself cut off from the rest of the world, "a lone island," as FDR was to put it in June 1940, "in a world dominated by the philosophy of force."[82]

Acheson's return to the fold of the Roosevelt administration, culminating in his appointment by Hull as an assistant secretary of state for economic affairs in February 1941, was part of the reemergence of an "ultra-British party," along with Roosevelt's cooptation of the Progressive Republicans Stimson and Knox.[83] In September 1939, Adolf Berle wrote that "the Morgans, the Harvard New Englanders and the like who really influenced our entry into war in 1917" were mobilizing once again. Frankfurter's chief foreign policy henchman, Berle believed, was Acheson. This was not an implausible view. Yet Acheson required no prompting from his friend. By the spring of 1941, Acheson was arguing for a declaration of war or its equivalent by ordering the fleet to battle stations, while Frankfurter believed that such a move was politically unwise.[84]

Acheson's efforts began with a speech, "An American Attitude toward Foreign Affairs," delivered at Yale in November 1939. Acheson attempted to provide a historical explanation for the present catastrophe: "The economic and political system of the Nineteenth Century, which

82. FDR quoted by John A. Thompson, "The Exaggeration of American Vulnerability: The Anatomy of a Tradition," *Diplomatic History*, 16 no. 1 (Winter 1992), 35.
83. Acheson's 1933 experience had given him high-level British connections, including Lindsay and Leith-Ross. En route to the Cotswolds and Devonshire in 1935, he lunched with Neville Chamberlain, Walter Runciman, and Lord Halifax and spent an evening with the Labour Party leader Sir Stafford Cripps. See Acheson to George Rublee, Sept. 3, 1935, DAP-SL. He visited England again (and France) in 1938 and corresponded with his friend Raymond Lee, military attaché at the U.S. Embassy in London. British behavior caused him concern. In early 1935 he noted that the British were "hoping rather wistfully like the three little pigs, that the Big Bad Wolf [Germany] is not going to 'blow in their house.'" British policy in the Abysinnian crisis he described as "no hits, no runs, all errors," and the Baldwin government's European policy as "the most incredible bungle." See Acheson to Mr. and Mrs. M. D. Truesdale, Mar. 29, 1935; Acheson to Raymond Lee, Mar. 16 and May 28, 1936, DAP-SL. He did not feel that the victors of 1919 were blameless for the rise of Hitler but, in contrast to Bullitt or Berle, was inclined to see Paris rather than London as the culprit: the French invasion of the Ruhr in 1923 had brought inflation and the Nazis and was thus "the most disastrous single step taken in Europe during this century." Acheson to his son David Acheson, May 4, 1936, in *Among Friends*, 27.
84. Adolf Berle Diary, Sept. 30, 1939, FDRL. For an account of the Acheson–Frankfurter disagreement, see J. M. Keynes to Horace Wilson, May 25, 1941, in Moggridge, ed., 23: 95.

throughout the world produced an amazing increase in the production of wealth and population, has been for many years in the obvious process of decline." The system, he observed, was now "deeply impaired." It probably could not be "reestablished in anything approaching its old form, if at all." Acheson spelled out a series of consequences:

> We can see that the credits which were once extended by the financial center of London no longer provide the means for the production of wealth in other countries. We can see that the free trade areas, which once furnished both a market of vast importance and a commodities exchange, no longer exist. We can see that British naval power no longer can guarantee security of life and investment in distant parts of the earth and a localization of conflict near home.... With credits unavailable, markets gone, and with them the means of attaining the price of needed raw materials, with population pressing upon restricted resources, the stage was set for the appearance of the totalitarian military state.

As an immediate response, "we must make ourselves so strong that we shall not be caught defenseless or dangerously exposed in any even possible eventuality." Powerful military and naval forces would be needed "to secure ourselves, if the disintegration of the world order cannot be checked and the system revised and revived," and, he added more optimistically, "to take an effective part in the attempt to recreate it."[85] Acheson called for aid to the British and French up to and including the dispatch of air and naval units to Europe. Much of the speech was devoted to the essential American contribution "to reestablishing the foundations of peace," including "making capital available to those parts of Europe which need productive equipment upon condition that Europe does its part to remove obstructions to trade within itself."[86]

By the fall of 1940, Acheson was, with the possible exceptions of Francis Miller (animator of the "Century Group") and William Allen White (head of the Committee to Defend America by Aiding the Allies), the most active private campaigner on behalf of aid to Britain. Acheson did not work closely with the Century Group;[87] he operated mainly in Washington through his own connections. His most important effort

---

85. Acheson, "An American Attitude Toward Foreign Affairs," in *Morning and Noon*, 267–75.
86. Ibid.
87. At least he later denied connection with the group. See Acheson's letter to D. Dillinger, Apr. 27, 1967, and to J. M. D. Alexander, Nov. 2, 1966, DAP-SL. It may be that Acheson had brief contact with the group – some of whose members were personal friends – when he was in New York in early August to prepare the legal opinion on U.S. destroyers.

was the famous legal opinion, written with Ben Cohen of the White House, arguing that the release of U.S. destroyers did not violate existing law and was possible without congressional action. The opinion, printed in the *New York Times*, prompted Attorney General Robert Jackson to argue that the transfer was legal. Acheson persuaded British Ambassador Lord Lothian to convince Canadian Prime Minister MacKenzie King to pressure Roosevelt on the destroyer transfer.[88] Acheson's files contain a memo, dated July 3, 1940, outlining U.S., British and Canadian defense cooperation and the continuation of aid once British financial resources were exhausted. He tried unsuccessfully to persuade Lippmann to write in favor of the destroyer deal and collaborated on campaign speeches with Harry Hopkins and Samuel Rosenman in October 1940.[89]

Acheson wrote later, "The only interest the President took in foreign affairs during his first two terms was in the good neighbors of Latin America." The international crisis "burst upon a president unprepared intellectually and militarily." Acheson's later criticism centered on what he and the interventionists considered Roosevelt's failure to lead in 1940–41. Their role had been to speed up the president's agonizingly slow advance.[90] In effect, what Acheson found incomprehensible were the president's Europhobic and hemispheric instincts. Solidarity with Britain was the alpha and omega of Acheson's approach. Sentimental and geopolitical considerations were inseparable, as they had been for John Hay, Edward House, and Oliver Wendell Holmes.

Acheson's urge in 1940 was also to help Franklin Roosevelt himself. His service to the administration was, among other things, a kind of penance for what Acheson came to think had been his own rashness and failure to appreciate the president's political necessities in 1933. Just as Acheson's refusal to devise a legal opinion to permit the president to buy gold was an act of defiance, his (by his own admission less than airtight) legal opinion that the president could transfer the destroyers was a gesture of reconciliation. In 1933 FDR had lectured Acheson that lawyers were supposed to find out what their clients *could* rather than

88. See Acheson, *Morning and Noon*, 224. For text of the opinion see "No Legal Bar Seen to Transfer of Destroyers," *New York Times*, Aug. 11, 1940.

89. See Acheson memo, July 3, 1940, DAP-HSTL, box 3. On Lippmann, whom Acheson invited to his farm in early September, see Acheson to Frankfurter, Sept. 9, 1940, DAP-SL. On speeches see Acheson, *Morning and Noon*, 225–26; Princeton Seminar transcript, 116, DAP-HSTL.

90. Dean Acheson, "The Eclipse of the State Department," *Foreign Affairs*, 49, no. 4 (July 1971), 593–606; Acheson, *Present*, 21–22; Acheson to Anthony Eden (undated) 1965, DAP-SL; Acheson, *Morning and Noon*, 267.

what they could not do. In 1941, FDR called Acheson "without question the ablest lawyer in Washington."[91]

The "true" liberals and the "real"

In the twenties Keynes made a distinction between the "true" liberals and the "real." According to Roy Harrod, the "true" liberals "adhered unflinchingly to the old doctrines even, and not least, when it required courage to do so." The "real" liberals were "more concerned with the future than the past." In 1931, Keynes wrote, "Free trade unbesmirched invokes old loyalties and recalls one of the greatest triumphs of reason in politics which adorns our history... [but] one must not let one's sense of the past grow stronger than one's sense of the present and the future, or sacrifice the substance to the symbol."[92]

These sentiments, along with the Englishman's caustic intellect and charm, attracted Felix Frankfurter to Keynes. Frankfurter considered himself a "real" liberal, intent on saving the substance of a private enterprise system from those too obtuse to see that this required systematic intervention by the state. Holmes and Brandeis had also been "real" Victorian liberals. Just as Keynes was trying to demonstrate the obsolesence of strict free trade and the gold standard to the purposes of a liberal society, they had tried to sweep away the cant and legalistic cobwebs in the path of prudential adaptation and reform.

In mid-1941, Acheson was still hostile to deficit spending and especially to trade and exchange controls. There was an expedient "shorttermism"[93] and fashionable anti-Victorian iconoclasm about "Keynesianism" that continued to grate on his Evangelical conscience. For his part, Keynes no longer viewed Americans with his old superciliousness.[94] He had numerous sympathizers in the United States. Still, his preliminary sparring with U.S. officials over the concessions to be attached to lend-lease prompted fear that "true" liberalism reigned in the

91. On Acheson's reflection on his own behavior see Acheson, *Morning and Noon*, 191. For his private comments on the legal opinion see Acheson to Quincy Wright, Aug. 29, 1940; Acheson to John McCloy, Sept. 12, 1940, DAP-SL. See also Princeton Seminar transcript, 116. On FDR see Acheson, *Morning and Noon*, 178; FDR memo to William Knudsen et al., on appointments, Feb. 8, 1941, copy in DAP-SL.

92. Keynes quoted in Harrod, 378, 340; also in Robert Skidelsky, "Keynes's Middle Way," Special Ford Lecture delivered at Oxford University, May 3, 1991, mimeo, 6. Keynes was speaking of the Liberal Party but, by inference, of people of liberal economic and political views generally.

93. On "shorttermism," see Robert Skidelsky, "Keynes's Middle Way," 5.

94. See Robert Skidelsky, *John Maynard Keynes*, vol. 1: *Hopes Betrayed* (London: Macmillan, 1983), 342.

State Department. He referred to a July 28, 1941, American draft of Article VII of the lend-lease "consideration" agreement as "the lunatic proposals of Mr. Hull."[95]

Acheson met Keynes in late May 1941, and dined with him at Frankfurter's apartment.[96] Acheson recalled, "Keynes was not only one of the most delightful and engaging men I have ever known but also, in a true sense of the word, one of the most brilliant. His many-faceted and highly polished mind sparkled and danced with light."[97] Keynes's magnetism worked like a solvent on Acheson's Smilesian reservations. Keynes, in turn, was buoyed by Acheson's pro-British interventionism.[98] Certainly he belonged to the presentable category of Americans and was a potential "real" liberal. The process of conversion was to leave a mark on both teacher and adept.

Acheson rejected Keynes's draft lend-lease proposal of July 15, 1941, as "wholly impossible" since it contemplated virtually no British obligations.[99] It was a Welles–Acheson counterdraft that touched a raw nerve in Keynes on July 28. Article VII included a joint commitment to end "discrimination" against each other's exports. Keynes reacted emotionally to what he called an "ironclad formula from the Nineteenth Century." The "only hope of the future was to maintain economies in balance without great excesses of either exports or imports, and this could only be through exchange controls, which Article VII seemed to ban." Acheson replied coldly that Keynes was taking "an extreme and unjustified position." According to Acheson's record, Keynes then explained:

> There were some who believed that Great Britain should return to a free trade policy; there was a middle group, among whom he classified himself, who believed in the use of control mechanisms; and there was a third group who leant toward imperial policies. I said that I realized this and that we hoped that in his discussion of the Article he would not take a narrow or technical view regarding the language as a draftsman's product... but would try to direct attention to the major purpose.... At the end of our talk he seemed more reconciled to the Article, but by no means wholly so.[100]

95. Harrod, 512. See also Richard N. Gardner, *Sterling–Dollar Diplomacy in Current Perspective: The Origins and the Prospects of Our International Economic Order* (New York: Columbia University Press, 1980), 57.
96. For Keynes's account of that occasion, see Moggridge, ed., 23: 95.
97. Acheson, *Present*, 29. He also spoke of his "cherished friendship" with Keynes (22).
98. Moggridge, ed., 23: 95.
99. Acheson, *Present*, 29; Moggridge, ed., 23: 162–63.
100. *FRUS*, 1941, 3: 10–15.

It was an emotional exchange. Acheson's evident goodwill prompted a handwritten note ("My Dear Acheson") from Keynes on July 29:

> My so strong reaction against the word "discrimination" is the result of my feeling so passionately that our hands must be free to make something new and better of the postwar world.... But the word calls up, and must call up – for that is what it means strictly interpreted – all the old lumber; most-favored-nation clause and the rest which was a notorious failure and made such a hash of the old world.... It is the clutch of the dead, or at least the moribund hand.... We must be free to work out new and better arrangements which will win in substance and not in shadow what the President and you and others really want.[101]

Subsequent events suggest that Keynes had opened Acheson's eyes to the factors affecting Britain's willingness to return to a liberal regime: the inevitability of a huge U.S. balance-of-payments surplus and British deficit after the war, likely to be aggravated by a return to depression and protectionism in the United States.[102] Acheson henceforth worked for a version of Article VII that assuaged British concerns. The final American draft of Article VII, presented by Acheson to the British ambassador on December 2, 1941, incorporated "mutually dependent obligations."[103] The British commitment to move toward the elimination of discrimination was made contingent on American domestic expansion and liberal tariff policies. "We were," Acheson said, "embracing the Keynesian ideas of an expanding economy. If it needed to be managed, let us do it together and not separately."[104]

Thus Acheson threw his weight behind Keynes when he became convinced that the Englishman's instincts were for a return to cooperation,[105] and embraced Keynesian domestic policies of managed growth as the means to restore the substance of a liberal *international* economy. The "real" Victorians were all Keynesians now. The stunning World War II growth of the U.S. economy, stimulated by government spending, reinforced the point. After 1945, in any event, Acheson was no longer a fiscally conservative Democrat. When arguments were advanced to show how, through economic stimulation, the United States might keep

---

101. Ibid., 16–17.
102. McClellan notes that "Acheson learned from this encounter" (48). See also Acheson, *Present*, 30. Acheson observes that Keynes spoke (on July 28) "wisely about a postwar problem that he foresaw far more clearly than I did – our great capacity to export, the world's need for our goods and the problems of payment."
103. Richard N. Gardner, 59.
104. Acheson, *Present*, 32. See also *FRUS*, 1941, 3: 43–45; E. F. Penrose, *Economic Planning for the Peace* (Princeton, N.J.: Princeton University Press, 1953), 19.
105. On Keynes's internationalist instincts see Harrod, 525.

its high standard of living and at the same time pay for the military power necessary to maintain its international position, Acheson was prepared to go along.[106]

Keynes's own ideas were in flux in the summer of 1941. "So far from its being my opinion that the bilateral arrangements to which the Americans object are the ideal solution," he wrote, "I have been spending some time since I came back in elaborating a truly international plan which would avoid these difficulties.... Let us start constructively, offering them [the Americans] something which would give them all they ask, provided they are really prepared to be truly internationally minded."[107] Keynes had begun work on plans for an international clearing union (ICU) whose role would be to provide sufficient liquidity to permit countries to pursue liberal commercial policies. He was convinced that there were enough educable and well-intentioned Americans to make such a project worthwhile. It was Keynes's "actual experience of the cooperative spirit of the Americans," observes Harrod, "and their willingness to temper their principle of non-discrimination by all manner of safe-guarding expedients, that made him veer back to favouring an open international system" and an Anglo-American special relationship.[108]

By "present at the creation," Acheson meant to stress his role in setting up the "Free World": the Truman Doctrine, the Marshall Plan, and the North Atlantic Treaty. He had also been at the center of the earlier, more grandiose and ambitious effort to lay the foundations of "One World." Few came more honestly by their belief in that program or expended more energy trying to achieve it. For guidance, Acheson looked less to Hull, Morgenthau, or Harry White than to Keynes. If Acheson helped to rekindle Keynes's internationalism, Keynes encouraged Acheson's belief in the practicality of the administration's program. It was Keynes who "opened up the far reaching complexities" of the postwar relief problem with which Acheson became involved as a planner of the Food and Agricultural Organization and the United Nations Relief and Rehabilitation Administration (UNRRA).[109] Acheson and Keynes saw each other frequently in September–October 1943. Keynes wrote him ("My Dear Dean") before leaving, "We have

106. On the impact of World War II expansion on attitudes toward economic policy see Herbert Stein, *Presidential Economics* (Washington, D.C.: American Enterprise Institute, 1988), 65.

107. Keynes to Sir Horace Wilson, Sept. 19, 1941, in Moggridge, ed., 23: 209. Harrod, 526–27.

108. See Harrod, 469; Keynes in Moggridge, ed., 24: 221.

109. See Acheson, *Present*, 65, 76–77.

greatly enjoyed this visit to Washington. . . . Not the least part of our enjoyment came from our meetings with you and your family . . . we have felt that our bonds to several of our American friends have come a great deal closer and more intimate."[110]

Acheson's role at the Bretton Woods conference was a secondary one. Where possible he facilitated agreement with the British.[111] On closing the conference, Keynes paid "a particular tribute" to the lawyers. "All the more so because I have to confess that, generally speaking, I do not like lawyers. . . . Too often lawyers busy themselves to make commonsense illegal . . . [and] to turn poetry into prose." Not so at Bretton Woods. The lawyers – Acheson foremost among them – had "turned our jargon into prose and our prose into poetry. And only too often they have had to do our thinking for us."[112] Acheson also played a minor role in the talks to obtain Stage II (post–VE Day) lend-lease aid for Britain, but Keynes praised him privately "for what I believe that he did, without confessing it or blabbing in the too frequent Washington way, behind the scenes."[113]

Acheson's wartime letters indicate that he was frustrated by the "major foolishness of small men" and the department's isolation. In June 1944, he wrote, only half facetiously: "Exhaustion and spiritual degeneration are my present difficulties"; in October, he was "tired and somewhat at a dead end."[114] But he had a deep wellspring of stamina. As assistant secretary of state for congressional affairs, he was a key spokesman during the passage of the postwar economic program. In speeches to business audiences, Acheson argued for a large postwar

110. Moggridge, ed., 23: 298–99. Keynes wrote to Sir Wilfred Eady on October 3, 1943: "People in Washington are extraordinarily kind. . . . The (I suppose rather high brow) group where Lydia and I are most comfortable are the Walter Lippmann's, Dean Acheson's and the Archie Macleishes. . . . We have really enjoyed ourselves extraordinarily on several occasions in their most hospitable company." See ibid., 25: 354.

111. See letter to Noel Hall, Aug. 1, 1944, DAP-SL. See also Acheson, *Present*, 84; Blum, ed., *Morgenthau Diaries*, 3: 271–78.

112. See Keynes speech, July 22, 1944, at Bretton Woods closing plenary session. Moggridge, ed., 26: 102.

113. See Keynes to Sir John Anderson, Dec. 12, 1944, in Moggridge, ed., 24: 214. See also 190 on Acheson's role.

114. See Acheson letter to David Acheson, Jan. 17, 1945, DAP-SL. He is probably referring to the Treasury Department. Being chairman of the UNRRA conference "meant that, in addition to attempting to run a large and somewhat unwieldy American delegation, I have had to take on the responsibility for the Conference and the endless meetings and discussions in which we persuade and cajole people not to do foolish things." See Acheson to his mother, Nov. 27, 1943, in *Among Friends*, 43–45; Acheson to David Acheson, June 20 and Oct. 2, 1944, DAP-SL.

outflow of U.S. private capital – something he had foreseen in his 1939 Yale speech – to finance recovery abroad and for lower U.S. tariffs permitting foreign countries to repay their debts by exporting to the United States. Trade liberalization went hand in hand with Keynesian domestic policies: "Over the years we must by means of an adequate domestic policy attain expanding income and employment at home, so that fluctuations in our volume of business do not destroy economic progress abroad."[115]

Acheson's final accomplishment as assistant secretary was Senate approval of the United Nations Charter in July 1945. One observer wrote, "No other man did as much on behalf of the organization he thought necessary." This may be an exaggeration, but it is closer to the truth than Acheson's own dismissive comments.[116] Acheson had little to do with the preparation of the charter, but he said privately of Hull's efforts, "It has been a very great service of the old gentleman to his country."[117] When asked what was the most important feature of the Yalta agreement, he replied, "From a long-range viewpoint, I should say completion of the Dumbarton Oaks proposals . . . and the agreement on the treatment of Germany." On the same occasion he said, "We will either get order by organized international cooperation, or we won't get it."[118] On hearing the news of the atomic bomb on August 6, 1945, he wrote, "If we can't work out some sort of organization of great powers, we shall be gone geese for fair."[119]

The facts of the situation

"The conversion of Acheson to a hard line stance," write Issacson and Thomas, "was perhaps the most dramatic and significant of any postwar American statesman."[120] Acheson was not exactly Saul on the road to Damascus in mid-1946, but his shift did have an impressive finality when it came. As in any such event there was an elusive personal element in the timing. As much as a conversion it was a conscious decision to suspend doubt about whether the United States and the

---

115. See Acheson speech of Dec. 7, 1944, "The Interest of the American Businessman in International Trade." See also speech of Apr. 16, 1945 (untitled) to the Economic Club of New York, DAP-SL.
116. See John Kenneth Galbraith, "Dean Acheson Recalls His Good Life and Good, Brawling Times" (review of *Present*), *Washington Post Book World*, Oct. 12, 1969, 3. See also Acheson, *Present*, chap. 1, 111–12.
117. Acheson to David Acheson, June 20, 1944, DAP-SL.
118. NBC Radio University of the Air broadcast, Mar. 1945, transcript in DAP-SL.
119. Acheson, *Present*, 113.
120. Issacson and Thomas, 362.

Soviet Union could get along – doubt of the kind that paralyzed constructive action. That somewhere doubt survived is at least suggested
by the way Acheson recalled the events of 1946–47 (in 1953): "It
seemed to us that... behind this experience was the attempt of the
Soviet Union... to produce weakness and disintegration in Western
Germany.... That seemed to be the program." Russian action in Iran
in 1945–46 "and the years following in Greece and Turkey; and at the
same time in Italy and France – seemed to show a very large pincer
movement going on."[121] Later he said that this scenario, presented at a
famous White House meeting in February 1947, was "enough true but
not completely."[122]

Acheson's retrospective statements about the Russians are not the
most reliable guide to his views at the time.[123] He was part of the dominant camp within the Roosevelt administration that believed the
United States "could do business with the Russians." As Berle later
told the House Un-American Activities Committee investigating charges
against Alger Hiss (the brother of Acheson's protégé Donald Hiss),
Acheson's appointment as assistant secretary for congressional affairs in
November 1944 was part of a shake-up in which Berle, who favored a
"pretty clear-cut show down" with Russia, ended up in Rio de Janiero.
In early 1946, Acheson's own name appeared on an FBI list of "high
government officials operating an alleged espionage network" – along
with Hiss and Henry Wallace.[124]

While Acheson never idealized Soviet–American relations, his
firsthand experience had counseled cautious optimism. Acheson worked
successfully with the Russians to set up UNRRA; at Bretton Woods he
regarded the Soviet concession on the International Bank quota issue
"as a great diplomatic victory... and as a matter of great political

121. Princeton Seminar transcript, 292, DAP-HSTL.
122. See transcript of interview of Acheson prepared from notes taken by Bob Woodward
   and transmitted to Acheson on April 22, 1970, DAP-SL. On the February 26, 1947,
   meeting, see Acheson, *Present*, 219.
123. When asked in 1953 what his view of Soviet power had been in 1939, he said, "I
   don't think I can answer that now.... I think if I answered it now I would intend to
   say that I thought in 1939 what I think now." Princeton Seminar transcript, July 2,
   1953, session, 74, DAP-HSTL. In 1970, he told a reporter that he had had problems
   dealing with Vishinsky – "who was a louse" – in 1941. "I always had a feeling that
   things weren't going to work out with them." See transcript of interview sent by
   Woodward to Acheson, Apr. 22, 1970. Acheson answered Woodward, "I am afraid
   your notes are pretty well mixed up. I didn't know Vishinsky in 1941, and so on.
   The point is, do not rely on them." Acheson to Woodward, May 4, 1970, DAP-SL.
124. See Berle testimony to the House Un-American Activities Committee, Aug. 30,
   1948, concerning Alger Hiss. Copy in Messer, 269 n. 2. Post-Administration file,
   box 89, DAP-SL. See also Issacson and Thomas, 322.

significance." Probably he would have agreed with Keynes, who wrote that personal relations with the Russians had been "very cordial. . . . They *want* to thaw and collaborate."[125]

The first signs of serious worry in Acheson's case surface in a letter written on April 2, 1945. Acheson was stunned to learn that Roosevelt had agreed at Yalta to three votes for the Soviet Union in the General Assembly:

> When one adds to this the failure of the Russians to send Molotov [to the San Francisco UN conference] and the present demand that the Lublin Committee without changes be represented, it begins to look as though the whole program had received some pretty damaging body blows. The added trouble is that all of these things seem to be so inexplicable. They make so little sense from the point of view of any participant and therefore become even more difficult to explain.

Still, he also wrote – using a phrase remarkably like FDR's own in his final message to Churchill on April 11, 1945 – "I think that granted a reasonable amount of good luck the situation can be more or less straightened out."[126] By May, Acheson was more suspicious of Moscow, but he opposed the abrupt cutoff of lend-lease and Harriman's advice to "get tough." "There is great gloom over the imminence of World War III," he wrote. "This I do not believe."[127]

In September 1945, retiring Secretary of War Stimson recommended a private approach to the Russians with a view to creating an international atomic energy regime: "If we fail to approach them now, and merely continue to negotiate with them, having this weapon rather ostentatiously on our hip, their suspicion and their distrust of our purposes will increase." At a September 21 cabinet meeting, Stimson argued that the Russians had "been our traditional friends." Also present, Acheson endorsed the Stimson line: "He could not conceive of a world in which we were hoarders of military secrets from our Allies."[128] On September 25, 1945, Acheson advised Truman that the Soviet Union would have the bomb within five years. "The advantage of being ahead in such a race is nothing compared with not having the race," while a U.S.–British–Canadian monopoly could only be seen by

125. See Acheson, *Present*, 68, 78, 85–86; Blum, ed., *Morgenthau Diaries*, 3: 277.
126. Acheson to David Acheson, Apr. 2, 1945, in *Among Friends*, 49–50. See also Kimball, ed., *Correspondence*, 3: 277.
127. See Acheson, *Present*, 132; Acheson to Mary Acheson Bundy, May 12 and 16, 1945, DAP-SL. Portions printed in *Among Friends*, 54–59.
128. Stimson memo, Sept. 12, 1945, *FRUS*, 1945, 2: 41–44. See also Henry Stimson and McGeorge Bundy, *On Active Service in Peace and War* (New York: Harper Bros., 1947), 642–47; Larson, 213, 215–16; Blum, ed., *The Price of Vision*, 482.

Moscow as evidence of an anti-Soviet bloc. "To their minds there is much other evidence of this." Like Stimson – or Frankfurter and FDR himself – Acheson favored a private approach to the Russians on the subject.[129] On November 14, 1945, in a speech to the National Council of American–Soviet Friendship, Acheson made a classic statement of the FDR–Stimson–Lippmann thesis about Soviet–American relations. For nearly a century and a half, he said,

> we have gotten along well – remarkably well, when you consider that our forms of government, our economic systems and our social habits have never been similar. . . . [N]ever, in the past, has there been any place on the globe where the vital interests of the American and Russian peoples have clashed or even been antagonistic – and there is no objective reason to suppose that there should, now or in the future, ever be such a place.[130]

This thesis was under systematic attack in late 1945. Truman rejected the Stimson–Acheson approach on the bomb and appeared – under the advice of Forrestal and other hard-liners – to favor an Anglo-American monopoly. Coming at a time of Soviet intrigue in Iranian Azerbaijan, the president was infuriated with Secretary of State Byrnes's independent, conciliatory stance at Moscow in December 1945. In January 1946, he wrote that he was "tired [of] babying the Soviets." Acheson attended a meeting in December to discuss the recently nego-tiated $3.75 billion loan to Britain where he heard Vandenberg oppose "the loan to England because he thought that meant a loan to Russia." Loy Henderson's December 28, 1945, memo to Acheson was straight out of Mackinder: "The Soviet Union seems to be determined to break down the structure which Great Britain had maintained so that Russian power and influence can sweep unimpeded across Turkey and through the Dardenelles into the Mediterranean, and across Iran and through the Persian Gulf into the Indian Ocean." On February 9, Stalin gave a famous speech warning that war was inherent in the nature of capitalism.

129. Acheson wrote, "Overall disagreement with the Soviets seems to be increasing. Yet I cannot see why the basic interests of the two nations should conflict. Any long-range understanding based on firmness and frankness and mutual recognition of the others' [sic] basic interests seems to me impossible under a policy of Anglo-American exclusion of Russia from atomic development. If it is impossible there will be no organized peace but only an armed truce." *FRUS*, 1945, 2: 48–50. See also Larson, 218–19. On Frankfurter and FDR see Chapter 3, this volume.

130. Copy of the speech in DAP-SL. See also Acheson, *Present*, 130–31. Lippmann had written in 1943, "Each has always opposed the dismemberment of the other. Each has always wished the other to be strong. They have never had a collision which made them enemies. Each has regarded the other as a potential friend in the rear of potential enemies." *U.S. Foreign Policy*, 143.

On February 28, Byrnes endorsed the Truman–Vandenberg line: "We cannot allow aggression to be accomplished by coercion or pressure or subterfuges."[131]

But Acheson was in no hurry to climb aboard the anti-Soviet bandwagon. He dismissed Forrestal's view that Stalin's speech was a "delayed declaration of war." There is little evidence that he was convinced by Kennan's "long telegram" in early March.[132] When Stalin kept troops in Iran after the March 2, 1946, deadline, Byrnes requested their immediate withdrawal. After heavy Soviet troop movements were reported nonetheless, Acheson recommended expressing concern but leaving "a graceful way out."[133] After lengthy discussions in the Security Council, a Soviet–Iranian accord was reached and the Red Army left in May. Acheson devoted much of February–March 1946 to a scheme to control the atomic bomb. Liberals and Rooseveltians praised the resulting Acheson–Lilienthal report, which represented an effort to create an international authority with control over all dangerous activities related to atomic energy. When Truman and Byrnes abruptly transferred responsibility for the plan to the Democratic Party financial backer Bernard Baruch, Acheson vigorously protested. He believed that Baruch's provisions for "swift and sure punishment" of violators "could be interpreted in Moscow only as an attempt to turn the United Nations into an alliance to support a United States threat of war against the USSR."[134] In late April, Acheson endorsed a plan conceived by junior officials for the creation of a European-wide council under UN auspices to head off the emerging split of Europe into two blocs. Byrnes chose not to put Soviet intentions to the test, rejecting the plan by "pocket veto."[135] During the same period Acheson fought and lost a bitter battle to set up a new intelligence organ within the State Department, staffed by former members of the Office of Strategic Services (OSS). A principal reason for his defeat was what Acheson called "a pre-McCarthyite attack" from Congress and within the department itself on the new personnel – and implicitly Acheson himself – for allegedly

131. See Messer, 158–66; 188; Blum, ed., *The Price of Vision*, 526; *FRUS*, 1946, 7: 2.
132. Issacson and Thomas, 350–51, 356; Acheson, *Present*, 151.
133. See Byrnes to Molotov, Mar. 6, 1946, *FRUS*, 1946, 7: 340–42; see also Mar. 8, 1946, message to Moscow, on the basis of Acheson's recommendation, ibid., 348. On this point see Bruce R. Kuniholm, *The Origins of the Cold War in the Near East: Great Power Conflict and Diplomacy in Iran, Turkey and Greece* (Princeton, N.J.: Princeton University Press, 1980), 322.
134. Acheson, *Present*, 145. See also Robert J. Donovan, *Conflict and Crisis: The Presidency of Harry S. Truman, 1945–1948* (New York: Norton, 1977), 204–6.
135. On this plan, see Walt W. Rostow, *The Division of Europe after World War II* (Aldershot: Grover Press, 1982), 8, 126–33.

favoring "a socialized America in a world commonwealth of Communist and Socialist states."[136]

Mid-1946, Acheson recalled, was "a time of almost uninterrupted troubles."[137] The definitive crumbling of Roosevelt's design and its replacement by a "cold war consensus" during the first six months of the year coincided with a moment of crisis and disillusionment in his career. The Yalta agreements – the Far Eastern protocol was published for the first time on February 11, 1946 – were widely discredited. Acheson had embarrassed the administration by claiming at a January 22, 1946, press conference that the United States had not agreed at Yalta to permanent Soviet sovereignty over the Kurile Islands.[138] By April 1946, Acheson was becoming a lame duck within the Truman administration. No one was more aware of this than Acheson himself. Referring to the atomic energy and intelligence controversies, he wrote, "Both experiences, occurring almost coincidentally, led me to review my position carefully and to attempt a precautionary measure." On April 17, he wrote a letter of resignation to Byrnes and Truman, to take effect July 1, 1946.[139]

Why did Acheson decide to place his considerable energies and intellect behind the policy of confrontation and become its leading spokesman? According to Acheson it was because the "facts" – Soviet conduct – had changed. As a good Brandeisian, he changed his views accordingly.[140] But the "facts" of the situation were personal as well as objective. One was that he had more than paid his dues to the Roosevelt administration and its policies. The "debt" incurred by his 1933 "disloyalty" had been made good with interest by mid-1946. Another fact was that Acheson wished to avoid the trauma and controversy of a second 1933 – the impression that he was once again allowing sour grapes to take precedence over the interests of an embattled president.

136. Joseph Panuch, assistant to the assistant secretary for administration Donald Russell (Byrnes's law partner), made the charges in the department. See Acheson, *Present*, 161–62.

137. Ibid., 184.

138. See Messer, 169, 174–75.

139. Acheson, *Present*, 156, 163, 746. Messer, chaps. 8 and 9. Byrnes also gave Truman his letter of resignation in April – ostensibly for reasons of health – to become effective at the end of the peace treaty negotiations in which he was involved for most of 1946.

140. According to James Reston, who talked to Acheson during the summer of 1946, although his "bias" had been toward conciliation of the Soviet Union, "he was never doctrinaire about it, and when the facts seemed to him to merit a change – as he seems to think they now do in the case of the Soviet Union – he switched with

This was another point where a political choice resolved itself into a question of personal conscience. The right thing to do this time was to stay. Staying entailed burying personal reservations about the anti-Soviet line and observing his own advice, "Whatsoever thy hand findeth to do, do it with thy might."[141]

A reinforcing fact was the president himself and their developing relationship. Truman was a man in serious trouble. "While you yourself are an orderly person," his budget director told him, "there is disorder all around you."[142] Truman needed a loyal, strong-willed inner circle. Acheson saw that Truman was foundering. The lawyer's instinct was to be his advocate. By doing so he could vindicate himself. When Forrestal took to organizing informal cabinet meetings without the president during the summer of 1946, Acheson reported the practice to Truman – who ordered it stopped. When Truman returned to Washington after the heavy Democratic electoral defeat in November 1946, Acheson alone was there to meet the train.[143] Truman was a congenial, gratifying chief; his small-town bonhomie, his absence of pretention, his appetite for advice made him the opposite of FDR.

As for the external "facts," by June 1946 the sensation had taken hold among liberals that the United Nations was not working as intended and that Soviet "unilateral aggrandizement in violation of the Atlantic Charter" was the reason.[144] Kennan's message – rather, its first part – was now the consensus. Acheson was finally moving with the general liberal trend. He realized Soviet suspicions of the "Baruch Plan" were justified. If, as Litvinov asserted in June, Stalin had returned to an "outmoded concept of geographical security"[145] and feared Anglo-American "encirclement," his fears were not altogether unreasonable from Acheson's point of view. But once Stalin had made his choice, it was useless to try to construct "One World" in concert with him. The fact that the Russians may have been acting out of defensive motives did not necessarily make the results of their actions reassuring.

the facts." See "The No. 1 No. 2 Man in Washington," *New York Times Magazine*, Aug. 25, 1946, 8.

141. Acheson quoted Holmes, himself quoting this biblical advice in his November 1939 Yale speech. Acheson, *Morning and Noon*, 268.

142. Donovan, 171.

143. Acheson, *Present*, 184–85. Donovan, 237. The Democrats lost their majority in both the House and the Senate. On the Truman–Acheson relationship, see also McCullough, 751–56.

144. See the editorial "The Road to Peace," *New York Times*, June 17, 1946.

145. See Moscow Embassy account of Litvinov's interview with CBS correspondent Richard C. Hottelet, June 21, 1946, *FRUS*, 1946, 6: 763.

The Turkish Straits were a dramatic case in point. Moscow was correct to assume that in a future war Turkey could not be relied on to maintain an evenhanded neutrality. Once the Allies had gained the upper hand in World War II, Ankara had thrown the Montreux Convention (regulating the passage of warships) out the window and acted in their favor. In August 1946, the Soviet Union asked Turkey for a new Straits regime, including a Soviet base on the Mediterranean side of the Dardenelles.[146] Acheson was perceptive enough to see that this request might have arisen from defensive considerations, but also that granting it would place Turkey in the Soviet political orbit and facilitate Soviet offensive action in the Mediterranean. Acheson threw his weight behind a policy of resisting the Soviet demand, if necessary by force.[147]

A final fact figured heavily, maybe decisively, in Acheson's "conversion": Anglo-American relations. In January 1946, Acheson congratulated Keynes on his defense of the loan and Anglo-American Financial Agreement (negotiated in late 1945) before the House of Lords. Despite provisions (the British promised to make sterling convertible for current transactions within one year) both considered unrealistic, Keynes argued that the agreement was "an essential condition of the world's best hope, an Anglo-American understanding which brings us together and others together in international institutions." Acheson told Keynes that Congress would probably approve the loan by mid-March. "I think that there will be a good deal of vocal opposition and some real opposition, which, with luck, may fade, as did that to Bretton Woods."[148]

But the administration's luck had run out. A year earlier, Acheson had helped to persuade Congress to approve Bretton Woods on the grounds that it would guarantee the transition to multilateralism without additional aid to Britain. No one had foreseen the magnitude of Britain's financial troubles. The early 1946 argument that the loan would guarantee British acceptance of "the principle of fair and non-discriminatory currency and trade practices" met with disbelief.[149] At the first meeting of the Bretton Woods institutions (in Savannah, March 8–18), meanwhile, Treasury Secretary Vinson rammed through a U.S.

---

146. On this point see State Department comment on the Soviet request for a revised Straits regime, Aug. 9, 1946, *FRUS*, 1946, 7: 832. For Soviet note of Aug. 7, 1946, see ibid., 827–29. The note called for "joint means of defense of the straits."
147. See the Joint Chiefs of Staff memo on this subject, Aug. 23, 1946, ibid., 857–58. See also Aug. 15, 1946, memo to Truman, recommending a strong stand, ibid., 840–42.
148. Keynes quoted in Richard N. Gardner, 233. Acheson to Keynes, Jan. 2, 1946, DAP-SL.
149. Richard N. Gardner, 245–46.

proposal for the organization of the fund and the bank. For Keynes, who had "regarded Anglo-American cooperation, with mutual give and take, as the only means of saving the world, Savannah seemed to show that this was an unattainable ideal. There he had seen power used, for irrelevant motives, to frustrate a good purpose." Keynes left Savannah exhausted and depressed.[150]

As Keynes faded from the scene, Winston Churchill stepped forward with his own argument for the loan – and alternative vision harking back to 1940 and 1898. On March 5, he intoned:

> It is necessary that constancy of mind, persistency of purpose, and the grand simplicity of decision shall guide and rule the conduct of the English speaking peoples.... Before we cast away the solid assurances of national armaments for self-preservation, we must be certain that our temple is built, not upon shifting sand or quagmires [like Roosevelt's] but upon the rock.[151]

Acheson's feelings for Churchill, he later wrote, "were not very different from that combination of deep respect, veneration, and affection, warm but not intimate, which a loyal but sophisticated Catholic might have for the pope."[152] If Anglo-Saxon brotherhood was Acheson's basic creed, Churchill was his pontiff. Acheson's visceral reaction to Churchill's speech was to endorse it.[153] But Keynes had been his mentor-confessor. Acheson was loath to choose between Keynes's concept of Anglo-American cooperation with a hand extended to the Russians and Churchill's Anglo-American alliance in opposition to them.

Acheson argued for the loan on economic, not geopolitical, grounds and continued to favor a loan to the Soviet Union. As David McClellan argues, he resisted the notion that "one constructive action [the British loan] could only be gained at the expense of constructive alternatives forgone in another direction [a possible loan to Moscow]."[154] But it was too late for economic arguments. Vandenberg called for passage of

---

150. Keynes had favored a fund located in New York whose part-time directors would be Treasury officials from the member countries and thus well connected and well informed regarding political realities at home. The Americans favored Washington as the headquarters and highly paid "professional" directors. See Harrod, 636–39.

151. See Churchill's "iron curtain" speech, delivered at Fulton, Missouri. Reprinted in William Safire, ed., *Lend Me Your Ear: Great Speeches in History* (New York: Norton, 1992), 783–95.

152. Dean Acheson, *Sketches from Life of Men I Have Known* (New York: Harper Bros., 1959), 83.

153. See Issacson and Thomas, 364.

154. See Acheson's speech to Economic Club of Detroit, Mar. 1946, DAP-HSTL. McClellan, 77, 94–95.

the loan agreement on the grounds that the Russians would stand to gain from its defeat.[155] On May 10, the Senate approved the loan. Keynes had had a serious heart attack on the train north from Savannah, and died on April 24.[156] No event symbolized more poignantly the eclipse of the One World effort. Multilateralist appeals fell flat in the House, and the loan agreement almost failed before its narrow passage in July. Even before the return of an inward-looking, budget-cutting Republican majority in November, it was clear that as a means of obtaining the kind of multilateral world based on Anglo-American cooperation that Acheson still believed in, Keynesian arguments were obsolete.

"This was my crisis"

In June 1946, in the midst of the British loan controversy, Acheson publicly deplored what he called

> the new psychology of crisis – exemplified by the common expression "to build a fire under him." Now in my archaic profession to do that is to commit arson. . . . The evil is not merely that the perpetuator of crisis misjudges his own skill and involves us all in disaster, but that, as with all these practices, a Gresham's law of politics and words sets in. The baser practice drives out the better. The cheaper, the more fantastic, the more adapted to prejudice, the more reckless the appeal or the maneuver, the more attention, and excited attention, it receives.[157]

Years later, however, he argued:

> The task of a public officer seeking to explain and gain support for a major policy is not that of the writer of a doctoral thesis. Qualification must give way to simplicity of statement, nicety and nuance to bluntness, almost brutality. . . . If we made our points clearer than truth we did not differ from most other educators and could hardly do otherwise.[158]

The British loan was the beginning of a hard lesson. People could not always be moved to behave constructively through appeals to their loftier instincts. Fear of punishment and loathing of the enemy were the fount of self-discipline, cohesion, and action. If Cobden, in his serene midcentury surroundings had forgotten this lesson, the earlier

155. Richard N. Gardner, 250.
156. That is, shortly after his return to England.
157. "Random Harvest," a talk given on June 4, 1946, *State Department Bulletin*, June 16, 1946, 1045.
158. Acheson, *Present*, 375.

Evangelicals had not. The Devil probably existed. If he had not, it probably would have been necessary to invent him. To a degree, he had been.

When on February 26, 1947, following the diplomatic note announcing the imminent end of British aid to Greece and Turkey, Truman, Acheson, and the new secretary of state George Marshall faced congressional leaders at the White House, Acheson "knew we were met at Armageddon.... This was my crisis."[159] It was "his crisis" not simply because "for a week [he] had nurtured it," orchestrating support for a major commitment to Greece and Turkey, but because as late as November–December 1946 he had continued to look to Britain "to take the lead in maintaining the eastern Mediterranean and sharing with us the burdens of occupation and defense of Europe." Acheson's ideal was never America in Britain's place, but America and Britain side by side. Despite the accumulating evidence of British weakness, when part of the foundation of his belief in Anglo-American partnership seemed to give way, Acheson was genuinely dismayed.[160] To perturbation could be added embarrassment at having to face his "Congressional masters" again.[161] The British withdrawal did little to bolster the "Britain as geopolitical partner" argument that had helped to carry the British loan debate – just as the "Bretton Woods as key to multilateralism" argument had been discredited by events. It was Acheson's crisis because the credibility of the department over which he exercised effective authority was now on the line: "Everyone knew that the State Department was facing its last clear chance to get a job done." Acheson no doubt saw the occasion as a last clear chance to bury doubts about his own political reliability, which Marshall appeared to share.[162]

February 1947 was *Acheson's* special, personal crisis because it marked the end of the kind of political innocence suggested in the June speech. Marshall – a Galahad-like figure for Acheson as well as

159. Ibid., 219.
160. See ibid., 212. On Acheson's hope that Britain would continue to be the chief supplier of military aid to the Greek government, see memo, Nov. 8, 1946, *FRUS*, 1946, 7: 262–63. On November 18, 1946, Frankfurter reported that Acheson was "disturbed by his conversation with the British regarding the financing of a unified Anglo-American zone [in Germany]. The British professed to be absolutely up against it.... Dean made it plain that neither Congress nor American opinion would stand for that and the British seemed rather hopeless about it." Lash, ed., *The Diaries of Felix Frankfurter*, 301.
161. Acheson's expression; see *Present*, 212.
162. Ibid., 220. On his new authority in the department see 213. Marshall had been told by his friend Bernard Baruch that Acheson could not be trusted. On this point see ibid., 216.

Kennan[163] – made a measured appeal for aid to the congressional leaders, but it failed to move them. Perhaps in that moment Acheson fully grasped that wielding power meant playing with fire. At times the means justified the ends. Sometimes something "cheaper and more fantastic" was needed. Acheson asked for the floor:

> Never had I spoken under such a pressing sense that the issue was up to me alone.... Like apples in a barrel infected by one rotten one, the corruption of Greece would infect Iran and all to the east. It would also carry infection to Africa through Asia Minor and Egypt and to Europe through Italy and France.... The Soviet Union was playing one of the greatest gambles in history at minimal cost.[164]

Acheson's shaping of Truman's March 12 message was a sincere attempt to emphasize the fundamental moral issues at stake in the conflict with the Soviet Union, as he saw them. Unlike Lippmann, with whom he nearly came to blows, Acheson did not think the question was one of maintaining the balance of power alone.[165] The clash was between a system that, like the nineteenth century pax, safeguarded freedom of choice and a system that did not. Acheson's Cleveland, Mississippi, speech of May 8, 1947, calling for new aid to Europe was an appeal to the economic self-interest of his listeners: how else could Europe pay for U.S. exports? It foreshadowed Marshall's Harvard address of June 5, 1947.[166] The problem was that henceforth the baser appeal tended to drive out the reasoned argument, exactly as Acheson had foreseen. Kennan himself had committed rhetorical arson when composing the "long telegram" a year before. He had begun to regret it by March 1947, and that is one of the reasons he deplored the Truman speech. But Acheson's code did not allow for crying over spilled milk, only bending to the plough.

Finally, the Greek–Turkish and subsequent Western European efforts were Acheson's crises because, of all high executive figures, he was the most cosmopolitan in his cultural background while at the same time lacking an intimate knowledge of Europe. As a first-generation British-American, he did not have – he could not emotionally fathom – the Europhobic baggage and residual trepidation about involvement in Europe of Roosevelt and countless others. His legal education made

163. See ibid., 213–16.
164. Ibid., 219.
165. On Acheson and the preparation of the Truman Doctrine speech see Kuniholm, 413; Larson, 308–9. On Lippmann's view and his clash with Acheson see Steel, 439; Acheson, *Present*, 223.
166. See Department of State *Bulletin*, May 26, 1947, 991–94.

him suspicious of dusty formulas and open to the unprecedented features of any situation. Unlike Kennan he did not subscribe to an ideal, Platonic notion of the separate fates and identities of the Old and New Worlds or see the Atlantic as an unbridgable historical divide. Nor did he possess the kind of firsthand knowledge of Europe (or the Soviet Union) that might have made him rather more skeptical of the cries of desperation emanating from abroad. In 1947, he felt the parallels with 1940–41: the task was to prevent Europe and the United States – the essential components of One World – from being isolated from each other.

Acheson personally did not set foot in Europe between 1938 and 1949. After 1944, his European contacts were mainly with ambassadors like Lord Inverchapel, Henri Bonnet, and Alberto Tarchiani whose job was to obtain financial aid by dramatizing the situation at home. He later wrote – and presumably believed at the time – that in early 1947 "the life of Europe as an organized industrial community had come well-nigh to a standstill, and with it, so had production and distribution of goods of every sort." This statement is somewhat at variance with the facts. Those who knew Europe better – Kennan or the shrewd Treasury official Henry Tasca – realized that the crisis of 1947 was, to a considerable extent, psychological.[167] They were more wary than Acheson of European dependency and manipulation of the United States. The point is not that Acheson fundamentally misjudged the situation – Europe was running out of foreign exchange in 1947; rather, his lack of preconceptions about Europe made him a uniquely appropriate vehicle of the U.S. departure from isolationism after 1946. Entanglement in Europe was certainly not Acheson's conscious goal, but if it came to that he was the least Jeffersonian of Americans.

167. Acheson, *Present*, 213. Compare Acheson's claim with the industrial production figures provided by Milward in *The Reconstruction of Western Europe*, 8. On Kennan's view see his memo of May 16, 1947, *FRUS*, 1947, 3: 225–27. On Tasca's 1947 analysis of the Italian situation, see Harper, *America and the Reconstruction of Italy*, chaps. 7 and 8.

7

Acheson and Europe,
1949–1953:
a statesman's progress

Introduction

During the debate on the Marshall Plan in March 1948, Acheson said:

> During the period of crisis and present weakness, the United States has to
> stay in Europe and will stay. In this sense our presence in Germany
> operates as a shield behind which the health of free Europe can return.
> When that health has been restored, the community of these 16 [ERP]
> nations will inevitably be bound together in a much closer union or
> association. . . . A natural balance in Europe would begin to emerge.[1]

This view, typical of the time, saw Europe's salvation in greater unity
and contemplated a transitional U.S. role.

Much water had passed over the dam by early 1949. The European
situation Acheson inherited then was one, in effect, where joint Anglo-
Soviet control had long since proved a chimera, where Marshall Plan
dreams of early European union and self-sufficiency were starting to
fade, where neither French nor British leadership was readily forthcoming, where German leadership was unthinkable to most and Soviet
hegemony greatly feared. It was still the kind of situation in which,
Acheson had said, "we have chaos but not enough to make a world."[2]
It was a situation in which American leadership seemed necessary by
default. But this does not mean that Acheson's views had fundamentally
changed since early 1948. The relationship of the New World to the
Old did not necessarily have to be an unequal one. The important thing
was that the two essential components of One World not be separate or
antagonistic. Acheson also shared the general belief that the initial
political success of the Marshall Plan had had to do with offering the

---

1. Acheson, Philadelphia speech, based on Bohlen notes, Mar. 10, 1948, DAP-HSTL, box
4.
2. Acheson, quoting Sir Wilmott Lewis in a speech on Apr. 18, 1947, DAP-SL.

initiative to the Europeans. Likewise, the British foreign secretary Ernest Bevin had taken the lead in tying the United States to Western Europe in a collective security arrangement. The pattern of Europe as initiator, America as respondent was an established one in 1949.

Commenting on the new secretary of state, the British ambassador Sir Oliver Franks told his superiors, "Acheson though . . . a man of high character and standing *is essentially a lawyer* and a person who, if confronted with a difficulty, will examine it from all sides in the hope of finding some compromise way around it rather than give a clear cut yes or no."[3] Franks had not yet taken the measure of his friend's incisiveness or understood that when political choices resolved themselves into questions of conscience Acheson might eschew compromise with a vengeance. But Franks's observation contained an essential element of truth. Acheson's lawyerly instinct was to take the particular interests

3. Franks to the FO, Jan. 11, 1949, FO 371/74174, PRO; emphasis added.

and agendas of his various European "clients" as the starting point of action and to find a common formula. For Acheson, the "facts" of the situation necessarily included what America's European interlocutors themselves wanted or could be persuaded to accept.

Acheson came to think in terms of what he called a "pattern of responsibility." This notion combined two basic strains in his makeup, the Evangelical ideal of self-abnegation and service and the advocatory-propitiatory approach: "We must act with the consciousness that our responsibility is to interests which are broader than our immediate American interests. . . . We must operate in a pattern of responsibility which is greater than our own interests. . . . We must not confuse our own opinions with the will of God." Acheson's ideal was a kind of leadership that the Europeans "believe considers their interests as deeply as it does [the United States'] own."[4] Coalitions were held together mainly by force used by the leader "or predominantly by the *consent* of the members." In the latter case they must see that their basic interests were recognized by the leader and served by the coalition.[5] The leader's – or the lawyer's – effectiveness and legitimacy depended on his capacity both to defend and to forbear his individual followers. The cohesion of the coalition was partly a function of its flexibility; consent was granted to its confining features because the coalition brought its members greater independence. Speaking of the central problem, Germany, in 1952, Acheson said: "We have been deeply guided by those who know that problem far better than we do" – including the Germans themselves. "We have deferred to our friends. . . . We have supported plans which they have supported."[6] Therein lay a key to both the striking achievements and the shortcomings of the Acheson approach.

In the process of trying to promote the unity and cohesiveness of Europe, U.S. diplomacy necessarily relied on and strengthened bilateral channels of influence or "special relationships" that, however, served to perpetuate the separate visions of the individual states. In progressively extending the political-military "umbrella" without which – the Europeans were the first to insist – an integrated Europe would never emerge, the United States also fostered a situation in which the incentives for collective European self-reliance and autonomy were reduced. Washington's accurate perception of continuing dependency and division among the Europeans translated into a permanent anxiety about

4. Acheson, press conference, June 29, 1951, DAP-HSTL, box 69.
5. Dean Acheson, "Instant Retaliation: The Debate Continues," *New York Times Magazine*, Mar. 28, 1954; emphasis in original.
6. Acheson off-the-record talk in London, June 26, 1952, DAP-HSTL box 67.

the credibility of the American guarantee to defend them and fear that the Europeans would "go neutral," or worse, if they perceived a weak United States.

American anxiety about losing Europe and eagerness to appease European doubts translated into a European capacity to call forth an ever tighter American political-military embrace. The American price, however – Congress and the Pentagon demanded it after the beginning of the Korean War – was European rearmament. This in turn struck many in Europe as apt to provoke either the attack it was supposed to deter or else fatal economic damage to the subjects of the "protectorate." American officiousness – not the same thing as influence – bred European resentment and resistance, which in turn engendered American impatience and mistrust. Not the least paradoxical aspect of the situation in which the Americans gradually found themselves enveloped was that few things were more subversive than success: if strength brought forth concessions on the part of the adversary, the coalition tended to fall apart as a result.

By its very nature, such a leader's work is never done. Pervasive evidence – real, invented, and imagined – that his clients will lose faith and revert to their old habits beclouds his original purpose. The leader's indispensability – or at least his own sense thereof – increases over time. Perseverance becomes the ultimate value.[7] Keeping the coalition together becomes an end in itself: "The purpose of the coalition must be to strengthen the coalition and bind it more closely together – or to weaken an opposing coalition.... This rule must be an ever present guide."[8] To discomfit the opposing coalition, however, is only to undermine one's own. To push the boulder up the hill is only to have it roll down once again. An account of the experience, "despite its successes, inevitably leaves a sense of disappointment and frustration.... How often what seemed almost within grasp slipped away."[9]

The shadow of the umbrella

"The real issue," Acheson wrote on the question of Italy's adherence to the North Atlantic Treaty, grows "out of the position into [sic] which we now [find] ourselves."[10] This sums up Acheson's attitude toward three of the main questions he inherited in 1949: the Atlantic pact, Germany, and European integration. Even if he had been inclined –

7. On perseverance see Acheson's quotation from William the Silent, in *Present*, 728.
8. Acheson, "Instant Retaliation."
9. Acheson, *Present*, 725.
10. Acheson to Truman, Mar. 2 1949, *FRUS*, 1949, 4: 141.

which he was not – to reverse the policies of his predecessor, he would have found it very difficult to do so. Acheson's handling of the negotiations he inherited confirmed Oliver Franks's view: the secretary as seeker of compromise among the interested parties, including the U.S. Senate. Several of the North Atlantic Treaty's main features were undefined when Acheson took office. These included Italian membership, strongly favored by France on the grounds that Italy was an important strategic frontier and that membership would facilitate extension of the pact to include Algeria, but opposed by Truman, the Senate, and the British government on the grounds that Italy was a liability. Acheson became convinced that Italy's exclusion might foster an Italian "isolation complex" and drift toward neutrality[11] – a view skillfully advanced by the Italian government – but the compelling factor in his thinking was French insistence. France, Acheson told the president, "was so emphatically in favor.... that she would have to reconsider her whole relation to the Pact if Italy was not to be included."[12] Without France there could be no pact worthy of the name. Without a pact, as Acheson told Senators Vandenberg and Connally, "it was doubtful... the French would ever be reconciled to the inevitable diminution of direct allied control over Germany." The pact would provide France "a greater sense of security against Germany as well as the Soviet Union."[13] The "intra-European" rationale of the alliance was explicit from the start.

The most controversial part of the treaty was Article V defining the members' obligations in case of war. The negotiations became "a contest between our allies, seeking to impale the Senate on the specific, and the Senators, attempting to wriggle free."[14] In his public interpretation of Article V, Acheson underlined the unavoidable U.S. legal and moral obligation – as well as interest – in observing the contract in case of war and, according to Article III, in helping the parties to develop their capacity to resist by providing military aid.[15] Article III gave rise to Senator Bourke Hickenlooper's famous question: would the United States "be expected to send substantial numbers of troops over there as a more or less permanent contribution of the development of these countries' capacity to resist?" Acheson replied: "The answer to that

11. Acheson, *Present*, 279.
12. Acheson to Truman, Mar. 2, 1949, cited in note 10. On this episode see also Irwin M. Wall, *The United States and the Making of Postwar France, 1945–1954* (Cambridge: Cambridge University Press, 1991), 145–47.
13. Acheson conversation with Senators, Feb. 14, 1949, *FRUS*, 1949, 4: 109.
14. Acheson, *Present*, 280.
15. McClellan, 151–52; Acheson, *Present*, 281.

question, Senator, is a clear and absolute 'NO!'"[16] There is no reason to believe that this did not reflect Acheson's sincere hope and conviction at the time.

Along with the signing of the North Atlantic Treaty in April 1949, the foreign ministers of the United States, Great Britain, and France agreed to simplify the German occupation regime through the Occupation Statute and Allied High Commission. Plans for the Federal Republic of Germany were well advanced, and Acheson was inclined to follow the advice of those who knew the problem better than he did. Among these was Kennan, who had advanced the idea of a statute ceding broad autonomy to the Germans, as well as Foreign Ministers Schuman and Bevin.[17] Acheson skillfully presided over talks leading to final agreement on the statute while postponing the controversial question of dismantling. Acheson was guided by the sensation – and Kennan's explicit argument – that damming up Germany's energies would produce a dangerous reaction: it was simply not possible "to sit on such a great country."[18]

By the same token, strong French, British, and *German* reservations about schemes for Soviet–American disengagement, reunification, and neutralization of Germany convinced Acheson to reject Kennan's Program A. German leaders did not believe that the forthcoming council of foreign ministers would lead to satisfactory terms for reunification, namely, the extension of the West German Basic Law to the East.[19] Kennan later wrote that the views of Bevin and Schuman on Germany "made a deep impression on Mr. Acheson: first, I think, because while he did not know much about Europe, he assumed that they did; secondly because they largely coincided with those of our own military establishment; and thirdly, because they had the support of the Western European Division in the Department of State."[20] Kennan is correct; at the same time, however, Schuman and Bevin – and through them Acheson – were more in touch with Adenauer's strong opposition to reunification by compromise with Moscow than Kennan himself. Kennan may also be correct in suggesting that the secretary was later inclined to write off the Germans east of the Elbe because of a belief that they had been

16. Acheson, *Present*, 285; McClellan, 154–55.
17. See *FRUS*, 1949, 3: 141, 159. See also Chapter 5, this volume.
18. Acheson, Princeton Seminar transcript, 339, DAP-HSTL.
19. On the views of Adenauer and other German officials see *FRUS*, 1949, 3: 870–71, 874–75. See also Chapter 5, this volume.
20. Miscamble, 171, n. 125, quoting Kennan's personal letter to the author. On the U.S. military view see *FRUS*, 1949, 3: 875–76.

"baptized late and badly."[21] If so it was an attitude that Acheson had picked up from Adenauer himself.

Acheson did not meet Adenauer until November 1949, but by the time of the Paris CFM (May–June 1949) he had more or less embraced the Rhinelander's basic view: "The reunification of Germany should not be regarded as the chief end in itself." Acheson told reporters on May 18, 1949: "Our fundamental attitude is to go ahead with the establishment of a West German government, come hell or high water. Any reunification must be on the basis of the Bonn constitution."[22] The Palais de Marbre Rose CFM became the first of several elaborate charades designed mainly to propitiate public opinion by fostering the impression that the West was willing to negotiate on Germany while the Soviets were not. By now Acheson had sensed that few things could complicate the project upon which he was embarked like genuine Soviet concessions. Paul Nitze was "very much concerned" that the Russians would make a troop withdrawal offer, something that would have been "highly embarrassing to us." But when they did not, the lesson Acheson took was that Russian motives were the mirror image of his own: "They would make no concessions of any sort" that would weaken their hold on the East.[23]

When civil government began in Germany in September 1949, Chancellor Adenauer immediately asked the Allies to reexamine their policy of dismantling heavy industry for reparations, an explosive issue in Germany. The French strongly opposed the request, while Bevin was sure that "the Germans would take whatever we give them and then ask for more."[24] Acheson faced what was to be his classic dilemma: how to propitiate his most important clients at the same time. He did not disagree with Bevin and was irritated by U.S. High Commissioner John McCloy's criticism of "aimless dismantling." McCloy was told that "nothing must be done which could give rise to the inference that the U.S. is seeking to impose a solution on the French or British." But it was useless to deny that the Germans held high cards: "We are likely to

21. See *Memoirs*, 1: 445.
22. Off-the-record press conference, May 18, 1949, Press Conferences, June–July 1949 file, DAP-HSTL. On the same occasion he called Program A schemes "entirely impractical at this time." He later wrote, "A reunited Germany bought at the price of military insecurity in Europe, or milked by reparations, or paralyzed politically and economically by Soviet veto power or stultifying Soviet control over the East German economy, would fatally prejudice the future of Europe." Acheson, *Present*, 291–93.
23. Princeton Seminar transcript, 432, DAP-HSTL. Nitze was deputy head of the Policy Planning Staff and succeeded Kennan as head on Jan. 1, 1950. Acheson developed the lesson of May 1949 in a letter to Alan Bullock, Feb. 25, 1955, DAP-SL.
24. Memo of tripartite conversation, Sept. 15, 1949, *FRUS*, 1949, 3: 599–601.

yield eventually under German pressure and not because of our policy decision. Wouldn't it be better to yield now as a conscious move?"[25] To hasten the inevitable concessions he appealed to the self-interest and anxiety of the British and the French: "I believe that we shall probably never have any more democratic or more receptive atmosphere in Germany in which to work than we have at the present moment. . . . I believe it would be wise to give an 'advance' of good will to the Germans."[26] This was the message that Adenauer himself liked to repeat; in effect, "Help me win the concessions I need to stay in power because *'après moi le déluge.'* "[27]

In exhausting talks with Bevin and Schuman in Paris in early November Acheson argued that Germany must be integrated into the West. If Germany became "a separate entity . . . the German Government would be in a position to hold itself up to auction against the bids of East and West." These talks laid the basis for the Petersberg Protocols embodying major concessions on dismantling and other issues.[28] There were several reasons for the unexpected French and British concessions, including U.S. financial leverage, and rising fear of the Soviet Union following its recent atomic test and the creation of the German Democratic Republic. Adenauer helped by making highly conciliatory statements on Franco-German relations.[29] But Acheson's achievement should also be seen in the context of the "special relationships" he had managed to shore up with London and Paris in 1949.

Acheson compared Anglo-American relations to a "common law marriage," something that seemed to him "the very heart of what we must do to try to hold the world together." "My own attitude," he later said, "had long been and was known to have been, pro-British."[30] Even

25. Ibid., 600, 635. On McCloy statements see Thomas Alan Schwartz, *America's Germany: John J. McCloy and the Federal Republic of Germany* (Cambridge, Mass.: Harvard University Press, 1991), 74.

26. Acheson letter to Schuman, Oct. 30, 1949, *FRUS*, 1949, 3: 623–24.

27. In fact, Adenauer may have been playing for time. "The stronger his position became, the less likely the Allies were to 'rock the boat'" with issues like denazification or dismantling. Schwartz, 82.

28. See memo of tripartite conversation, Nov. 11, 1949, FO 800/448 Bevin Papers, PRO. The protocols embodied significant reductions in the Allied dismantling program and the creation of a German consular service. See *FRUS*, 1949, 3: 343–48. See also Alan Bullock, *Ernest Bevin, Foreign Secretary, 1945–1951* (New York: Norton, 1983), 737–39.

29. Schwartz, 75.

30. Princeton Seminar transcript, 883, DAP-HSTL; Acheson, *Present*, 387. On this subject see Lawrence Kaplan, "Dean Acheson and the Atlantic Community," in Douglas Brinkley, ed., *Dean Acheson and the Making of U.S. Foreign Policy* (New York: St. Martin's Press, 1993), 29–33.

if the wily ambassador may not always have deserved it, Acheson had implicit faith in the clergyman's son and logician Franks. He liked and admired Bevin, even if the foreign secretary's judgment began to fail, in his view, in 1950–51.[31] Matrimony implied an intimate but not idyllic relationship, and one apt to provoke misunderstanding, envy, even rancor on the part of others. If nothing ever seemed truer to Acheson than that the marriage existed, "nothing has ever seemed...more dangerous than talking about it, and certainly writing it down."[32] Acheson's constant effort was to preserve the substance – rather than the mere shadow – of ties dating from 1898.

In August 1949, Acheson told Franks that the delicate U.S.–British–Canadian talks upcoming in Washington were "like the rare, inevitable and very difficult evenings when husband and wife had to go into their mutual way of life and after about three hours one felt that it was all too dreadful for anything. Nevertheless it had to be done." If Franks found Acheson "extremely vague and unprepared," it was because the secretary wanted London to make the positive suggestions. If the British were to devalue, he told reporters off the record, "they must do so by themselves without U.S. pressure. They must not be able to say that the U.S. made them do so."[33] As we have seen, Acheson agreed with Kennan that the British should not be forced to assume leadership of European integration. Though the long-term results of the talks were meager, Acheson would have agreed with Franks's assessment that "the previous crisis of confidence was resolved.... It was clear that the Americans decided to regard us once more as their principal partner in world affairs and not just a member of the European game."[34] If Acheson did not accept Kennan's idea of a separate U.S.–British–

---

31. For Acheson on Bevin, see Acheson, *Sketches from Life*, chap. 1. Acheson described his practice of private talks with Franks "in complete confidence, about any international problem we saw arising. Neither would report or quote the other unless... he got the other's consent and agreement on the terms of a reporting memorandum or cable." Acheson, *Present*, 323.

    Before one such meeting Acheson told his staff, "It was understood that the [Acheson–Franks] meeting would be on a personal basis and that Sir Oliver would not report to London about the discussion." Memo of conversation, Mar. 7, 1950, DAP-HSTL, box 65. In fact, Franks sent a detailed account of the conversation the following day. See personal letter to Bevin, Mar. 8, 1950, FO/800/517, PRO.

32. Princeton Seminar transcript, 832–33. DAP-HSTL.

33. Franks to Bevin, Aug. 11, 1949, FO 800/516, PRO. Acheson's "*strictly* off the record" press conference, Aug. 26, 1949, DAP-HSTL, box 68.

34. Franks to FO, Sept. 19, 1949, FO 800/516, PRO. Acheson had also done his best in 1949 to restore full Anglo-American cooperation on atomic energy. See Acheson, *Present*, chap. 35.

Canadian bloc detached from the Continent, one reason is that the British themselves did not. Their aim was to tie the United States closer to Europe through the Atlantic pact and they argued – maybe disingenuously – that integration could prosper only in the shadow of the American umbrella.

David McClellan writes, "Neither by intellect nor temperament was Acheson sympathetic to plans for European unity."[35] It is true that he was not inclined to see European integration as an end in itself, but McClellan's statement does not really do justice to Acheson's views at the time. In January 1948, Acheson told the House Foreign Affairs Committee that Europe contained "human and physical resources that if properly used can make this area one of great strength and stability. But our own experience teaches us and has taught our European friends that proper use requires union." When Bevin asked him what he meant by "integration," Acheson replied, "conditions in which it was possible to have free movement of goods, of labour and of funds in Europe."[36] Removing economic barriers had been the essence of the "One World" project. But he favored more than a unified market. In October 1949, he urged "the earliest possible decisions by the Europeans as to objectives and commitments among them on a timetable for the creation of supra-national institutions."[37] This was only partly to appease pro-unity politicians in the United States.

Acheson was skeptical of a "United States of Europe" – the ultimate goal of true believers in Congress – but he was willing to try Monnet's technique of applying supranationalism to specific problems between states. Like Monnet he referred to this as "a method of progressing without being sure where you want to go."[38] Acheson had a natural affinity for Monnet the man, the English-speaking, cosmopolitan offspring of Cognac merchants whose great market was the Anglo-Saxon world and who had named a street in their town in honor of Cobden. Monnet's ultimate aim – he had once worked for the League of Nations

35. McClellan, 347. He adds, "especially when they [the plans] threatened to interfere with or delay the realization of his more immediate objective [after 1950]: the rearming of Germany."
36. Acheson statement to House Foreign Affairs Committee, Jan. 28, 1948, copy in DAP-HSTL. Memo of conversation between Bevin and Acheson, Nov. 11, 1949, FO/800/448, PRO.
37. *FRUS*, 1949, 4: 472.
38. Acheson quoted in Minutes of PPS meeting, Oct. 19, 1949, PPS Records, box 32, RG 59, NA. On Monnet's reluctance to spell out a specific point of arrival see François Fontaine, "Forward with Jean Monnet," in Douglas Brinkley and Clifford Hackett, eds., *Jean Monnet and the Path to European Unity* (New York: Macmillan, 1991), 55.

– was not a European superstate rivaling the United States, but a kind of world federation whose key components were North America and Europe. In any event, Acheson believed, the form and extent of unity were for the Europeans to decide: "Our position here should be to encourage, to help, to constantly remind, to urge all the speed that is possible, but basically to understand. . . . We have to have an attitude of forbearance in watching, helping, encouraging the Europeans to greater economic and political unity."[39]

The State Department warned ECA administrator Paul Hoffman against attempts to link requests for congressional appropriations to progress toward European integration. Acheson later criticized the ECA for meddling in European affairs. "It was resented and it was not necessary."[40] Still, he did not wish the British to think they were completely off the hook. This was especially true after top U.S. officials meeting in Paris (October 21–22, 1949) had endorsed the view that "European integration without the U.K. was impossible." On October 26, 1949, Acheson told Bevin that

> any suggestion that the U.K.'s integration with Western Europe should impair her relations with the Empire and the Commonwealth or undermine her position as a world power would be as unfortunate for the U.S. alone as it might be disastrous for the whole Western world. This however did not imply that there were not steps of a more far-reaching character than any so far taken by the U.K. and the participating countries toward economic commonality.[41]

When the ECA wanted to increase the political stature and supranational character of the OEEC by appointing a major European figure to head it, the British tried to block the candidacy of the Belgian unity enthusiast Paul Henri Spaak. Acheson supported the "superman" idea, but refused to impose Spaak on the British and told them that the

---

39. Acheson press conference, Feb. 9, 1949, Press Conferences, DAP-HSTL, box 68. On Monnet's background and ultimate aims, see Fontaine, "Forward with Jean Monnet." See also François Duchene, "Jean Monnet's Methods," in Brinkley and Hackett, eds., *Jean Monnet*, 203–5. On Acheson and Monnet see also Douglas Brinkley, "Dean Acheson and European Unity," in Francis H. Heller and John R. Gillingham, eds., *NATO: The Founding of the Alliance and the Integration of Europe* (New York: St. Martin's Press, 1992), 120–60.

40. See memo of conversation by James Webb, Nov. 3, 1949, recounting the meeting of Hoffman, Treasury Secretary Snyder, and Acheson on October 25, shortly before Hoffman's trip to Paris, where he made a major speech urging rapid progress toward unity. DAP-HSTL, box 64. See also Princeton Seminar transcript, 74, DAP-HSTL.

41. *FRUS*, 1949, 4: 493, 437.

importance of the position was essentially "symbolic."[42] When the British representative to the OEEC visited Washington in February 1950, he wrote home: "There are strong pressures towards integration and with it towards treating us as just another European country to be cajoled and bullied into a common policy." On the other side there were "strong sections inside and outside the Administration who recognize our special position and wish to buttress it."[43] By instinct Acheson was in the latter camp. At the same time, as Monnet's approach proved its worth and Acheson became more involved in the French–German problem, his faith in European integration, and in his own capacity to promote it, grew.

Acheson began to emphasize French–German reconciliation in September–October 1949. French leadership of Europe was a connected theme. Kennan was virtually alone in seeing Germany as the inevitable leader. Those who thought Britain could take up the reins did so in the face of mounting evidence to the contrary. For Acheson the conclusion was inescapable. As he told Schuman on September 15, 1949: "The best chance and hope seems to us to be under French leadership. It doesn't work for us to take the lead. We are too far away."[44] When Paris seemed to interpret such statements as presaging U.S. abandonment of France, Acheson assured Schuman and less phlegmatic colleagues like Prime Minister Henri Queuille that American policy meant "the increasing association of the U.S. with the Atlantic Community." But he stuck to the theme of a French initiative. Despite Ambassador Bruce's reservations, Acheson told Schuman on October 30, 1949, that the time had come for French leadership "to integrate the German Federal Republic promptly and decisively into Western Europe."[45]

The fall of 1949 established the basic pattern of Acheson's dealings with France. America was "far away." Only France could avert the

---

42. Ibid., 436. See also memo of conversation between Acheson and Franks, Jan. 20, 1950, DAP-HSTL, box 65; Franks to Sir William Strang, Nov. 27, 1949, FO 371/ 81637, PRO; Hogan, *The Marshall Plan*, 330.

43. Sir Edmund Hall-Patch to FO, sometime in Feb. 1950, FO 371/87050, PRO.

44. *FRUS*, 1949, 3: 600–1.

45. For a fuller discussion of the controversy see Chapter 5. See also Bruce to Secretary, Sept. 23, 1949, *FRUS*, 1949, 4: 663–65. On Schuman–Acheson meeting, Sept. 26, 1949, see ibid., 338–39. On French initiative see his statement during the PPS meeting, Oct. 11, 1949, *FRUS*, 1949, 1: 400. See also department instructions to the ambassador's meeting, *FRUS*, 1949, 4: 470. For Bruce's skepticism see his statement during the ambassador's meeting, Oct. 21, 1949, ibid., 492. See also his cable to Acheson, Oct. 22, 1949, ibid., 343. For Acheson's Oct. 30, 1949, message, see *FRUS*, 1949, 3: 623.

worsening German situation. Like Monnet, Acheson was not averse to warning Paris of the consequences if it did not.[46] Still the French themselves left him little choice but to accept the Bruce–Bohlen thesis that getting France to lead required ironclad American guarantees. If in Kennan's analysis European unity based on Franco-German reconciliation was meant to obviate American tutelage, Acheson's experience was teaching him that European unity could come about – if at all – only by tying the United States closer to the Continent. During this same period France's precarious Indochina position became a perennial subject. After "deplorable delays and errors,"[47] the French had transferred power to the Emperor Bao Dai and were looking for U.S. support. Years later when asked if U.S. aid had been given in order to secure French support on European questions, Acheson said, "Entirely fair. The French blackmailed us. . . . One discovers in dealing with the French that they expect their allies to accept their point of view without question on every issue." Needless to say, the Americans had rendered themselves vulnerable to blackmail by accepting the dubious thesis that the war "involved nothing less than the extention [*sic*] of Soviet control to Southeast Asia."[48] While Acheson never agreed to the French point of view without question on any issue, he usually accepted something close to it in the end.

ON NOVEMBER 13, 1949, Acheson faced Adenauer across a mahogany table in Bonn. There were two important moments in the forging of their special relationship: this meeting and a later one, in November 1951. Adenauer captivated Acheson with his analysis of the German character. The Germans were an impressionable people who took on the color of their environment. Thus they must be tied firmly to Western Europe, a task for which the Rhineland Catholic Adenauer was naturally suited. The common heritage of France and Germany "had come down the Rhine, on the successors of Charlemagne, who guarded European civilization when human sacrifice was still practiced in eastern Germany." In Kurt Schumacher, head of the pro-unification Socialists, Adenauer told Acheson, he "would meet a typical East German." Acheson was impressed by Adenauer's pro-Western sentiments, shrewdness, and self-possession.[49] Acheson lacked the deep distrust of Germany

---

46. See Acheson's letter to Schuman, cited in note 45. For his description of Schuman, see Princeton Seminar transcript, 317, DAP-HSTL.
47. In Bruce's words. *FRUS*, 1949, 4: 495.
48. See Acheson interview with Gaddis Smith in the *New York Times Magazine*, Oct. 12, 1969. See also Bruce comment in *FRUS*, 1949, 4: 495.
49. See *FRUS*, 1949, 3: 309–14, Acheson, *Present*, 341; Schwartz, 78; Konrad Adenauer, *Memoirs, 1945–1953* (London: Weidenfeld & Nicolson, 1966), 206–8.

that characterized most Europeans – and Americans like FDR – while Adenauer was inclined to trust the Americans more than the British or the French. Bonn and Washington also found themselves drawn together by a fear and loathing of the Soviet Union that London and Paris did not feel to the same degree.

If Acheson had intellectually accepted the Adenauer thesis about reunification before coming to Germany, from now on defending it was a question of personal loyalty to his friend. Acheson had also been convinced that the Russians would never compromise on Germany. He now took to heart what might be called the Ernst Reuter corollary to Adenauer's "policy of strength." Any idea, the mayor of Berlin told him, "that the Soviet Union could be *persuaded* to withdraw its troops from East Germany was utterly absurd. The moment they were withdrawn, the local Communist collaborators would be swept aside in a bloody purge." It was henceforth comforting to Acheson to assume that one did not have to make serious negotiating proposals of one's own, because the other side could not possibly be dealing in good faith.[50]

"A descending spiral"

On January 31, 1950, President Truman announced the historic decision to develop the hydrogen bomb. The same day he ordered the State and Defense departments to undertake "a reexamination of our objectives in peace and war and of the effect of the objectives on our strategic plans in light of the probable fission bomb capability and possible thermonuclear capability of the Soviet Union." The resulting study, NSC 68, was completed in early April. On February 16, 1950, Acheson gave a speech in which he said, "The only way to deal with the Soviet Union we have found from hard experience is to create situations of strength." In a private conversation in March, he said, "The American people have a false sense of security and do not realize that the world situation, which is called a cold war, is in fact a real war. . . . During the last six to nine months there had been a trend against us which, if allowed to continue, would lead to a considerable deterioration in our position."[51]

50. Acheson, *Present*, 347; emphasis added.
51. *FRUS*, 1950, 1: 207, 236. Department of State *Bulletin*, Feb. 20, 1950, 274. On this period see also Gaddis, *Strategies of Containment*, chap. 4; Samuel F. Wells, "Sounding the Tocsin: NSC 68 and the Soviet Threat," *International Security*, 4, no. 2 (Fall 1977), 116–58; Mark Trachtenberg, *History and Strategy* (Princeton, N.J.: Princeton University Press, 1991), 107–13; Steven L. Rearden, "Frustrating the Kremlin Design: Acheson and NSC 68," in Brinkley, ed., *Dean Acheson and the Making of U.S. Foreign Policy*.

By any measure the fall of China and the Soviet atomic test in September–October 1949 had produced a relative weakening of the U.S. position. Acheson pointed out that the loss of China had been "expected," however, and he had not seen it as an enormous calamity at the time.[52] The loss of the atomic monopoly was more serious, since the bomb had compensated for America's conventional inferiority. The United States had seven active divisions in 1949; the Soviet Union was thought to have 175. In early 1950, the Joint Chiefs of Staff warned the NSC 68 study group (headed by Paul Nitze) of "a new type of Pearl Harbor attack of infinitely greater magnitude than that of 1941." But Acheson himself had predicted in 1945 that the U.S. atomic monopoly would end within five years. Nitze had assumed that the monopoly and its "strategic significance" would "progressively decline."[53] Neither believed the Soviet Union would deliberately attack Western Europe in the near future, and both believed in the overwhelming actual and potential economic and technological superiority of the United States. NSC 68's suggestion that the Soviet Union might be capable (regardless of its intentions) of delivering a surprise one-hundred-A-bomb attack on American soil by 1954 was based on military estimates concerning which the authors themselves expressed some doubt.[54]

A case can be made that the Truman administration felt compelled to fend off the "attack of the primitives" by adopting a more anti-Communist line of its own. There was a "tremendous boiling" of the domestic political kettle in early 1950. Acheson's famous statement on the Alger Hiss perjury verdict on January 25 was a gallant and charac-

---

52. *FRUS*, 1950, 1: 207. On China policy see Nancy Tucker, *Patterns in the Dust: Chinese–American Relations and the Recognition Controversy* (New York: Columbia University Press, 1983).

53. Joint Chiefs of Staff statement quoted in Talbott, 56. On Acheson's prediction see his Sept. 25, 1945, memo to Truman, *FRUS*, 1945, 2: 48–50. On Nitze's view see Nitze, "The Development of NSC 68, a Reply to John Lewis Gaddis, 'NSC 68 and the Soviet Threat,'" *International Security* 4 no. 4, (Spring 1980), 172. On conventional capabilities see Matthew Evangelista, "Stalin's Postwar Army Reappraised," *International Security*, 7 (Winter 1982–83), 110–38.

54. See Nitze "The Development of NSC 68," 172, and Nitze memo of Feb. 8, 1950, *FRUS*, 1950, 1: 145. See also text of NSC 68, *FRUS*, 1950, 1, esp. 248, 282–91. According to NSC 68, "We do not know accurately what the Soviet atomic capability is. . . . This estimate [of the Soviet weapons stockpile] is admittedly based on incomplete coverage of Soviet activities and represents the production capabilities of known or deducible Soviet plants." Others might exist, raising the estimate. Still, the Soviets might have operating difficulties, reducing the estimate. Ibid., 251. See Talbott, 56, on the exaggeration of Soviet delivery capabilities. On the significance of the 1954 date see also Nitze, *From Hiroshima to Glasnost: At the Center of Decision* (New York: Grove Weidenfeld, 1989), 97.

teristic gesture, but it brought down the fury of the demagogues on himself.[55] After seeing Acheson in March, Franks told Bevin that the Americans appeared "to be groping desperately for ideas on foreign policy." One reason was that Acheson and Truman were trying to escape the pressure of the Right. He added, however, that this did not *determine* Acheson's view. The secretary was more "objective."[56]

The "objective" factor that bothered Acheson most was Western Europe. In essence, the fear was that the perception of a loss of U.S. strategic superiority and resolve would translate into an erosion of European confidence in the United States. The crisis of confidence would prompt the "Allies" to place their bets on neutralist or pro-Soviet accommodationist leaders and policies, ultimately leading to Soviet domination of the Continent. The essence of the NSC 68 program was to take the steps necessary to reverse this perception and to prevent a European sellout, which would leave the United States isolated in the world. Doing what had to be done necessarily implied a closer U.S. connection with the Continent. The essence of the NSC 68 program, in other words, was the propitiation of Europe.[57]

Acheson later said that the purpose of NSC 68 was "to so bludgeon the mass mind of 'top government' that not only could the President make a decision but that the decision could be carried out."[58] This meant that in order to gain the support of domestic skeptics – including Truman and Defense Secretary Louis Johnson, committed to a defense budget ceiling of $13.5 billion for 1950–51 – NCS 68 exaggerated the *direct* threat to U.S. soil. NSC 68 envisioned a rearmament program costing around $50 billion per year. But NSC 68 was not lacking in statements of what its authors feared most. Speaking of the new situation created by atomic "duopoly," the document observed:

> The risk that we may thereby be prevented or too long delayed in taking all needful measures to maintain the integrity of our system is great. The risk that our allies will lose their determination is greater. And the risk that in this manner a descending spiral of too little and too late, of doubt and

55. See Acheson, *Present*, chaps. 39–40; Princeton Seminar transcript, 807, DAP-HSTL; Merle Miller, *Plain Speaking: An Oral Biography of Harry S. Truman* (New York: Berkley Books, 1982), chap. 33.
56. Franks to Bevin, Mar. 8, 1950, FO 800/517, PRO.
57. Nitze said as much in his memoirs: "One of our first concerns was the security of Europe, where our North Atlantic Treaty Organization allies were in serious need of reassurance that the balance of power was not tipping in favor of the Soviet Union." Nitze, *Hiroshima*, 93. On this point see also Melvyn P. Leffler, *A Preponderance of Power: National Security, the Truman Administration and the Cold War* (Stanford, Calif.: Stanford University Press, 1992), 345, 357.
58. Acheson, *Present*, 374–75.

recrimination, may present us with ever narrower and more desperate alternatives, is the greatest risk of all.[59]

The authors warned of

> indications that a decline in morale and confidence in Western Europe may be expected. In particular, the situation in Germany is unsettled. Should the belief or suspicion spread that the free nations are not now able to prevent the Soviet Union from taking, if it chooses, the military action outlined in Chapter V [overrunning Western Europe] the determination of the free countries to resist probably would lessen and there would be an increasing temptation for them to seek a position of neutrality.[60]

"Continuation of present trends," NSC 68 argued, would "lead progressively to the withdrawal of the United States from most of its present commitments in Europe and Asia and to our isolation in the Western Hemisphere and its approaches." This would not be the result of a "conscious decision" but "withdrawal under pressure," and such "pressure might come from our present Allies." The conclusion repeated that "unless our combined strength is rapidly increased, our allies will tend to become ... increasingly anxious to seek other solutions, even though they are aware that appeasement means defeat."[61]

Kennan was disgusted by Europe's wish to cower under the American umbrella and inclined to dismiss European fear of Soviet attack as contemptible and neurotic. By early 1950, however, Acheson had lost faith in Kennan's views, especially on the nuclear issue, which he found muddled and pacifistic. Kennan's friend Nitze he found more practical and "a joy to work with because of his clear, incisive mind." The two had a common passion for the "facts" – the "knowable" capabilities of the Soviet Union as opposed to its elusive intentions. But Nitze made basic assumptions about European intentions that were rooted in his interwar isolationism-cum-hostility toward the Old World. Acheson, needless to say, did not carry Europhobic baggage, but he now had Nitze (the main author of NSC 68) at his side arguing that the Europeans – especially the British and the French – could not really be trusted and that the fate of Europe was far too important a matter to be left to Europeans alone to decide.[62]

The air was full of such warnings at the time. For Bohlen, Europe

---

59. *FRUS*, 1950, 1: 264.
60. Ibid., 277.
61. Ibid., 279–80, 284.
62. Acheson's break with Kennan at this point had to do with the hydrogen bomb project, which the latter opposed. See Chapter 5, this volume. See also Acheson, *Present*, 373.

was "a patient whom we have been treating and whom we can now say will not die, but who...is showing decided tendencies to drift back to its former bad habits of disunity." From London the Embassy reported tendencies leading to "the resurgence of the neutrality complex in Western Europe." The Germans, of all people, respected strength and despised weakness. Thus their loyalty was very much "up for grabs." McCloy noted a "growing sense of fear that has been permeating the country for the last six months or so due largely to the obviously increasing Soviet propaganda and to what the Germans consider a lack of power in the West." For the Dutch foreign minister Dirk Stikker, "the world political situation was gradually deteriorating." On the first anniversary of the North Atlantic pact, the French journalist Jean Jacques Servan-Schreiber wrote that the treaty had not succeeded in creating a sense of security in Europe, that U.S. isolationism and European neutralism were still possible, and that the West was unable to stop a Soviet attack. A U.S. Embassy official in Paris believed that Servan-Schreiber's paper, *Le Monde*, was "poisoning the mind of France" and was more dangerous than the Communist Party.[63]

European requests for military aid had begun right after the signing of the treaty, with France "the most importunate of the allies on the subject."[64] Reflecting French insistence, Brussels pact planners had decided that Europe should be defended "as far east in Germany as possible" – that is, east of the Rhine – while awaiting U.S. intervention. The Joint Chiefs of Staff and Congress had very reluctantly begun to accommodate themselves to European pressure while trying to dictate their own terms – the basic pattern of 1949–52. After the adoption of a North Atlantic Treaty "strategic concept" in December 1949, the Mutual Defense Assistance Program (U.S. military aid) had begun. The NATO Medium Term Defense Plan (January 1950) contemplated a "maximum initial effort" to hold the enemy rather than the rapid withdrawal to the Pyrenees and the Channel that the Joint Chiefs preferred, but with the Europeans providing the "hard core" of the ground defense. The Joint Chiefs' "off-tackle" plan (December 1949) – disclosed only to the British and Canadians – presumed that all forces mobilizable by mid-1954 *might* be able to hold the Rhine, Scandinavia, and Italy. The Europeans were justified in thinking that the Joint Chiefs

63. For Bohlen's January 1950 comment see *FRUS*, 1950, 3: 620; London Embassy to Secretary, Feb. 17, 1950, ibid., 810; McCloy to Secretary, Mar. 1950, ibid., 29; On Servan-Schreiber see Lawrence Kaplan, *The United States and NATO: The Formative Years* (Lexington: University Press of Kentucky, 1984), 153. U.S. official quoted in Alexander Werth, *France, 1945–1955* (Boston: Beacon Press, 1966), 394.
64. Kaplan, 123.

of Staff had little desire to entangle the United States in the "forward defense" of Europe.[65]

The spring of 1950 was also the time when inflated American hopes surrounding Britain's role as promoter of European unity collapsed. Acheson expressed irritation with British foot dragging on the proposed European Payments Union. He told Stikker that he had "gone pretty easily on the British ... in view of the elections" (in February, won by Labour) "and Bevin's poor health and that it ... was now time to have a talk with Sir Oliver Franks." Acheson subsequently told Franks:

> We could not hold our position defensively, we would slip back. It was, therefore, necessary to find some new idea or new step which would retain the initiative.... We had thought about the possibility of stepping up the activities and tempo of existing organizations such as NATO, the Council of Europe, OEEC, and in particular the NATO might be used a vehicle since we were members.

With Europe seemingly adrift toward neutralism, Acheson concluded that a tighter Atlantic relationship under U.S. leadership was inevitable. The spirit behind this choice was not "Finally our opportunity has arrived," but rather "Our friends seem to demand it and need it and are leaving us little choice."[66]

This was all the more true if (as U.S. officials had by now concluded) German "manpower and industrial capabilities" would have to be used in order to retain German political loyalty and to strengthen Western Europe. Accepting that necessity in principle, the French and British tried, consequently, to draw the United States into a tighter political embrace. At the tripartite meeting in London in May 1950, Schuman told Acheson that "it was necessary for some more lasting relationship between the U.S., Canada and Western Europe to be established" before the ERP ended in 1952. France promoted the OEEC as an entity that could bind North America and Europe – including Germany – together. The British were willing to consider German NATO membership but told Acheson that European morale could recover only under "a kind of 'Atlantic umbrella.'" Those were the *only* conditions under which France and Britain would be prepared to live with a resuscitated Germany.

65. See Christian Greiner, "The Defense of Western Europe and the Rearmament of West Germany, 1947–1950," in Riste, ed., 152–56. See also *FRUS*, 1950, 4: 353–56. Kaplan, 142–44. As for NATO force objectives, a U.S. official noted in March, "Figures developed on the subject were so far apart from reality that the element of discouragement was becoming evident." See Charles Bonesteel during the meeting of U.S. ambassadors in Rome, Mar. 22–24, 1950, *FRUS*, 1950, 3: 820.

66. *FRUS*, 1950, 3: 639–40; see also Franks to Bevin, Mar. 8, 1950, FO 800/517, PRO.

Ambassador Bruce had concluded that since Britain was not interested, "purely European integration" was already hopeless. Instead, he recommended "a broadening of the conception of an Atlantic Treaty Community that will comprise most of Western Europe as well as the U.S., U.K. and Canada and eventually Western Germany." Acheson was inclined to follow the advice of a closer adviser, Ambassador-at-Large Philip Jessup, who favored trying to trade a U.S. role in Europe after 1952 for French and British support for some kind of European integration involving both Germany and Britain. Acheson must have been at least dimly aware of growing European dependency on the United States. But if the basic choice in the spring of 1950 was between Kennan's three-world vision and the closer Atlantic solidarity urged by the Europeans, it seemed to him "that we had to do the latter, whether it was right or wrong."[67]

Under the circumstances, the French offer (May 9, 1950) to negotiate a European coal and steel community (ECSC) was manna from heaven for the secretary of state. He was awed and puzzled by Monnet's brilliant, inchoate plan. Only half facetiously he said, "The most terrible preparation for diplomatic life is the training in Anglo-Saxon law. That gives you a spurious desire for the specific: you try to find out categorically what things mean. People who have really great constructive ideas don't really know what they mean." Understandable or not, the proposal was a source of personal satisfaction. Acheson had been urging the Europeans – and especially the French – to take the initiative all along.[68] The French move suggested an unexpected degree of European political vitality and independence, so perhaps the indefinite extension of American tutelage was not inevitable after all. Most important, the coal and steel pool was a means of consummating Franco-German reconciliation and German integration into the West. This is what the Americans wanted to accomplish without knowing exactly how.

---

67. On Germany see McCloy comment, *FRUS*, 1950, 3: 815; Schuman comment, ibid., 1040; memo of conversation between Bevin and Acheson, May 9, 1950, FO 800/449, PRO; Bruce to Secretary, Apr. 25, 1950, *FRUS*, 1950, 3: 64; Jessup to Secretary, May 5, 1950, ibid., 910–11. Acheson said as much to Schuman on May 9. See ibid., 1015. See also Princeton Seminar transcript, 835–37. The concrete result of the London meetings was the creation of a permanent council of deputies to the North Atlantic Council, responsible for defense planning.

68. When Bevin began to give Schuman "absolute hell" – the British had not been consulted and did not like the plan – Acheson reminded him that the French had not been consulted before the devaluation of sterling. Schuman told Acheson, "You have a large deposit in my bank." Princeton Seminar transcript, 341–42, 826, DAP-HSTL. Acheson, *Present*, 382–87.

A "shocking turn of events"

Acheson himself later encouraged the myth that the Korean War somehow facilitated U.S. European diplomacy. He wrote of the NSC 68 program, "It is doubtful if anything like what happened in the next few years could have been done had not the Russians been stupid enough to have instigated the attack." Two weeks after the invasion, Franks reported that Harriman favored "the rapid intensification of defense under the Atlantic Pact." For Harriman, "Congress was in an emotional state. Korea gave the chance."[69] But the Schuman Plan had provided reason to hope that something short of a full-scale American protectorate would suffice to counter the negative tendencies identified in NSC 68. Korea dashed those hopes and brought dramatically to the surface the anxiety and mutual mistrust that had preoccupied Acheson since early 1950. The fear animating American policy was not so much that the Soviet Union would attack Western Europe directly; rather, it was that European doubts about the United States – by late 1950 the United States had suffered a full-scale disaster in the Far East – would translate into neutralism or worse.

Now reinforcing that tendency were European fears that American pressures to rearm Germany would lead to World War III. Mixed with fear was animosity arising from the raw material shortages, higher taxes, inflation, and falling living standards that rearmament entailed. Korea also injected new poison into the domestic atmosphere: Acheson was blamed for having invited the North Korean attack. (In his January 12, 1950, Press Club speech, he had left South Korea outside the U.S. defense perimeter.) What Acheson had feared in mid-1946 actually happened four years later: he became a political liability to the administration. Republican senators vilified him. Walter Lippmann demanded his resignation. "At home as well as abroad," said the *Washington Post* in April 1951, "he is a political deadweight."[70] Korea did not help Acheson. It was his personal hell.

DURING THE SUMMER AND FALL OF 1950, U.S. officials convinced themselves, once and for all, that responding to Moscow's putative challenge on the periphery was essential in order to preserve U.S. credibility in more vital parts of the world. The Europeans themselves certainly did not discourage the belief that there was far more at stake in the war than

69. Acheson, *Present*, 374; Franks to Sir William Strang, July 12, 1950, FO 371/81637, PRO.
70. On Lippmann's demand in December 1950 see Steel, 473–74. See also *Washington Post* editorial (by Herbert Ellison), Apr. 28, 1951, calling for Acheson's resignation.

Korea itself. They now took the initiative to do what they had been trying to do since 1948: to engage the United States directly in the forward defense of Europe.

In July 1950, Bohlen warned "of definite signs that the United States reverses in Korea have brought discouragement and dismay to our friends and it is to be expected that as long as these reverses continue this feeling will deepen." Acheson warned that the "feeling in Europe was changing from one of elation that the United States had come into the Korean crisis to petrified fright." Kennan himself could not rule out a chain of events leading to "the break-up of the Atlantic Pact organization, the political defection of Germany, and the eventual strategic withdrawal of the U.S. from the European continent." In Bonn, many feared – or professed to fear – occupation by East German paramilitary forces. McCloy warned that if Germany was not to be lost politically, it must be convinced not only that the United States was able to defend it but that "some opportunity would be afforded" Germans to defend themselves. Prompted by Adenauer – who had recognized the potential link between rearmament and the recovery of sovereignty since 1948 – McCloy said publicly that "there would be very many Germans who would be prepared and anxious to defend Germany in the event of an attack."[71]

The French government's message was not simply that Europe must be defended "as far east as possible," but that American and British troops had to be there "to help meet the initial shock." Typically, the French attempted to make this a condition of their own contribution: they "would not again be willing to support the major share of the burden of land war in Europe, unless they were assured that massive mutual support from their allies would be on the spot upon the outbreak of hostilities." The French, British, and Dutch urged a unified command under an American officer. Bevin wrote Acheson that the number of U.S. troops on the Continent was "now the key question."[72]

In early August, Acheson told the president that "we must now make up our mind to accept the responsibility of a unified command and of additional American forces." The State Department proposal for a

71. *FRUS*, 1950, 1: 343, 345, 367; ibid., 3: 201. McCloy quoted in Schwartz, 127–28. See also Bark and Gress, *A History of West Germany*, vol. 1: *From Shadow to Substance, 1945–1963* (London: Basil Blackwell, 1989), 276, 77; Samuel Wells, "The First Cold War Build Up," in Riste, ed., 181–97.
72. U.S. deputy to the North Atlantic Council Charles Spofford, summarizing the position of his French colleague, Hervé Alphand, July 28, 1950, *FRUS*, 1950, 3: 148; Bruce reporting Prime Minister René Pleven's views, Aug. 1, 1950, ibid., 170; On U.S. commander and troops see ibid., 132, 171, 269, 272.

"European defense force" (August 1950) including U.S. and German units was an attempt to satisfy both France and Germany. According to Bruce a German army was out of the question for Paris, but "if Germans are made soldiers in an Atlantic Community army or even a European army, the question will be viewed in a quite different light." On August 21, Acheson informed his envoys that he was now in "complete agreement" with their "general thesis."[73]

Melvyn Leffler argues that the differences that emerged at this point between Acheson and the Pentagon were "primarily tactical." Acheson would agree. Like the Pentagon he believed that trying to defend Germany east of the Rhine without German help was absurd. He favored the individual elements of the "one-package" proposal endorsed by Truman on September 8, 1950: increasing U.S. troop strength from about two to about six divisions, an integrated Western army including German contingents, and a U.S. supreme commander. This historic departure was designed to remove doubts about the U.S. interest "in the defense, rather than the liberation, of Europe" – a French prime minister had told the Americans: "The next time you would probably liberate a corpse." When the objective of deterring and meeting an attack had been achieved, it was "hoped that the United States would be able to leave to the European nation members the primary responsibility, with the collaboration of the United States, of maintaining and commanding such a force."[74] Acheson, however, was a tactician par excellence. Bad tactics might be fatal to one's strategic objectives, and he considered the Pentagon's "murderous" in this case. Trying to force the French to accept the immediate inclusion of German soldiers would "delay and complicate the whole enterprise," but the Pentagon had its way. Acheson's position was further complicated by the Germans themselves. In August, Adenauer had asked publicly for a 150,000-man "defense force" and presented a memorandum offering German contingents for a European army. An accompanying memo asked for the restoration of full sovereignty in foreign and domestic affairs. Just as the French government demanded Anglo-American involvement on the Continent as a condition of its own indispensable contribution, the German government insisted, "If Germans are to make sacrifices of every kind then the road to

---

73. McCloy wanted to accommodate the Germans' wish to defend themselves, by creating a "genuine European army." Ibid., 157, 181, 183, 211–19, 231. See also Schwartz, 129–32.

74. Leffler, 386; Acheson, *Present*, 438; State–Defense memo, Sept. 8, 1950 (later NSC 82), *FRUS*, 1950, 3: 273–78. Henri Queuille quoted in McClellan, 148.

freedom must be open to them just as it is to all other Western European peoples."[75]

Here was Acheson's classic dilemma again: how to propitiate France and Germany at the same time. At the September 1950 tripartite and NATO meetings, he was obliged to argue a case that risked creating a full-scale political crisis in France. His appeal to Paris was essentially "Allow us to do what you have insisted that we do." Without a German contribution, the Pentagon and Congress would never agree to place American troops on the front line. In fact, he stretched his "one-package" brief by telling the French, "We could decide now on German participation without getting it into effect for some time." He also persuaded the new secretary of defense, George Marshall, that the one-package deal would not work. At the same time, he feared that either Germany would be allowed to join the West "and take a full part and help, or it will begin to hedge its bets." Avoiding this meant pressing the French very hard "in private."[76]

Acheson's reaction to the October 1950 Pleven Plan, calling for mere German battalions – and only after an elaborate supranational structure had been created – was skeptical: "Aside from the minimal accretion to European defense ... the second-class status accorded Germany was all too plain." Though "cautiously favorable" in public, Acheson was shocked by French Defense Minister Moch's "extreme intransigence" on the question. Other NATO members were openly contemptuous. For once – and on behalf of the others – Acheson threatened France: "If France insist[ed] on the present plan ... it is obvious that we will be obliged to reverse our entire policy toward the defense of Western Europe."[77] But he was intent on finding, "if possible, some means of giving France hope as regards her aims on the Continent and particularly that we are not deliberately working against France." Bruce suggested endorsing the underlying principle of the French plan, "as long as deliberations to create an integrated army did not delay the raising of

75. In an October 1950 memorandum, German planners contemplated a force of twelve German divisions under Atlantic–European command. Acheson, *Present*, 438; Bark and Gress, 282; Norbert Wiggershaus, "The Decision for a West German Defense Contribution," in Riste, ed., 206–7.

76. See memo of conversation between Acheson and Schuman, Sept. 14, 1950, *FRUS*, 1950, 3: 293, 298–99; Acheson report to Truman, Sept. 15, ibid., 1230; Acheson to Acting Secretary, Sept. 17, ibid., 320; Acheson to Truman, Sept. 20, ibid., 1246; Acheson, *Present*, 444, 458. Marshall replaced Louis Johnson, whom Truman dismissed in September.

77. Acheson, *Present*, 458; *FRUS*, 1950, 3: 385, 411–13, 426–30. Acheson asked Bruce to convey his message to Schuman on November 3, 1950.

German contingents and the force would be within the NATO chain of command." This idea anticipated the so-called Spofford Plan adopted by NATO in December 1950.[78]

By the time of the December meeting, however, the Chinese had routed MacArthur's army in Korea. In a letter to Schuman, Acheson wrote of "the far-reaching and tragic significance of the shocking turn of events. . . . I am convinced that our response must be to forge ahead without delay in our efforts to build defensive strength in Western Europe." Between the lines was an appeal to Schuman to help shore up American credibility in Europe and the Truman administration's tottering position at home. Acheson was more than ever worried about Germany. The Germans had received significant concessions in response to their August demands, but Adenauer's problems were now compounded by a Soviet note calling for Four Power talks on "fulfillment of the Potsdam Agreement regarding demilitarization of Germany." In November, Adenauer reiterated a call for "contractual agreements" ending the occupation and other concessions to counter "defeatist" attitudes. "Do as we ask," the Germans seemed to be saying, "or it may be Rapallo all over again." Adenauer was inclined – and obliged – to drive a hard bargain with the Allies in return for overcoming strong domestic opposition to rearmament. Acheson warned Schuman, "The situation in Germany, as it seems to me, is noticeably deteriorating, or at any rate tending to harden unfavorably." In mid-December, he told the secretary of the army that the European situation was "getting more and more critical every minute."[79]

The December compromise involving France, the Pentagon, and the other NATO allies allowed for negotiations aiming at a modified version of the Pleven Plan (eventually called the European Defense Community, or EDC). In the meantime, steps would be taken to raise German forces, and a U.S. supreme commander would be sent without delay. The French were not satisfied, but they had won significant concessions.

78. Acheson to Bruce, Nov. 14, 1950, ibid., 451; Bruce to Acheson, Nov. 17, ibid., 466. See also Spofford, U.S. representative to the NAT Council of Deputies, to Acheson, recommending such a plan, Nov. 16, 1950, ibid., 457–60.

79. At the September New York meeting the Allies agreed to German mobile police forces on a *land* basis and announced that their troops in Germany were now acting in an external security capacity. The German government was authorized to create a foreign ministry and to enter into diplomatic relations with foreign governments. Restrictions on heavy industry and exports were further modified. The three powers reaffirmed their intention to remain in Berlin. See *FRUS*, 1950, 3: 1296–99. On the Soviet note of November 3, 1950, see ibid., 4: 903. Acheson to Schuman, Nov. 29, 1950, ibid., 3: 497; memo of conversation with Secretary Pace, Dec. 14, 1950, ibid., 570. See also Schwartz, 145, 148–49.

While accepting negotiations in good time on contractual agreements designed to give Germany substantial freedom and equality "at such time as she would enter defense arrangements," Acheson reassured Schuman that there would be no hasty offer of participation to the Germans that they might reject and attempt to counter.[80]

The French had also tried to tie agreement on German rearmament to the successful outcome of the Schuman Plan negotiations, but those talks had reached an impasse over the question of decartelization. Acheson decided on a major additional effort to sweeten the rearmament pill. Adenauer was to be told that progress toward the "contractuals" would be heavily influenced by the outcome of the ECSC and upcoming EDC negotiations. In early 1951, McCloy and Monnet conducted the "bashing of the Ruhr," the use of heavy pressure to break down the bitter resistance of Bonn and local business magnates to "law 27" requiring the reduction of vertical integration in the steel and coal industries and the breakup of the coal industry's combined sales agency, the DKV. Even if its terms were never really carried out, the agreement allowed for the signature of the ECSC treaty in April 1951, a badly needed political success for the French and U.S. governments at the time.[81]

IF LATE 1950 MARKED THE NADIR of U.S. postwar fortunes, the same could be said of the Anglo-American special relationship. The Truman–Atlee emergency meeting of December 1950 found both sides shaken and alarmed by the weakness of the other. The Labour government faced the agonizing prospect of rearmament at the expense of domestic social achievements and fond hopes of financial independence from the United States. Bevin, dying of heart disease, did not attend the talks. In Washington, Anglophobe Republicans demanded that any agreement with the British be submitted to them for ratification. The two governments were themselves far apart on fundamental issues. The British

---

80. Acheson, *Present*, 486–87. The German units were to be regimental combat teams (6,000 men), a compromise between the divisions (12,000) that the Pentagon wanted and Pleven's battalions (1,000). On the contractual negotiations see Acheson to British Embassy, Dec. 14, 1950, *FRUS*, 1950, 4: 801. On the need to "put the German matter on ice for a little while" see Acheson conversation with Lovett, Dec. 15, ibid., 3: 579. On reassurance to Schuman see minutes of tripartite meeting, Dec. 19, ibid., 806–9.

81. See Acheson to London Embassy, Dec. 14, 1950, ibid., 802. See also Hogan, *The Marshall Plan*, 377–78; Schwartz, 186–203; John Gillingham, *Coal, Steel and the Rebirth of Europe, 1945–1955: The Germans and the French from Ruhr Conflict to European Community* (Cambridge: Cambridge University Press, 1991), 266–83. The expression "bashing of the Ruhr" is Gillingham's.

feared a wider war with China leading to the loss of Hong Kong and defensive strength in the West and favored appeasement of Peking. The Americans insisted that their credibility in both Europe and the Far East would be shattered by a withdrawal from Korea.[82]

Acheson also told the British that they would have to accept something less than automatic prior consultation by Washington on the use of the atomic bomb. An accord of the kind sought by Atlee (and nearly agreed to by Truman) "would open a most vicious offensive against both." Acheson the propitiator was for once empty-handed. It was Britain's turn to give in. But the British understood that his basic message was "Help us to do what you have insisted that we do" – to maintain our commitment to Europe and the substance of the special relationship. After all the attention paid by the United States to France and Germany, an essential part of what the British sought in Washington they received: psychological reassurance. Atlee cabled home that Britain had now been "lifted out of the 'European queue' and . . . treated as a partner, unequal no doubt in power but still equal in counsel."[83]

The period of "greatest sensitivity"

A year after NSC 68, the likelihood that both America and Europe might revert to their historical bad habits seemed stronger than ever. Herbert Hoover's call for a peripheral strategy founded on a "Western Hemisphere Gibraltar" turned the argument of NSC 68 on its head. The Korea disaster also raised the possibility that the United States might abandon Europe in favor of an all-out crusade in Asia. In Europe, fear was no longer the only reaction: "When MacArthur's troops were driven back from the Yalu . . . there was an unmistakable feeling of *Schadenfreude* in France – as there was, indeed, in England." Once the mid-1951 Korea stalemate had begun "to sap all urgency" about a military buildup, even friendly opinion began to cast a suspicious eye upon the "youthful, headstrong giant." By mid-1951 the feeling was widespread that war with the Soviet Union was unlikely unless the Americans provoked it. The Canadian foreign minister was prompted

82. *FRUS*, 1950, 3: 1732; see also 1710, 1711–14, 1716. In the midst of the talks, McCloy cabled that in view of the Chinese success "certain elements in West Germany" were disposed to examine the so-called Grotewohl letter – a recent East German offer to set up an all-German constitutional assembly – "most carefully rather than turn it down flat." See ibid., 4: 669.
83. Atlee to FO, Dec. 10, 1950, FO 371/81637, PRO; Hogan, *The Marshall Plan*, 401. See also Franks to FO, Dec. 11, 1950, FO 371/81637, PRO.

to warn his friend Acheson of the impression in his country "that the United States had come to accept the inevitability of war and was, accordingly, launched on a program not to win the peace but to win the war."[84]

Irwin Wall aptly writes of Franco-American relations that it was "the pull of the French, rather than the push outward from Washington that characterized the different aspects of American involvement, diplomatic, economic, political, and military, between 1945 and 1954. Invariably, though, having invited the Americans in, the French quickly became dissatisfied with what their guests brought with them." What they brought in 1951 were new air bases, rail lines, oil-storage depots, extravagant headquarters, and thousands of personnel. Hervé Alphand of the French Foreign Ministry said in June 1951 that "it was increasingly important to explain NATO, NATO airfields, infrastructure, etc. to the French people, portraying it as a triumph of French diplomacy which had requested and finally obtained such protection." That is exactly what it was, but Frenchmen did not believe it. Wall's thesis applies especially to Franco-American financial relations. What the French – at first somewhat absent-mindedly – invited the Americans to do in this case was to scrutinize their national budget in search of ways to raise French defense spending, as a condition of American aid. The two governments fell into a series of bitter – to the French, humiliating – arguments over who was not doing enough for the other. The June 1951 elections shifted the country to the right. "We want the Western powers to be our allies not our masters" was a successful Gaullist slogan. The October return of the British Conservative Party to power was directly attributable to the economic consequences of rearmament.[85]

The Americans themselves were no longer worried about a worldwide Soviet offensive. The new supreme commander, General Eisenhower, told Truman's cabinet in January 1951 that the Soviet leaders could not "see their way through to winning a war now and I don't think they'll

---

84. Hoover radio talk published in the *Washington Evening Star*, Dec. 21, 1950; Werth, 475; Robert E. Osgood, *NATO: The Entangling Alliance* (Chicago: University of Chicago Press, 1962), 75; Bruce characterizing the French view of the U.S. "giant," Sept. 2, 1951, *FRUS*, 1951, 4: 421; memo of conversation between U.S. and Canadian foreign ministers, June 14, 1951, ibid., 1: 848.

85. Wall, *The United States and the Making of Postwar France*, 300 and chap. 7 in general. McCloy to Secretary, June 4, 1951, quoting Alphand, *FRUS*, 1951, 1: 785–86. Werth, 540. The French election, partly because of the new, less proportional system introduced by the government, brought major gains by the Gaullist Rassemblement du Peuple Français and lesser gains by the traditional Right and Radicals. The losers included the Communists and to a lesser extent the Catholic Mouvement Républicain Populaire, the party of Schuman.

start one." Acheson told reporters a week later that he "doubted that the Soviet Union would act in Germany." Paul Nitze wrote, "If they do not launch World War III now it may be because they realize better than we admit the basic strength of our position and because they believe our allies can be split and our position softened by the war of nerves." If Nitze knew his Europeans, the Soviets were right. A visit by Pleven to Washington in January 1951 was designed "to assist the French Prime Minister in his efforts to combat the psychological depression that exists in France."[86]

The essence of American fear was that the Yalu defeat, followed by the January–April 1951 "Great Debate" on sending troops to Europe, conveyed the image of weakness and unreliability. If, as Hoover claimed, the Europeans' "will to defend themselves [was] feeble and their disunities [were] manifest," did not the dispatch of a mere four U.S. divisions constitute a dangerous provocation? In Washington, Pleven wanted to be reassured that the "United States' predominant position in the atomic field was being maintained." As usual, Germany was thought to be hypersensitive to the way the wind blew. McCloy warned: "We had to adopt a vigorous, consistent policy if we aspired to keep Germany on our side.... Time was running out."[87]

Officials like Eisenhower were not inclined to attach strings to U.S. aid: "Let's go ahead and give them the stuff." But the instinct to propitiate the Europeans was now at war with the necessity to prod them to do the things that would counteract anger and cynicism toward Europe in the United States. The conservative-isolationist attack also had to do with the Truman administration's economic policies, including higher taxes, price controls, budget deficits, and "give-aways" to Europe. The dubious "Keynesian" hopes, if not explicit assumptions, contained in the NSC 68 analysis came home to roost. The administration won the Great Debate about U.S. troops. In April a Senate resolution authorized the sending of four divisions to Europe. But the Republicans won the financial Great Debate. Congress cut Truman's (worldwide) nonmilitary aid request from $2.5 to 1.4 billion and weakened the State

86. Eisenhower, quoted in *FRUS*, 1951, 3: 457. According to his biographer, "Within Europe, Eisenhower considered morale to be his biggest problem." Stephen Ambrose, *Eisenhower*, vol. 1: *Soldier, General of the Army, President Elect, 1890–1952* (New York: Simon & Schuster, 1983), 506. Acheson off-the-record press conference, Feb. 8, 1951, Press Conferences, 1951, DAP-HSTL. Nitze, in *FRUS*, 1950, 3: 1049. See also Leffler, 442. On Pleven, see Jessup to Marshall, Jan. 24, 1951, *FRUS*, 1951, 4: 300.
87. Hoover speech, cited in note 84. On the debate see Osgood, 77–79; *FRUS*, 1951, 3: 14, 22, 24. On Pleven, see ibid., 4: 318. McCloy, ibid., 3: 156.

Department's control over its disbursement by creating the Mutual Security Administration.[88]

CHARLES BOHLEN BELIEVED that the personal attacks leveled at Acheson in 1950–52 made him "more rigid in his anti-Soviet attitude after he left the government. Some of the bitterness welled up later. He became much more caustic in his descriptions of people and downright dogmatic in his view of events." In reality these effects were felt before 1953. Late 1950 to early 1951 was another period in Acheson's life when a great political issue resolved itself into a matter of personal conscience. Increasingly he displayed the temperamental rigidity that had always been at war with the lawyer's inclination to accommodate. Emotionally, the Great Debate of 1951 was 1941 revisited. The dramatis personae were much the same, with Hoover, Kennedy, and Taft leading the opposition. "The stench of spiritless defeat, of death of high hopes and broad purposes given off by [their statements]," wrote Acheson, "deeply shocked me." His reaction to the isolationist challenge was to redouble his efforts, as in 1941.[89]

At the same time, Acheson and Nitze shared the preoccupation that the very steps being taken to deter a Soviet attack might indeed provoke it: "A program for building strength, prior to the time the strength has been achieved, tends to increase the likelihood of USSR counteraction. We would like to see the period of build-up and therefore of greatest sensitivity shortened as much as possible."[90] Trying to accelerate rearmament at the very moment when conditions in Europe were growing less hospitable meant increasing friction with Britain and France and increasing congruity of outlook with Bonn. Acheson had pledged himself to defend Adenauer's "policy of strength" in November 1949. Adenauer now emerged as the strongest European supporter of the U.S. effort to create a "situation of strength" in Europe, a project he had in part inspired.

Still, one had to try to propitiate all sides. To a degree that seems remarkable in retrospect, this remained Acheson's approach. Propitiation

88. Eisenhower to the cabinet, Jan. 31, 1951, *FRUS*, 1951, 3: 453. A typical question from Eisenhower's business friends was "Why in hell should we support a bunch of pinkos?" Ambrose, 505. Hogan, *The Marshall Plan*, chap. 9, is a lucid recounting of the domestic economic battle. On the hopes, if not solid assumptions, that government-stimulated expansion of the economy would permit, and "might even be aided by," rearmament without squeezing civilian consumption see NSC 68, *FRUS*, 1950, 1: 258; see also 285–86.

89. Bohlen, 302. Acheson, *Present*, 489. Acheson referred specifically to a Kennedy statement and Hoover's December 20 speech.

90. Nitze to Acheson, July 31, 1951, *FRUS*, 1951, 1: 111. See also Leffler, 439–40.

entailed another diplomatic charade at the Palais du Marbre Rose in Paris designed to cater to European public opinion and governments while persuading them that the Soviet bid for a CFM session on Germany was itself a hoax. The State Department decided upon a drawn-out preliminary meeting to discuss an agenda for the eventual CFM. As Acheson feared, a degree of Soviet flexibility created problems with the French and British. "They obviously regard us as stubborn, rigid and overly suspicious and probably averse to a conference any-way," a department official accurately noted.[91] Acheson reluctantly conceded the Soviet demand for an agenda item on the "demilitarization of Germany." Adenauer warned that the Russians "would 'play on every available flute' to appeal to every soft element in the West." Fortunately for Acheson, the Soviets were not overly astute – or maybe their German clients feared a deal on Germany as much as Bonn. Moscow rejected an apparently reasonable Western offer to choose among three possible agendas.[92] With the French elections out of the way, Washington obtained an adjournment of the talks.

It was at this point that the State Department also decided, as Acheson later put it, "that the time had come to really make a bet on the EDC."[93] This was hardly a foregone conclusion at the time. The British and Dutch wanted no part of the scheme. The Germans were scarcely less hostile to something they considered politically discriminatory and militarily risible. The American discussion of the issue revolved around some classic themes. The main supporter of the EDC in the State Department was David Bruce, whose inclination was always to ap-pease France. To a degree, he shared the enthusiasm of McCloy and Eisenhower for European federation and their concern to create a rela-tively self-sufficient European structure as soon as possible. Eisenhower's much-publicized conversion to the EDC had to do with the need for "some spectacular accomplishment" to shore up U.S. popular support for the European commitment, also with a set of assumptions that linked him to Mackinder, Coudenhove-Kalergi, Bullitt, Berle, and Kennan: the purpose of a Continental federation was to allow Europe to counterbalance Soviet Russia without having to rely heavily on

---

91. "We should approach the exploratory talks and, if it eventuates, a CFM, with the belief that their value lies in a) gaining time; b) propaganda advantage; c) convincing the Soviets that we are determined and confident. We should not be sanguine of reaching any real settlements although we should always seek them." PPS paper, Dec. 28, 1950, *FRUS*, 1950, 3: 1051; Laukhuff to Byroade, Mar. 23, 1951, ibid., 1951, 3: 1105. See also Bohlen, 296–97.

92. See McCloy to Secretary, Mar. 16, 1951, *FRUS*, 1951, 3: 1026–27. On the "triple play" see ibid., 1133–34; Acheson, *Present*, 554–55.

93. Princeton Seminar transcript, 1040, 1050, DAP-HSTL; McClellan, 347–48.

American support. Once the Europeans had built up an adequate force with trained reserves, Eisenhower believed, the Americans could come home.[94]

Acheson and his advisers also foresaw the day when there might no longer be "substantial numbers of U.S. forces on the continent." They hoped "therefore that a complete and workable European army concept could be perfected." Moreover, he had developed higher hopes for European unity than a year before – higher, certainly, than his later derisive talk about EDC "cultists" suggests. The completion of the ECSC treaty was a fillip in this regard. At the same time, Acheson was more open than most to the unprecedented aspects of the situation and did not see an extended American stay as necessarily "abnormal." His experience told him, in any case, that integration proceeded hand in hand with the extension of the American umbrella, not with its removal.[95]

As of late June 1951, Acheson was still inclined to separate the raising of German forces from the political aspect of EDC – supporting the latter, but not letting it stand in the way of the essential goal. On July 3, 1951, Bruce warned him that "after U.S. troops and the U.S. commander are withdrawn, national components in NATO will surely revert to separate national armies unless there is a permanent European political structure." He also made what appeared an eminently practical point: setting up the European defense force would actually be the *fastest* way to obtain German forces. The Germans were refusing to rearm until the contractual agreements had been negotiated, but the French were sure to delay them until their security concerns had been met. Within a European army framework, Bruce argued, France would allow the contractuals to go forward and accept larger German military units.[96]

Perhaps reasoning independently – as he suggests in his memoirs – but undoubtedly influenced by McCloy, Bruce, and Eisenhower, Acheson arrived at a similar conclusion. A European force, for the indefinite future backed by U.S. and British forces, was the best way to reconcile French, German, and American demands. A State–Defense recommendation to the president (July 30, 1951) called for the settlement of

94. He told Truman that U.S. forces could begin to come home in four to eight years. See Ambrose, 506–8. See also his statement to the cabinet, *FRUS*, 1951, 3: 456. For McCloy's similar view see Schwartz, 218–19. Schwartz shows how McCloy and Monnet lobbied Eisenhower on the subject.

95. On the EDC "cult" see Princeton Seminar transcript, 1040, 1050, DAP-HSTL. See also Acheson to Bruce, June 28, 1951, *FRUS*, 1951, 3: 801–4.

96. Bruce to Acheson, July 3, 1951, *FRUS*, 1951, 3: 805–12. Acheson, *Present*, 557. Martin Herz (an officer in the Paris Embassy at the time), *David Bruce's "Long Telegram" of July 3, 1951* (Lanham, Md.: University Press of America, 1986).

three questions by November 1, 1951: the creation of a European defense force under NATO; a specific plan for raising German forces; arrangements for restoring substantial German sovereignty. "The United States position would be that our support of point no. 1 would be contingent upon the three points being treated simultaneously and within the indicated time period."[97]

The real complexity of the European venture on which Acheson had embarked was becoming more evident day by day. Rapid European rearmament was essential to disarm Europhobic-isolationist critics and to reduce the risk of a sudden Soviet attack that rearmament itself was thought to entail. But the Europeans had reached the end of their financial tether; Acheson admitted to Schuman and Herbert Morrison, the new foreign secretary, that "it would be obviously unwise to bring about the destruction of the economic stability of various member countries in order to provide defense." The squaring of the circle was left to a "Temporary Council Committee," whose task was to study the plight of each NATO country – including the United States – and devise a plan of "burden sharing."[98]

Adenauer's political survival was now linked to his capacity to deliver German sovereignty and equality through the contractual agreements, which depended on successful negotiation of the European defense force in Paris. With each intractable problem laid to rest, a thornier one loomed in its place. Washington's November 1 deadline was soon forgotten. The closer the Europeans came to the prospect of a self-reliant and autonomous European entity based on Franco-German reconciliation, the more the United States became entangled in the details of the structure, and seemingly essential to its capacity to stand "on its own." Neither Paris nor Bonn was prepared to become friends unless each was sure it could count on Washington to protect it from the other. But Washington could not provide the necessary guarantees – Congress would never agree unless and until the Europeans had settled their differences. This was Acheson's particular circle to square.

At Paris in November, the so-called General Agreement was nonetheless concluded, and the Allies satisfied Adenauer with a statement that the status of the territories east of the Oder–Neisse line remained open pending a final peace settlement. But Adenauer was looking for the kind of propitiation that only Washington could provide. Acheson describes their private meeting on this occasion:

97. *FRUS*, 1951, 3: 813–19, 838–39, 848–52. Once approved by Truman, the July 30, 1950, document became NSC 115. On Eisenhower influence see Schwartz, 230.
98. *FRUS*, 1951, 3: 1290. On the activities of the Temporary Council Committee (presided over by Harriman, Monnet, and Sir Edwin Plowden) see ibid., 279–392.

We were sitting in the living room after lunch and he just blurted out the question: were we and the French and the British playing around with the idea that we were using Germany to back the Russians into a corner? But at any time when we had accomplished that purpose we would make a deal with the Russians and sell the Germans out? . . . He made it reasonably clear that he had the gravest worries about our associates – the British and the French.

Acheson – McCloy was also present – told Adenauer that such "was not the way Americans carried on business and that in asking him to come along as a partner, this partnership was going to hold and decisions were going to be made together and nothing of that sort would occur." When asked later whether the United States had, in effect, conceded Germany a veto over any future deal with the Soviet Union, Acheson replied, "In fact we did not after that enter into any arrangements or send notes or do anything else with the Russians, without laying the matter before the Germans and getting the Germans' observations and in many cases, modifying what we were doing in response to their views."[99]

Having previously conceded France a veto of sorts over its plans to rearm Germany, Washington now faced the prospect that the French Parliament would refuse to ratify a European defense force treaty once deputies became aware of the concrete implications – supranational control over the French army and membership in an entity that Great Britain and the United States did not deign to join. A State Department official believed that the United States should now consider political "shock treatment," explicitly linking U.S. aid to the "condition that Europe immediately take decisive steps toward federation." Shock treatment was the opposite of Acheson's approach. Still, he hazarded a warning concerning the European army negotiations going on in Paris. At the Rome session of the North Atlantic Council in late November, Acheson took Schuman aside to say that the negotiations "must be completed by the end of the year and success or failure registered by that time." What would happen in case of failure, Acheson did not say or know. Ironically, the initially skeptical Germans had by now decided to put all their eggs in the EDC basket. Adenauer saw no other solution to problems such as "security restrictions, support of U.S. and U.K. forces and an adequate financial contribution to defense, and the demand for equality of treatment. He clearly feels he must carry the EDC through in view of his domestic political situation, fear of many

99. Adenauer had been invited to Paris to meet with the three Allied foreign ministers for the first time. Princeton Seminar transcript, 1084–86, DAP-HSTL. The person asking the "veto" question was Herbert Feis. See also Acheson, *Present*, 583–84.

Germans of revival of national militarism, and his own settled policy to build a European community."[100] Bonn's commitment made it doubly difficult for Washington to switch to some alternative to the EDC.

At Rome, "the atmosphere was heavy almost to the point of pessimism." The Europeans feared economic dislocation due to the defense effort more than the risk of Soviet attack. When General Alfred Gruenther, Eisenhower's chief of staff, gave a "hair raising description" of an all-out Soviet offensive, Acheson did not find it the height of sagacity. Maybe Acheson suspected that Eisenhower had ulterior motives in pushing for the buildup of "battle worthy forces as soon as possible, [while] de-emphasizing somewhat the longer range force requirements." It was around this time that Eisenhower told his backers that "his success in Europe was the *sine qua non* of a successful bid for the Presidency."[101]

All was not bleak at the end of 1951. The French Parliament had ratified the ECSC treaty. Under the pressure of Acheson's "ultimatum" to Schuman, a meeting of the European foreign ministers in late December made progress toward the EDC treaty. Acheson seemed genuinely proud of a Western disarmament proposal presented to the UN General Assembly meeting in Paris in November. There he had become close friends with the new foreign secretary, Anthony Eden. Acheson, son of a penniless emigrant, had been fond of the rough-hewn trade unionist Bevin, but Eden was his favorite kind of Englishman. It was a matter of historical outlook and personal style, the same Tory attributes in Eden that had alienated FDR.[102]

A diplomatic grand finale

When the curtain lifted on the new year, the Americans found themselves facing a kind of twentieth century European psychodrama. French fears, set out in a dramatic letter from Schuman, were classic: Germany would either dominate the European army – the flower of the French army was dying in Indochina – or throw it over to pursue a militarist-

100. See Ridgway Knight to Secretary, Nov. 26, 1951, *FRUS*, 1951, 3: 723–25. See also Acheson to Truman, Nov. 30, 1951, ibid., 747–51, reporting on the Rome meeting; Bruce to Secretary reporting his conversation with Adenauer, Dec. 29, 1951, ibid., 981–83.
101. See Knight's assessment of the Rome meeting, *FRUS*, 1951, 3: 751–54, including remark about Eisenhower's emphasis. See also Acheson, *Present*, 731–34. Eisenhower was being actively courted by internationalist Republicans at the time. On his December 1951 statement see Ambrose, 521. Ambrose is paraphrasing him.
102. On the EDC see Bruce to Secretary, Jan. 3, 1952. *FRUS*, 1951, 3: 985–89. See also Acheson, *Present*, 578, 590–92.

revanchist course. As if to hedge its bets, the French government took steps in January 1951 to consolidate its hold on the disputed Saar district. Halfway through a debate on the EDC in February, Bruce spoke of an atmosphere of "irritation, frustration, and assertiveness" in the French Parliament. The Germans, meanwhile, were demanding equality of treatment – McCloy spoke of their "almost hysterical attitude" on the subject – across the board. Bonn told its prospective EDC partners, all NATO members, that "it did not wish to issue an ultimatum but simply to state that any arrangement that totally excluded Germany from NATO membership would be unacceptable." The German government feared American isolationism. It feared a stab in the back by the British and the French. It feared that its own public opinion might prefer a deal with Moscow promising reunification to integration with the West.[103]

The smaller European powers were not the least of Washington's problems. Once the United States had embraced the EDC, Italy followed suit and became a staunch supporter. In turn, however, Rome importuned Washington for additional aid, the easing of U.S. immigration laws, revision of the 1947 peace treaty, UN membership, and backing for territorial claims against Yugoslavia. Of Prime Minister de Gasperi's visit to Washington in September 1951, Acheson could say only that the Italians had been received "on the same basis of respect and cordiality as those states with whom they so desperately hoped to equate themselves." The Dutch government feared that an EDC without Britain would lead to German domination or a more detached United States. If the EDC spoke with a single voice in NATO councils, Dutch influence would be drowned out. The Belgian prime minister also deplored the absence of his country's traditional protector, Britain – backed by the United States: " 'Belgians,' he said, 'do not trust either France or Germany (he referred to an incident during the period of the Franco-Prussian war when Napoleon III was ready to agree with Bismarck for the territorial division of Belgium).' "

Needless to say, the British had no intention of joining the EDC. Eden was ready to help with more explicit political statements and pressure on the Benelux countries, but the Churchill government's objective was to refurbish a semiexclusive special relationship with the

---

103. See Schuman to Acheson, Jan. 29, 1952, *FRUS*, 1952–54, 5: 7–11; Bruce's analysis, ibid., 12–13. See also memo of conversation between Bohlen and Daridan of the French Embassy, Feb. 7, 1952, ibid., 610–11; Bruce to Secretary, Feb. 12, ibid., 613. McCloy to Secretary, Feb. 1, ibid., 15; on Germany and NATO, see department report on EDC, undated, ibid., 604. See also minutes of meeting between Eisenhower and State Secretary Hallstein, Jan. 28, ibid., 595–96.

United States, while coping with Britain's third postwar balance-of-payments crisis and gaining support for what even Acheson saw as increasingly dubious policies in Egypt and Iran.[104] The thread running through these interconnected European anxieties, grievances, and ambitions was that only the United States – or so it appeared – could put things right. As never before, the Western Europeans looked to Washington and not to each other, or rather to each other only insofar as they could rely on Washington, for the solution to their problems.

"With firmness in the right," Acheson had said at the end of 1951, "as God gives us to see the right, let us strive on to finish the work we are in."[105] But the work that the Truman administration was now in was nearly as ambitious as the programs of Wilson or Roosevelt, and under conditions no more ideal. By early 1952, the "Soviet threat" brought diminishing returns in terms of alliance cohesion. An official NATO report admitted that among the few factors that could cause an enemy attack was the rearmament of Germany and Japan. Moreover, as Truman told Churchill in January, in one of the great understatements of the era, 1952 "was going to be a very political year." Truman's foreign policy had precious little to show for itself after 1949 without the EDC and contractual agreements. In an election year, those agreements had to be before the Senate by midsummer to ensure ratification. If the Europeans had never needed the Truman administration more, the converse was hardly less true. It was indeed an entangling alliance.[106]

THE LISBON CONFERENCE of the North Atlantic Council (February 20–26, 1952) – preceded by frenetic talks in London – was Acheson's Yalta: a "supreme gamble," the culmination of his career as a statesman, an apparent success followed by disappointment, a house of cards built on some results of lasting significance. These intense weeks saw Acheson at his finest: the skilled mediator and fashioner of formulas, the man, as Lewis Douglas had put it, with the "queer ability to untie mental knots and snarls." His awe-inspiring reserves of stamina, forbearance, loyalty

104. Acheson, *Present*, 573, on Italy; see also memos of conversations with various Dutch officials in Jan. 1952, *FRUS*, 1952–54, 5: 584, 89, 91. On Belgium, see Ambassador Murphy to Secretary, reporting on conversation with Prime Minister Van Houtte, Jan. 17, 1952, ibid., 586. See also ibid., 598. On U.S. worry over British Middle East policy, see Acheson, *Present*, chaps. 58, 62, and 71. On the January 1952 Churchill visit to Washington, see *FRUS*, 1952–54, 6: 693–861.

105. This quote from an end-of-the-year press conference was from Lincoln. Acheson, *Present*, 593.

106. See report by the Council of Deputies to the NAC on Soviet Foreign policy, Feb. 6, 1952, *FRUS*, 1952–54, 5: 286. See also memo of Truman–Churchill talk, Jan. 19, 1952, ibid., 6: 854.

to his clients, and native tactical skill were put to their great test. These qualities, along with the political debts he had accumulated vis-à-vis his European counterparts, allowed him to persuade the parties to set aside the "extraneous" Saar and Germany-in-NATO issues and to broker a compromise on the problems of Germany's financial contribution to Western defense and security controls (in effect, the military items that Germany would not be able to manufacture). Acheson used liberal amounts of cajolery, moral suasion, and reminders of the dire consequences of failure. With Schuman, he pleaded, "We have put our hands to the plough and we cannot look back." His successful last-minute appeal to Adenauer for concessions included the words "What is needed now is another of those acts of statesmanship of which you have proved yourself so capable in the past – an act of help to me in my efforts – which only you can give. I am counting on it."[107]

Bonn gained temporary satisfaction through a formula permitting Germany to call joint sessions of the North Atlantic and EDC councils, and the North Atlantic Council approved a protocol extending the provisions of Article V of the 1949 treaty to include all members of the EDC. The French received the promise of a statement reiterating U.S. resolve to keep troops in Europe and abiding interest in the integrity of the EDC. To be sure, this was less than a guarantee to stay in Germany "as long as necessary" to prevent German secession from the EDC – something that struck Acheson as an affront to Bonn and exceeding existing congressional authorizations. But the Americans would have preferred to have Germany in NATO immediately; not pushing for this was itself a major concession. Above all, the French received the pledge of an aid package of $600 million, including $200 million in "offshore procurement" (OSP) orders by the U.S. government. Together with an adequate German financial contribution – thanks to Adenauer's last-minute concession – and promised increases in French military spending, this aid would permit Paris to pay for an EDC force (twelve divisions) on a par with the German contingent, while at the same time financing France's Indochina effort and providing orders for the French armaments industry.[108] At Lisbon the pieces also fell into place for adoption

---

107. "Lisbon was to be the supreme gamble upon which we would stake our whole prestige, skill and power." Acheson, *Present*, 609. For Douglas remark see Chapter 6, this volume. Acheson letter to Schuman, Feb. 4, 1952, *FRUS*, 1952–54, 5: 23; memo of conversation among Acheson, Schuman, and Eden, Feb. 15, ibid., 43–44; Acheson letter to Adenauer, Feb. 26, ibid., 260.

108. On the EDC–NATO link see *FRUS*, 1952–54, 5: 82, 249, 255. For the draft promise, agreed to at London, to be issued on the signing of the German contractual agreements see Acheson to Acting Secretary, Feb. 18, 1952, ibid., 78–79. See also

of the Temporary Council Committee's recommendation: "to increase the number of effective divisions available within a month of the outbreak of war from the present thirty-four to fifty-five by the end of 1952." Finally, the North Atlantic Council approved the entry of Greece and Turkey into the alliance and a new structure providing for permanent representatives and a secretary general. Acheson was exultant. He cabled Truman at the end of the conference: "We have something pretty close to a grand slam."[109]

Looking back on the period after Lisbon, Acheson said, "I think there was a momemtum going forward which everybody in Europe at the time believed would result in EDC being ratified by the end of '52." The subsequent problems arose, he believed, because "we ceased to operate for a year – the American government went out of the business of being a government for a year, from the time that the Convention met in '52 to the time the new Administration came in and spent six months getting used to things."[110] With the United States government out of business, Acheson was unable to offer more of the kind of propitiation that had underpinned his diplomacy. The ambivalent now had ample opportunity to dither over EDC, and the opponents to obstruct.

Acheson has a strong case. In the months after Lisbon – a time nearly as crowded and exhausting as January–February – the Truman administration survived the famous "battle of the notes," oversaw the conclusion of the EDC Treaty and German contractual agreements in late May, and achieved Senate approval of the latter on July 1, 1952. The Soviet note of March 10 challenged the very premises of the Adenauer–Acheson "policy of strength." It proposed a reunited and nonaligned Germany with its own armed forces and armaments industry, UN

Acheson to Truman, Feb. 21, ibid., 85. For the French–U.S. memo of understanding of Feb. 25, 1952, see ibid., 273–77. See also Acheson, *Present*, 623–24.

In late January, the French defense minister had threatened to reduce the French EDC contribution to seven divisions, rendering French approval of twelve German divisions out of the question. Acheson later said that it had been necessary to underwrite the Indochina war in order to keep the French in NATO. This was true in a literal financial sense. But Washington had also convinced itself of Indochina's vital importance to Japanese and general Western security – and now feared a large-scale Chinese assault, à la November 1950. On the seven-division proposal and the Lisbon deal see Wall, 224–26. On Indochina see minutes of meeting between State and Defense officials, Feb. 6, 1952, *FRUS*, 1952–54, 6: 1145–50; Leffler, 469–70, 471–75. Acheson's point about Indochina and Europe was made during a conversation with Richard Nixon, Mar. 19, 1969. See memo of conversation, DAP-SL.

109. The NAC adopted the recommendations of approximately 70 divisions by the end of 1953 as a "provisional goal" and of 87 divisions by the end of 1954 "for planning purposes." See *FRUS*, 1952–54, 5: 204, 221; Acheson, *Present*, 625–26.

110. Princeton Seminar transcript, 1001, DAP-HSTL. See also Acheson, *Present*, 709.

membership, the end of foreign trade and internal economic restrictions, and the restoration of civil and political rights for all. Eden and the French Foreign Ministry believed the Russians had made a serious offer. When Acheson was asked whether the West would go along with free elections, he answered, "We'll have to answer that question when we get to it. I'm convinced the Russians will not release the control over Eastern Germany they already have." Like Adenauer, however, he did not really want to put Soviet intentions to the test. The Allied reply (March 26, 1952) – prepared after consultation with Bonn – was designed to appease public opinion while buying time for last-minute EDC and contractual negotiations, and to produce a negative Soviet response.[111]

When a second Soviet note (April 9) raised the ante by proposing free elections in a united Germany, Schumacher demanded that Adenauer request Four Power talks on Germany. The State Department considered a dilatory meeting "to discuss plans for having the UN Commission or some neutral body investigate conditions throughout Germany" to see if free elections were possible, but Adenauer concluded that even this might abet those who wanted to stop the contractual accords in favor of a deal with Moscow. Acheson agreed on the grounds that "our European friends are better qualified than we are to appraise this danger which certainly must be avoided." On May 24, adopting a more familiar – and under the circumstances, welcome – tone, Moscow accused the West of simply trying to gain time for the "restoration of a West German army under the leadership of Fascist Hitlerite generals." The contractual agreements and EDC Treaty were signed, respectively, on May 26 and 27, 1952. On May 28, Eden declared the "battle of the notes" won for now.[112]

The end of May 1952 was the moment when "nightmarish weeks of being held immovable by difficulties as the clock ticked away time for action came to an end." Mindful of the U.S. electoral deadline and Adenauer's internal problems, McCloy and the State Department had

---

111. For text of the note, department comment, and Allied reply, see *FRUS*, 1952–54, 7: 169–72, 176, 189–90. See also Schwartz, 262–64; Acheson, *Present*, 630–31; Bark and Gress, 297–98; Acheson off-the-record press conference, Mar. 26, 1952, DAP-HSTL.

112. See Acheson to Truman, May 9, 1952, *FRUS*, 1952–54, 7: 237–38. In its reply (May 13, 1952) to the second Soviet note, the U.S. government reiterated its support for the integration of the Federal Republic in a "peaceful European community" and repeated its demand that a UN commission be allowed to carry out an "impartial inquiry" in the East. For texts of U.S. note of May 13 and Soviet reply of May 24, see ibid., 242–52. For Eden comment, ibid., 256. See also Schwartz, 266–67; Bark and Gress, 297–98.

pressed the Allies (and the Pentagon) for concession after concession to Bonn on the contractual agreements. Once again Acheson himself made the real difference – or so it seemed at the time. He personally negotiated the outstanding issues at Bonn with Adenauer, Eden, and Schuman.[113] On May 27, Acheson was in Paris to witness the christening of the cherished stepchild of American diplomacy, the EDC. Meeting that appointment entailed another eleventh-hour tour de force. Acheson had originally tried to set the date of May 9 and to combine the EDC and contractual ceremonies at The Hague: to separate them would have been "absurd" for both logistical and political reasons. Once again, however, he deferred to his clients. A more serious problem was renewed French demands for concrete guarantees against German secession. Britain offered a treaty providing automatic armed assistance to all EDC parties – but valid only as long as Britain remained within NATO. Two days before Acheson's scheduled departure for Europe, he learned of "considerable sentiment" in the French cabinet in favor of postponing the EDC and contractuals. Serious financial doubts had reappeared in Paris. The Dutch, meanwhile, were refusing to sign unless the EDC Treaty were made coterminous with NATO and the British guarantee – that is, only seventeen years instead of fifty.[114]

Acheson told Eden that he did not "want to land in Europe just in time to find that we are all faced with a most insoluble dilemma resulting from possible agreement on the contractuals and a deadlock on the EDC." Eden and Truman urged him to depart. The Dutch were persuaded to accept a formula requiring consultations within the EDC in the event the NATO treaty expired. Schuman asked for a promise from the United States and Britain to augment their forces in Germany should the latter withdraw from the EDC, to be included in a tripartite declaration accompanying the EDC Treaty. Acheson and Eden implored the French to content themselves with the declaration as it stood (stating, inter alia, U.S., British, and French interest in the integrity of the EDC) and a separate presidential declaration reiterating the U.S. interest in keeping troops on the Continent. With the clock ticking and Schuman dozing, the French cabinet was persuaded to accept a last-minute, face-saving change of wording in the declaration. The treaty, along with

---

113. These included the German defense contribution and the question of the international rights and obligations of a future unified Germany. Acheson, *Present*, 640–42; Schwartz, 270–75; *FRUS*, 1952–54, 7: 202–3, 107–8.

114. See *FRUS*, 1952–54, 5: 639–42, 663–65. On British guarantee, see Edward Fursdon, *The European Defence Community: A History* (London: Macmillan, 1980), 44–45. The North Atlantic Treaty, with a duration of twenty years, was three years old at this point.

protocols pledging NATO and the EDC to come to each other's aid, was ready for the formalities – held, appropriately, in the Clock Room of the Quay d'Orsay.[115]

Looking at the first half of 1952 as a whole, Acheson's argument about the subsequent loss of momentum because of the U.S. elections does not seem so much inaccurate as misleading and incomplete. What Acheson's thesis omits is that the somewhat miraculous falling into place of the various pieces of the puzzle between January and May – the NATO force levels, French finances, the EDC Treaty, and German contractual agreements – would never have happened *in the absence* of the U.S. electoral deadline and the temporary additional leverage it afforded American diplomacy. It would not be much of an exaggeration to say that the agreements were a kind of elaborate election-year offering on the part of European governments to the Truman administration. Washington's impressive 1952 handiwork, on closer examination, was of a hastily patched-together quality. The midyear deadline hastened agreements that created the impression of momentum and imminent success but that had exhausted the administration's political capital and because of their artificial nature were likely to unravel.

Acheson titled the section in his memoirs on the Soviet notes and SPD campaign against Adenauer "Thunder on the left." In late May 1952, there were also violent, Communist-organized riots in Paris against the EDC and the new NATO supreme commander, General Matthew Ridgway. Referring specifically to German rearmament, the journalist Alexander Werth speaks of "something like a European rebellion" that broke out in 1952. As a description of what was happening in Europe at the time, Werth's is probably an apter catchphrase than Acheson's. Washington's most serious problems were created not by thunder on the left but by storm clouds on the bourgeois and nationalist side of the political spectrum.[116]

It is interesting to compare the 1952 "rebellion" with the 1944 reaction of Churchill and de Gaulle to Roosevelt's vision of Europe. In contrast to Roosevelt, Acheson had defended the French presence in Indochina, Morocco, and Tunisia as essential to the West. The same was true of the British position in Egypt and Iran. Now his – in truth not very wholehearted – efforts to persuade Paris and London to begin granting timely concessions to local nationalism involved him in a series

---

115. *FRUS*, 1952–54, 5: 666–67, 677–78, 680–83, 686–88. Acheson, *Present*, 644–45.

116. Acheson, *Present*, 629; Werth, 592, 638. The riots were accompanied by a government crackdown on the French Communist Party, during which one of its leaders, Jacques Duclos, was arrested on trumped-up charges.

of rows with conservative forces whose economic interests, credibility, and *amour propre* were hopelessly wrapped up in the colonial status quo.[117] Acheson's skill and sympathy could fashion no compromise formulas. In 1944, the Europeans had reacted against an American policy of entente with Moscow that threatened to leave them naked in the face of advancing Soviet power. In 1952, they reacted against an American policy based on assumptions about Soviet aggressiveness that they did not share. In both cases, the Europeans reacted against what they saw as American efforts to consign them to arrangements that limited their independence and left them more vulnerable than before.

On the first day of the Lisbon conference, Churchill had announced that the pace of the British defense effort would be "stretched out." This decision reflected both a basic shift in British strategy toward reliance on nuclear weapons and the view that the danger of Soviet attack by 1954 was not what U.S. experts claimed. By mid-1952, writes Robert Osgood, the Lisbon force goals were a "mirage on the bleak arms horizon in the aftermath of the Korea stalemate." The Eisenhower administration would announce major cuts in defense spending in 1953. At the April 1953 meeting of the North Atlantic Council, the provisional 1953 and 1954 force goals were postponed until an unspecified future date.[118]

The ink on the Franco-American memo of understanding signed at Lisbon was hardly dry when Ridgway Knight – the same official who had predicted that EDC would not be ratified – wrote, "No one to whom I have spoken really believes the agreement is realistic and that the French have the capacity to live up to it."[119] One can only wonder what Acheson himself believed. Four days later, the government of Premier Edgar Faure fell over the issue of a 15 percent tax increase designed to pay for France's Lisbon commitments. Faure was replaced by Antoine Pinay, a traditional conservative with populist leanings – "I am Mr. Consumer" – who formed a government with breakaway Gaullist backing. His program was no new taxes and a crackdown on Communists and Arab nationalists. In effect, he was gambling on a "gold loan" – in the event undersubscribed – and U.S. aid in the form of OSP contracts beyond the $200 million already promised. The Americans had unwisely, but understandably, agreed to consider this at

117. See Acheson, *Present*, chaps., 62, 66, 70, 71.
118. Osgood, *The Entangling Alliance*, 87–90. The British tested an atomic weapon for the first time in October 1952.
119. Knight to Bonbright, Feb. 25, 1952, *FRUS*, 1952–54, 4: 1175.

Lisbon. When the administration replied that it could not provide anything close to Pinay's request of $625 million in additional OSP (over three years), the French warned of rising unemployment that would fuel Communism and of rising fear of German "military hegemony" that would undermine the EDC. Pinay called the negative U.S. answer a "most disastrous blow," as it surely was to his own position. The U.S. Embassy in France urged support for Pinay's request of $650 million in total aid for 1953. Washington's reply, prepared by third-level officials, offered $525 million and only "on the assumption of a French defense budget in 1953 considerably larger than in 1952." Pinay publicly denounced this as an "inadmissible" interference in French affairs – to widespread applause in France. Knight spoke of "tactics which border on open blackmail" – Pinay was linking EDC's passage to more U.S. aid – but recommended finding another $125 million for 1953. The French paper *Combat* commented, "You cannot combine a hat-in-hand attitude with national dignity."[120]

The Pinay government represented both the logical outcome and the beginning of the end of the early cold war phase of Franco-American relations. Pinay's popularity rested on his promise to neutralize the economic effects of what was seen as an American-imposed rearmament, but in order to do so he had to go hat-in-hand to the Americans and promise to rearm to their standards. Since those standards could never be satisfied and since the Americans themselves had now run out of money, a showdown was inevitable. Pierre Mendès-France, leader of a more serious rebellion against the Americans in 1954, summarized the situation in December 1952: "The governments of the last two years had a bad habit of assuring the Americans that France would do this and that and telling the French that the Americans would pay. Since neither was quite true, there was grumbling and discontent on all sides."[121] With a strong anti-EDC reaction under way, Pinay inevitably tried to use that issue to extract more dollars from Washington. Less than a month after the EDC Treaty was signed, the U.S. Embassy in Paris noted:

> The fact that the EDC represents fulfillment of French policy for which France has obtained U.S. support has been almost entirely lost from sight. Psychological picture is of U.S. forcing a reluctant France to accept EDC which has become synonymous in French thinking with German rearma-

120. Ibid., 1204, 1208–14, 1221–23, 1227–29, 1234–35, 1245, 1248–56, 1266–67, including fn. 2, 1270–71. See also the admirable accounts of Wall, 227–32, and Werth, 564–96, upon which I have relied.
121. Quoted in Werth, 552.

ment. Result is general impression ... that France is in a position to
demand concessions from us in connection with ratification.[122]

Washington had accelerated the diplomatic pace for its own purposes,
while French governments had grown accustomed to winning games of
diplomatic "chicken" with the United States. By late 1952, however,
there was little that the French or U.S. governments, even if both had
been in stronger positions, could have done for the EDC. The whole
complex of objections – fear of German domination, preference for
negotiations with Moscow, resentment of France's second-rate status
vis-à-vis the Anglo-Saxons, anger that French sacrifices in Indochina
were not appreciated, outrage over the loss of the national army and the
supranational features – now came to the fore. The EDC was also in
trouble in Germany, where Adenauer had first requested a ruling of the
Constitutional Court as to whether the EDC and contractuals required
a two-thirds majority in the Bundestag. When a second reading of the
legislation was approved (December 6, 1952) by less than a two-thirds
majority, Adenauer withdrew his request to the court and challenged its
right to make a binding decision. Adenauer delayed the third reading in
the Bundestag, pending action by France.[123]

On November 8, 1952, Acheson personally answered the Paris
Embassy's request for more aid to Pinay. His mood was philosophical –
as well it might have been. The Republicans had won an overwhelming
victory on November 4. Acheson observed:

> For more than two years we have been seeking every possible way to ease
> the problem of German participation in the defense of the West. . . . At
> no time have we hinted at what the French themselves fear in the back
> of their minds nor sought by any means whatever to foster a German
> military effort without an equivalent French effort. . . . This patience does
> not result only from the sentimental and human values which we place on
> France – rather it reflects our mature judgment that European security and
> thereby our own rests on France and Germany and not on France or
> Germany.

The problem with France, said Acheson, seemed to arise from the fact
that "while we are able to support them and agree with them up to
90% of their views and wishes, we cannot do so 100%." This was a
fair summary of his general European policy. If in November he did not
see how France could now be promised the extra money outside of

---

122. Paris Embassy to Secretary, June 20, 1952, *FRUS*, 1952–54, 5: 689. Werth, 552.
123. *FRUS*, 1952–54, 5: Editorial note, 699; Acheson, *Present*, 708.

NATO channels, on Christmas Eve 1952, with the Pinay government collapsing and Schuman's position in jeopardy, he nevertheless made a final, futile attempt to increase 1953 aid to France.[124]

"The World stopped moving"

In late 1952 U.S. officials turned their attention to the future of Europe. It was generally assumed that European unity was in the American interest over the long run. Experience suggested both that Congress and public opinion demanded a degree of visible progress toward unity as a condition of their support for a Eurocentric policy and that the Europeans would not move very far toward unity without U.S. guarantees. That one could not have unity in Europe without the Americans or the Americans in Europe without unity might have struck William Bullitt or George Kennan as a bizarre state of affairs, but it was now accepted truth.

During a discussion in September 1952, William Draper, U.S. permanent representative to NATO, raised a new question: were there fears in Washington "regarding the emergence of the Community of Six as a '3rd Force' which would not be subject to U.S. influence and might in fact oppose it"? Bruce (after March 1952, under secretary of state) thought that "little consideration had been given in the U.S. to this possibility." In fact, the Office of European Regional Affairs of the State Department had given it some consideration and concluded, "Continued integration of the six leading to a solid core ... requires concomitant evolution of a well-knit larger grouping of Atlantic states within which the new EUR grouping can develop, thus assuring unity of purpose of the entire group and precluding the possibility of European union becoming a third force or opposing force." Theodore Achilles dared to raise a related question: whether a solid European core, or "pillar," was really a good thing for NATO:

> A Europe united outside the framework of the Atlantic community would not be in our interest.... A Europe united within a developing Atlantic unity may or may not be in our national interest.... [A]s Atlantic unity develops, we may find a six-nation knot within it an unnecessary and possibly harmful complication.

124. Acheson to Ambassador Dunn, Nov. 8, 1952, *FRUS*, 1952–54, 6: 1276–78. On aid see memos of Acheson telephone conversations, Dec. 24, ibid., 1286–88. The René Mayer government, formed in January 1953, ended Schuman's long career as foreign minister. He was replaced by Georges Bidault, a far less fervent supporter of EDC.

But this was not the conventional wisdom. An unidentified Mutual Security Administration official, perhaps Harriman, admitted the risks of a European federation but concluded:

> Integration of the six continental countries is complementary to the continued growth and strengthening of the Atlantic community as a whole. The two developments mutually reinforce and strengthen one another.... In the military field, this implies treating the EDC, once it has been established, as a *single* but key element in all NATO plans, as well as in bilateral relations with the U.S.[125]

Acheson did not take a direct part in these discussions. Under the circumstances they might have struck him as rather idle. There would be plenty of time to worry about the EDC–NATO relationship if and when it was a fact.

Acheson's personal views about Europe, in any event, were by now skeptical and ambivalent. For a variety of reasons, he had embraced the goal of unity. He was guided by the model of the nineteenth century integrated world economy. Unity seemed to be the premise of U.S. public support for aid to Europe. Some degree of unity was what European leaders themselves professed to want – partly to appease the Americans, partly for their own compelling political, economic, and psychological reasons in the wake of World War II. The thrust of Acheson's approach had been to assist the concrete initiatives of his European clients. Even as the United States responded to invitations from the Europeans to entangle itself in their affairs, Acheson continued to believe that American power was no substitute for local cohesion and strength. The two statesmen whom he came to rely on and support most were also the strongest advocates of European unity, Adenauer and Schuman. Acheson could take some of the credit for the seminal accomplishment of these years, the European Coal and Steel Community and the beginnings of Franco-German political reconciliation. The experience of February–June 1952 had confirmed for Acheson what American leadership and mediation could achieve.

The experience of July–December 1952, however, gave rise to a different view. If at midyear Acheson believed that American propitiation and prowess had exorcised discord and cleared a path toward diplomatic success, his parting perspective was of a collection of basically egocentric and unreliable European states, stronger in an absolute sense but more

---

125. For the exchange between Draper, U.S. permanent representative to NATO, and Bruce see *FRUS*, 1952–54, 6: 655. See also Secretary to Paris Embassy, Sept. 19, 1952, ibid., 5: 324. For Achilles memo see ibid., 6: 242. At the time, Achilles was deputy chief of mission at the Paris Embassy. Mutual Security Administration memo, Jan. 9, 1953, ibid., 262–64; emphasis added.

dependent on U.S. tutelage and protection than in 1949. When Monnet told him of progress in setting up the ECSC, Acheson replied:

> I was glad to be encouraged because the situation had seemed to me most depressing indeed. Last June, I had hoped and believed that there was a spirit and momentum toward European unity, including ratification of the EDC, which would in the year 1952 carry all of these matters so far along the road that neither Soviet obstructionism nor the natural hesitancy of nations to take such far-reaching steps could prevent the accomplishment of something almost unparalleled in history. However, it had seemed to me that the momemtum had been lost, retrogression had set in, and that we might now be on the verge of complete disaster.... I did not see that there was very much, if anything, that I could do now.... I could not say that we had overlooked or neglected anything which we could have done in the past.

These words contain the sense of helplessness in the face of incipient calamity, of defeat tragically snatched from the jaws of success, of personal disillusion that marked Acheson's attitude toward Europe "after the creation." He had been the unfaltering paladin of European interests. He had tried to establish a "pattern of responsibility." His conscience was clean.[126]

Acheson's pessimistic vision of the Old World was compounded by the now-overwhelming evidence of British and French imperial decline. There was serious talk in Washington about replacing France in Indochina and Britain in the Middle East. Acheson resisted this, but the handwriting was on the wall.[127] Surveying crowds at King George VI's funeral in February 1952, Acheson said, "They looked like a tired people." In July, he made a farewell visit to Europe and South America. England, he wrote Felix Frankfurter, left him "sad and depressed.... There is much sorrow and anxiety in store for us there." On his first trip to Brazil, he found the contrast spectacular: "The amazing greatness of Brazil one has to see to apprehend. It is altogether fantastic.... I am in love with it." France, in its decadence, could not be counted on to lead Europe. Germany was economically dynamic but politically immature. How Adolf Berle, the old Europhobe, Latinophile, and opponent of Frankfurter and Acheson, would have smiled.[128]

126. Memo of Acheson–Monnet conversation, Dec. 14, 1952, ibid., 249–52. See also Acheson speech, "The American Interest in European Unity," Sept. 18, 1963, DAP-HSTL. "It is not boastful to say," he said, that the early strivers after European unity had been supported by America "at least as loyally as the royal champions of the earlier explorers supported them."
127. See Leffler, 469–92.
128. Acheson, *Present*, 613, 658–70; Acheson to Frankfurter, July 10, 1952, DAP-SL.

Acheson took leave of the State Department on January 16, 1953, with Bunyan's words: "My sword I give to him who shall succeed me in my pilgrimage, and my courage and skill to him that can get it. My marks and scars I carry with me to be a witness for me that I have fought his battles who now will be my rewarder."[129] A more detached observer, less scathed by the fight, would no doubt have seen that the battle had not really been won or lost in 1952. Over the course of time Acheson had led himself to believe that American power and insight, and his personal strength and skill, might cut the Gordian knot and bring the European Question to a breakthrough of historic dimensions. There was an element of hubris and self-delusion in Acheson's spring optimism, just as there was an element of self-righteousness and (uncharacteristic) self-pity in his December gloom. In part because his personal conduct had been scrupulous to a fault about avoiding overbearing interference, in part because his closest interlocutors were the advocates of unity, Acheson was slow, at least reluctant, to grasp the dynamics of the European reaction – across the spectrum – to the physical implantation of American power or the wounded pride and hostility generated by a sense of growing dependence on the United States. The same could be said of the depth of national feeling and even of conscious dissimulation surrounding the EDC affair. The EDC was not exactly an elaborate hoax perpetrated on the Americans to delay German rearmament while allowing American aid to continue, but it did serve this purpose for a time. Alexander Werth concludes: "The fundamental fact of all these tortuous negotiations spreading over nearly four years is that ... all the French governments from the end of 1950 till the actual rejection of EDC in 1954, knew that *at no time* was there a majority in the National Assembly or in the country, to sanction EDC."[130] Adenauer, Schuman, Monnet, and de Gasperi cultivated Acheson not because they were under any illusion about becoming his partners but because they hoped to use American power and influence to advance their own agendas.

After the beginning of the Korean War, the Truman administration had also been the object of a conservative rebellion in the United States. To a degree, the administration had been done in by the kind of facile "Keynesian" assumptions that Acheson himself would have rejected twenty years before. Acheson was justified in thinking that from the standpoint of U.S. foreign policy 1952 was a most inconvenient time to hold a presidential election. But the people who designed the U.S. politi-

129. Acheson, *Present*, 720.
130. Werth, 603; emphasis in original.

cal system were the same who had warned against involvement in "the toils of European ambition, rivalship, interest, humor, or caprice."[131]

THE EUROPE OF LATE 1952 that had so disappointed Acheson became an *idée fixe*. "The World stopped moving" for him from that year. Acheson's final vision was of a Western Europe too divided – by its own choice – and vulnerable to be trusted, but too important to let go. In effect, the only way not to lose it was to hold it fast. Speaking of the Fourth Republic's anarchic politics in 1953, he asked, "Is the Western alliance doomed because of a rotten core?" But signs of European renewal or independence – the Mendès-France government of 1954–55 and later de Gaulle – or of East–West détente, raised the specter of neutralization or worse. The answer was always a redoubling of the pressure on the East and more forceful leadership of the West – the propitiatory, kid-gloves approach having failed. In early 1955, Acheson wrote, "Europe seems to be unravelling fast. I am afraid that we have had our chance and have lost it. I doubt whether it comes again." Certainly his would not. When Kennan advanced his old disengagement thesis in the 1957 Reith Lectures, Acheson replied with what the *Washington Post* called a "savage" attack. Acheson wrote a friend: "I felt savage about it." Kennan's ideas were not simply "woolly-headed" or "mischievous" – that would not have mattered – but "destructive in the extreme." The Germans might see signs of American weakness in Kennan's words – Eisenhower and Dulles had already given signs enough – and begin to shift their bets.[132]

During the 1958 Berlin crisis he did not see where the "vigor or leadership" would come from before 1961. "Then it will be too late." In 1961–62 he favored a confrontation with Moscow over Berlin, backed by five more U.S. divisions in Europe: "Perhaps, indeed probably, our allies would have been scared to death and unwilling to go through with such a program; but, even so, it is better to have the followers desert the leader, than to have the leader follow the followers." Is this what had happened in 1949–52? Adenauer – by 1961 he had answered

131. Washington's Farewell Address (1796).
132. "The World stopped" was Harriman's comment on Acheson. See transcript of interview with Elie Abel, Harriman Papers. Acheson on France in Princeton Seminar transcript, reading copy, notes for meeting, DAP-HSTL, box 73. Acheson admired de Gaulle's conduct during the Cuba crisis of 1962. For his judgment of de Gaulle's European and NATO policies, however, see "Dean Acheson's Word for de Gaulle: 'Nonsense,'" *U.S. News and World Report*, 60, no. 16 (Apr. 12, 1966), 79–81 (an interview with Acheson). See also Acheson to Charles Gary, Feb. 25, 1955, DAP-SL; Acheson to F. Leith-Ross, Jan. 29, 1958, DAP-SL; Acheson press release, "Reply to Kennan," Jan. 11, 1958, copy in DAP-SL.

de Gaulle's siren call – Acheson found "aged, slower, and, so I thought, confused." When he was called with other "wise men" to talk to Lyndon Johnson about Vietnam in July 1965, he found his fellow advisers merely "fighting the problem." As he described the scene to Truman:

> Finally I blew my top and told him [LBJ] that he was wholly right in...Vietnam, that he had no choice except to press on, that explanations were not as important as successful action; and that the trouble in Europe...came about because under him and Kennedy there had been no American leadership at all. The idea that the Europeans could come to their own conclusions had led to an unchallenged de Gaulle.

Having negotiated with the Russians on Berlin, Acheson told the German ambassador in 1970 he "saw no more likelihood now than in earlier periods for any improvement in access or other recognition of interests other than Russian or East German interests." Around the same time he wrote of Monnet, "I am sure that when I see him next he will tell me, as he always does, that the unification of Europe is just around the corner, although it does seem to me that that corner is a receding one."[133]

In the end Acheson was too harsh with the Europeans and, as someone who had once believed in them, with himself. To call the idea "that the Europeans could come to their own conclusions" mistaken and foolish was a far cry from an earlier notion according to which "we must not confuse our own opinions with the will of God." When the latter notion had been genuinely put into practice, when Acheson had assisted his clients in doing what they genuinely wished to do – when the leader also knew how to follow – American policy, more often than not, had been successful. What the European states had genuinely wished to do during the years 1947–53 was to enhance their security and independence as individual states. The North Atlantic Treaty, the stationing of U.S. troops in Europe, an American Supreme Commander, the ECSC, Franco-German friendship, the restoration of German sovereignty all helped them to do so, and these were the achievements of the Achesonian period that stood. Acheson's legacy was the kind of American entanglement, or hegemony, in Europe that the Europeans themselves wanted or were prepared to accept.

That German rearmament five years after World War II, and then the

---

133. Acheson to William Tyler, Dec. 17, 1958, DAP-SL; Acheson to Lucius Clay, Jan. 4, 1962, DAP-SL; Acheson to Marshall Shulman, Nov. 23, 1961, DAP-SL; Acheson to Truman, July 10, 1965, DAP-SL; memo of Acheson's conversation with the German ambassador, Dec. 11, 1970, DAP-SL; Acheson to Shepard Stone, Jan. 3, 1970, DAP-SL.

EDC, did not fit into the acceptable category, Acheson's first instincts had told him at the time. That exerting perpetual pressure on the Soviet Union was not an acceptable solution for those living on the front lines – not even for Adenauer – was something that Acheson was never able to accept. This is probably because he had paid dearly in public life for having been associated with the Roosevelt–Stimson thesis about the Russians, because opposition to the Moscow regime sooner or later resolved itself into a question of conscience, and because he was convinced that a relaxation of tension in Europe would undermine all he had labored to create. Whatever Acheson himself came to think of the handiwork he had crafted together with the Europeans – unfinished, haphazard, prone to fall apart – it no doubt exhausted the objective possibilities – the facts – of the European situation at the time. As such it was an appropriate monument to the protégé of Brandeis who thrived on doing "hard, pioneering things."[134]

134. See Oliver Franks's comment on Acheson, Chapter 6, this volume.

Conclusion

For years historians will debate the causes, deep-seated and proximate, of the Soviet collapse and American victory in the cold war some forty-five years after it began – and whether the end of the cold war represents an "American victory" at all.[1] When the costs to the American economy are tallied up, it will have proved, at the very least, an expensive triumph. If, as has been claimed, the outcome of the ongoing political struggle between conservatives and reformers in Russia will prove "decisive for the entire continent," the next century is as likely to bring a new period of East–West conflict as it is a "new world order."[2] Any balance sheet concerning cold war winners and losers seems provisional and liable to be overthrown by new facts. The same is no doubt true of conclusions – though observers have not hesitated to draw them – concerning which of the protagonists of this book has been vindicated by history "in the end."[3]

1. For John Lewis Gaddis and Samuel Wells, for example, the collapse vindicated Truman's original policy and was due, among other causes, to sustained Western pressure. Other commentators – including Raymond Garthoff, Ronald Steel, and Hermann-Josef Rupieper – stress the enormous economic cost to the United States and emphasize that changes in Soviet policy are to be attributed to factors other than U.S. pressure, such as the example of the European Community and the independent decision of Gorbachev to abandon the notion of inevitable world conflict, in 1986. See Michael J. Hogan, ed., "The End of the Cold War: A Symposium" (Part 2), *Diplomatic History*, 16, no. 2 (Spring 1992), 223–318. During the 1992 presidential campaign, Kennan himself disputed the Republican claim that the United States had won the cold war. See "Who Won the Cold War? Ask Instead What Was Lost?" *International Herald Tribune*, Oct. 29, 1992.
2. On the Moscow political struggle and its possible implications see Franco Venturini, "Nuovi spettri a mosca," *Corriere della Sera*, Aug. 3, 1992. Yeltsin's armed conflict with the Russian Parliament – an event that does not bode well for the future of democracy in Russia – occurred during the final revisions of this book.
3. See, e.g., A. M. Schlesinger, Jr., "FDR's Vision Is Vindicated by History," *Wall Street Journal*, June 22–23, 1990, and Evan Thomas, "An Icon of the Cold War: Gorbachev

For now, FDR would seem to have been vindicated by the emergence of China as a great power, by the fall of the European empires, and above all by Russo-American cooperation within the Security Council of the United Nations. Kennan, by the same token, has been vindicated by the mellowing and breakup of Soviet power and by the emergence of an at least potentially autonomous European bloc with a powerful reunited Germany at its heart. It is doubtful that a continuous, unreconstructed Achesonian (or Adenauerian) policy of confrontation with Moscow and nonrecognition of East Germany – even if it had proved tolerable to Western public opinion – would have produced the end of the Soviet empire. Periods of détente and "change through rapprochement," to use the German Social Democratic phrase, were indispensable in order to plant the seeds of 1989.[4] Yet it is hard to believe that the changes of 1985–91 would have occurred in the absence of the Acheson-inspired policies of the late Carter and early Reagan years. Each of the three protagonists, in other words, has an indisputable claim to the partial vindication of his ideas. But equally striking are the ways in which hopes were betrayed or unfulfilled. "Alas," as Acheson says, quoting Holmes, at the end of his memoirs, "we cannot live our dreams."[5]

IN *THE AMBASSADORS*, Henry James's favorite novel, a middle-aged, mustachioed New Englander, Lambert Strether, long absent from the Old World, is sent by his patroness-fiancée, the formidable Mrs. Newsome, to bring home her twenty-eight-year-old son Chad, thought to be dissipating himself in the bohemian world of Paris. Instead, Strether finds the young man moving in the most rarefied of circles and refined and matured by his friendship with an older woman, the exquisite Marie de Vionnet. "'I came out to find myself in presence of new facts –,'" he says, "'facts that have kept striking me as less and less met by our old reasons.'" His self-appointed mission is now to "save" the relationship, which, in his naive and idealized vision of the couple, is "virtuous" in nature. Even after suffering disillusion on this last point, he loyally perseveres in his aim to keep the two together, at the cost of his own break with Mrs. Newsome. But neither is Chad really – he is tired of the Comptesse de Vionnet and ready for the new world of

Is Vindicating George Kennan's Views," *Newsweek*, Apr. 17, 1989. For arguments vindicating Acheson and Truman see the contributions by Gaddis and Wells in Hogan, ed., "The End of the Cold War."

4. On this point see Timothy Garton Ash, "Germany Unbound," *New York Review of Books*, 37, no. 18 (Nov. 22, 1990), 11–15.

5. Acheson, *Present*, 725.

American advertising – what Strether had imagined him to be: that is, what he himself at the same age under the same circumstances might have become. Strether is empty-handed – except for his dearly purchased knowledge and untroubled conscience – in the end.[6]

Kennan, on a Jamesian wavelength late in his life, wrote that the results of statesmanship never "bear anything other than an ironic relation to what the statesman in question intended to achieve and thought he was achieving."[7] Even allowing for the hyperbole, this observation applies with a certain frequency to twentieth century American statesmen and their dealings with the Old World. Roosevelt's announced plans to leave Europe ultimately made it more likely that the United States would stay; Kennan's analysis of the Soviet Union, which he hoped would provide the basis for preventing a freezing of the blocs, had, if anything, the opposite effect; Acheson's attempt to force the pace of European unification in 1951–52 may have helped to slow it down.

Kennan's aperçu is no doubt partly to be explained by the fact that a statesman's goals, or at least the means for achieving them, themselves change and adapt according to what circumstances – the facts – will permit. For example, the UN blueprint that emerged in anticipation of the 1944 election campaign was a far cry from what Roosevelt had originally intended and ill-suited to his vision of great-power regional hegemony. Kennan's call for negotiations with Moscow over Germany in 1948–49 was not something he had imagined in 1946–47. The intention to keep large numbers of U.S. troops permanently on the Continent was one that Acheson had honestly denied. But the deeper reason for the often ironic relation between conscious intentions and perceptions, on one hand, and concrete results, on the other, is the inevitable element of wishfulness and self-deception in the statesman's vision.

The visions under consideration here were composites of widely shared ideas and lucid insights melded with feelings and aspirations unique and personal to the point of producing an obliviousness to reality – of the kind affecting Strether when he fails to recognize the element of vicariousness in his view of Chad. How else can one explain the persistence with which Roosevelt believed in the possibility of reviving something resembling the good old pre-1870 Germany? The same question could be asked of Kennan's belief that it was simply not in the historical cards for the United States to become a European power. It is

6. Henry James, *The Ambassadors* (1903) (Harmondsworth: Penguin, 1986), 300.
7. GFK, "The Gorbachev Prospect."

the similar, wishful element that explains Acheson's persistent belief in the viability of the nineteenth century European empires.

The deep, private, quasi-obsessive nature of certain convictions fostered self-deception as to the views and reactions of others – of the kind affecting Strether when he has difficulty seeing that Chad's family do not see, and have no interest in seeing, what he sees and that he himself is being used. Unshakable in his view of American superiority and European decadence, Roosevelt underestimated the depth of Europe's will to survive and renew itself, a reaction galvanized, moreover, by his own plans. He also deceived himself about his ability to pull the wool over the eyes of his Wilsonian constituency while simultaneously reassuring the Russians that they were not going to be deceived. Kennan deceived himself in thinking that his lay colleagues would grasp from his cogent prose and then act upon his highly intuitive sense of Soviet weakness, also in thinking that the Europeans themselves – the survivors of World War II – might share his aspiration for an autonomous Continental unit including Germany. Acheson deceived himself when he came to believe that his propitiatory style of diplomacy might foster a historic breakthrough in Europe and when he convinced himself that he truly understood the Soviet Union after having traded one stereotypical view of that country for another. Each of the three deceived himself or fell short of his objectives when he imagined that America, or he personally, held the key to resolving the European Question in ways that ran against the grain of what the Europeans themselves wanted or could accept.

IF THE VISIONS OF STATESMEN tend to crack on hard reality, often producing ironic results, the more suggestive and resonant elements nonetheless survive as part of diplomatic culture. The notion of the Old World shackled and semiretired – the visceral worry being German power, ambition, and diplomatic mobility – while a loose concert of new, non-European status quo powers including China and the Soviet Union collaborates to run the world is present in the outlook of Henry Kissinger, as is Roosevelt's preoccupation with economy in the management of a global foreign policy. Kissinger did not really believe a united, federal Europe was in America's interest anymore than did FDR. Such a Europe "might be forced into an anti-American mold because its only sense of identity could be what distinguished it from America." A safer kind of European unity, wrote Kissinger, was one that "would enable the United States to maintain an influence at many centers of decision rather than be forced to stake everything on affecting the views of a single, supranational body" – a kind of "unity," FDR would have understood, permitting Washington to pursue a policy of *divide et impera.* "For us," Kissinger said in announcing his "Year of Europe" initiative in 1973, "European unity is...not an end in itself but a means to the strengthening of the West." The Soviets captured something of the spirit animating Kissinger's détente diplomacy when they decided to hold the final Nixon–Brezhnev summit near the site of the Crimea conference.[8]

With the East bloc starting to crumble in early 1989, Kissinger's former State Department assistant, Helmut Sonnenfeldt – who had propounded the "Sonnenfeldt Doctrine" in 1975 – called for the "Finlandization" of Moscow's satellites. Such had been Roosevelt's hope, if not really his expectation, in 1943–45: to tie the "loose cannon" states of Eastern Europe to Moscow in a way that would satisfy Soviet security concerns while preserving a degree of internal pluralism. During the same month Kissinger himself proposed a plan for high-level East–West talks leading to new arrangements for Europe that were quickly dubbed "Yalta II." A basic objection of State Department officials to the plan was that instead of working to overcome the division of Europe, it might "involve U.S. complicity in consigning Eastern Europe permanently to the Soviet sphere of influence." Franklin Roosevelt, finally, would surely have endorsed the argument of one of Kissinger's former Harvard colleagues who wrote of the emerging Europe of the late 1980s: "The political integration of the European Community, if that should occur, would also bring into existence an extraordinarily powerful entity which could not help but be perceived as a major threat to American interests." The United States should therefore promote the "evolution of the European Community in the direction of a looser, purely economic entity with broader membership rather than a tighter political entity with an integrated foreign policy." To paraphrase FDR's suggestion at Tehran, the rest of the world was better off when Europe was divided into "107 provinces."[9]

The difference between the outlook just described and the opposite postwar view is a continuation of the early twentieth century difference of opinion between those (Theodore Roosevelt, Stimson, and FDR) who

8. Kissinger, "What Kind of Atlantic Partnership?" 31, 33; Kissinger, "A New Atlantic Charter," *Atlantic Community Quarterly,* 2, no. 3 (Summer 1973), 155.
9. See Cesare de Carlo, "Cosa cambia per l'URSS dopo Kabul" (interview with Helmut Sonnenfeldt), *Il Resto del Carlino* (Bologna), Feb. 15, 1989. On Kissinger "plan" see Don Oberdorfer, "Kissinger Offers Bush an East–West Plan on Central Europe," *International Herald Tribune,* Feb. 13, 1989. See also Samuel Huntington, "America's Changing Strategic Interests," *Survival,* 33 (Jan. 1991), 12. Roosevelt quoted in *FRUS, Conferences at Cairo and Tehran,* 603.

tended to see Germany and Japan as permanent threats to the United States, with autocratic Russia as a suitable collaborator, and those (Mackinder, Mahan, the elder Kennan, and their followers) who sought to use German and Japanese power to contain Russia.[10] In its postwar, or Kennan-esque, incarnation, this latter tendency of thought has emphasized the overcoming of the division of Europe, or "Yalta system," the American interest in a relatively autonomous European Third Force, and the transformation of the Soviet Union as a prerequisite of its collaboration with the West. Kennan had no personal liking for John Foster Dulles, the man who ended his Foreign Service career in early 1953 and who failed to protect friends and colleagues like John Paton Davies and Charles Thayer. Of Dulles's policies, however, he wrote: "He knew he was going to have to follow *in practice* the line I had laid down, and I think he didn't want me around Washington in any resident capacity, because he didn't want it to be said that I was inspiring his ideas." By his "line" Kennan meant a diplomatic approach to getting the Soviets out of Eastern Europe, as opposed to the bombastic "roll back" with which Dulles became associated during the 1952 campaign. Kennan believed that his 1957 disengagement proposal "disconcerted" Dulles because the secretary of state "knew there was something in it, but it was all, in his opinion, much too fast for the development of Congressional opinion here and in this he was probably right." In fact, the "unexpected Dulles," to use John Lewis Gaddis's description, himself toyed with a similar proposal for "broad zones of restricted armament" in Europe. He shared Kennan's sense that the Soviet system was basically weak and that time was on the side of the West. Both were committed to the idea of a strong Japan and a solid federal Europe that would be able to counterbalance Russia with limited help from abroad.[11]

The most Kennan-esque of major postwar figures – at least in his basic vision of Europe – is probably Zbigniew Brzezinski, someone who given his nationality and social extraction might have risked ending in the Katyn Forest had he been born in 1918 instead of 1928. Perhaps because he learned something from the official reception accorded

---

10. See the discussion of this point in Chapter 1, this volume.
11. The Eisenhower administration failed to find a State Department assignment for GFK (though Allen Dulles offered him a CIA job), obliging him to retire a year earlier than he would have liked. For Kennan's view of Dulles see the interview he gave on March 3, 1967, to Richard Challener for the Dulles Oral History project, Seeley Mudd Library, Princeton University; emphasis in original. See also John Lewis Gaddis, "The Unexpected John Foster Dulles: Nuclear Weapons, Communism, and the Russians," in Richard Immerman, ed., *John Foster Dulles and the Diplomacy of the Cold War: A Reappraisal* (Princeton, N.J.: Princeton University Press, 1990), 63–76.

Kennan's Reith Lectures, Brzezinski's personal design for the liberation of Eastern Europe through mutual disengagement consisted of a gradual, step-by-step process in which the Europeans themselves were important actors rather than a signed and sealed accommodation between the Soviet Union and the United States. On the fortieth anniversary of the Yalta Conference, he called for the kind of phased withdrawals of U.S. troops from Western Europe that, he believed at the time, were the premise of political liberalization in the East.[12] The underlying reasoning was identical to Kennan's own.

By the mid-eighties, and probably well before, Brzezinski saw the USSR as "a giant with steel hands but rotten innards." Like Kennan, he stressed the potential political-ideological pull of a united Western Europe on the Eastern countries and saw – from his fundamentally Mackinderian perspective – a more cohesive and militarily self-reliant European Community as something to be *welcomed*, not feared, by an America with its hands full at other points on the periphery of Eurasia. Both Kennan and Brzezinski were in basic sympathy, despite some reservations, with the great denouncer of the "Yalta system" and apostle of European autonomy, de Gaulle. Speaking of the notion "Europe from the Atlantic to the Urals," Kennan said, "I was a Gaullist before de Gaulle." In truth, Kennan's had been a Europe from Brest to Brest-Litovsk, but he shared de Gaulle's hope for an *inherent* European balance – that is, one with minimal reliance on Anglo-Saxon backing. Like de Gaulle, Brzezinski believed in the "organic connection between the willingness to defend yourself and your internal political health." With cold war tensions still running high in 1986, he said that reducing the U.S. military presence in Europe "would compel Europeans to undertake a sober assessment of the security position and of their responsibility in regard to it." Not surprisingly, the Polish emigrant and the former diplomat who had favored a showdown with Moscow after the Warsaw uprising found themselves together in opposing what they saw as Kissinger's proposal for artificially prolonging the division of Europe in early 1989. The striking difference between the two concerned the role of human rights in foreign policy – Brzezinski preferring an activist approach, Kennan practically none at all. The message of both, however, was that the American example – the successful functioning of the domestic system – is, or should be, the nation's fundamental asset in foreign affairs.[13]

12. See Zbigniew Brzezinski, *Alternative to Partition* (New York: McGraw, 1965). See also Brzezinski, "The Future of Yalta," *Foreign Affairs*, 63, no. 2 (Winter 1984–85), 279–302, esp. 298–99.
13. See Zbigniew Brzezinski, *Game Plan: A Geostrategic Framework for the Conduct of the U.S.–Soviet Contest* (Boston: Atlantic Monthly Press, 1986); "A Conversation

IF THERE HAS BEEN a predominant tendency in U.S. policy toward the Old World since the early fifties, it has been neither Rooseveltian nor Kennan-esque. Rather, it has been the kind of compromise that emerged during Acheson's tenure as secretary of state – reflecting the wishes of the Europeans themselves – between the impulse to control Europe and the desire to restore it. Following Acheson's example, U.S. policy makers have with few exceptions been sincere supporters of European integration on the grounds that a united Europe would provide a growing market for U.S. goods and generate the resources and cohesiveness to allow Europe to share America's burdens both on the Continent and "out of area." But the same policy makers have had ample reason to doubt the willingness of the European states themselves to enter into arrangements seriously impairing their sovereignty or bilateral channels of (reciprocal) influence with Washington, and they have developed serious reservations about the desirability of such arrangements from the U.S. point of view.

The Americans have feared economic exclusion and greater competition but, above all, a loss of political control. Both Acheson's personal and subsequent general American experience have suggested to Washington that with or without the Soviet Union the European states, left to their own devices, would be incapable of organizing an effective political-military coalition and that the European state system tends, as Jefferson, Wilson, and Roosevelt believed, toward national egoism and war. By and large, the Western European elites themselves have accepted this point of view.[14] Yet if the Europeans did succeed in organizing themselves into an effective and relatively autonomous third force, there is little reason to believe that it would see eye to eye on important questions with the United States. The North Atlantic Treaty framework has therefore served to promote a degree of European cohesion and unity – the Europeans themselves were the first to argue that the Atlantic umbrella was indispensable to that end – while acting as a

with Zbigniew Brzezinski" (conducted by Owen Harries), *National Interest*, no. 5 (Fall 1986), 29–30; Brzezinski, "Selective Global Containment," *Foreign Affairs*, 70, no. 4 (Fall 1991), 9–10. On Kennan's view of the Gaullist project see his letter to Countess Marion Dönhoff, Mar. 15, 1965, GKP. On Brzezinski's opposition to the Kissinger plan see Stephen S. Rosenfeld, "Eastern Europe: Neither 'Yalta' nor Silent Inertia," *International Herald Tribune*, Apr. 25, 1989; on Kennan's opposition, see Thomas. See also GFK, "Morality and Foreign Policy," *Foreign Affairs*, 64, no. 2 (Winter 1984–85), 205–18; Zbigniew Brzezinski, *Power and Principle: Memoirs of the National Security Adviser, 1977–1981* (New York: Farrar, Strauss, & Giroux, 1985), 124–28.

14. For a sophisticated European expression of this point of view, arguing for the abiding need for U.S. leadership, see Josef Joffe, "Europe's American Pacifier," *Foreign*

ceiling beyond which it cannot go. By and large, as Kissinger said, "American policy has been extremely ambivalent: it has urged European unity while recoiling before its probable consequences."[15] In so doing, he might have added, American policy has faithfully reflected the feelings of the European states themselves.

Ambivalence became the established pattern in the early sixties when Kennedy's "grand design" clashed with the European Economic Community's Common Agricultural Policy and de Gaulle's vision of a European confederation and greater political-military autonomy. On one hand, the Kennedy administration enthusiastically supported the notions of a "deepened" federal Europe and an "equal Atlantic partnership."[16] On the other, it encouraged Britain, the least federalist of nations, to take the lead of Europe in order to turn the European Community in the outward-looking, liberal direction congenial to U.S. commercial interests and to counterbalance Gaullist France. Washington also tried to tighten its military hegemony through the "flexible response" strategy while getting the Europeans to pay more for their defense. The outcome was stalemate. De Gaulle blocked British entry into the community. Under French pressure the Europeans set up the Common Agricultural Policy and henceforth dealt with the United States on trade questions as a single bloc. At the same time, Washington isolated France by inviting Bonn to reject de Gaulle's design for Franco-German security arrangements that would have weakened NATO.

It is instructive to compare the late fifties and early sixties with the late eighties and early nineties. The European Single Market program and progress toward political and military integration triggered a similar set of reactions. The United States gave its blessing to the 1992 initiative, but only in the context of a high-pressure campaign to prevent the emergence of "Fortress Europe," accompanied by the effort to forge a tighter political link between Washington and Brussels. For his part, George Bush proclaimed that his administration had gone beyond America's "historic ambivalence" toward a united Europe. Faced with rising U.S. budget deficits and the problems of how to help the former Eastern satellites and safely house a reunited Germany, Washington saw its interest in a more cohesive, self-reliant Europe, as it had thirty years

Policy, no. 54 (Spring 1984), 64–82. For Joffe, Europe is a "continent whose strategic importance in this century has been dwarfed only by its inability to manage its own security affairs when left alone" (82).

15. Kissinger, "What Kind of Atlantic Partnership?" 30.

16. See George Ball, "NATO and World Responsibility," *Atlantic Community Quarterly*, 2, no. 2 (Summer 1964), 216.

before. Nonetheless, Bush's claim was dubious when measured against subsequent events.[17]

The American reaction to the Franco-German appeal for "European Union," including "a common foreign and security policy," was not overly enthusiastic. European behavior during the Persian Gulf crisis of 1990–91 allowed the Americans to express the doubts about a European defense pillar that they would have advanced in any case, but more forcefully and cogently than otherwise would have been the case. The European states reacted to the crisis according to considerations of traditional national interest. The Germans, preoccupied with their internal problems, did not really react at all. When Bonn and Paris nonetheless entertained the idea of a European Community–controlled defense caucus that would speak with a single voice within the alliance, Washington warned them in no uncertain terms to abandon the idea. It was the kind of structure, Washington feared, that would prove incapable of acting in an emergency; an unspoken fear was perhaps that it might eventually work all too well.

Washington's pressure seemed aimed at splitting the nascent Franco-German security axis, as in 1963. As in the early sixties – and the early fifties – London and The Hague opposed European arrangements that might short-circuit their direct relationships with Washington or give the Americans an excuse to go home. The eventual compromise within NATO, adopted a month before the signature of the Maastricht Treaty, endorsed the notion of a "European defense identity," but reaffirmed that NATO was the "essential forum for consultation . . . and the venue for agreement on policies bearing on the security and defence commitments of Allies under the Washington Treaty [of 1949]."[18] Europe's hesitant, ineffectual reaction during the agony of Bosnia in 1992–93 did little to alter either Washington's old conviction that a more dynamic, responsible, and cohesive European entity was needed in order to share America's burdens – or its belief that the Europeans were incapable of taking incisive action on their own.

17. The November 1990 U.S.–European Community joint declaration institutionalized a series of consultations at all levels between Washington and Brussels. For Bush's May 1989 Boston University commencement speech see Department of State *Bulletin*, July 1989, 18–19. For this period I rely heavily on my "The United States and the European Community on the Eve of 1993," in Sergio Romano, ed., *L'Impero riluttante* (Milan: ISPI, 1992), 93–126.

18. See Harper, "The United States and the European Community." See also "Rome Declaration on Peace and Cooperation," Nov. 8, 1991, adopted by the heads of state and government during the Rome meeting of the North Atlantic Council, Nov. 7–8, 1991, NATO Press Service, Brussels.

In general, the experience of the early nineties suggested that genuine European union was incompatible with the kind of hegemony to which the Americans had grown accustomed and which – despite the novel flexibility toward Europe on security questions, and domestic priorities, of the Clinton administration – they were hesitant to give up. The period also indicated that despite the end of the cold war, the Western Europeans, as well as the former Soviet satellites, still preferred American leadership and protection to the alternative of European union involving the real surrender of sovereignty in the fields of defense and foreign policy and the dilution of their autonomous national links to the United States. By the mid-nineties neither party to the relationship saw the status quo as either salutary or tenable. But American ambivalence about greater European unity and autonomy from the United States continued to be matched and reinforced by European ambivalence, the enduring pattern since 1952.

Bibliography

Unpublished material

The Library of Congress, Manuscripts Division
Joseph Davies Papers
W. Averell Harriman Papers

The George C. Marshall Foundation, Lexington, Va.
C. Ben Wright Kennan Biography Project

The Seeley G. Mudd Manuscript Library, Princeton University
George F. Kennan Papers

The National Archives, Washington, D.C.
Record Group 59, General Records of the Department of State
Decimal Files
Records of the Policy Planning Staff

The Public Record Office, Kew
Record Class FO 371, General Records of the Foreign Office
Record Class FO 800, General Records of the Foreign Office (Ernest Bevin
Papers)
Record Class FO 954, General Records of the Foreign Office (Anthony Eden
Papers)

The Franklin D. Roosevelt Library, Hyde Park, New York
Adolf A. Berle Diaries
Adolf A. Berle Papers
Copies of Materials from Other Repositories
Delano Family Papers
Harry L. Hopkins Papers
Henry Morgenthau, Jr., Presidential Diary
Roosevelt Family: Papers Donated by the Children of Franklin D. and Eleanor
Roosevelt
Roosevelt Family Papers
Franklin D. Roosevelt Papers
Papers Pertaining to Family, Business and Personal Affairs

Papers as Assistant Secretary of the Navy, 1913–20
Papers as Vice-Presidential Candidate, 1920
Papers, 1920–28
Papers as President: Map Room Papers (MR)
Papers as President: Official File (OF)
Papers as President: President's Personal File (PPF)
Papers as President: President's Secretary's File (PSF)
James Roosevelt Papers

The Sterling Memorial Library, Yale University
Dean G. Acheson Papers
Henry L. Stimson Diary, Microfilm version
Arthur Willert Papers

The Harry S. Truman Library, Independence, Mo.
Dean G. Acheson Papers
Clark M. Clifford Papers
George M. Elsey Papers
Harry B. Price Papers (Interviews on the Marshall Plan)
Frank N. Roberts Papers
Charles W. Thayer Papers
Harry S. Truman Papers
    President's Secretary's Files, 1945–53
    White House Central Files, 1945–53
Oral History Interviews
    Dean Acheson
    Theodore Achilles
    Konrad Adenauer
    Edward W. Barrett
    Lucius Battle
    Richard Bissell
    Henri Bonnet
    David K. E. Bruce
    Robert L. Dennison
    Elbridge Durbrow
    George M. Elsey
    Oliver Franks
    W. Averell Harriman
    John D. Hickerson
    Walter H. Judd
    Robert A. Lovett
    Roger M. Makins
    H. Freeman Matthews
    Livingston Merchant
    Jules Moch
    Paul H. Nitze
    Dirk U. Stikker
    James E. Webb

Published primary sources

Acheson, David, and David McClellan, eds. *Among Friends: Personal Letters of Dean Acheson.* New York: Dodd, Mead, 1980.

Berle, Beatrice, and Travis Beal Jacobs, eds. *Navigating the Rapids, 1918–1971: The Papers of Adolf A. Berle.* New York: Harcourt Brace Jovanovich, 1973.

Bland, Larry, ed. *George C. Marshall Interviews and Reminiscences for Forrest C. Pogue.* Lexington, Va.: George C. Marshall Research Foundation, 1991.

Blum, John Morton, ed. *From the Morgenthau Diaries.* 3 vols. Boston: Houghton Mifflin, 1959–67.

The Price of Vision: The Diary of Henry Wallace, 1942–1946. Boston: Houghton Mifflin, 1973.

Bullitt, Orville H., ed. *For the President, Personal and Secret: Correspondence Between Franklin D. Roosevelt and William C. Bullitt.* Boston: Houghton Mifflin, 1972.

Campbell, Thomas, and George Herring, eds. *The Diaries of Edward Stettinius, Jr., 1943–1946.* New York: New Viewpoints, 1975.

Colville, John. *The Fringes of Power: Downing Street Diaries, 1939–1953.* London: Hodder & Stoughton, 1976.

Correspondence between the Chairman of the Council of Ministers of the U.S.S.R. and the Presidents of the U.S.A. and the Prime Ministers of Great Britain during the Great Patriotic War, 1941–1945. Moscow: FLPH, 1957.

Dilkes, David, ed. *The Diaries of Sir Alexander Cadogan, O.M., 1938–1945.* London: Cassell, 1971.

Dodd, William E., Jr., and Martha Dodd, eds. *Ambassador Dodd's Diary, 1933–1938.* New York: Harcourt Brace, 1941.

Freedman, Max, ed. *Roosevelt and Frankfurter: Their Correspondence, 1928–1945.* Boston: Little, Brown, 1967.

Gwynn, S., ed. *The Letters and Friendships of Cecil Spring-Rice.* Vol. 1: *A Record.* London: Constable, 1929.

Hassett, William D. *Off the Record with FDR, 1942–1945.* New Brunswick, N.J.: Rutgers University Press, 1958.

Hendrick, Burton J., ed. *The Life and Letters of Walter Hines Page.* London: William Heinemann, 1930.

Hooker, N. H., ed. *The Moffat Papers.* Cambridge, Mass.: Harvard University Press, 1956.

Howe, Mark de Wolfe, ed. *Holmes–Laski Letters: The Correspondence of Mr. Justice Holmes and Harold J. Laski, 1916–1935.* Cambridge, Mass.: Harvard University Press, 1953.

Holmes–Pollock Letters: The Correspondence of Mr. Justice Holmes and Sir Frederick Pollock, 1874–1932. 2 vols. Cambridge, Mass.: Harvard University Press, 1961.

Ickes, Harold L. *The Secret Diary of Harold L. Ickes.* Vol. 2: *The Inside Struggle, 1936–39.* London: Weidenfeld & Nicholson, 1955.

Kimball, Warren F., ed. *Churchill and Roosevelt: Their Complete Correspondence*. 3 vols. Princeton, N.J.: Princeton University Press, 1984.

Lash, Joseph P., ed. *From the Diaries of Felix Frankfurter*. New York: Norton, 1974.

Loewenheim, Francis L., Harold D. Langley, and Manfred Jonas, eds. *Roosevelt and Churchill: Their Secret Wartime Correspondence*. New York: Dutton, 1975.

Moggridge, Donald, ed. *The Collected Writings of John Maynard Keynes*. Vols. 23, 24, and 26. London: Macmillan; Cambridge: Cambridge University Press, 1979.

Moran, Lord. *Churchill: Taken from the Diaries of Lord Moran*. Boston: Houghton Mifflin, 1965.

Morison, Elting, ed. *The Letters of Theodore Roosevelt*. 8 vols. Cambridge, Mass.: Harvard University Press, 1951.

Nixon, Edgar, ed. *Franklin D. Roosevelt and Foreign Affairs*. New York: Clearwater, 1969.

Nowell, Elizabeth, ed. *The Letters of Thomas Wolfe*. New York: Scribners, 1956.

Rauch, Basil, ed. *Franklin D. Roosevelt: Selected Speeches, Messages, Press Conferences, and Letters*. New York: Holt & Rinehart, 1957.

Roosevelt, Elliott, ed. *FDR: His Personal Letters*. 4 vols. New York: Duell, Sloan & Pearce, 1947–50.

Roosevelt, Franklin Delano. *Development of U.S. Foreign Policy: Addresses and Messages of FDR*. Washington, D.C.: U.S. Government Printing Office, 1942.

Rosenman, Samuel L., ed. *The Public Papers and Addresses of Franklin D. Roosevelt*. 13 vols. New York: Russell & Russell, 1938–50.

Safire, William, ed. *Lend Me Your Ear: Great Speeches in History*. New York: Norton, 1992.

Seager, Robert III, and D. Maguire, eds. *The Letters and Papers of Alfred Thayer Mahan*. 3 vols. Annapolis, Md.: Naval Institute Press, 1975.

U.S. Department of State, *Foreign Relations of the United States*. Various vols. Washington, D.C.: U.S. Government Printing Office, 1933–53.

Vandenberg, Arthur H., Jr., ed. *The Private Papers of Senator Vandenberg*. Boston: Houghton Mifflin, 1952.

Van Der Poel, Jan, ed. *Selections From the Smuts Papers*. Vol. 4. Cambridge: Cambridge University Press, 1973.

Books and dissertations

Acheson, Dean. *A Democrat Looks at His Party*. New York: Harper Bros., 1955.

Morning and Noon. Boston: Houghton Mifflin, 1965.

Present at the Creation: My Years at the State Department. New York: Norton, 1969.

Sketches from Life of Men I Have Known. New York: Harper Bros., 1959.

Adams, Brooks. *America's Economic Supremacy* (1900). New York: Harper Bros., 1947.

Adams, Henry. *The Degradation of the Democratic Doctrine* (1919). New York: Peter Smith, 1949.

The Education of Henry Adams: An Autobiography. Boston: Houghton Mifflin, 1918.

A History of the United States of America During the Administrations of Jefferson and Madison. One-volume ed. based on 1921 ed. Chicago: University of Chicago Press, 1967.

Adenauer, Konrad. *Memoirs, 1945–1953.* London: Weidenfeld & Nicolson, 1966.

Aglion, Raoul. *Roosevelt and De Gaulle: Allies in Conflict – A Personal Memoir.* New York: Free Press, 1988.

Alsop, Joseph. *FDR, 1892–1945: A Centenary Remembrance.* New York: Viking Press, 1982.

Alsop, Joseph, with Alan Platt. *"I've Seen the Best of It": The Memoirs of Joseph Alsop.* New York: Norton, 1993.

Ambrose, Stephen. *Eisenhower.* Vol. 1: *Soldier, General of the Army, President Elect, 1890–1952.* New York: Simon & Schuster, 1983.

Anderson, Harry, ed. *German-American Pioneers in Wisconsin and Michigan: The Frank Kerber Letters, 1849–1864.* Milwaukee, Wis.: Milwaukee County Historical Society, 1971.

Anderson, Terry H. *The United States, Great Britain, and the Cold War, 1944–47.* Columbia, Mo.: University of Missouri Press, 1981.

Auchincloss, Louis. *The Romantic Egoists.* Boston: Houghton Mifflin, 1954.

Backer, John H. *The Decision to Divide Germany: American Foreign Policy in Transition.* Durham, N.C.: Duke University Press, 1978.

Bark, Dennis L., and David R. Gress. *A History of West Germany.* Vol. 1: *From Shadow to Substance, 1945–1963.* London: Basil Blackwell, 1989.

Barnett, Correlli. *The Collapse of British Power.* New York: William Morrow, 1972.

Beale, Howard. *Theodore Roosevelt and the Rise of America to World Power.* Baltimore: Johns Hopkins University Press, 1956.

Beecroft, J., ed. *The Gentleman from Indianapolis: A Treasury of Booth Tarkington.* Garden City, N.Y.: Doubleday, 1957.

Beneš, Eduard. *The Memoirs of Dr. Eduard Beneš.* New York: Arno Press, 1972.

Ben-Moshe, Tuvia. *Churchill: Strategy and History.* New York: Lynne Rienner, 1992.

Berlin, Isaiah. *Personal Impressions.* Harmondsworth: Penguin, 1982.

Beschloss, Michael R. *Kennedy and Roosevelt: The Uneasy Alliance.* New York: Norton, 1980.

Blum, John Morton. *The Republican Roosevelt.* Cambridge, Mass.: Harvard University Press, 1954.

Bogart, Earnest, and Donald Kemmerer. *Economic History of the American People.* New York: Longman Green, 1942.

Bohlen, Charles E. *Witness to History, 1929–1969.* New York: Norton, 1973.

Bowen, Catherine Drinker. *Yankee from Olympus: Justice Holmes and His Family.* Boston: Little, Brown, 1943.

Bowers, Claude. *Jefferson and Hamilton.* Boston: Houghton Mifflin, 1925.

Brinkley, Douglas. *Dean Acheson: The Cold War Years, 1953–71.* New Haven, Conn.: Yale University Press, 1992.

Brinkley, Douglas, ed. *Dean Acheson and the Making of U.S. Foreign Policy.* New York: St. Martin's Press, 1993.

Brinkley, Douglas, and Clifford Hackett, eds. *Jean Monnet and the Path to European Unity.* New York: Macmillan, 1991.

Broadberry, S. N. *The British Economy Between the Wars.* Oxford: Basil Blackwell, 1986.

Brownell, Will, and Richard N. Billings. *So Close to Greatness: A Biography of William C. Bullitt.* New York: Macmillan, 1987.

Brzezinski, Zbigniew. *Alternative to Partition.* New York: McGraw-Hill, 1965.

Game Plan: A Geostrategic Framework for the Conduct of the U.S.–Soviet Contest. Boston: Atlantic Monthly Press, 1986.

Power and Principle: Memoirs of the National Security Adviser, 1977–1981. New York: Farrar, Strauss, & Giroux, 1985.

Buckley, Peter, ed. *Essential Papers on Object Relations.* New York: New York University Press, 1986.

Bullock, Alan. *Ernest Bevin, Foreign Secretary, 1945–1951.* New York: Norton, 1983.

Burk, Katherine. *Britain, America and the Sinews of War, 1914–1918.* Boston: Allen & Unwin, 1985.

Burns, James MacGregor. *Roosevelt: The Lion and the Fox.* New York: Harcourt, Brace, 1956.

Roosevelt: The Soldier of Freedom. New York: Harcourt Brace Jovanovich, 1970.

Butler, R. B., ed. *The Conservatives: A History from Their Origin to 1965.* London: Allen & Unwin, 1970.

Callaghan, David. *Dangerous Capabilities: Paul Nitze and the Cold War.* New York: Harper & Row, 1990.

Calleo, David P. *The German Problem Reconsidered.* New York: Cambridge University Press, 1978.

Careless, J. M. S., and R. Craig Brown, eds. *The Canadians, 1867–1967.* Toronto: Macmillan Co. of Canada, 1967.

Carlton, David. *Anthony Eden.* London: Allen & Lane, 1981.

Chadwin, Mark. *The Hawks of World War II.* Chapel Hill: University of North Carolina Press, 1968.

Chekhov, Anton. *The Cherry Orchard.* London: Heinemann, 1963.

Child, Clifton J. *The German-Americans in Politics, 1914–1917.* Madison: University of Wisconsin Press, 1939.

Churchill, Winston S. *The Second World War.* 6 vols. Boston: Houghton Mifflin, 1948–53.

Clay, Lucius. *Decision in Germany.* Garden City, N.Y.: Doubleday, 1950.

Clemens, Diane Shaver. *Yalta*. New York: Oxford University Press, 1970.

Clough, Shepard. *European Economic History*. New York: McGraw-Hill, 1968.

Cook, Blanche Wiesen. *Eleanor Roosevelt*. Vol. 1: *1884–1933*. Harmondsworth: Penguin, 1993.

Cooper, John Milton, Jr. *The Warrior and the Priest: Woodrow Wilson and Theodore Roosevelt*. Cambridge, Mass.: Harvard University Press, 1983.

Crankshaw, Edward, and Strobe Talbott, eds. *Khrushchev Remembers*. London: Book Club Associates, 1971.

Croly, Herbert. *The Promise of American Life* (1909). New York: Anchon Books, 1963.

Dallek, Robert. *Franklin D. Roosevelt and American Foreign Policy, 1932–1945*. New York: Oxford University Press, 1979.

Daniels, Jonathan. *The End of Innocence*. Philadelphia: Lippincott, 1954.

Washington Quadrille. Garden City, N.Y.: Doubleday, 1968.

Daniels, Jonathan, Arthur Bestor, and David C. Mearns. *Three Presidents and Their Books*. Urbana: University of Illinois Press, 1955.

Daniels, Josephus. *The Wilson Era*. Vol. 2: *1917–1923*. Chapel Hill: University of North Carolina Press, 1946.

Davis, Kenneth. *FDR: The New Deal Years, 1933–37*. New York: Random House, 1986.

De Gaulle, Charles. *The Complete War Memoirs of Charles de Gaulle, 1940–46*. Vol. 2: *Unity*. New York: Simon & Schuster, 1964.

Deibel, T. L., and John Lewis Gaddis, eds. *Containing the Soviet Union: A Critique of U.S. Policy*. Washington, D.C.: Pergamon-Brassey's International Defense Publishers, 1987.

DePorte, Anton. *De Gaulle's Foreign Policy, 1944–46*. Cambridge, Mass.: Harvard University Press, 1968.

De Tocqueville, Alexis. *Democracy in America* (1836). Vol. 1. New York: Vintage Books, 1961.

Divine, Robert A. *The Illusion of Neutrality*. Chicago: University of Chicago Press, 1962.

The Reluctant Belligerent: American Entry into World War II. New York: Wiley, 1965.

Roosevelt and World War II. Baltimore: Johns Hopkins University Press, 1969.

Second Chance: The Triumph of Internationalism in America During World War II. New York: Atheneum, 1967.

Djilas, Milovan. *Conversations with Stalin*. New York: Harcourt, Brace, & World, 1962.

Donovan, Robert J. *Conflict and Crisis: The Presidency of Harry S. Truman, 1945–1948*. New York: Norton, 1977.

Drummond, Donald F. *The Passing of American Neutrality, 1937–1941*. Ann Arbor: University of Michigan Press, 1955.

Eden, Anthony. *The Reckoning*. London: Cassell, 1965.

Erickson, John. *Stalin's War with Germany*. Vol. 2: *The Road to Berlin*. London: Grafton Books, 1983.

Feis, Herbert. *Churchill–Roosevelt–Stalin: The War They Waged and the Peace They Sought.* Princeton, N.J.: Princeton University Press, 1957.

Europe: The World's Banker, 1870–1914. New York: A. M. Kelley, 1964.

1933: Characters in Crisis. Boston: Little, Brown, 1966.

Ferdon, Nora. "FDR: A Psychological Interpretation of His Childhood and Youth." Ph.D. diss., University of Hawaii, 1971.

Fitzgerald, F. Scott. *The Great Gatsby.* New York: Scribners, 1925.

This Side of Paradise (1920). New York: Collier Books, 1986.

Fowler, W. B. *British–American Relations, 1912–1918: The Role of Sir William Wiseman.* Princeton, N.J.: Princeton University Press, 1969.

Freidel, Frank. *Franklin D. Roosevelt: The Apprenticeship.* Boston: Little, Brown, 1952.

Franklin D. Roosevelt: The Ordeal. Boston: Little, Brown, 1954.

Franklin D. Roosevelt: A Rendezvous with Destiny. Boston: Little, Brown, 1990.

Fursdon, Edward. *The European Defense Community: A History.* London: Macmillan, 1980.

Gabriel, Jürg Martin. *The American Conception of Neutrality after 1941.* London: Macmillan, 1988.

Gaddis, John Lewis. *Strategies of Containment: A Critical Appraisal of Postwar American National Security Policy.* New York: Oxford University Press, 1982.

Gannon, Robert. *The Cardinal Spellman Story.* Garden City, N.Y.: Doubleday, 1962.

Gardner, Lloyd C. *Architects of Illusion: Men and Ideas in American Foreign Policy, 1941–1949.* Chicago: Quandrangle Books, 1970.

A Covenant with Power: America and World Order from Wilson to Reagan. London: Macmillan, 1984.

Gardner, Lloyd C., Arthur M. Schlesinger, Jr., and Hans J. Morgenthau. *The Origins of the Cold War.* Waltham, Mass.: Ginn-Blaisdell, 1970.

Gardner, Richard N. *Sterling–Dollar Diplomacy in Current Perspective: The Origins and the Prospects of Our International Economic Order.* New York: Columbia University Press, 1980.

Gay, Peter. *Weimar Culture.* New York: Harper & Row, 1968.

Gellman, Barton. *Contending with Kennan.* New York: Praeger 1984.

Gellman, Irwin F. *Good Neighbor Diplomacy: United States Policies in Latin America, 1933–1945.* Baltimore: Johns Hopkins University Press, 1979.

George, Alexander, and Juliette George. *Woodrow Wilson and Colonel House: A Personality Study.* New York: Dover, 1964.

Gibbon, Edward. *The Decline and Fall of the Roman Empire.* 2 vols. Chicago: Encyclopedia Britannica Great Books Edition, 1952.

Gietz, Axel. *Die neue Alte Welt: Roosevelt, Churchill und die europaische Nachkriegsordnung.* Munich: Wilhelm Fink, 1986.

Gilbert, Martin. *Winston S. Churchill.* Vol. 7: *The Road to Victory, 1941–1945* Boston: Houghton Mifflin, 1986.

Gillingham, John. *Coal, Steel and the Rebirth of Europe, 1945–1955: The*

Germans and the French from Ruhr Conflict to European Community. Cambridge: Cambridge University Press, 1991.

Goldschmidt, Bertrand. *The Atomic Complex: A Worldwide Political History of Nuclear Energy.* La Grange Park, Ill.: American Nuclear Society, 1982.

Graebner, Norman, ed. *Ideas and Diplomacy.* New York: Oxford University Press, 1964.

Greenfield, Kent Roberts. *American Strategy in World War II: A Reconsideration.* Baltimore: Johns Hopkins University Press, 1963.

Gromyko, Andrei Andreevich. *Memories.* London: Hutchinson, 1989.

Hamalian, Leo, and Vera Von Wiren-Garczynski, eds. *Seven Russian Short Novel Masterpieces.* New York: Popular Library, 1967.

Harbutt, Fraser J. *The Iron Curtain: Churchill, America and the Origins of the Cold War.* New York: Oxford University Press, 1986.

Harper, John L. *America and the Reconstruction of Italy, 1945–1948.* Cambridge: Cambridge University Press, 1986.

Harriman, W. Averell, and Elie Abel. *Special Envoy to Churchill and Stalin, 1941–1946.* New York: Random House, 1975.

Harrod, Roy F. *The Life of John Maynard Keynes.* New York: St. Martin's Press, 1963.

Heinrichs, Waldo H. *Threshold of War: Frankin D. Roosevelt and American Entry into World War II.* New York: Oxford University Press, 1988.

Heller, Francis H., and John R. Gillingham, eds. *NATO: The Founding of the Alliance and the Integration of Europe.* New York: St. Martin's Press, 1992.

Herz, Martin. *David Bruce's "Long Telegram" of July 3, 1951.* Lanham, Md.: University Press of America, 1986.

Hingley, Ronald. *Joseph Stalin: Man and Legend.* London: Hutchinson, 1974.

Hixson, Walter. *George F. Kennan: Cold War Iconoclast.* New York: Columbia University Press, 1989.

Hobsbawn, Eric. *The Age of Capital, 1848–1875.* London: Weidenfeld & Nicholson, 1975.

Hofstadter, Richard. *The American Political Tradition and the Men Who Made It.* New York: Knopf, 1948.

Hogan, Michael. *The Marshall Plan: America, Britain, and the Reconstruction of Western Europe, 1947–1952.* Cambridge: Cambridge University Press, 1987.

Holsti, Ole R., Randolph M. Silverson, and Alexander L. George, eds. *Change in the International System.* Boulder, Colo.: Westview, 1980.

Howard, Michael. *Grand Strategy.* Vol. 4: *August 1942–September 1943.* London: HMSO, 1970.

Hull, Cordell. *The Memoirs of Cordell Hull.* 2 vols. London: Hodder & Stoughton, 1948.

Hurstfield, Julian. *America and the French Nation, 1939–1945.* Chapel Hill: University of North Carolina Press, 1986.

Immerman, Richard, ed. *John Foster Dulles and the Diplomacy of the Cold War: A Reappraisal.* Princeton, N.J.: Princeton University Press, 1990.

Iriye, Akira. *The Origins of the Second World War in Asia and the Pacific.* London: Longmans, 1987.

Issacson, Walter, and Evan Thomas. *The Wise Men: Six Friends and the World They Made.* New York: Simon & Schuster, 1986.

James, Henry. *The Ambassadors* (1903). Harmondsworth: Penguin, 1986.

The American (1876). Harmondsworth: Penguin, 1986.

The Europeans (1878). Harmondsworth: Penguin, 1986.

Hawthorne (1879). Ithaca: Great Seal Books, 1963.

An International Episode (1879). Harmondsworth: Penguin, 1985.

The Wings of the Dove (1902). Harmondsworth: Penguin, 1982.

Kaplan, Lawrence. *The United States and NATO: The Formative Years.* Lexington: University Press of Kentucky, 1984.

Kazin, Alfred. *On Native Grounds.* New York: Harcourt, Brace, & World, 1942.

Kellogg, Frederic Roger. *The Formative Essays of Justice Holmes: The Making of an American Legal Philosophy.* Westport, Conn.: Greenwood Press, 1987.

Kennan, George. *Siberia and the Exile System* (1891). With an introduction by George F. Kennan. Chicago: University of Chicago Press, 1958.

Kennan, George F. *American Diplomacy, 1900–1950.* New York: Mentor Books, 1951.

Around the Cragged Hill: A Personal and Political Philosophy. New York: Norton, 1992.

The Decline of Bismarck's European Order: Franco-Russian Relations, 1875–1890. Princeton, N.J.: Princeton University Press, 1979.

Democracy and the Student Left. Boston: Little, Brown, 1968.

The Fateful Alliance: France, Russia, and the Coming of the First World War. Manchester: Manchester University Press, 1984.

From Prague after Munich: Diplomatic Papers, 1938–1940. Princeton, N.J.: Princeton University Press, 1968.

Memoirs. Vol. 1: *1925–1950.* Boston: Little, Brown, 1967.

Memoirs. Vol. 2: *1950–1963.* Boston: Little, Brown, 1972.

Russia and the West Under Lenin and Stalin. Boston: Little, Brown, 1960.

Sketches from a Life. New York: Pantheon, 1989.

Soviet–American Relations. 2 vols. Princeton, N.J.: Princeton University Press, 1956–58.

Kennan, T. L. *Genealogy of the Kennan Family.* Milwaukee, Wis.: Cannon Printing Co., 1907.

Keynes, J. M. *The Economic Consequences of the Peace* (1919). London: Macmillan, 1921.

Kimball, Warren F. *The Juggler: Franklin Roosevelt as Wartime Statesman.* Princeton, N.J.: Princeton University Press, 1991.

Swords into Plowshares: The Morgenthau Plan for Defeated Nazi Germany, 1943–1946. Philadelphia: Lippincott, 1976.

Kindleberger, Charles. *A Financial History of Western Europe.* London: Allen & Unwin, 1984.

Kirkpatrick, Carroll, ed., *Roosevelt and Daniels*. Chapel Hill: University of North Carolina Press, 1952.

Kleeman, Rita Halle. *Gracious Lady: The Life of Sara Delano Roosevelt*. New York: Appleton-Century, 1935.

Konefesky, Samuel. *The Legacy of Holmes and Brandeis*. New York: Dacapo Press, 1974.

Korbel, Joseph. *Twentieth-Century Czechoslovakia*. New York: Columbia University Press, 1977.

Korman, Gerd. *Industrialists, Immigrants and Americanizers: The View from Milwaukee*. Madison: State Historical Society of Wisconsin, 1967.

Kuniholm, Bruce. *The Origins of the Cold War in the Near East: Great Power Conflict and Diplomacy in Iran, Turkey and Greece*. Princeton, N.J.: Princeton University Press, 1980.

Lacouture, Jean. *De Gaulle*. Vol. 1: *Le Rebelle, 1890–1944*. Paris: Editions du Seuil, 1984.

Langer, William L., and S. Everett Gleason. *The Challenge to Isolation, 1937–1940*. New York: Harper Bros., 1952.

The Undeclared War, 1940–41. New York: Harper Bros., 1953.

Laqueur, Walter. *Stalin: The Glasnost Revelations*. New York: Scribners, 1990.

Larrabee, Eric. *Commander in Chief: Franklin Delano Roosevelt, His Lieutenants, and Their War*. New York: Harper & Row, 1987.

Larson, Deborah Welch. *Origins of Containment: A Psychological Explanation*. Princeton, N.J.: Princeton University Press, 1985.

Lash, Joseph P. *Eleanor and Franklin*. New York: New American Library, 1973.

Roosevelt and Churchill, 1939–1941: The Partnership That Saved the West. New York: Norton, 1976.

Lea, Homer. *The Day of the Saxon*. New York: Harper Bros., 1912.

The Valor of Ignorance. New York: Harper Bros., 1909.

Leahy, William. *I Was There*. New York: Whittlesey House, 1950.

Leffler, Melvin P. *A Preponderance of Power: National Security, the Truman Administration and the Cold War*. Stanford, Calif.: Stanford University Press, 1992.

Lewis, Sinclair. *Dodsworth*. New York: Signet, 1929.

Main Street (1920). New York: Signet, 1980.

Lewis, W. L. *One Man's Education*. New York: Knopf, 1967.

Link, Arthur. *Wilson*. Vol. 5: *Campaigns for Progressivism and Peace, 1916–1917*. Princeton, N.J.: Princeton University Press, 1965.

Woodrow Wilson: Revolution, War and Peace. Arlington Heights, Ill.: Harlan Davidson, 1979.

Lippmann, Walter. *The Cold War*. New York: Harper Bros., 1947.

U.S. Foreign Policy: Shield of the Republic. Boston: Little, Brown, 1943.

U.S. War Aims. Boston: Little, Brown, 1944.

Louis, William Roger. *Imperialism at Bay: The United States and the Decolonization of the British Empire, 1941–45*. Oxford: Oxford University Press, 1977.

Lukacs, John A. *A New History of the Cold War*. Garden City, N.Y.: Anchor Books, 1966.

Lundestad, Geir. *The American Non-Policy towards Eastern Europe, 1943– 1947: Universalism in an Area Not of Essential Interest to the United States*. Oslo: Universitetsforlaget, 1978.

Lush, C. *The Autocrats: A Novel*. New York: Doubleday, Page, 1904.

Lynn, Kenneth, ed. *The American Society*. New York: G. Braziller, 1963.

MacDonald, Callum A. *The United States, Britain and Appeasement, 1936– 1939*. New York: St. Martin's Press, 1981.

Mackinder, Halford John. *Democratic Ideals and Reality: With Additional Papers* (1919). New York: Norton, 1962.

Maddux, Thomas. *Years of Estrangement: American Relations with the Soviet Union, 1933–41*. Tallahassee: University Press of Florida, 1980.

Mahan, Alfred Thayer. *The Problem of Asia*. New York: Harper Bros., 1900.

The Interest of America in Sea Power. New York: Harper Bros., 1897.

Malone, Dumas. *Jefferson the President: Second Term, 1805–1809*. Boston: Little, Brown, 1974.

Marks, Frederick W. III. *Wind over Sand: The Diplomacy of Franklin Roosevelt*. Athens: University of Georgia Press, 1988.

Mason, A. T. *Brandeis: A Free Man's Life*. New York: Village Press, 1956.

Mastny, Vojtech. *Russia's Road to the Cold War*. New York: Columbia University Press, 1979.

Matlaw, Ralph E., ed. *Anton Chekhov's Short Stories*. New York: Norton, 1979.

Matloff, Maurice. *Strategic Planning for Coalition Warfare*. Vol. 2: 1943–1944. Washington, D.C.: Office of the Chief of Military History, 1959.

Matloff, Maurice, and Edwin M. Snell. *Strategic Planning for Coalition Warfare*. Vol. 1: 1941–1942. Washington, D.C.: Office of the Chief of Military History, 1953.

May, Ernest, ed. *The Ultimate Decision: The President as Commander-in-Chief*. New York: G. Braziller, 1960.

Mayers, David. *George Kennan and the Dilemmas of U.S. Foreign Policy*. New York: Oxford University Press, 1988.

McClellan, David S. *Dean Acheson: The State Department Years*. New York: Dodd, Mead, 1976.

McCullough, David. *Truman*. New York: Simon & Schuster, 1992.

McJimsey, George. *Harry Hopkins*. Cambridge, Mass.: Harvard University Press, 1987.

McNeill, William Hardy. *America, Britain and Russia: Their Cooperation and Conflict, 1941–46*. London: Oxford University Press, 1953

Messer, Robert. *The End of an Alliance: James F. Byrnes, Roosevelt, Truman and the Origins of the Cold War*. Chapel Hill: University of North Carolina Press, 1982.

Miller, James E. *The United States and Italy, 1940–1950: The Politics and Diplomacy of Stabilization*. Chapel Hill: University of North Carolina Press, 1986.

Miller, Merle. *Plain Speaking: An Oral Biography of Harry S. Truman.* New York: Berkley Books, 1982.

Miller, Nathan. *FDR: An Intimate History.* Garden City, N.Y.: Doubleday, 1983.

Milward, Alan. *The Economic Effects of the World Wars on Britain.* London: Macmillan, 1970.

    The Reconstruction of Western Europe, 1945–51. Berkeley: University of California Press, 1984.

Miner, Steven M. *Between Churchill and Stalin: The Soviet Union, Great Britain, and the Origins of the Grand Alliance.* Chapel Hill: University of North Carolina Press, 1988.

Miscamble, Wilson D. "George F. Kennan, the Policy Planning Staff, and American Foreign Policy, 1947–1950." Ph.D. diss., Notre Dame University, 1980.

    George F. Kennan and the Making of American Foreign Policy, 1947–1950. Princeton, N.J.: Princeton University Press, 1992.

Monnet, Jean. *Memoirs.* Garden City, N.Y.: Doubleday, 1978.

Morgan, Ted. *FDR: A Biography.* New York: Simon & Schuster, 1985.

Murphy, Bruce Allen. *The Brandeis–Frankfurter Connection: The Secret Political Activities of Two Supreme Court Justices.* New York: Oxford University Press, 1982.

Murray, Arthur. *At Close Quarters.* London: J. Murray, 1946.

Nation, R. Craig. *Black Earth, Red Star: A History of Soviet Security Policy, 1917–1991.* Ithaca, N.Y.: Cornell University Press, 1992.

Nevins, Allan. *Ordeal of the Union.* Vol. 2. New York: Scribners, 1947.

Niebuhr, Reinhold. *The Children of Light and the Children of Darkness.* New York: Scribners, 1944.

Nisbet, Robert. *Roosevelt and Stalin: The Failed Courtship.* New York: Simon & Schuster, 1989.

Nitze, Paul H. *From Hiroshima to Glasnost: At the Center of Decision.* New York: Grove Weidenfeld, 1989.

Noshpitz, Joseph, ed. *Basic Handbook of Child Psychiatry.* Vol. 1. New York: Basic Books, 1979.

Offner, Donald. *American Appeasement: U.S. Foreign Policy and Germany, 1933–38.* Cambridge, Mass.: Harvard University Press, 1969.

Osgood, Robert E. *Ideals and Self Interest in American Foreign Policy.* Chicago: University of Chicago Press, 1953.

    NATO: The Entangling Alliance. Chicago: University of Chicago Press, 1962.

Parsons, Edward B. *Wilsonian Diplomacy: Allied–American Rivalries in War and Peace.* St. Louis, Mo.: Forum Press, 1978.

Penrose, E. F. *Economic Planning for the Peace.* Princeton, N.J.: Princeton University Press, 1953.

Perkins, Bradford. *The Great Rapprochement: England and the United States, 1895–1914.* New York: Atheneum, 1968.

Perkins, Frances. *The Roosevelt I Knew.* New York: Viking Press, 1946.

Peterson, Merrill. *The Jefferson Image in the American Mind.* New York: Oxford University Press, 1960.

Pierson, G. W. *Yale College: An Educational History, 1871–1921.* New Haven, Conn.: Yale University Press, 1952.

Pocock, J. G. A. *Virtue, Commerce and History.* Cambridge: Cambridge University Press, 1985.

Pogue, Forrest. *George C. Marshall: Ordeal and Hope, 1939–1942.* New York: Viking Press, 1966.

Polley, Michael. *A Biography of George Kennan: The Education of a Realist.* Lewiston, N.Y.: Edwin Mellen Press, 1990.

Potter, Jim. *The American Economy Between the Wars.* New York: Macmillan, 1974.

Pritchett, V. S. *Chekhov: A Spirit Set Free.* New York: Random House, 1988.

Range, Willard. *Franklin D. Roosevelt's World Order.* Athens: University of Georgia Press, 1959.

Ratner, Sidney, James Soltow, and Richard Sylla. *The Evolution of the American Economy.* New York: Basic Books, 1979.

Reynolds, David. *The Creation of the Anglo-American Alliance: A Study in Competitive Cooperation.* London: Europa Publications, 1981.

Rhodes, Richard. *The Making of the Atomic Bomb.* London: Simon & Schuster, 1986.

Riste, Olav, ed. *Western Security: The Formative Years – European and Atlantic Defense.* Oslo: Norwegian University Press, 1985.

Rock, William R. *Chamberlain and Roosevelt: British Foreign Policy and the United States, 1937–1940.* Columbus: Ohio State University Press, 1988.

Romano, Sergio, ed. *L'Impero riluttante.* Milan: ISPI, 1992.

Roosevelt, Eleanor. *This I Remember.* New York: Harper, 1949.
This Is My Story. New York: Harper, 1937.

Roosevelt, Elliott. *As He Saw It.* New York: Duell, Sloan & Pearce, 1946.

Roosevelt, James. *My Parents: A Different View.* Chicago: Playboy Press, 1976.

Roosevelt, James, and Sidney Shallet. *Affectionately, FDR: A Son's Story of a Lonely Man.* New York: Harcourt, Brace, 1959.

Roosevelt, Sara, with Isabel Leighton and Gabrielle Forbush. *My Boy Franklin.* New York: Long & Smith, 1933.

Roosevelt, Theodore. *Autobiography.* New York: Scribners, 1913.

Rosenman, Samuel. *Working with Roosevelt.* New York: Harper Bros., 1952.

Rosenthal, Joel H. *Righteous Realists: Political Realism, Responsible Power, and American Culture in the Nuclear Age.* Baton Rouge: Louisiana State University Press, 1991.

Rostow, Walt W. *The Division of Europe after World War II.* Aldershot: Grover Press, 1982.

Rothwell, Victor. *Britain and the Cold War, 1941–1947.* London: Cape, 1982.

Ruddy, T. Michael. *Cautious Diplomat: Charles E. Bohlen and the Soviet Union.* Kent, Ohio: Kent State University Press, 1986.

Russell, Ruth B. *A History of the United Nations Charter,* Washington, D.C.: Brookings Institution, 1958.

Schilling, Warner R., Paul Y. Hammond, and Glenn H. Snyder. *Strategy, Politics, and Defense Budgets.* New York: Columbia University Press, 1962.

Schlesinger, Arthur M., Jr. *The Age of Roosevelt.* Vol. 1: *The Crisis of the Old Order.* Boston: Houghton Mifflin, 1957.

   The Age of Roosevelt. Vol. 2: *The Coming of the New Deal.* Boston: Houghton Mifflin, 1958.

Schmitz, David. *The United States and Fascist Italy, 1922–1940.* Chapel Hill: University of North Carolina Press, 1988.

Schwartz, Thomas Alan. *America's Germany: John J. McCloy and the Federal Republic of Germany.* Cambridge, Mass.: Harvard University Press, 1991.

Schwarz, Jordan. *Liberal: Adolf A. Berle and the Vision of an American Era.* New York: Free Press, 1987.

Sharp, Tony. *The Wartime Alliance and the Zonal Division of Germany.* Oxford: Clarendon Press, 1975.

Sherwin, Martin. *A World Destroyed: The Atomic Bomb and the Grand Alliance,* New York: Random House, 1977.

Sherwood, Robert. *Roosevelt and Hopkins: An Intimate History.* New York: Harper, 1950.

Simmons, Ernest J. *Chekhov: A Biography.* Chicago: University of Chicago Press, 1962.

Skidelsky, Robert. *John Maynard Keynes.* Vol. 1: *Hopes Betrayed.* London: Macmillan, 1983.

Sloan, G. R. *Geopolitics in U.S. Strategic Policy, 1890–1987.* Brighton: Wheatsheaf Books, 1988.

Smiles, Samuel. *Self Help* (1859). New York: J. W. Lovell, 1884.

Smith, Gaddis. *American Diplomacy During World War II.* New York: Wiley, 1965.

   Dean Acheson. New York: Cooper Square, 1972.

Smith, M. L., and Peter M. R. Stirk, eds. *Making the New Europe: European Unity and the Second World War.* New York: Pinter Publishers, 1990.

Spengler, Oswald. *The Decline of the West.* Edited by Helmut Werner. New York: Modern Library Edition, 1962.

Steel, Ronald. *Walter Lippmann and the American Century.* Boston: Atlantic Monthly Press, 1980.

Stein, Herbert. *The Fiscal Revolution in America.* Chicago: University of Chicago Press, 1969.

   Presidential Economics. Washington, D.C.: American Enterprise Institute, 1988.

Stephanson, Anders. *Kennan and the Art of Foreign Policy.* Cambridge, Mass.: Harvard University Press, 1989.

Stettinius, E. Edward. *Roosevelt and the Russians: The Yalta Conference.* Garden City, N.Y.: Doubleday, 1949.

Still, Bayard. *Milwaukee: The History of a City.* Madison: State Historical Society of Wisconsin, 1965.

Stiller, Jesse. *George Messersmith: Diplomat of Democracy.* New York: New York University Press, 1987.

Stimson, Henry, and McGeorge Bundy. *On Active Service in Peace and War.* New York: Harper Bros., 1947.

Stoler, Mark A. *George C. Marshall: Soldier-Statesman of the American Century.* Boston: Twayne, 1989.

The Politics of the Second Front. Westport, Conn.: Greenwood Press, 1977.

Stourzh, Gerald. *Alexander Hamilton and the Age of Republican Government.* Stanford, Calif.: Stanford University Press, 1970.

Strout, Cushing. *The American Image of the Old World.* New York: Harper & Row, 1963.

Talbott, Strobe. *The Master of the Game.* New York: Knopf, 1988.

Taubman, William. *Stalin's American Policy.* New York: Norton, 1982.

Taylor, Telford. *Munich: The Price of Peace.* Garden City, N.Y.: Doubleday, 1979.

Trachtenberg, Mark. *History and Strategy.* Princeton, N.J.: Princeton University Press, 1991.

Travis, Fredrick, Jr. *George Kennan and the American–Russian Relationship, 1865–1924.* Athens: Ohio University Press, 1990.

Trefousse, Hans. *Carl Schurz: A Biography.* Knoxville: University of Tennessee Press, 1982.

Trollope, Anthony. *North America* (1862). New York: Knopf, 1951.

Tucker, Nancy. *Patterns in the Dust: Chinese–American Relations and the Recognition Controversy.* New York: Columbia University Press, 1983.

Tucker, Robert C. *Stalin in Power: The Revolution from Above, 1928–1941.* New York: Norton, 1990.

Tugwell, Rexford. *The Democratic Roosevelt.* Garden City, N.Y.: Doubleday, 1957.

Twain, Mark. *Innocents Abroad.* New York: Harper Bros., 1911.

Van Minnen, Cornellis A., and John F. Sears, eds. *FDR and His Contemporaries: Foreign Perceptions of an American President.* New York: St. Martin's Press, 1992.

Volkogonov, Dmitri. *Stalin: Triumph and Tragedy.* New York: Grove Weidenfeld, 1991.

Wall, Irwin M. *The United States and the Making of Postwar France, 1945–1954.* Cambridge: Cambridge University Press, 1991.

Ward, Geoffrey. *Before the Trumpet: Young Franklin Roosevelt, 1882–1905.* New York: Harper & Row, 1985.

A First-Class Temperament: The Emergence of Franklin Roosevelt. New York: Harper & Row, 1989.

Weil, Martin. *A Pretty Good Club: The Founding Fathers of the U.S. Foreign Service.* New York: Norton, 1978.

Weinberg, Gerhard L. *The Foreign Policy of Hitler's Germany: Starting World War II, 1937–1939.* Chicago: University of Chicago Press, 1980.

Welles, Sumner. *Naboth's Vineyard.* 2 vols. New York: Payson & Clarke, 1928.

The Time for Decision. New York: Harper Bros., 1944.

Seven Decisions That Shaped History. New York: Harper Bros., 1950.

Werth, Alexander. *France, 1945–1955.* Boston: Beacon Press, 1966.

Wharton, Edith. *The Age of Innocence* (1920). New York: American Library ed., 1962.

Wheeler-Bennett, J. *King George VI: His Life and Reign.* New York: St. Martin's Press, 1958.

Willert, Sir Arthur. *The Road to Safety: A Study in Anglo-American Relations.* New York: Praeger, 1953.

Woods, Randall Bennett. *A Changing of the Guard: Anglo-American Relations, 1941–1946.* Chapel Hill: University of North Carolina Press, 1990.

Woodward, Sir Ernest Llewellyn. Abridged ed. *British Foreign Policy in the Second World War.* London: HMSO, 1962.

Yergin, Daniel. *The Shattered Peace: The Origins of the Cold War and the National Security State.* Boston: Houghton Mifflin, 1977.

Young, G. M. *Victorian England: Portrait of an Age* (1936). London: Oxford University Press, 1959.

Young, J. W. *France: The Cold War and the Western Alliance, 1944–49.* Leicester: University of Leicester Press, 1990.

Ziegler, Philip. *Mountbatten: The Official Biography.* London: Collins, 1985.

Zurcher, Arnold. *The Struggle to Unite Europe, 1940–1958.* New York: New York University Press, 1958.

Articles and papers

Acheson, Dean. "Dean Acheson's Word for de Gaulle: 'Nonsense.'" *U.S. News and World Report* 60, no. 16 (April 18, 1966):79–81. (Quotations from a Columbia Broadcast System TV–radio interview with former secretary of state Dean Acheson on April 4, 1966.)

"The Eclipse of the State Department." *Foreign Affairs* 49, no. 4 (July 1971):593–606.

"Instant Retaliation: The Debate Continues." *New York Times Magazine* (March 28, 1954):13+.

"Lawyers in the Republic." *Esquire* 56 (July 1961):100–3.

"The Prelude to Independence." *Yale Review* 48, no. 4 (June 1959):481–90.

Aga-Rossi, Elena. "Reorganizing the Postwar World: Roosevelt and the Future of Europe." Typescript courtesy of the author.

Alsop, Joseph, with Adam Platt. "The WASP Ascendency." *New York Review of Books* 36, no. 17 (November 9, 1989):48–56.

Ash, Timothy Garton. "Germany Unbound." *New York Review of Books* 37, no. 18 (November 22, 1990):11–15.

Atkinson, Justin Brooks. "America's Global Planner." *New York Times Magazine* (July 13, 1947):9+.

Ball, George. "NATO and World Responsibility." *Atlantic Community Quarterly* 2, no. 2 (Summer 1964):208–17.

Beneš, Eduard. "Czechoslovakia Plans for Peace." *Foreign Affairs* 23, no. 1 (October 1944):26–38.

Berlin, Isaiah. "President Franklin Delano Roosevelt." *Political Quarterly* 26, no. 4 (October–December 1955):340–41.

Bernstein, Barton. "Roosevelt, Truman and the Atomic Bomb: A Reinterpretation." *Political Science Quarterly* 90, no. 1 (Spring 1973):23–40.

Bess, Demaree. "The Cost of Roosevelt's 'Great Design.'" *Saturday Evening Post* 216 (May 27, 1944):17+.

Brzezinski, Zbigniew. "The Future of Yalta." *Foreign Affairs* 63, no. 2 (Winter 1984–85):279–302.

"Selective Global Containment." *Foreign Affairs* 70, no. 4 (Fall 1991):9–10.

Buchan, Alastair. "High Postured Leader." *Listener* 40, no. 15 (April 23, 1970):11–13.

Bullitt, William C. "How We Won the War and Lost the Peace." *Life* 25 (August 30, 1948):82–4+; (Sept. 6, 1948):86–8+.

Bush, George. Commencement Address, Boston University, May 23, 1989. Department of State *Bulletin* (July 1989):18–19.

Combs, Jerald A. "The Compromise That Never Was: George Kennan, Paul Nitze, and the Issue of Conventional Deterrence in Europe, 1949–1952." *Diplomatic History* 15, no. 3 (Summer 1991):361–86.

Davis, Forrest. "Roosevelt's World Blueprint." *Saturday Evening Post* 115 (April 10, 1943):20–21, 109–11.

"What Really Happened at Teheran." *Saturday Evening Post* 216 (May 13, 1944):12–13+; 217 (May 20, 1944):22–3+.

Davis, Kenneth. "FDR as a Biographer's Problem." *American Scholar* 53 (Winter 1983–84):100–8.

Evangelista, Matthew. "Stalin's Postwar Army Reappraised." *International Security* 7 (Winter 1982–83):110–38.

Gaddis, John Lewis, "Containment: A Reassessment." *Foreign Affairs* 55, no. 4 (July 1977):873–87.

"Intelligence, Espionage and Cold War Origins." *Diplomatic History* 13, no. 2 (Spring 1989):196–206.

"NSC 68 and the Soviet Threat." *International Security* 4, no. 4 (Spring 1980):164–70.

Gaddis, John Lewis, ed. "The Soviet Side of the Cold War: A Symposium." *Diplomatic History* 15, no. 4 (Fall 1991):523–63.

Halle, Louis. "The World of George Kennan." *New Republic* 145 (August 7, 1961):21–3.

Harper, John L. "Henry Stimson and the Origin of America's Attachment to Atomic Weapons." *SAIS Review* 5, no. 2 (Summer–Fall 1985):17–28.

Harries, Owen. "A Conversation with Zbigniew Brzezinski." *National Interest* no. 5 (Fall 1986):28–35.

Hilton, Stanley E. "The Welles Mission to Europe, February–March 1940: Illusion or Realism?" *Journal of American History* 58 (1971):93–120.

Hogan, Michael J., ed. "The End of the Cold War: A Symposium" (Part 2). *Diplomatic History* 16, no. 2 (Spring 1992):223–318.

Huntington, Samuel P. "America's Changing Strategic Interests." *Survival* 33, no. 1 (January 1991):3–17.

Jahanbegloo, Ramin. "Philosophy and Life: An Interview." *New York Review of Books* 39, no. 10 (May 28, 1992):46–54.

Joffe, Josef. "Europe's American Pacifier." *Foreign Policy* no. 54 (Spring 1984): 64–82.

Kateb, George. "George F. Kennan: The Heart of a Diplomat." *Commentary* 45, no. 1 (January 1968):21–26.

Kennan, George F. "Allied Leadership during World War II." *Survey* 21 (Winter–Spring 1975):29–36.

"George Kennan Replies [to C. Ben Wright]." *Slavic Review* 35, no. 1 (March 1976):32–36.

"The Gorbachev Prospect." *New York Review of Books* 34, nos. 21–22 (January 21, 1988):3–7.

"Morality and Foreign Policy." *Foreign Affairs* 64, no. 2 (Winter 1984–85): 205–18.

"The National Interest of the United States." *Illinois Law Review* 37 (January–February 1951):52–60.

"The Passing of the Cold War." *International House of Japan Bulletin* 3 (October 1964):2–7.

"The Sources of Soviet Conduct." *Foreign Affairs* 25, no. 4 (July 1947): 566–82. (Originally signed anonymously by Mr. "X.")

Kent, George P. "Towards Containment: The Impact of George Kennan's Views of the Russian National Character and the Soviet Regime on His Policy Formulation, 1944–47." Master's thesis, Johns Hopkins University, 1992.

Kimball, Warren. "Naked Reverse Right: Roosevelt, Churchill and Eastern Europe from Tolstoy to Yalta – and a Little Beyond." *Diplomatic History* 9, no. 1 (Winter 1985):2–7.

"Wheel Within a Wheel: Churchill, Roosevelt, and the Special Relationship." Typescript courtesy of the author, 1992.

Kissinger, Henry. "A New Atlantic Charter." *Atlantic Community Quarterly* 2, no. 3 (Summer 1973):151–60.

"What Kind of Atlantic Partnership?" *Atlantic Community Quarterly* 7, no. 1 (Spring 1969):18–38.

Lasky, Melvin. "A Conversation with George Kennan." *Encounter* 14, no. 3 (March 1960):46–57.

Leffler, Melvin P. "Adherence to Agreements: Yalta and the Experience of the Early Cold War." *International Security* 11, no. 1 (Summer 1986):88–123.

"Was the Cold War Necessary?" *Diplomatic History* 15, no. 2 (Spring 1991):265–75.

Lippmann, Walter, and Sumner Welles. "The Big Four and World Peace: A Debate by Welles and Lippmann." *Newsweek* 24 (August 21, 1944): 96–107.

Mark, Eduard, "American Policy Toward Eastern Europe and the Origins of the Cold War, 1941–46: An Alternative Explanation," *Journal of American History* 68, no. 2 (September 1981):313–37.

"Charles E. Bohlen and the Acceptable Limits of Soviet Hegemony in Eastern Europe: A Memorandum of 18 October 1945," *Diplomatic History* 3 (Spring 1979):201–13.

"The Question of Containment: A Reply to John Lewis Gaddis." *Foreign Affairs* 56, no. 3 (January 1978):430–41.

McNally, Robert C. "Sledgehammer: An Examination of the Motives and Objectives of a 1942 Cross-Channel Attack proposed by General George C. Marshall." Master's thesis, Johns Hopkins University, 1992.

Mosley, Philip. "Dismemberment of Germany: The Allied Negotiations from Yalta to Potsdam." *Foreign Affairs* 28, no. 3 (April 1950):487–98.

Ninkovich, Frank. "Theodore Roosevelt: Civilization as Ideology." *Diplomatic History* 10, no. 3 (Summer 1986):221–45.

Nitze, Paul. "The Development of NSC 68, a reply to John Lewis Gaddis, 'NSC 68 and the Soviet Threat,'" *International Security* 4, no. 4 (Spring 1980): 170–6.

Pfaff, William. "The Fallen Hero." *New Yorker* 65, no. 12 (May 8, 1989):105–15.

Resis, Albert. "The Churchill–Stalin 'Percentages' Agreement on the Balkans, Moscow, October, 1944." *American Historical Review* 83, no. 2 (April 1978):368–87.

Reston, James. "The No. 1 No. 2 Man in Washington." *New York Times Magazine* (August 25, 1946):8+.

Roosevelt, Franklin D. "Shall We Trust Japan?" *Asia: Journal of the American Asiatic Association* 23 (July 1923):475–8.

Schlesinger, Arthur M., Jr. "Some Lessons from the Cold War." *Diplomatic History* 16, no. 1 (Winter 1992):47–53.

Sheehan, Thomas. "Heidegger and the Nazis." *New York Review of Books* 35, no. 10 (June 26, 1988):38–47.

Sherwin, Martin. "The Atomic Bomb and the Origins of the Cold War: U.S. Atomic Energy Policy and Diplomacy, 1941–45." *American Historical Review* 78, no. 4 (October 1973):945–68.

Thomas, Evan. "An Icon of the Cold War: Gorbachev Is Vindicating George Kennan's Views." *Newsweek* 113 (April 17, 1989):34.

Thompson, John A. "The Exaggeration of American Vulnerability: The Anatomy of a Tradition." *Diplomatic History* 16, no. 1 (Winter 1992):23–43.

Tucker, Robert W., and David C. Hendrickson. "Thomas Jefferson and American Foreign Policy." *Foreign Affairs* 69, no. 2 (Spring 1990):135–56.

Urban, George, and George F. Kennan. "A Conversation with George Kennan." *Encounter* 47, no. 3 (September 1976):10–43.

Watt, D. Cameron. "Britain and the Historiography of the Yalta Conference and the Cold War." *Diplomatic History* 13, no. 1 (Winter 1989):67–98.

Wells, Samuel F. "Sounding the Tocsin: NSC 68 and the Soviet Threat." *International Security* 4, no. 2 (Fall 1977):116–58.

Wills, Gary. "The Power of Impotence." *New York Review of Books* 36, no. 18 (November 23, 1989):3–4.

Wright, C. Ben. "Mr. 'X' and Containment." *Slavic Review* 35, no. 1 (March 1976):1–31.

Index

Acheson, Alexander, 237, 238
Acheson, David C., 264 n. 114
Acheson, Dean, 3; and Edward
  Acheson, 237, 238, 239, 240; and
  Eleanor Gooderham Acheson, 237, 239,
  243, 264 n. 114, and Adenauer,
  283–84, 285, 290–91, 300, 302, 307,
  308, 310, 311, 315, 316, 317, 318, 319,
  326, 327, 329; and American
  reformism, 239; on the American
  Revolution, 242; and Anglo-American
  relations (see and Great Britain); and
  Atlee, 304; and atomic energy, 267–68,
  269, 270–71, 291, 292; and Baruch
  Plan, 271; and "battle of the notes"
  (1952), 316–17; and Berle, 256, 325;
  and Berlin crisis of 1948–49, 284; and
  Berlin crisis of 1958, 327; and Berlin
  crisis of 1961–62, 327, 328; and Bevin,
  212, 279, 283, 285, 286, 287, 288, 293,
  296, 297 nn. 67, 68; 299, 303; 312;
  Bohlen on, 307; and Brandeis, 246–47,
  248, 249, 250, 255, 270; on Brazil, 325;
  and Bretton Woods Conference, 264,
  266, 272, 275; and British loan, 268,
  272–74, 275; and Bruce, 297, 309; and
  Byrnes, 270; and Century Group, 258;
  character of, 235–36, 242–43, 244,
  250; childhood of, 241–44; and China,
  292, 302; Churchill, admiration for,
  273; and Clayton, 255; and Benjamin
  Cohen, 259; and Connecticut Valley,
  241, 242; and Covington and Burling
  (see law career of); and de Gasperi, 313,
  326; and de Gaulle, 327, 328; and
  destroyers for bases deal, 259;
  and Douglas, 250, 251, 252, 314; and
  Dumbarton Oaks Conference, 265; and
  Eden, 312, 318; education of, 242, 243,

244, 245; and Eisenhower, 309, 312;
and Ernst Reuter corollary, 291; and
European Coal and Steel Community,
297, 303, 309, 310, 312; and European
Defense Community, 301, 302, 303,
308, 309, 310, 312, 314, 316, 318, 326;
and European Recovery Program (see
and Marshall Plan); and European unity,
281, 287–89, 296–97, 308–9, 324,
325, 326, 327, 328; and Food and
Agricultural Organization, 263; and
France, 219, 220, 282, 283, 285,
289–90, 296, 297, 299, 300, 301,
302–3, 305, 307, 308, 310, 311, 313,
315–16, 318, 319–23, 325, 327; and
Franco-German relations, 285, 289–90,
297, 300–1, 309, 310–11, 315,
318–19, 321, 322, 324; and
Frankfurter, 246, 249, 251, 252, 257,
268, 275 n. 160, 325; and Franks, 235,
236, 251, 279, 282, 286, 296; and
Germany, 216, 219–20, 265, 280, 281,
282–83, 290–91, 296, 297, 298, 299,
300, 301, 308, 309, 310, 311, 313, 315,
317–18, 322, 324, 325, 326, 328–29;
and Germany rearmament, 298, 299,
302, 303, 307, 308–9, 310, 311, 313,
315, 316–19, 320–22, 328–29; gold
purchase program, opposition to,
(1933), 251–53; and Great Britain, 218,
220, 235–36, 242–43, 249, 250, 259,
261–62, 268, 272–74, 275, 285–87,
296–97, 303–4, 307, 308, 313–14,
318, 319–20, 325; and "Great Debate"
of 1951, 306–7; and Greece, 266, 275,
276; and Harriman, 267, 327 n. 132;
Hickenlooper, answer to, on U.S. troops
in Europe, 282–83, 333; Alger Hiss
verdict, statement after, 292–93; and